D1458498

Pediatric Traumatic Brain Injury

New Frontiers in Clinical Research

Pediatric Traumatic Brain Injury

New Frontiers in Clinical and Translational Research

Edited by

Vicki Anderson
Murdoch Children's Research Institute and Royal Children's Hospital, Melbourne, Australia

Keith Owen Yeates
The Ohio State University and Nationwide Children's Hospital, Columbus, OH, USA

CAMBRIDGE
UNIVERSITY PRESS

CAMBRIDGE UNIVERSITY PRESS
Cambridge, New York, Melbourne, Madrid, Cape Town, Singapore,
São Paulo, Delhi, Dubai, Tokyo

Cambridge University Press
The Edinburgh Building, Cambridge CB2 8RU, UK

Published in the United States of America by
Cambridge University Press, New York

www.cambridge.org
Information on this title: www.cambridge.org/9780521763325

First published 2010

Printed in the United Kingdom at the University Press, Cambridge

A catalogue record for this publication is available from the British Library

Library of Congress Cataloging-in-Publication Data

Pediatric traumatic brain injury / edited by Vicki Anderson, Keith
Owen Yeates.
  p. ; cm.
  Includes bibliographical references and index.
  ISBN 978-0-521-76332-5 (hardback)
  1. Brain-damaged children.   2. Brain-damaged children–Rehabilitation.
I. Anderson, Vicki, 1958–   II. Yeates, Keith Owen.   III. Title.
  [DNLM: 1. Brain Injuries.   2. Child.   3. Infant. WS 340 P3719 2010]
  RJ496.B7P436 2010
  618.92′8–dc22

                                                              2009042288

ISBN 978-0-521-76332-5 Hardback

Contents

Contributors

P. David Adelson
Children's Neuroscience Center
Phoenix Children's Hospital,
Phoenix, AZ, USA

Vicki Anderson
Department of Psychology
Australian Centre for Child
Neuropsychology Studies
Murdoch Childrens Research Institute,
Royal Children's Hospital,
University of Melbourne,
Melbourne, Victoria, Australia

Stephen Ashwal
Division of Pediatric Neurology
Department of Pediatrics
Loma Linda University School of Medicine,
Loma Linda, CA, USA

Rachel P. Berger
Children's Hospital of Pittsburgh
Safar Center for Resuscitation Research,
Pittsburgh, PA, USA

Cathy Catroppa
Research Fellow
Australian Centre for Child
Neuropsychology Studies
Murdoch Childrens Research Institute,
Royal Children's Hospital,
University of Melbourne,
Melbourne, Victoria, Australia

Brittany Coats
Department of Bioengineering
University of Pennsylvania,
Philadelphia, PA, USA

Robbin Gibb
Department of Neuroscience
University of Lethbridge,
Lethbridge, Alberta, Canada

Christopher C. Giza
Division of Pediatric Neurology,
Mattel Children's Hospital, UCLA
Department of Neurosurgery
UCLA Brain Injury Research Center
David Geffen School of Medicine at UCLA,
Los Angeles, CA, USA

Ronald L. Hayes
Chairman, Clinical Programs Director
Banyan Biomarkers Inc.,
Alachua, FL, USA

Erik Hessen
Department of Neurology
Akershus University Hospital,
Oslo, Norway

Barbara A. Holshouser
Department of Radiology
Loma Linda University School of Medicine,
Loma Linda, CA, USA

Ingrid van't Hooft
Neuropediatric Rehabilitation Unit
Astrid Lindgren Children's Hospital
Karolinska University Hospital/Karolinska
Institute
Stockholm, Sweden

David A. Hovda
UCLA Brain Injury Research Center
Department of Neurosurgery
David Geffen School of Medicine at UCLA,
Los Angeles, CA, USA

Michael W. Kirkwood
Department of Physical Medicine
and Rehabilitation
University of Colorado,
The Children's Hospital,
Aurora, CO, USA

Patrick Kochanek
Safar Center for Resuscitation Research,
Pittsburgh, PA, USA

Bryan Kolb
Department of Neuroscience
Canadian Centre for Behavioural
Neuroscience
University of Lethbridge,
Lethbridge, Alberta, Canada

Susan S. Margulies
Bioengineering Graduate Group
Department of Bioengineering
University of Pennsylvania,
Philadelphia, PA, USA

Andre Obenaus
Department of Radiology
Loma Linda University School of Medicine,
Loma Linda, CA, USA

Mayumi L. Prins
UCLA Brain Injury Research Center
Department of Neurosurgery
David Geffen School of Medicine at UCLA,
Los Angeles, CA, USA

H. Gerry Taylor
Case Western Reserve University and
Rainbow Babies & Children's Hospital
University Hospitals Case Medical Center,
Cleveland, OH, USA

Karen A. Tong
Department of Radiology
Loma Linda University School of Medicine,
Loma Linda, CA, USA

Shari L. Wade
Division of Physical Medicine and
Rehabilitation
Cincinnati Children's Hospital Medical
Center
University of Cincinnati College of
Medicine,
Cincinnati, OH, USA

Kevin K. W. Wang
Banyan Biomarkers Inc.,
Alachua, FL, USA

Keith Owen Yeates
The Ohio State University
Nationwide Children's Hospital,
Columbus, OH, USA

Acknowledgments

This book evolved from a research conference held in San Diego, California, November 8–10, 2007, entitled 'New Frontiers in Pediatric Traumatic Brain Injury'. The editors served as the conference organizers. The conference was held with support from a grant (R13 HD55078) awarded to the editors by the National Center for Medical Rehabilitation Research of the National Institute of Child Health and Human Development, the National Institute of Neurological Disease and Stroke, and the National Center for Injury Prevention and Control of the Centers for Disease Control and Prevention. We would like to acknowledge the additional support for the conference provided by the Murdoch Childrens Research Institute, Melbourne, Australia; the Research Institute at Nationwide Children's Hospital, Columbus, Ohio; and the Australian Society for the Study of Brain Impairment. We would like to thank David Hovda, Ph.D., Linda Noble, Ph.D., and Patrick Kochanek, M.D., for serving on the conference organizing committee. We would also like to acknowledge the Office of Continuing Medical Education at the University of California at San Diego, which provided logistical support for the conference, and Kate Anderson who provided administrative assistance in compiling and editing the book. Dr. Yeates received support for preparation of the conference grant and this book in part through an Independent Scientist Career Development Award from the National Institutes of Health (K02 HD44099).

Introduction: Pediatric traumatic brain injury: New frontiers in clinical and translational research

Vicki Anderson and Keith Owen Yeates

Introduction

Traumatic brain injury (TBI) is a major public health problem among children and adolescents. Surveillance data reveal that 1 in every 20 emergency department presentations at pediatric hospitals is for a TBI, making TBI more common than burns or poisonings. For children, such injuries represent a common interruption to normal development, with population estimates ranging from 200 to over 500 per 100 000 a year, and with well-established variations across age and gender (Crowe *et al.*, in press; Langlois *et al.*, 2006). The majority of TBI in children and adolescents are mild, typically with few long-term consequences; however, a significant proportion of children will suffer more serious injuries and will experience a range of residual physical, cognitive, educational, functional, and social and emotional consequences, requiring the lifelong involvement of health professionals across a range of disciplines and leading to a significant social and economic burden for the children's families and for the community more broadly (Cassidy *et al.*, 2004).

This book, *New Frontiers in Pediatric Traumatic Brain Injury*, aims to evaluate what we have learned about TBI in childhood to date and, perhaps more importantly, to articulate the challenges we face and how we should go forward in the future. Over the past two or three decades, researchers and clinicians working with children with TBI have become aware that injuries to the developing brain cannot be understood or treated in exactly the same manner as those occurring in adulthood. Although we may be guided by science and practice in adult TBI, unique developmental and contextual issues need to be taken into account at all stages of recovery and treatment in children. Thus, a separate knowledge base is needed for pediatric TBI. As a consequence, until recently our understanding of recovery and outcomes in pediatric TBI has lagged behind that for adults. This is changing. Research in pediatric TBI now has more solid foundations. A number of principles have been established, some consistent with the adult literature, such as the predictive value of injury severity (Anderson *et al.*, 2004; Taylor *et al.*, 2008). Others are specific to early brain injury, such as the unique mechanics and characteristic pathology of inflicted injury in children (Coats & Margulies, 2006; Prange & Margulies, 2002), or reflect the importance of developmental and contextual factors, such as the age at injury, developmental stage of brain development, and functional maturation (Anderson *et al.*, 2005; Taylor & Alden, 1997), the key role of the family, and implications of life tasks specific to children (Yeates *et al.*, 1997).

Pediatric Traumatic Brain Injury: New Frontiers in Clinical and Translational Research, ed. V. Anderson and K. O. Yeates. Published by Cambridge University Press. © Cambridge University Press 2010.

To this point, we have been reasonably successful in describing the consequences of pediatric TBI. The natural history of pediatric TBI has also been studied extensively, and we have a working understanding of the acute and long-term effects of injury for the child and family. At a group level, research has demonstrated that children with milder injuries are likely to recover well, with few residual problems. With increasing severity, recovery is less complete, and we know that those with severe injury are at risk for ongoing difficulties across a range of physical, cognitive, and socio-emotional domains, and that these difficulties may persist through childhood and into adulthood (Hessen et al., 2007; Jaffe et al., 1995; Yeates et al., 2004). In contrast, at the individual level, these trends may not necessarily apply, and clinical reports confirm that outcomes are highly variable, leading to uncertainty with respect to prognosis and key predictive factors. More precise information is critical to determining which children are at high risk and to effectively allocating limited resources for management and treatment. To date, our research has been only modestly successful in providing guidance with respect to which factors contribute most to recovery and outcome, with much past research focused within specific domains or silos. For example, medical researchers may examine the impact of raised intracranial pressure or neurological signs on long-term outcome, while others may look at biochemical markers, radiological results, or environmental factors. To date, progress using this narrow focus has been disappointing, suggesting that a more multi-dimensional model is required, in which researchers across disciplines come together with a more holistic view of the child.

A further challenge exists in the area of management and treatment. At present, the evidence base for effective treatment, at both acute and more chronic stages of recovery post-TBI, is largely lacking, across medical, pharmacological, and behavioral domains (Anderson & Catroppa, 2006; Laatsch et al., 2007; Ylvisaker et al., 2005). As a result, health professionals have little direction with respect to which interventions may lead to better outcomes. Reflecting this problem, clinical practice guidelines, where established, vary dramatically across the world, and even within individual centers. As a result, care pathways are disparate and clinical decisions are typically made on the basis of previous training and experience, rather than on empirical grounds. Treatment research and clinical trials in this domain are costly and difficult, but are critical to improving child outcomes.

So, there is a way to go yet, and the challenge for the next decade is to begin to translate empirical findings into clinically relevant information that will lead to improved and appropriately targeted care and better outcomes for the child and family. To do this, we need to ask why, despite the commitment of clinicians and researchers alike, we have been unable to achieve more. In considering this question, we can identify a number of very real obstacles, many specific to this particular population. To begin, pediatric TBI has not attracted the public attention received by other childhood disorders. As a result, funding for this population is surprisingly low, and does not reflect the high cost to the community of such injuries in childhood. To some extent, this may reflect the traditional view that children recover well from brain injury and that their needs are few. The observation that the consequences of TBI are "masked" is also of relevance, with most children appearing "normal" after injury, despite suffering from functionally significant impairments. But perhaps we as a field have not been sufficiently proactive in informing the community of the needs of these children and their families, and need to consider an increased focus on advocacy and public policy.

Even with adequate funding, substantive studies are difficult to conduct. TBI in children has a low base rate, and individual centers struggle to recruit sufficient numbers of children to conduct studies that can help answer the outstanding questions regarding management, treatment, and prognosis. At a practical level, contemporary health systems worldwide are not set up to facilitate this research, instead focusing on acute care and rapid discharge and paying limited attention to the transition home or to community reintegration.

An additional complication is that children who suffer TBI are not representative of the healthy population, and are more likely to have pre-existing behavioral and learning problems as well as social disadvantage (Taylor & Alden, 1997). These factors may impact negatively on recovery, and confound our ability to determine which post-injury difficulties are due to TBI and which might have predated the injury. These unique characteristics also lead to challenges in selecting appropriate comparison groups for determining injury-related consequences, and differentiating them from pre-existing problems. Researchers to date have either ignored these issues by using normal control groups, employed recruitment criteria that exclude children with pre-injury problems, or selected comparison groups deemed similar to TBI cohorts on key characteristics such as social background or behavioral function.

The developmental context creates its own challenges. In contrast to colleagues studying adult TBI, pediatric researchers cannot assume that all children are at the same level of development, or that the same injury will have an equal impact across childhood. In fact, increasing evidence indicates that age and skill attainment at the time of injury are important considerations in assessing likely recovery. Further, some argue that, in contrast to the recovery patterns described in adults, children may in fact "grow into their difficulties" as they progress through childhood, as environmental demands increase but age-appropriate developmental milestones fail to be mastered. This view is supported by an emerging literature that describes adult survivors of pediatric TBI as experiencing educational failure, restricted vocational options, psychological adjustment difficulties, and poor quality of life (Anderson *et al.*, 2009; Cattelani *et al.*, 1998; McKinlay *et al.*, 2002). The child's need to acquire new skills and knowledge and meet educational demands, in the context of increased risk of physical, cognitive, and behavioral impairment, generates unique challenges for rehabilitation and reintegration following pediatric TBI.

Associated with developmental issues is the problem of identifying acceptable "gold standards" to measure outcomes that are relevant from infancy to adolescence (Fletcher *et al.*, 1995). This dilemma impacts on acute outcome measurement, because most widely used measures of levels of consciousness and post-traumatic amnesia are inappropriate for infants and young children. Radiological measures, in particular functional neuroimaging, are also problematic with children, because of practical issues around brain scanning, as well as given the lack of normative comparisons. However, perhaps the greatest challenge is in the area of cognitive and behavioral outcomes, where few if any measures are available which are applicable across the desired age range. As a result, studies utilize a wide range of outcome measures and findings are difficult to compare.

'Pediatric Traumatic Brain Injury: New Frontiers in Clinical and Translational Research' emerged from an international research conference held in San Diego, California, USA, in 2007, with financial support from the National Institutes of Health, the Centers for Disease Control, the Murdoch Children's Research Institute, the Research Institute at Nationwide Children's Hospital, and the Australian Society for the Study of Brain Impairment. The conference was attended by over 200 delegates, representing many disciplines, cultures, and levels of training and experience. The program for the meeting comprised keynote addresses from a panel of international experts across a range of specialties relevant to pediatric TBI, ranging from bench scientists to clinical researchers. Our intent was to bring together people with similar goals and interests to facilitate communication across disciplines and to encourage those in the field to begin to work together.

In designing the program, we placed an emphasis on research and evidence-based practice, and its potential to contribute to clinical practice and better child outcomes. The meeting was designed not so much to present specific research findings as to illustrate multi-level, integrative, and translational research and to consider how best to promote such research in the future, as well as to encourage both new and established investigators to undertake research consistent with this goal. Our aim with the conference, as well as with this book, was to highlight the need to move away from simple comparisons of children with and without TBI to investigations of factors across a range of levels that account for variations in outcomes, and to translate this information into evidence-based models for intervention with these children.

As will be illustrated in the following chapters, the past few decades have seen an explosion of interest in this field that has led to advances in acute medical treatments for childhood TBI. Researchers have begun to study the biomechanics of TBI using non-human models, including animals and simulations, such as "crash dummies." This work has provided important insights into the mechanisms of TBI and its unique impact on the developing brain. Within the human domain, a major research focus in recent years has been the reduction of more preventable secondary brain insult, via implementation of more rapid medical response, investigation of potentially predictive biomarkers for early detection of injury, and interventions such as hypothermia.

Advances in brain imaging have assisted in early diagnosis and guiding appropriate treatment, with current high-resolution imaging enabling the identification of even subtle brain damage in the context of mild TBI. Growing evidence, from both structural and functional imaging technologies, indicates common patterns of brain pathology resulting from childhood TBI, both macroscopic and microscopic, and changes that occur over time in response to damage to the developing brain.

Further, research has established that the mechanisms of injury often vary with developmental stage. For example, inflicted injuries due to child abuse are almost exclusive to infants, whereas in preschool children, the majority of injuries occur as a result of falls from furniture or play equipment. These early injuries are likely to be linked closely to environmental factors, such as family dysfunction and social disadvantage. In contrast, in older children, injuries are more likely to be due to sporting or motor vehicle accidents, and can be more directly associated with the child's own actions and behavior. These epidemiological data have implications for prevention and community education, and small steps are beginning to be made in this direction. For example, mandatory helmet usage for bicycle riders and for certain contact sports has been introduced in some countries.

Other research findings, from a range of mostly discipline-specific research endeavors, describe an increased risk for a multitude of residual impairments following childhood TBI, both acutely and in the long term. Persisting neurological symptoms, motor dysfunction, communication difficulties, poor attention and information processing, reduced memory, executive dysfunction, and social and emotional disorders have been consistently reported for many children with serious TBI. In association with these impairments, functional outcomes are also impacted, with solid evidence of low school attainment, reduced vocational opportunities, poor adaptive skills, and lowered quality of life. Unfortunately, although these problems are now accepted as frequent consequences of serious TBI, findings have yet to be successfully translated into more precise prognoses or acceptable evidence-based treatments for victims and their families.

Of crucial importance is growing evidence for a developmentally specific response to injury, demonstrating that adult knowledge and theories cannot be simply translated to the child population. The relative vulnerability of the young brain to the impact of TBI and the increased behavioral consequences in terms of reduced skill and knowledge acquisition is a relatively new concept, but is now supported by animal research, neuroimaging data, and behavioral findings. Again, these findings are yet to be incorporated into clinical practice or reflected in availability of appropriate medical and rehabilitative resources.

In an effort to improve the precision of prognoses, and to facilitate the development of treatment and management models, attempts have been made to link child outcomes with a variety of injury-related, environmental, family, and developmental factors, with only modest success. We believe that this stalling of progress may be due to a variety of factors. In particular, prior research has often occurred in separate silos, with little integration across domains or disciplines. The scientific advances that have occurred within domains (e.g. genomics and proteomics of neural recovery, neuroimaging, neuropsychology) are unlikely to result in significant progress in the clinical management of children with TBI until they become the topic of collaborative research that cuts across levels and specialties. In comparison to the field of TBI, we can learn much from the study of other childhood disorders, such as childhood cancer, where international collaborative consortia have been in existence for many years and have led the way in developing and implementing evidence-based, life-saving treatment protocols that have reduced mortality rates from 70% in the 1970s to closer to 10% in the past decade.

The time appears ripe for an interdisciplinary and collaborative approach to pediatric TBI that promotes integrative and translational research efforts. We believe that 'New Frontiers in Pediatric TBI' will help advance the state-of-the-art of research in the field and promote networking and collaboration among investigators. The chapters that constitute the book describe the state of the art in research across a variety of disciplines, all of which contribute to developing knowledge about pediatric TBI. This body of work makes it clear that the challenges and obstacles we face are similar, regardless of discipline, and that the solutions for progress will require a concerted effort by investigators that cuts across disciplines and other artificial boundaries.

References

Anderson, V. & Catroppa, C. (2006). Advances in post-acute rehabilitation after childhood acquired brain injury: a focus on cognitive, behavioural and social domains. *American Journal of Physical Medicine and Rehabilitation*, **85**(9), 767–787.

Anderson, V. A., Morse, S. A., Catroppa, C., Haritou, F. & Rosenfeld, J. V. (2004). Thirty month outcome from early childhood head injury: a prospective analysis of neurobehavioural recovery. *Brain*, **127**, 2608–2620.

Anderson, V. A., Catroppa, C., Morse, S., Haritou, F. & Rosenfeld, J. (2005). Functional plasticity or vulnerability after early brain injury? *Pediatrics*, **116**, 1374–1382.

Anderson, V., Brown, S., Hewitt, H. & Hoile, H. (2009). Educational, vocational, psychosocial and quality of life outcomes for adult survivors of childhood traumatic brain injury. *Journal of Head Trauma Rehabilitation*, **24**(5), 303–312.

Cassidy, J. D., Carroll, L. J., Peloso, P. M. *et al.* (2004). Incidence, risk factors and prevention of mild traumatic brain injury:

results of the WHO Collaborating Centre Task Force on Mild Traumatic Brain Injury. *Journal of Rehabilitation Medicine,* suppl. **43**, 28–60.

Cattelani, R., Lombardi, F., Brianti, R. & Mazzucchi, A. (1998). Traumatic brain injury in childhood: intellectual, behavioural and social outcomes into adulthood. *Brain Injury,* **12**, 283–296.

Coats, B. & Margulies, S. S. (2006). Material properties of human infant skull and suture at high rates. *Journal of Neurotrauma,* **23**, 1222–1232.

Crowe, L., Babl, F., Anderson, V. & Catroppa, C. (2009). The epidemiology of paediatric head injuries: data from a referral centre in Victoria, Australia. *Journal of Paediatrics and Child Health,* **45**(6), 346–350.

Fletcher, J. M., Ewing-Cobbs, L., Francis, D. J. & Levin, H. S. (1995). Variability in outcomes after traumatic brain injury in children: a developmental perspective. In S. H. Broman & M. E. Michel, eds. *Traumatic Head Injury in Children.* New York: Oxford University Press, pp. 3–21.

Hessen, E., Nestvold, K. & Anderson, V. (2007). Neuropsychological function 23 years after mild traumatic brain injury. A comparison of outcome after pediatric and adult head injuries. *Brain Injury,* **21**, 963–979.

Jaffe, K. M., Polissar, N. L., Fay, G. C. & Liao, S. (1995). Recovery trends over three years following pediatric traumatic brain injury. *Archives of Physical Medicine and Rehabilitation,* **76**, 17–26.

Laatsch, L., Harrington, D. & Hotz, G. (2007). An evidence-based review of cognitive and behavioral rehabilitation treatment studies in children with acquired brain injury. *Journal of Head Trauma Rehabilitation,* **22**(4), 248–256.

Langlois, J. A., Rutland-Brown, W. & Thomas, K. E. (2006). *Traumatic Brain Injury in the United States: Emergency Department Visits, Hospitalizations, and Deaths.* Atlanta: Centers for Disease Control and Prevention, National Center for Injury Prevention and Control.

McKinlay, A., Dalrymple-Alford, J. C., Horwood, L. J. & Fergusson, D. M. (2002). Long term psychosocial outcomes after mild head injury in early childhood. *Journal of Neurology, Neurosurgery & Psychiatry,* **73**, 281–288.

Prange, M. & Margulies, S. (2002). Regional, directional, and age-dependent properties of brain undergoing large deformation. *Journal of Biomechanical Engineering,* **124**, 244–252.

Taylor, H. G. & Alden, J. (1997). Age-related differences in outcomes following childhood brain insults: an introduction and overview. *Journal of the International Neuropsychological Society,* **3**, 1–13.

Taylor, H. G., Swartwout, M. D., Yeates, K. O., Walz, N. C., Stancin, T. & Wade, S. L. (2008). Traumatic brain injury in young children: post-acute effects on cognitive and school readiness skills. *Journal of the International Neuropsychological Society,* **14**, 1–12.

Yeates, K. O., Taylor, H. G. *et al.* (1997). Pre-injury family environment as a determinant of recovery from traumatic brain injuries in school-age children. *Journal of the International Neuropsychological Society,* **3**, 617–630.

Yeates, K. O., Swift, E. E., Taylor, H. G. *et al.* (2004). Short- and long-term social outcomes following pediatric traumatic brain injury. *Journal of the International Neuropsychological Society,* **10**, 412–426.

Ylvisaker, M., Adelson, P. D., Willandino Braga, L. W. *et al.* (2005). Rehabilitation and ongoing support after pediatric TBI: twenty years of progress. *The Journal of Head Trauma Rehabilitation,* **20**, 95.

Chapter

1

Biomechanics of pediatric TBI

Susan S. Margulies and Brittany Coats

Traumatic brain injury (TBI) is a leading cause of death and disability among children and young adults in the United States (NCIPC, 2000). Each year TBI results in approximately 3000 childhood deaths, 29 000 hospitalizations, and 400 000 emergency department visits. The predominant causes of TBI in young children are motor vehicle accidents, firearm incidents, falls, and child abuse.

Since the 1940s biomechanics has made a significant contribution to understanding the mechanisms and tolerances of adult traumatic brain injury and it continues to play a crucial role in forming guidelines for adult motor vehicle occupancy and sports safety (Goldsmith, 2001; Goldsmith & Monson, 2005). Biomechanical research specific to pediatric traumatic brain injury did not begin until the late 1970s and the paucity of pediatric biomechanical data at the time forced researchers to make assumptions regarding the relationship of infant material properties to adult material properties (Mohan et al., 1979). Since then, biomechanical researchers have measured many pediatric tissue properties directly. Biomechanical studies of the intact skull and brain and the properties of individual tissues have demonstrated that the pediatric brain and skull respond differently to loads than adult tissue, and previous linear extrapolation from adult data does not provide an accurate estimate of pediatric properties (Coats & Margulies, 2006; Prange & Margulies, 2002).

Despite the increased research in the field, not enough key pieces of information are in place to establish realistic injury tolerances for children. The Head Injury Criterion (HIC) was initially established as an estimate of linear acceleration head injury in adults from lateral impact car crashes. Despite ongoing research to create better predictors of head injury in adults (Deck & Willinger, 2008), the HIC is still used as the standard predictor of head injury severity in pediatric biomechanical studies (Bertocci et al., 2003; Kapoor et al., 2005). In a somewhat arbitrary manner, the adult HIC value is reduced for predicting head injury severity in children, but this metric is not based on measurements of the types of forces and accelerations that actually produce injuries in children. Biomechanical data that define an age-specific response of the body to loading and define age-specific tissue thresholds for injury are necessary to improve our understanding of pediatric TBI and to develop more effective prevention, diagnosis, and treatment strategies for kids.

Biomechanics of traumatic brain injury

Large impact forces to the head can cause skull fracture, epidural hemorrhages, and focal contusions to the brain and scalp, but subdural hemorrhages (SDH) and axonal injury are primarily caused during rapid accelerations or decelerations of the head. These rapid

Pediatric Traumatic Brain Injury: New Frontiers in Clinical and Translational Research, ed. V. Anderson and K. O. Yeates. Published by Cambridge University Press. © Cambridge University Press 2010.

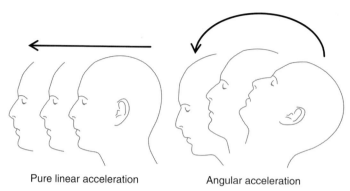

Pure linear acceleration   Angular acceleration

Fig. 1.1. Schematic of linear and angular acceleration to the head. In animal studies, large angular accelerations are more often correlated to subdural hemorrhage and traumatic axonal injury than linear accelerations. However, a combination of linear and angular acceleration is the most common loading mechanism in motor vehicle accidents, falls, and assault.

accelerations may be linear or rotational in nature (Fig. 1.1), but high angular accelerations are more often correlated with SDH and traumatic axonal injury than linear. One early biomechanical study on primates reported that all animals subjected to a primarily angular motion of the head showed immediate onset of unconsciousness that varied for 2–10 minutes, but animals with only a translational (linear) motion of the head never became unconscious (Gennarelli *et al.*, 1971). Subsequent biomechanical experiments focusing on mechanisms of rapid, non-impact head rotation to primates and pigs resulted in widespread axonal injury (Gennarelli *et al.*, 1972; Gennarelli *et al.*, 1982; Gennarelli, 1996; Raghupathi & Margulies, 2002; Smith *et al.*, 2000) and SDH (Gennarelli *et al.*, 1979; Gennarelli & Thibault, 1982; Meaney, 1991).

These rapid angular accelerations can occur without head impact, but they are most commonly associated with an impact to the head (e.g. motor vehicle accident, falls, assault). Assessing the mechanism of injury is challenging in children because there is often no reliable witness to the incident, particularly in the case of abusive head trauma. Additionally, the absence of evidence of a contact injury (i.e. skull fracture, cranial bruising, or scalp swelling) does not establish that there was no impact. A forceful impact of an infant head to a 4-inch thick piece of soft foam dissipates the force to the head possibly eliminating external evidence of impact, but producing a head angular acceleration that is on average three times greater than that of shaking (Prange *et al.*, 2003). Additionally, several clinical studies have reported bruising (Atwal *et al.*, 1998), extracranial swelling (Strouse *et al.*, 1998), and skull fracture (Alexander *et al.*, 1990) that are only found after autopsy and not during clinical examination.

Computational and physical models of angular acceleration mimicking the animal experiments mentioned above have correlated axonal injury with the amount of deformation (strain) in the brain tissue and not the stress (force applied per unit area) of the tissue (Margulies *et al.*, 1990; Miller *et al.*, 1998). Experiments on unmyelinated squid axons support these data (Galbraith, 1988; Galbraith *et al.*, 1993). Specifically, uniaxial tensile strain, not stress, in the axon produced short- and long-term neural dysfunction. In primate models of SDH from non-impact rotational loading, it was also observed that the deformation of the parasagittal bridging veins, and not the stress, correlated with the presence or absence of SDH (Meaney, 1991). Together, these data show that the deformational response of brain tissue due to angular acceleration/deceleration of the head is tightly linked with primary axonal and vascular damage found in traumatic axonal injury and SDH.

Biomechanical tools for understanding TBI

Biomechanics draws from several different engineering approaches to answer questions that are difficult or impossible to answer from clinical and epidemiological studies. The most common biomechanical tools are *material property testing, event reconstruction using instrumented surrogates, animal studies*, and *computational modeling*. Each of these tools provides valuable information to increase our understanding of pediatric traumatic brain injury.

Material property testing

Human brain tissue from children is difficult to obtain, and the majority of pediatric brain material property data have been from immature pigs (Prange *et al.*, 2000; Prange & Margulies, 2002) and rodents (Gefen *et al.*, 2003). In both species, the immature brain was reported to be approximately twice as stiff as adult pig and rodent tissue when undergoing large deformation. Similar testing on a single specimen of human temporal cortex gray matter obtained and tested within 3 hours of excision from a 5-year-old patient during a temporal lobectomy procedure was reported to be stiffer than human adult specimens, correlating with the age-dependent findings of the pig and rodent studies (Prange, 2002). This increase in stiffness means that it takes a larger amount of force to deform the pediatric brain compared to the adult. However, it is unknown how much deformation is required to produce injury in the pediatric brain, so an increase in tissue stiffness does not necessarily denote a protective benefit.

The material property differences between the adult and pediatric brain may be due to the degree of myelination. Biomechanical studies have suggested that the axons, rather than the surrounding matrix of astrocytes and oligodendrocytes, contribute more to the effective stiffness of the brain (Arbogast & Margulies, 1999). Thus, the progress of axon myelination during development of the pediatric brain may contribute to the differences reported in material properties of children and adults. Lipids, such as myelin, have a low shear modulus (Yamada, 1970) and may decrease the stiffness of the composite material as the amount of myelin in the brain increases to adult levels.

Because traumatic brain injury events often involve contact to the head, the material properties of the pediatric skull play an important role in defining the underlying brain injury. The developing skull begins as a single layer of mesenchyme in utero, and by birth an infant has several single-layer bony plates approximately 1 mm thick. These bony plates are connected by a membranous material called suture. As a child ages, the bony plates begin to fuse together, eliminating the suture, and becoming a solid encasing for the brain. During childhood the bone begins to differentiate from a single cortical bone layer into a three-layered structure containing a layer of cortical bone on the inner table, followed by a middle layer of spongy diploe, and then another layer of cortical bone on the outer table. The entire thickness of the final composite structure is approximately 5–6 mm. Material property studies on fetal cranial bone have reported that the stiffness (elastic modulus) of the bone significantly increases with donor age (McPherson & Kriewall, 1980a). More recent studies on pediatric cranial bone from infants < 1-year-old also report a significant increase in stiffness with donor age (Coats & Margulies, 2006). The material properties of

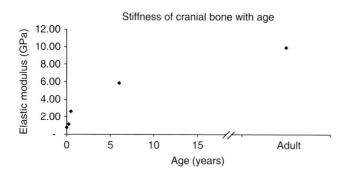

Fig. 1.2. The elastic modulus (stiffness) of cranial bone increases with age, but the relationship is not linear. (Data<1-year-old from McPherson and Kriewall (1980a) and Coats and Margulies (2006). Data from single 6-year-old sample reported in McPherson and Kriewall (1980a). Data from adult skull reported in Hubbard (1971).)

cranial bone in toddlers and adolescents are limited to a single specimen from a 6-year-old child (McPherson & Kriewall, 1980a). While this single specimen is over 7 times stiffer than newborn values, adult values of cranial bone (Hubbard 1971) are still 1.7 times stiffer than the 6-year-old. Overall, these data indicate that the stiffness of cranial bone increases with age, but the relationship is non-linear (Fig. 1.2).

When evaluating infant head injury, however, it is not just the cranial bone stiffness that reflects possible brain deformation upon head impact, but the presence of cranial sutures also contribute to the overall deformation of the skull. Tensile tests on human pediatric cranial suture report that this membranous material can deform over 100% before failure (Coats & Margulies, 2006), further emphasizing that the infant skullcase can undergo significantly larger distortions prior to fracture or rupture compared to the skulls of older children and adults.

Event reconstruction using instrumented surrogates

Biomechanics involves understanding the human body's response to applied forces. Injury severity will vary with the magnitude of the applied force, therefore it is important to quantify and compare the magnitude and types of loads (e.g. linear acceleration, rotational acceleration, impact force, etc.) being applied in events that cause traumatic brain injury. In children, the majority of incidents of TBI are caused by car crashes, accidental falls, and child abuse (CDC, 2005; Kraus *et al.*, 1987; Kraus *et al.*, 1990). Because children are not instrumented during these injurious events, biofidelic surrogates are used to re-enact injurious scenarios. The surrogates are usually instrumented with accelerometers to measure acceleration and/or load cells to measure force. Since the desire of these studies is to mimic the kinematic response of a real child, it is important that the mass, mobility, and deformation characteristics of the surrogate be based on biomechanical measurements in children.

In response to infant TBI from minor frontal car crashes, Klinich *et al.* (2002) used a commercially available 6-month-old surrogate (CRABI) to measure infant head angular acceleration from a passenger-side airbag impact to the back of a rear-facing child restraint system (CRS). In a car crash resulting in a 11 mph change in vehicle velocity, they report nearly an 8 times increase in infant head linear acceleration when the CRS is impacted with an airbag compared to no impact of the CRS by an airbag. Additionally, they report that even in a more severe car crash (30 mph change in vehicle velocity), a CRS system not impacted by an airbag still results in four times less infant head acceleration than the minor car crash with airbag–CRS impact. The use of anthropomorphic dummies (ATD), such as in this study, is common in motor vehicle research and provides valuable information for manufactures of pediatric safety equipment and motor vehicle design, and provides policy makers with data to make decisions regarding pediatric-specific safety regulations. However, it is noteworthy that the movement responses of these pediatric commercial surrogates have not been validated against live or cadaveric children.

Outside of the motor vehicle industry, anthropomorphic surrogates are used to help define load corridors for accidental and abusive events. Duhaime et al. (1987) created an instrumented surrogate to compare the loads experienced by an infant during abusive impact and shaking of an infant. They report that a violent impact of an infant's head against a hard surface creates 45 times greater angular acceleration of the head than violent shaking. Prange et al. (2003) later confirmed these findings and further reported that vigorous shaking produced accelerations significantly smaller than those from a head impact due to a 1 foot fall onto concrete. The same study also demonstrated that an aggressive impact to a 4-inch thick foam pad produced three times more head angular deceleration in an infant than vigorous shaking, suggesting that cases with no evidence of contact are not a guarantee that no head impact was involved.

A subsequent iteration of the instrumented infant surrogate by Coats and Margulies (2008) used new biomechanical data to create a skullcase with distinct cranial bone/suture structures and a neck with three-dimensional mobility. The addition of these structures significantly decreases measured head angular deceleration from impact during low height falls and suggests that a more deformable skullcase may lower the diffuse brain injuries caused by angular acceleration. Simultaneously, an increased deformation from this skullcase may increase the likelihood of local injury to the brain beneath the site of impact. More research is needed to assess the potential of brain injury from skull deformation upon impact.

Unfortunately, surrogates only yield insight into the accelerations and contact loads experienced during a fall or simulated abusive scenario, and cannot predict injuries. To better understand the biological response to these loads, they are often used in conjunction with animal studies and computational models as described below.

Animal studies

In adult head injury, relationships between head acceleration and concussion have been investigated in boxers (Breton et al., 1991) and football players (Pellmen et al., 2003), and primates have provided information regarding loading thresholds and diffuse axonal injury and SDH. In pediatric head injury, there is no human data on load tolerances causing concussion, SDH, or axonal injury. Instead, pediatric animal models are used to investigate mechanisms of brain injury under controlled experimental conditions.

The majority of animal models of pediatric TBI involve contusion injury in the immature rodent (Bittigau et al., 1999; Grundl et al., 1994; Prins et al., 1996). These focal injury studies have been valuable in elucidating the effect of cortical injury on behavior and investigating the biochemical cascade of events that follow head trauma. However, there are key characteristics of the rodent that limit its investigation into the full spectrum of TBI. First, the rodent has very little white matter, making characterization of axonal injury difficult. Second, the lissencephalic morphology of the brain and small brain mass pose unique challenges when investigating rotational head injury. The presence of a gyral brain pattern significantly affects the movement of the brain within the skullcase (Cloots et al., 2008) and results in significantly more brain deformation than a brain without gyri. Additionally, the magnitude of acceleration necessary to cause rotational brain injury is inversely related to brain mass, meaning that extremely high rotational forces would need to be applied to the rodent brain to simulate loads experienced in children. Lastly, the peak growth spurt of the rodent brain occurs before birth, while it occurs at birth in humans (Dobbing, 1974), bringing to question the developmental similarity between the two species.

In contrast, pigs and humans share several parallels in their brain morphology and development that make immature piglets a promising large-animal model for pediatric traumatic brain injury. The peak growth spurt of the pig occurs at birth, like humans, and the myelination and water content changes during development parallel to that in humans (Dickerson & Dobbing, 1966; Dobbing & Sands, 1973). Furthermore, cerebrovascular development (Buckley, 1986), cerebral blood flow and metabolism (Wagerle et al., 1986), and brain electrical activity (Pampiglione, 1971) in the immature pig closely resemble that in human infants. Morphologically, the piglet brain has gyri and differential development of white and gray matter (Dickerson & Dobbing, 1966).

Because of these similarities, pigs have been used not only to study the effect of age on injury, but also to study the effect of injury mechanism. Some fluid percussion studies report the pediatric brain to be more vulnerable to injury (Armstead & Kurth, 1994; Prins et al., 1996), while other contusion studies report no significant differences between adult and immature animals (Adelson et al., 1996). However, it is difficult to compare data across studies because the applied loads were not scaled according to differences in brain size between adult and immature animals. In a study with the applied load scaled to age, Duhaime et al. (2000) applied cortical impact to three age groups of piglets (5-day "infant," 1-month "toddler," and 4-month "adolescent"). One week following injury, piglets in the infant group had the smallest cortical lesion and the adolescent group of piglets had the largest cortical lesion, suggesting that the younger infant brain was either less vulnerable to acute injury and/or was able to recover more quickly than the older pigs. A follow-up study by Duhaime et al. (2003) reports that lesion volume 1 day after cortical impact in infant pigs was larger than adolescent pigs. However, lesion volume in infant pigs 7 and 30 days following cortical impact was smaller than adolescent pigs, confirming that piglets were more susceptible to injury and were able to recover more quickly than older pigs. In inertial injury studies in immature (Raghupathi & Margulies, 2002) and adult pigs (Smith et al., 2000) experiencing the same angular velocity and acceleration, the immature piglets had 3.4 times more injured axons per area than the adults 6 hours post-injury, agreeing with the Duhaime study in that the pediatric brain was more vulnerable to injury than the adult, even under a different mechanism of injury (rotational acceleration versus cortical impact).

Subsequent inertial studies from the same lab investigated the effect of repetitive rotation on TBI in immature piglets (Raghupathi et al., 2004). Animals underwent either a single rapid horizontal head rotation or a double rapid horizontal head rotation (induced 15 minutes following the initial rotation) and brains were evaluated by a neuropathologist. Animals with a double head rotation had significantly more injured axons within a region, and had significantly more regions with injured axons than animals with a single head rotation. These data imply a cumulative effect of injury when a second insult is applied shortly after the initial insult.

Another interesting finding to come out of animal studies of pediatric TBI is the effect of rotational direction on injury severity. In one study, rapid, non-impact head rotations in the sagittal, horizontal, and coronal directions produced very different brain injuries in immature piglets (Eucker *et al.*, 2008). The authors report significantly worse clinical findings, such as greater loss of unconsciousness, 100% apnea, and lower cerebral blood flow, in sagittal and horizontal rotation compared to coronal rotation. Inertial head injury studies in the adult primate also report significant effects of rotational direction on brain trauma (Gennarelli *et al.*, 1982; Gennarelli *et al.*, 1987), but differences between head and neck orientation in the biped compared to the quadruped make direct comparison to these piglet studies difficult.

In summary animal models have demonstrated that injury severity depends on developmental age, time after the injury, the number of insults to the brain, the time between those insults, and the rotational direction and/or impact location. While animal models are useful for determination of injury response and time course, as well as the development of new diagnosis and treatment strategies, they cannot be used to determine local tissue deformations that may be primarily responsible for acute traumatic brain injury. They also can not determine minimum accelerations or impact forces necessary to produce concussion, SDH, or traumatic axonal injury in humans. Instead, computational models are used to relate external loading forces and accelerations to finite deformations of tissue, and make predictions of injury in humans.

Computational modeling

Computational finite element models (FEM) are useful in investigating the effect of anatomical variances, biomechanical parameters, and injury mechanisms on resulting deformation and stress in the brain and skull. In order for these models to portray real-world scenarios accurately they require detailed geometry, biofidelic material property data, and realistic boundary conditions and applied loads. Justification for simplifying any of these parameters is dependent on the purpose of the model and should be supported with a parametric analysis (a series of model manipulations that evaluate the effect of various parameters on model predictions). FEM that have passed the above mentioned criteria can make predictions of injury given material property failure thresholds and prior validation of the model with real-world data.

The first FEM created specific for pediatric head trauma was by McPherson and Kriewall (1980b) and was later improved upon by Lapeer and Prageer (2001) to investigate the effect of uterine pressure on the pediatric skull during childbirth. The model showed good agreement with clinical experiments of uterine pressure and established the usefulness of using FEM to predict stress and strain in the pediatric head. Klinich *et al.* (2002) developed a FEM to predict the stress in an infant skull following airbag impact to the back of a rear-facing child restraint system. The skull stress patterns in her model correlated to varying severities of infant skull fractures in real-world cases, but development of skull fracture thresholds were hindered by the unavailability of accurate material property data in human cranial suture at the time of the study. Instead, the authors used material property data from immature pigs, which has since been shown to be 10 times stiffer than actual human infant suture (Coats & Margulies, 2006). Therefore, the thresholds determined in the study are likely higher than the actual thresholds for skull fracture.

More recently, Coats and Margulies (2008) developed a FEM to predict skull fracture in infants from head-first low height falls with occipital impact onto carpet pad, concrete, and an innerspring mattress. Validated first against cadaver (Coats *et al.*, 2007) and then against real-world data (Coats, 2007), they report a 99% probability of occipital skull fracture from an uninhibited head-first 2–3 feet fall onto concrete and a ¼-inch thick carpet pad. A 1 foot fall onto concrete and carpet pad resulted in a 84% probability of occipital skull fracture. All falls < 3 feet onto a 6 innerspring crib mattress resulted in only a 5% probability of occipital skull fracture. However, this FEM is only applicable to 0–2-month-old infants, only predicts the presence/absence of fracture and not the severity or type, and makes no predictions regarding underlying brain injury.

A recent series of infant FEM (Raul *et al.*, 2008; Roth *et al.*, 2006) have investigated the effect of an increased subarachnoid space and loading mechanism on strain in parasagittal bridging veins. There has been no validation of the model, so no predictions of injury can be made from these studies. Additionally, the method used to model the brain–skull interface has a significant effect on predicted brain–skull displacement and bridging vein strain (Wittek & Omori, 2003). Thus, further studies need to be done to ensure that the method for modeling this brain–skull interface in children is biofidelic before conclusions regarding bridging vein strain and brain–skull displacement can be made.

Translation of biomechanics to real-world applications

Each of these biomechanical tools offers a valuable perspective of mechanisms of TBI and can help in the development of prevention, detection, and treatment strategies. Life-like anthropomorphic surrogates can be used to re-enact events and directly measure the loads (forces, accelerations) experienced by the head. These surrogates must mimic the biomechanical response of children for these measurements to be relevant. Manufacturers can then use these loads to design safety equipment for children (e.g. helmets, child restraint systems, and playground surfaces) that reduce forces and acceleration to the head, and therefore reduce TBI risk. Load measurements for abusive and accidental scenarios (made with anthropomorphic surrogates) can be combined with the probabilities of injury at these load levels (determined from material property testing and computational models) to yield insight into injury mechanisms and help clinicians evaluate histories provided by caretakers suspected of abuse. Lastly, pediatric animal models can be used to investigate mechanisms of TBI, and develop or optimize treatment strategies that can be translated to clinical practice.

Despite the progress made in understanding mechanisms of pediatric head injury, there is still a paucity of pediatric-specific biomechanical data. Specifically, future directions in biomechanics should focus on defining age-specific tissue injury thresholds and better characterizing the pediatric neck and brain response to loads. Additionally, as computers become more powerful and able to represent biological materials more accurately, future models of pediatric head injury should strive to incorporate more detailed geometry and simulate more complex mechanisms of brain injury. Finally, future biomechanical research using animal models should focus on discovering improved treatment strategies for TBI specific to infants and older children.

References

Adelson, P. D., Robichaud, P., Hamilton, R. L. & Kochanek, P. M. (1996). A model of diffuse traumatic brain injury in the immature rat. *Journal of Neurosurgery*, **85**, 877–884.

Alexander, R., Sato, Y., Smith, W. & Bennett, T. (1990). Incidence of impact trauma with cranial injuries ascribed to shaking. *American Journal of Diseases of Children*, **144**, 724–726.

Arbogast, K. & Margulies, S. (1999). A fiber-reinforced composite model of the viscoelastic behaviour of the brainstem in shear. *Journal of Biomechanics*, **32**, 865–870.

Armstead, W. & Kurth, C. (1994). Different cerebral hemodynamic responses following fluid percussion brain injury in the newborn and juvenile pig. *Journal of Neurotrauma*, **11**, 487–497.

Atwal, G. S., Rutty, G. N., Carter, N. & Green, M. A. (1998). Bruising in non-accidental injured children; a retrospective study of the prevalence, distribution and pathological associations in 24 cases. *Forensic Science International*, **96**, 215–230.

Bertocci, G. E., Pierce, M. C., Deemer, E., Aguel, F., Janosky, J. E. & Vogeley, E. (2003). Using test dummy experiments to investigate pediatric injury risk in simulated short-distance falls. *Archives of Pediatrics and Adolescent Medicine*, **157**, 480–486.

Bittigau, P., Sifringer, M., Pohl, D. *et al.* (1999). Apoptotic neurodegeneration following trauma is markedly enhanced in the immature brain. *Annals of Neurology*, **45**, 724–735.

Breton, F., Pincemaile, Y., Tarriere, C. & Renault, B. (1991). Event-related potential assessment of attention and the orienting reaction in boxers before and after a fight. *Biological Psychology*, **31**, 57–71.

Buckley, N. (1986). Maturation of circulatory system in three mammalian models of human development. *Comparative Biochemistry and Physiology*, **83A**, 1–7.

CDC (2005). *Wisqar Database*. NCIPC – WISQAR Database.

Cloots, R. J. H., Gervaise, H. M. T., van Dommelen, J. A. W. & Geers, M. G. D. (2008). Biomechanics of traumatic brain injury: influences of the morphologic heterogeneities of the cerebral cortex. *Annals of Biomedical Engineering*, **36**, 1203–1215.

Coats, B. (2007). Mechanics of head impact in infants. Ph.D. thesis, Department of Bioengineering, University of Pennsylvania, Philadelphia.

Coats, B., Ji, S. & Margulies, S. S. (2007). Parametric study of head impact in the infant. *Stapp Car Crash Journal*, **51**, 1–15.

Coats, B. & Margulies, S. S. (2006). Material properties of human infant skull and suture at high rates. *Journal of Neurotrauma*, **23**, 1222–1232.

Coats, B. & Margulies, S. S. (2008). Potential for head injuries in infants from low-height falls. *Journal of Neurosurgery: Pediatrics*, **2**, 1–10.

Deck, C. & Willinger, R. (2008). Improved head injury criteria based on head fe model. *International Journal of Crashworthiness*, **13**, 667–678.

Dickerson, J. & Dobbing, J. (1966). Prenatal and postnatal growth and development of the central nervous system of the pig. *Proceedings of the Royal Society of London, Series B*, **166**, 384–395.

Dobbing, J. (1974). The later growth of the brain and its vulnerability. *Pediatrics*, **53**, 2–6.

Dobbing, J. & Sands, J. (1973). Quantitative growth and development of human brain. *Archives of Disease in Childhood*, **48**, 757–767.

Duhaime, A., Gennarelli, T., Thibault, L., Bruce, D., Margulies, S. & Wiser, R. (1987). The shaken baby syndrome: a clinical, pathological, and biomechanical study. *Journal of Neurosurgery*, **66**, 409–415.

Duhaime, A. C., Margulies, S. S., Durham, S. R. *et al.* (2000). Maturation-dependent response of the piglet brain to scaled cortical impact. *Journal of Neurosurgery*, **93**, 455–462.

Duhaime, A. C., Hunter, J. V., Grate, L. L. *et al.* (2003). Magnetic resonance imaging studies of age-dependent responses to scaled focal brain injury in the piglet. *Journal of Neurosurgery*, **99**, 542–548.

Eucker, S., Friess, S., Ralston, J. & Margulies, S. (2008). *Regional Cerebral Blood Flow Response Following Brain Injury Depends on Direction of Head Motion*. Orlando, FL: National Neurotrauma Society.

Galbraith, J. (1988). *The Effects of Mechanical Loading on the Electrophysiology of the Squid Giant Axon*. Philadelphia: University of Pennsylvania.

Galbraith, J. A., Thibault, L. E. & Matteson, D. R. (1993). Mechanical and electrical responses of the squid giant axon to simple elongation. *Journal of Biomechanical Engineering*, **115**, 13–22.

Gefen, A., Gefen, N., Zhu, Q., Raghupathi, R. & Margulies, S. (2003). Age-dependent changes in material properties of the brain and braincase of the rat. *Journal of Neurotrauma*, **20**, 1163–1177.

Gennarelli, T. (1996). The spectrum of traumatic axonal injury. *Neuropathology & Applied Neurobiology*, **22**, 509–513.

Gennarelli, T. A. & Thibault, L. E. (1982). Biomechanics of acute subdural hematoma. *Journal of Trauma*, **22**, 680–686.

Gennarelli, T. A., Ommaya, A. K. & Thibault, L. E. (1971). Comparison of linear and rotational accelerations in experimental cerebral concussion. *Proceedings of the 15th Stapp Car Crash Conference,* New York, Society of Automotive Engineers, pp. 797–803.

Gennarelli, T., Thibault, L. & Ommaya, A. (1972). Pathophysiologic responses to rotational and translational acceleration of the head. *Proceedings of the 16th Stapp Car Crash Conference*, New York, Society of Automotive Engineers, pp. 296–308.

Gennarelli, T., Abel, J., Adams, H. & Graham, D. (1979). Differential tolerance of frontal and temporal lobes to contusion induced by angular acceleration. *Proceedings of the 23rd Stapp Car Crash Conference*, New York, Society of Automotive Engineers.

Gennarelli, T., Thibault, L., Adams, J., Graham, D., Thompson, C. & Marcincin, R. (1982). Diffuse axonal injury and traumatic coma in the primate. *Annals of Neurology*, **12**, 564–574.

Gennarelli, T. A., Thibault, L. E., Tomei, G., Wiser, R., Graham, D. I. & Adams, J. H. (1987). Directional dependence of axonal brain injury due to centroidal and non-centroidal acceleration. *Proceedings of the 31st Stapp Car Crash Conference*, Warrendale, PA, Society of Automotive Engineers, pp. 49–53.

Goldsmith, W. (2001). The state of head injury biomechanics: past, present, and future: Part 1. *Critical Reviews in Biomedical Engineering*, **29**, 441–600.

Goldsmith, W. & Monson, K. (2005). The state of head injury biomechanics: past, present, and future: Part 2. *Critical Reviews in Biomedical Engineering*, **33**, 105–207.

Grundl, P., Biagas, K., Kochanek, P., Schiding, J., Barmada, M. & Nemoto, E. (1994). Early cerebrovascular response to head injury in immature and mature rats. *Journal of Neurotrauma*, **11**, 135–148.

Hubbard, R. (1971). Flexure of layered cranial bone. *Journal of Biomechanics*, **4**, 251–263.

Kapoor, T., Altenhof, W. & Howard, A. (2005). The effect of using universal anchorages in child restraint seats on the injury potential for children in frontal crash. *International Journal of Crashworthiness*, **10**, 305–314.

Klinich, K., Hulbert, G. & Schneider, L. (2002). Estimating infant head injury criteria and impact response using crash reconstruction and finite element modeling. *Stapp Car Crash Journal*, **46**, 165–194.

Kraus, J., Fife, D. & Conroy, C. (1987). Pediatric brain injuries: the nature, clinical course, and early outcomes in a defined united stated population. *Pediatrics*, **79**, 501–507.

Kraus, J., Rock, A. & Hemyari, P. (1990). Brain injuries among infants, children, adolescents, and young adults. *American Journal of Diseases of Children*, **144**, 684–691.

Lapeer, R. J. & Prager, R. W. (2001). Fetal head moulding: finite element analysis of a fetal skull subjected to uterine pressures during the first stage of labour. *Journal of Biomechanics*, **34**, 1125–1133.

Margulies, S., Thibault, L. & Gennarelli, T. (1990). Physical model simulations of brain injury in the primate. *Journal of Biomechanics*, **23**, 823–836.

McPherson, G. & Kriewall, T. (1980a). The elastic modulus of fetal cranial bone: a first step toward understanding of the biomechanics of fetal head molding. *Journal of Biomechanics*, **13**, 9–16.

McPherson, G. K. & Kriewall, T. J. (1980b). Fetal head molding: an investigation utilizing a finite element model of the fetal parietal bone. *Journal of Biomechanics*, **13**, 17–26.

Meaney, D. F. (1991). Biomechanics of acute subdural hematoma in the subhuman primate and man. Ph.D. thesis, Department of Bioengineering. University of Pennsylvania, Philadelphia.

Miller, R., Margulies, S., Leoni, M. *et al.* (1998). Finite element modeling approaches for predicting injury in an experimental model of severe diffuse axonal injury. *Proceedings of the 42nd Stapp Car Crash Conference*, Warrendale, PA, Society of Automotive Engineers, pp. 155–167.

Mohan, D., Bowman, B., Snyder, R. & Foust, D. (1979). A biomechanical analysis of head impact injuries to children. *Journal of Biomechanical Engineering*, **101**, 250–260.

NCIPC (2000). *Traumatic Brain Injury in the United States: Assessing Outcomes in Children*. Atlanta, Georgia Centers for Disease Control and Prevention: National Center for Injury Prevention and Control.

Pampiglione, G. (1971). Some aspects of development of cerebral function in mammals. *Proceeding of the Royal Society of Medicine*, **64**, 429–435.

Pellmen, E. J., Viano, D. C., Tucker, A. M., Casson, I. R. & Waeckerle, J. F. (2003). Concussion in professional football: reconstruction of game impacts and injuries. *Neurosurgery*, **53**, 799–814.

Prange, M. (2002). Biomechanics of traumatic brain injury in the infant. Ph.D. thesis, Department of Bioengineering. University of Pennsylvania, Philadelphia.

Prange, M. & Margulies, S. (2002). Regional, directional, and age-dependent properties of brain undergoing large deformation. *Journal of Biomechanical Engineering*, **124**, 244–252.

Prange, M., Meaney, D. & Margulies, S. (2000). Defining brain mechanical properties: effects of region, direction, and species. *Proceedings of the 44th Stapp Car Crash Conference*, Warrendale, PA, Society of Automotive Engineers, pp. 205–213.

Prange, M., Coats, B., Duhaime, A. C. & Margulies, S. (2003). Anthropomorphic simulations of falls, shakes, and inflicted impacts in infants. *Journal of Neurosurgery*, **99**, 143–150.

Prins, M., Lee, S., Cheng, C., Becker, D. & Hovda, D. (1996). Fluid percussion brain injury in the developing and adult rat:

a comparative study of mortality, morphology, intracranial pressure and mean arterial blood pressure. *Developmental Brain Research*, **95**, 272–282.

Raghupathi, R. & Margulies, S. S. (2002). Traumatic axonal injury after closed head injury in the neonatal pig. *Journal of Neurotrauma*, **19**, 843–853.

Raghupathi, R., Mehr, M., Helfaer, M. & Margulies, S. (2004). Traumatic axonal injury is exacerbated following repetitive close head injury in the neonatal pig. *Journal of Neurotrauma*, **21**, 307–316.

Raul, J. S., Roth, S., Ludes, B. & Willinger, R. (2008). Influence of the benign enlargement of the subarachnoid space on the bridging veins strain during a shaking event: a finite element study. *International Journal of Legal Medicine*, **122**, 337–340.

Roth, S., Raul, J. S., Ludes, B. & Willinger, R. (2006). Finite element analysis of impact and shaking inflicted to a child. *International Journal of Legal Medicine*, **121**, 223–228.

Smith, D. H., Nonaka, M., Miller, R. *et al.* (2000). Immediate coma following inertial brain injury dependent on axonal damage in the brainstem. *Journal of Neurosurgery*, **93**, 315–322.

Strouse, P. J., Caplan, M. & Owings, C. L. (1998). Extracranial soft-tissue swelling: a normal postmortem radiographic finding or a sign of trauma? *Pediatric Radiology*, **28**, 594–596.

Wagerle, L., Kumar, S. & Delivoria-Papadopoulos, M. (1986). Effect of sympathetic nerve stimulation on cerebral blood flow in newborn piglets. *Pediatric Research*, **20**, 131–135.

Wittek, A. & Omori, K. (2003). Parametric study of effects of brain–skull boundary conditions and brain material properties on responses of simplified finite element brain model under angular acceleration impulse in sagittal plane. *JSME International Journal Series C – Mechanical Systems Machine Elements and Manufacturing*, **46**, 1388–1399.

Yamada, H. (1970). *Strength of Biological Materials*. Baltimore: Williams and Wilkins Co.

Chapter

Neurobiology of TBI sustained during development

Mayumi L. Prins, Christopher C. Giza, and David A. Hovda

Introduction

Changes in brain growth and connectivity continue throughout an individual's lifespan. The most rapid period of cerebral changes are observed during infancy and childhood but have recently been shown to continue into early adulthood (Toga *et al.*, 2006). While the pediatric population as a whole shows robust differences across countless variables compared to the "adult" or mature brain, there are also significant differences between subgroups within the pediatric population. The pediatric population is not a homogenous group, but rather is made up of subgroups as defined by their developmental profiles for a given parameter. Despite the fact that increasing clinical and experimental evidence reveals age-related differences in response to traumatic brain injury (TBI) *within* the pediatric population, there remains a lack of appreciation for these differences when establishing standards of care for children. Many parameters (serum glucose management) continue to be "modified" from adult practice without direct knowledge of age-related responses. These findings emphasize the fact that developmental physiology impacts the pathophysiological response to traumatic brain injury and ultimately influences developmental disability.

Traumatic brain injury early in life
Myelination and compliance

Changes in cerebral myelination continue throughout adolescence into early adulthood (Courhesne *et al.*, 2000; Giorgio *et al.*, 2008; Paus *et al.*, 1999). As brain myelin content increases, brain water content decreases (Himwich, 1973) with consequent changes in the biomechanical properties of the brain. The younger brain with increased water content is less compressible and therefore more susceptible to elevations in intracranial pressure (ICP) based on the pressure volume index (Maset *et al.*, 1987; Muizelaar *et al.*, 1989). Age-related differences in brain water content and ICP have been examined after TBI. Postnatal day (PND) 24–32 rats were found to show earlier and greater increases in brain water content after weight drop injury than PND56–84 rats (Grundl *et al.*, 1994). Both age groups showed increased ICP at 24 hours post-injury. Following fluid percussion injury, PND17 rats showed a greater tendency for developing high ICP and low blood pressure compared to PND28 or 90 (Prins *et al.*, 1996). Their increased vulnerability was reflected in the 100% mortality rate after severe injuries. These findings have revealed how maturational differences increase cerebral vulnerability to elevated pressure, which interacts directly with changes in cerebral blood flow.

Pediatric Traumatic Brain Injury: New Frontiers in Clinical and Translational Research, ed. V. Anderson and K. O. Yeates. Published by Cambridge University Press. © Cambridge University Press 2010.

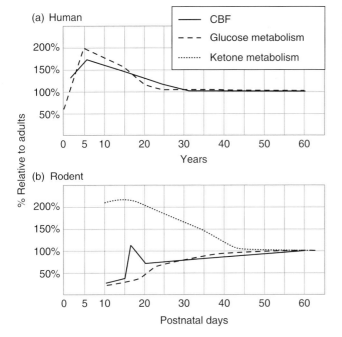

Fig. 2.1. Changes in cerebral blood flow (CBF), cerebral glucose metabolism, and cerebral ketone metabolism during human (a) and rodent (b) cerebral maturation.

Cerebral metabolism

Cerebral blood flow

Cerebral blood flow (CBF) is another physiological parameter that changes with cerebral maturation. It is the contrasting blood flow rates from critically ill neonates relative to adults that established an appreciation for the existence of age differences in blood flow to the brain. However, only a few studies have profiled CBF of normal children across various age groups (Chiron et al., 1992; Udomphorn et al., 2008). CBF as measured by ^{133}Xe single photon emission computed tomography and transcranial Doppler both indicate that neonates have the lowest blood flow rates (39 ml/min per 100 g tissue), which peak between 6–9 years of age (75 ml/min per 100 g) and then decrease towards adult rates (45 ml/min per 100 g; Fig. 2.1(a)). CBF remains coupled to glucose metabolism throughout brain development as reflected by the parallel changes in glucose metabolism (Chugani et al., 1987).

In contrast to the developing child, the postnatal rodent brain shows gradually increasing CBF rates from postnatal day 10 towards adult values, with only the PND17 age group exceeding adult values (Fig. 2.1(b); Nehlig et al., 1989). The apparent uncoupling of CBF and glucose metabolism at PND17 is thought to reflect cerebral ketone metabolism associated with the high circulating concentration of ketones at this age (Nehlig et al., 1987).

Experimental TBI models applied to the developing brain have revealed important age differences in CBF after injury. Scaled weight drop injury in PND32 and PND60–90 rats resulted in 74% and 58% decrease in CBF, respectively, in the injured cortex at 2 hours post-injury (Grundl et al., 1994). At 24 and 48 hours post-injury, PND28 rats showed global hyperemia with CBF rates over twofold greater than age-matched controls (Biagas et al., 1996). While the aged (PND420) rats did not show increased CBF, the mature (PND60–90) animals showed a 50% increase at 24 hours and 76% increase at 48 hours after injury relative to controls. Age differences were also observed after scaled cortical impact injury in the developing pig, where increased CBF above age-matched controls were observed in the PND5 piglet, but decreased CBF was observed in PND30 and PND120 pigs with time after injury (Durham et al., 2000). These models suggest that the immature brain may be more susceptible to increased CBF after TBI than the mature or aged brain.

Changes in CBF following TBI in children have produced conflicting findings. CBF changes after severe TBI in children 2–18 years old have shown increased CBF associated with malignant brain edema (Bruce et al., 1981; Muizelaar et al., 1989), no changes in CBF (Sharples et al., 1995), or decreased CBF (Adelson et al., 1997; Skippen et al., 1997). It is important to keep in mind that normal CBF in children can be significantly greater than in adults and comparisons of the changes after TBI in children should be made to age-matched controls. When pediatric TBI patients were compared to age-appropriate normative pediatric CBF data, hyperemia was not found to be common (Zwienenberg & Muizelaar, 1999). The term "hyperemia" may have to be age-specifically redefined. Despite the existence of increased blood flow among children, there is evidence that 43% of children show impaired autoregulation within 72 hours after severe TBI, which was associated with poor outcome (Vavilala et al., 2006).

Developmental cerebral metabolism

During cerebral maturation, the brain alters its reliance on various metabolic substrates. In utero, the developing brain relies on maternal glucose supplies. Shortly after birth the brain switches its metabolism briefly to lactate until suckling begins. The brain metabolizes a combination of glucose and ketone bodies during the suckling period, but switches reliance to glucose after weaning. These changes in cerebral substrate metabolism are accompanied by alterations in systemic substrate availability, substrate transport, and enzyme activities for substrate metabolism.

The pre-weaned animal is geared for cerebral ketone metabolism with higher circulating concentrations of ketones, greater number of blood brain barrier transporters, and greater enzymatic activities of ketone metabolizing enzymes (Booth et al., 1980; Vannucci & Simpson, 2003). During the period of peak ketone utilization, the brain's capacity to take up ß-hydroxybutyrate (ßOHB) is six times greater than the adult rat brain, as is the rate of ketone metabolism within the frontoparietal cortex (Cremer et al., 1976; Hawkins et al., 1971; Nehlig et al., 1991). Upon weaning, there is a decrease in arterial ketone concentrations, followed by a drop in cerebral uptake and finally a down-regulation of the monocarboxylate transporters (MCT).

In contrast to the abrupt changes in cerebral ketone metabolism, developmental changes in glucose metabolism are more gradual. At birth, circulating concentrations of glucose are 50% that of the adult. Plasma glucose concentrations gradually increase during early postnatal development to achieve adult levels at PND10. Changes in substrate availability occur before both the increased expression in cerebral glucose transporters (Glut 1 and Glut 3) (Vannucci & Simpson, 2003) and the increased activity of glycolytic enzymes (Leong & Clark, 1984). These parameters do not reach maturation until PND30 when adult levels of glucose metabolic rates are achieved (Nehlig et al., 1987).

During the acute phase ($\leq 1\,hr$) after fluid percussion (FP) injury, the adult rat brain shows an indiscriminate efflux of potassium, transient increase in extracellular glutamate (Katayama et al., 1990; Kawamata et al., 1992), accumulation of Ca^{2+} (Enerson & Drewes, 2003; Osteen et al., 2001), and transient increase in cerebral metabolic rate of glucose

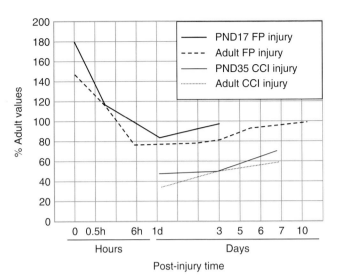

Fig. 2.2. Age differences in cerebral glucose metabolism as percentage of adult values with time after fluid percussion (FP) injury and controlled cortical impact (CCI) injury.

(CMRglc) (Hovda *et al.*, 1994; Sutton *et al.*, 1994; Yoshino *et al.*, 1991). This initial increase in CMRglc is due to increased cellular energy required to restore ionic balance and maintain the neuronal membrane potential (Hovda *et al.*, 1996). Following the transient increase in CMRglc is a prolonged period (10–14 days) of glucose metabolic depression. Similar to the adult glucose metabolic response, FP injured PND17 rats showed an immediate increase in CMRglc, followed by a period of glucose metabolic depression. However, the duration of the glucose metabolic depression is truncated (3 days) relative to adults (Thomas *et al.*, 2000) (Fig. 2.2). In addition to age-related differences in the duration of CMRglc depression after FP injury, there are age-related injury type differences in CMRglc after controlled cortical impact (CCI) injury. Following CCI injury in PND70 and PND35 rats, the CMRglc depression is greater in both magnitude and duration compared to changes after FP injury. While both age groups showed similar magnitude and duration of CMRglc depression in the cortical structures, PND35 rats showed earlier recovery of glucose metabolic rates within the hippocampus and thalamus (Prins & Hovda, 2009).

The reason for the prolonged decrease in CMRglc after TBI remains as yet unknown. There are numerous possible mechanisms that may explain this depression including disruption of mitochondrial metabolism by calcium accumulation (Fineman *et al.*, 1993; Osteen *et al.*, 2001), ionic flux disruptions (Katayama *et al.*, 1990), reduced CBF (Cherian *et al.*, 2004), or lactic acid accumulation (Kawamata *et al.*, 1995). Following the initial surge in neurotransmitter release and ionic fluctuations, brain activity may become quiescent and therefore require less substrate. Several studies have shown decreased ability of the brain to show stimulation-evoked increases in CMRglc as early as 4 hours and as long as 2 months post-injury (Dietrich *et al.*, 1994; Passineau *et al.*, 2000). This quiescent state may be a mechanism to reduce secondary injury from premature activation, which has been observed after direct cortical stimulation (Ip *et al.*, 2003).

Another possibility is that glucose metabolic pathways may be altered after injury, directly impacting cerebral glucose uptake. 2-deoxyglucose (2DG) autoradiography is a measure of glucose uptake, but it does not reveal how glucose is processed past hexokinase. Recently, the metabolic fate of $[1,2-^{13}C]$ glucose was determined using NMR spectroscopy

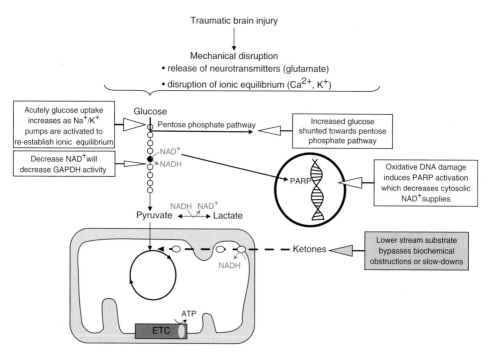

Fig. 2.3. Diagram of the biochemical changes after TBI that directly affect the metabolic fate of glucose and ultimately contribute to alterations in energy production. Under these conditions metabolism of alternative substrates, such as ketone bodies, has been shown to have therapeutic effects on histology and functional outcome.

after CCI injury in the PND90 rat (Bartnik-Olsen *et al.*, 2005). This study revealed a significant increase in lactate and glutamine pool at 3.5 hours post-injury. At 3.5 and 24 hours there was a 9%–12% increase in flux of glucose through the pentose phosphate pathway (PPP) in the ipsilateral cortex. Increased labeling was also reported in C3 glutamine, indicating increased pyruvate carboxylase activity, which is primarily glial. The decrease in oxidation of glucose and increased shunting of glucose towards NADPH synthesis suggests altered fates for glucose after TBI.

Contributing to this acute metabolic dysfunction during the first 24 hours post-TBI are production of reactive oxygen species (ROS) (Fig. 2.3) (Hall *et al.*, 1993; Marklund *et al.*, 2001) and activation of poly ADP-ribose polymerase (PARP) via DNA damage (LaPlaca *et al.*, 1999; Satchell *et al.*, 2003). The PARP-mediated DNA repair process requires nicotinamide adenine dinucleotide (NAD^+) (Satchell *et al.*, 2003). Depletion of the cytosolic NAD^+ pool has been shown to inhibit glyceraldehyde 3-phosphate dehydrogenase (GAPDH) (Berger *et al.*, 1985; Cosi & Marien, 1998; Sheline *et al.*, 2000; Ying *et al.*, 2003), which can cause rerouting of glucose to other biochemical destinations. Following ischemic brain injury in the adult rat, cytoplasmic expression of GAPDH increased within 3 hours with peak expression at 6–12 hours in the penumbra (Tanaka *et al.*, 2002). In the same region, there was also an increase in nuclear GAPDH expression at 3–24 hours with peak at 12–24 hours. The translocation of GAPDH to the nucleus has been associated with apoptosis (Ishitami *et al.*, 1998; Kim *et al.*, 2006). Alterations in GAPDH expression or activity will consequently reduce/inhibit glycolysis and alter the metabolism of glucose. Under conditions of impaired glycolytic metabolism, glucose becomes a less favorable energy substrate.

Alternative substrates after TBI

The capacity of the brain to increase its reliance on alternative substrates under conditions of stress has been well documented (Dahlquist & Persson, 1976; Hawkins *et al.*, 1971; Owen *et al.*, 1967). While the brain can metabolize various substrates (pyruvate, lactate, malate, etc.), ketone bodies are the only endogenously circulating alternative substrates that have been shown to significantly supplement cerebral metabolism (Dahlquist & Persson, 1976; Hawkins *et al.*, 1971; Owen *et al.*, 1967). Experiments utilizing fasting or starvation have revealed an inverse relationship between age and ketogenesis or cerebral ketone transport. The ability of the younger brain to achieve greater ketosis rapidly and to demonstrate greater cerebral uptake of ketones continues even after weaning and gradually decreases into adulthood.

The developmental difference in the brain's ability to shift towards ketone metabolism may ultimately make the juvenile brain the most receptive to alternative substrates as a therapeutic option after TBI. Robertson *et al.* (1991) showed that patients who were not administered intravenous glucose to maintain normoglycemia had arterial ßOHB approaching 1mM and extracellular lactate decreased by 23%. In these saline-infused patients, ketones accounted for 16% of brain energy production, suggesting that the use of insulin and glucose administration to maintain normoglycemia actually suppresses endogenous ketogenesis. In a subsequent study, the authors showed that TBI patients maintained on a "ketogenic" (KG)-type diet showed lower plasma glucose and lactate levels and had improved nitrogen balance (Ritter *et al.*, 1996). Ketosis has been suggested as a means to control plasma glucose in the past (Gumbiner *et al.*, 1996; Nakamura *et al.*, 1994). More recently, conditions of ketosis (induced by fasting or diet) have been shown to be neuroprotective in animal models of TBI (Appelberg *et al.*, 2009; Davies *et al.*, 2008; Prins *et al.*, 2004; Prins *et al.*, 2005). Administration of ketones after experimental TBI revealed age-dependent neuroprotection (Prins *et al.*, 2005). Postnatal day 35 and 45 rats placed on the ketogenic diet immediately after CCI injury had fewer fluoro-jade positive cells in the cortex and hippocampus at 6 hours post-injury and showed a 58% and 39% decrease in cortical contusion volume at 7 days post-injury. The ketogenic diet had no significant effect on PND17 or PND65 injured rats.

In order to ascertain whether the cortical preservation induced by ketones after injury was associated with functional recovery, motor and cognitive testing were conducted in PND35 and 75 rats maintained on standard or KG diet for 7 days after controlled cortical impact injury (Appelberg *et al.*, 2009). Motor assessment on the beam walking task revealed longer traverse times for both injured PND35 animals on the standard and KG diet, but KG-fed animals showed fewer footslips than standard-fed injured animals. PND35 injured rats on the KG diet showed shorter escape latencies in the Morris water maze task compared to standard-fed animals. The therapeutic effects of the KG diet in beam walking and cognitive performances were not observed in PND75 subjects.

Post-traumatic changes in neurotransmission

Age-dependent excitotoxicity and cell death

Traumatic brain injury is associated with indiscriminate excitatory neurotransmitter release, widespread potassium efflux, and membrane depolarization (Katayama *et al.*, 1990). Glutamate is the primary excitatory neurotransmitter in the nervous system and exerts its effects on the post-synaptic neuron through specific receptors. Glutamate receptors can transduce the excitatory signal either via the opening of an ion channel (in ionotropic glutamate receptors) or via activation of second messenger systems that enzymatically alters intracellular molecules (in metabotropic glutamate receptors). Ionotropic glutamate receptors come in two major subtypes: N-methyl-D-aspartate receptors (NMDARs) and α-amino-3-hydroxy-5-methyl-4-isoxazolepropionic acid receptors (AMPARs), both of which are important in plasticity and normal development.

Activation of NMDARs after TBI results in uncontrolled efflux of potassium and influx of sodium and calcium. Elevation of intracellular calcium can also result in a wide range of cellular perturbations. First, calcium flux can lead to phosphorylation of signaling molecules that can both activate or inactivate neural plasticity. Second, excess calcium is sequestered in mitochondria, where it results in dysfunction and loss of ATP-generating capacity, putting the cell into an energy crisis and tipping it towards cellular demise. Third, calcium flux can activate intracellular proteases (caspases, calpains) that, in turn, lead to programmed cell death/apoptosis. Massive ionic flux can result in acute cellular swelling and rupture, leading to excitotoxic cell death or necrosis (for review see Giza & Hovda, 2001).

The developing brain clearly shows an age-dependent response to TBI and other excitotoxic injuries. In the neonatal (<PND7) rat, both necrotic and apoptotic cell death occur after TBI, each with its own time course, necrosis occurring more rapidly (6 hours) and apoptosis peaking later (24 hours) (Bittigau et al., 1999). The vast majority of this neuronal death appears to occur via apoptotic mechanisms. Interestingly, 2–3-week-old (PND17–19) rats tend to show minimal acute cell death via either pathway (Adelson et al., 2001; Bittigau et al., 1999; Gurkoff et al., 2006). Adult rats tend to show substantial necrosis, as well as a delayed wave of apoptosis (Conti et al., 1998).

Given that overactivation of NMDARs results in cell death, agents that block this receptor have shown neuroprotective properties in many adult animal models of acute injury (Kroppenstedt et al., 1998; McIntosh et al., 1989; Rao et al., 2001). These neuroprotective responses have been difficult to translate into the clinical condition, and no neuron-specific protective therapies have shown efficacy in human brain injury. Furthermore, the young brain relies heavily on excitatory neurotransmission to maintain synaptic function and promote neural outgrowth (Hardingham & Bading, 2002, 2003), and use of NMDAR antagonists has actually shown a paradoxical worsening of cell death in the developing brain, both in normal controls and in traumatically injured rat pups (Bittigau et al., 1999; Ikonomidou et al., 1999). In fact, some argue that the inability to translate excitotoxic neuroprotection to effective therapies for stroke and trauma in human patients is due to underlying negative effects of these agents on neuronal survival and plasticity (Ikonomidou & Turski, 2002; Olney et al., 2004). If so, then the unintended consequences of agents that block neurotransmission are almost certainly even more relevant in the immature brain. Many studies have characterized the deleterious effects of sedatives, anesthetics and anticonvulsants on cellular survival, electrophysiological function, and cognition in the developing rat (Bittigau et al., 2002; Ikonomidou et al., 1999; Jevtovic-Todorovic et al., 2003; Kaindl et al., 2005). In children, it is well known that some anticonvulsants have chronic neurocognitive toxicity (Farwell et al., 1990), and a recent study has implicated repeated anesthetic exposure early in life with the later development of learning disabilities (Wilder et al., 2009).

Changes in neurotransmitters, receptors, and transporters

TBI has been shown to have widespread effects on multiple neurotransmitter systems. The alterations include but are not limited to GABAergic (gamma-amino butyric acid), cholinergic and glutamatergic systems. It has long been known that subpopulations of GABAergic neurons appear to be particularly vulnerable following TBI in the adult rat (Lowenstein *et al.*, 1992). This may result in an excitatory-inhibitory imbalance, particularly in hippocampal circuitry (Golarai *et al.*, 2001; Toth *et al.*, 1997). Receptor binding studies have also shown decreased GABA receptor binding after fluid percussion injury (Sihver *et al.*, 2001). While GABAergic systems have been implicated in processes such as epileptogenesis (Dudek & Sutula, 2007; Prince *et al.*, 2009), anxiety/post-traumatic stress disorder (Feusner *et al.*, 2001; Geuze *et al.*, 2008) and critical periods of neuroplasticity (Hensch *et al.*, 1998), the specific effects of TBI-induced GABAergic dysfunction have yet to be elucidated in detail in the immature brain.

Cholinergic neurotransmission also shows perturbations after TBI, but again, most of the studies have focused on injury in the adult animal. Decreases in choline acetyltransferase (Gorman *et al.*, 1996), muscarinic acetylcholine receptor (AChR) binding (Sihver *et al.*, 2001), and evoked release of ACh (Dixon *et al.*, 1997), have all been reported. These reductions in cholinergic transmission are associated with a (presumably) compensatory increase in vesicular ACh transporters (Shao *et al.*, 1999). In the developing brain, impaired regrowth of cholinergic projections to the hippocampus has been described after experimental TBI, which was associated with abnormal ultrastructural appearance to synaptic structures and with impaired cognitive performance (Prins *et al.*, 2003).

NMDAR receptors are down-regulated after adult TBI, as measured by receptor binding assays (Biegon *et al.*, 2004; Miller *et al.*, 1990) or molecular measures (Kumar *et al.*, 2002; Osteen *et al.*, 2004). In the developing brain, experimental TBI causes a selective reduction in hippocampal NR2A subunit levels during the first post-injury week (Giza *et al.*, 2006). Normally the NR2A subunit is up-regulated as the brain matures (Flint *et al.*, 1997; Roberts & Ramoa, 1999), and NR2A increases are also specifically associated with experience-dependent neuroplastic changes (Molteni *et al.*, 2002; Quinlan *et al.*, 1999). This TBI-induced reduction of NR2A has been related to impaired electrophysiological activation (Li *et al.*, 2005), diminished hippocampally based working memory (Reger *et al.*, 2005) and a loss of developmental plasticity in the young brain (Fineman *et al.*, 2000).

TBI-induced developmental disability: loss of developmental plasticity potential after TBI

Post-traumatic alterations in experience-dependent neuroplasticity

Studies of behavior following developmental TBI tend to show less obvious cognitive deficits than after comparable injuries in adults. Spatial learning, as measured using the Morris water maze, shows no significant deficit compared to age-matched controls in pre-weaning/weaning age rat pups (PND17–20), while juveniles (PND35) show a level of performance partway between that of weanlings and adults (Prins & Hovda, 2001). Some of this is due to age-related differences in Morris water maze (MWM) behavior, with younger animals showing different search strategies and slower latencies to find the hidden platform, with or without injury (Prins & Hovda, 1998; Rudy *et al.*, 1987).

When uninjured (sham) rat pups are reared in an enriched environment (EE), they show an enhancement in cognitive performance on the MWM (Fineman *et al.*, 2000; Giza *et al.*, 2005), a behavioral manifestation of intact experience-dependent neuroplasticity. This enhancement due to EE is also associated with increased cortical thickness and

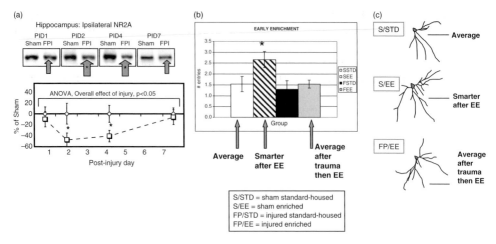

Fig. 2.4. Demonstration of altered experience-dependent plasticity after developmental TBI in the postnatal day 19 rat model of lateral fluid percussion (LFP) injury. (a) Immunoblots showing subunit-specific reductions of the NR2A subunit of the NMDA receptor during the 1st week post-LFP. NR1 and NR2B subunits (not shown) had no significant change (Giza *et al. J. Neurotrauma* 2006). (b) Target zone entries during the probe trail of the Morris water maze show enhanced performance by sham animals reared in enriched environment (EE). LFP rats showed no overt deficits, but failed to show any enhancement of cognitive abilities after EE rearing (Giza *et al.*, 2005). (c) Dendritic arborization is increased after EE in sham rats but not in rats that experienced LFP early in life (Ip *et al.*, 2002). In summary, this figure shows multiple lines of evidence for impaired experience-dependent neuroplasticity after developmental TBI.

expanded dendritic arborization in normal animals (Greenough *et al.*, 1973; Rosenweig & Bennet, 1996) and in uninjured (sham) rat pups (Fineman *et al.*, 2000; Ip *et al.*, 2002). However, when weanling rats (PND19) undergo early TBI (lateral FP injury) prior to EE rearing, they grow up and show cognitive performance as if they were never exposed to the EE. In other words, they have lost developmental potential and show impaired experience-dependent plasticity (Fig. 2.4).

Impaired neural activation after TBI

Activation of NMDAR by differential experience has been shown to alter the molecular composition of these receptors. Maturation of normal excitatory networks during brain development is associated with an increase in the NR2A subunit of the NMDAR, relative to the NR2B subunit. This shift from NR2B to NR2A appears in many brain regions, including somatosensory cortex (Flint *et al.*, 1997), visual cortex (Roberts & Romoa, 1999), hippocampus (Riva *et al.*, 1994; Tovar & Westbrook, 1999), and even cerebellum (Takahashi *et al.*, 1996).

This increase in NR2A appears to be linked to environmental experience in many cases. Dark-reared rat pups show reduced levels of NR2A expression in visual cortex; however, within hours of light exposure, visual cortex NR2A levels increase rapidly, while other NMDAR subunits remain stable (Quinlan *et al.*, 1999). Elevated levels of NR2A also occur in response to more nuturing maternal behaviors (Liu *et al.*, 2000), exercise (Molteni *et al.*, 2002), and even enriched environment (Giza *et al.*, 2000).

Following experimental TBI there is a period of altered NMDAR molecular composition, with evidence of impaired activation of glutamatergic systems. Adult studies have shown decreased NMDAR binding in the first 24–48 hrs post-experimental TBI (Biegon *et al.*, 2004; Miller *et al.*, 1990). In fact, following adult lateral FP injury, subunit selective reductions in NR2A are seen preferentially in ipsilateral cortex, and are associated with reduced NMDAR activation and NMDAR-mediated calcium flux in affected regions (Osteen *et al.*, 2004). After developmental TBI, hippocampal NR2A levels are selectively reduced by 40% over the first post-injury week (Giza *et al.*, 2006). This first post-injury week corresponds to a time window of dysfunctional neural activation and impaired experience-dependent neuroplasticity in the immature brain. Direct ex-vivo measurements of hippocampal NMDAR-mediated currents (evoked excitatory post-synaptic currents or eEPSCs) show reductions of nearly 50% within the first post-injury week (post-injury day [PID] 3–5) and recovery by PID 13–15 (Li *et al.*, 2005). Similarly, young rats show deficits on a hippocampally based, NMDAR-mediated working memory task (novel object recognition) during the first week post-injury (PID 4 & 7) that recovers by PID 14 (Reger *et al.*, 2005). Most importantly, the ability of the injured young rats to respond to rearing in EE is blunted during the first post-injury week, as described above. However, this loss of plasticity is not due to ongoing cell death (Gurkoff *et al.*, 2006). In fact, concordant with the data above, EE responsiveness post-FP injury appears to recover at least partially by PID 14, and FP pups once again show improvements in MWM latency/spatial learning if they are reared in EE beginning 2 weeks after injury (Giza *et al.*, 2005).

Clinical evidence of altered neural activation following pediatric TBI is also beginning to be reported. Certainly, age- and severity-dependent neurocognitive deficits have long been reported after TBI. Use of functional magnetic resonance imaging (fMRI) can now show quantifiable changes in neural activity during cognitive effort, and these fMRI signals are altered after TBI. Functional MRI signals reflect a change in blood oxygenation (blood oxygen level dependent – BOLD signal), which is increased in activated brain regions where neurovascular coupling is intact. While not a direct measure of neural activation, many investigators suggest that increased BOLD signal is an indication of increased excitatory glutamatergic neurotransmission (Bonvento *et al.*, 2002). This is further supported by animal studies showing that approximately 50% of the BOLD response to somatosensory stimulation can be blocked by administration of an NMDAR antagonist (Gsell *et al.*, 2006).

Functional MRI studies of head injured patients show changes in BOLD activation even weeks or months after injury. In young adults after mild TBI, low levels of working memory load appear to evoke a broader network of BOLD activation than in normal controls (McAllister *et al.*, 1999). However, at the highest levels of difficulty, the TBI patients show a noticeable loss of neural activation in the same paradigm (McAllister *et al.*, 2001). Reduced levels of BOLD activation in motor cortex early in the recovery phase after severe TBI are correlated with worse long-term functional outcomes in adults, while those showing more appropriate activation patterns went on to better functional motor outcomes (Lotze *et al.*, 2006). In an adolescent cohort of patients who underwent fMRI of a non-verbal working memory task, control patients showed broad regional activation of a bilateral fronto-temporo-parietal network, but those examined within several months of a moderate-severe TBI showed less structured overall activation (Cazalis *et al.*, 2007: Fig. 2.5).

In summary, TBI occurring in development shows distinctly different patterns of cell death, neurotransmission, and experience-dependent neuroplasticity. Underlying molecular

Condition 1 vs 3

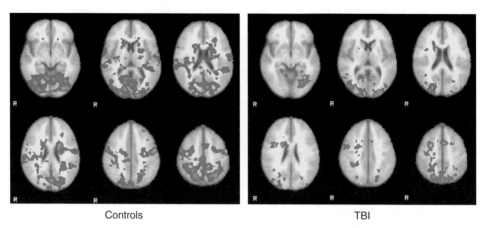

Controls   TBI

Fig. 2.5. Functional MRI activation maps during a non-verbal working memory task in adolescents. Control subjects show blood oxygen level dependent (BOLD) signal activation in a widespread bilateral fronto-temporo-parietal network that appears markedly attenuated in adolescents 3–6 months after moderate-severe TBI (Cazalis *et al.*, 2007). See color plate section.

changes in neurotransmitter receptors and transporters, and particularly those involved in glutamatergic neurotransmission, appear to underlie these impairments. NMDAR subunit composition changes after developmental TBI, with a temporal course that corresponds to measurable electrophysiological, cognitive, and neuroplastic deficits. This period of unresponsiveness can manifest itself in longer lasting changes, as the injured individuals appear to be unable to respond to critical environmental stimuli during the post-injury period of recovery. Advanced neuroimaging modalities are now able to shed light on functional neural activation in vivo in human patients, and studies show that significant perturbation of normal activation occurs following TBI. It is likely that these impairments of neural activation may be physiological biomarkers of neurobehavioral deficits and lost plasticity, and show great promise to advance the study of pediatric TBI and recovery of function in the near future.

Acknowledgments
Supported by the UCLA BIRC, NS27544, NS057420, NS052406,Winokur Family Foundation/Child Neurology Foundation and the Thrasher Research Fund.

References

Adelson, P., Clyde, B., Kochanek, P. M., Wisniewski, S., Marion, D. & Yonas, H. (1997). Cerebrovascular response in infants and young children following severe traumatic brain injury. *Pediatric Neurosurgery*, **26**, 200–207.

Adelson, P. D., Jenkins, L. W., Hamilton, R. L., Robichaud, P., Tran, M. P. & Kochanek, P. M. (2001). Histopathologic response of the immature rat to diffuse traumatic brain injury. *Journal of Neurotrauma*, **18**, 967–976.

Appelberg, S., Hovda, D. A. & Prins, M. L. (2009). The effects of a ketogenic diet on behavioral outcome after controlled cortical impact injury in juvenile and adult rat. *Journal of Neurotrauma*, **26**, 497–506.

Bartnik, B. L., Sutton, R. L., Fukushima, M., Harris, N. G., Hovda, D. A. & Lee, S. M.

(2005). Upregulation of pentose phosphate pathway and preservation of tricarboxylic acid cycle flux after experimental brain injury. *Journal of Neurotrauma*, **22**, 1052–1065.

Berger, N. A. (1985). Poly (ADP-ribose) in the cellular response to DNA damage. *Radiation Research*, **101**, 4–15.

Biagas, K. V., Grundl, P. D., Kochanek, P., Schiding, J. K. & Nemoto, E. M. (1996). Posttraumatic hyperemia in immature, mature, and aged rats: autoradiographic determination of cerebral blood flow. *Journal of Neurotrauma*, **13**, 189–200.

Biegon, A., Fry, P. A., Paden, C. M., Alexandrovich, A. & Tsenter, J. E. S. (2004). Dynamic changes in *N*-methyl-D-aspartate receptors after closed head injury in mice: implications for treatment of neurological and cognitive deficits. *Proceedings of the National Academy of Sciences, USA*, **101**, 5117–5122.

Bittigau, P., Sifringer, M., Pohl, D. et al. (1999). Apoptotic neurodegeneration following trauma is markedly enhanced in the immature brain. *Annals of Neurology*, **45**, 724–735.

Bittigau, P., Sifringer, M., Genz, K. et al. (2002). Antiepileptic drugs and apoptotic neurodegeneration in the developing brain. *Proceedings of the National Academy of Sciences, USA*, **99**, 15089–15094.

Booth, R. F. G., Patel, T. B. & Clark, J. B. (1980). The development of enzymes of energy metabolism in the brain of a precocial (guinea pig) and non-precocial (rat) species. *Journal of Neurochemistry*, **34**, 17–25.

Bonvento, G., Sibson, N. & Pellerin, L. (2002). Does glutamate image your thoughts? *Trends in Neuroscience*, **25**, 359–364.

Bruce, D., Alvai, A., Bilaniuk, L., Dolinskas, C., Obrist, W. & Uzzell, B. (1981). Diffuse cerebral swelling following head injuries in children: the syndrome of malignant brain edema. *Journal of Neurosurgery*, **54**, 170–178.

Cazalis, F., Babikian, T., Newman, N., Hovda, D. A., Giza C. C. & Asarnow, R. F. (2007). Longitudinal fMRI study of severe traumatic brain injury in adolescents. *Society for Neuroscience Abstracts*.

Cherian, L., Hlatky, R. & Robertson, C. S. (2004). Comparison of tetrahydrobiopterin and L-arginine on cerebral blood flow after controlled cortical impact injury in rats. *Journal of Neurotrauma*, **21**, 1196–1203.

Chiron, C., Raynaud, C., Maxiere, B. et al. (1992). Changes in regional cerebral blood flow during brain maturation in children and adolescents. *Journal of Nuclear Medicine*, **33**, 696–703.

Chugani, H. T., Phelps, M. E. & Mazziotta, J. C. (1987). Positron emission tomography study of human brain functional development. *Annals of Neurology*, **22**, 487–497.

Conti, A. C., Raghupathi, R., Trojanowski, J. Q. & McIntosh, T. K. (1998). Experimental brain injury induces regionally distinct apoptosis during the acute and delayed post-traumatic period. *Journal of Neuroscience*, **18**, 5663–5672.

Cosi, C. & Marien, M. (1998). Decreases in mouse brain NAD^+ and ATP induced by 1-methyl-4-phenyl-1,2,3,6-tetrahydropyridine (MPTP): prevention by the poly (ADP-ribose) polymerase inhibitor, benzamide. *Brain Research*, **809**, 58–67.

Courchesne, E., Chisum, H. J., Townsend, J. et al. (2000). Normal brain development and aging: quantitative analysis at in vivo MR imaging in healthy volunteers. *Radiology*, **216**, 672–682.

Cremer, J. E., Braun, L. D. & Oldendorf, W. H. (1976). Changes during development in transport processes of the blood–brain barrier. *Biochimica et Biophyica Acta*, **448**, 633–637.

Dahlquist, G. & Persson, B. (1976). The rat cerebral utilization of glucose, ketone bodies, and oxygen: a comparative in vivo study of infant and adult rats. *Pediatric Research*, **10**, 910–917.

Davis, L. M., Pauly, J. R., Readnower, R. D., Rho, J. M. & Sullivan, P. G. (2008). Fasting is neuroprotective following traumatic brain injury. *Journal of Neuroscience Research*, **86**, 1812–1822.

Dietrich, W. D., Alonso, O., Busto, R. & Ginsberg, M. D. (1994). Widespread metabolic depression and reduced somatosensory circuit activation following traumatic brain injury in rats. *Journal of Neurotrauma*, **11**, 629–640.

Dixon, C. E., Ma, X. & Marion, D. W. (1997). Reduced evoked release of acetylcholine in the rodent neocortex following traumatic brain injury. *Brain Research*, **749**, 127–130.

Dudek, F. E. & Sutula, T. P. (2007). Epileptogenesis in the dentate gyrus: a critical perspective. *Progress in Brain Research*, **163**, 755–773.

Durham, S. R., Raghupathi, R., Helfaer, M. A., Marwaha, S. & Duhaime, A. C. (2000). Age-related differences in acute physiologic response to focal traumatic brain injury in piglets. *Pediatric Neurology*, **33**, 76–82.

Enerson, B. E. & Drewes, L. R. (2003). Molecular features, regulation and function of monocarboxylate transporters: implications for drug delivery. *Journal of Pharmaceutical Science*, **92**, 1531–1544.

Farwell, J. R., Lee, Y. J., Hirtz, D. G., Sulzbacher, S. I., Ellenberg, J. H. & Nelson, K. B. (1990). Phenobarbital for febrile seizures–effects on intelligence and on seizure recurrence. *New England Journal of Medicine*, **322**, 364–369.

Feusner, J., Ritchie, T., Lawford, B., Young, R. M., Kann, B. & Noble, E. P. (2001). GABA(A) receptor beta 3 subunit gene and psychiatric morbidity in a post-traumatic stress disorder population. *Psychiatry Research*, **104**, 109–117.

Fineman, I., Hovda, D. A., Smith, M., Yoshino, A. & Becker, D. P. (1993). Concussive brain injury is associated with a prolonged accumulation of calcium: a 45Ca autoradiographic study. *Brain Research*, **624**, 94–102.

Fineman, I., Giza, C. C., Nahed, B. V., Lee, S. M. & Hovda, D. A. (2000). Inhibition of neocortical plasticity during development by a moderate concussive brain injury. *Journal of Neurotrauma*, **17**, 739–749.

Flint, A. C., Maisch, U. S., Weishaupt, J. H., Kriegstein, A. R. & Monyer, H. (1997). NR2A subunit expression shortens NMDA receptor synaptic currents in developing neocortex. *The Journal of Neuroscience*, **17**, 2469–2476.

Geuze, E., van Berckel, B. N., Lammertsma, A. A. *et al.* (2008). Reduced GABAA benzodiazepine receptor binding in veterans with post-traumatic stress disorder. *Molecular Psychiatry*, **13**, 74–83.

Giorgio, A., Watkins, K. E., Douaud, G. *et al.* (2008). Changes in white matter microstructure during adolescence. *NeuroImage*, **39**, 52–61.

Giza, C. C. & Hovda, D. A. (2001). The neurometabolic cascade of concussion. *Journal of Athletic Training*, **36**, 228–235.

Giza, C., Lee, S. M. & Hovda, D. A. (2000). Increased N-Methyl D-Aspartate (NMDA) receptor NR2A:NR2B subunit ratio induced by rearing in an enriched environment (EE). *Society for Neuroscience Abstracts*, 15.3.

Giza, C. C., Griesbach, G. S. & Hovda, D. A. (2005). Experience-dependent behavioral plasticity is disturbed following traumatic brain injury to the immature brain. *Behavioural Brain Research*, **157**, 11–22.

Giza, C. C., Maria, N. S. & D. A., H. (2006). N-methyl-D-aspartate receptor subunit changes after traumatic injury to the developing brain. *Journal of Neurotrauma*, **23**, 950–961.

Golarai, G., Greenwood, A., Feeney, D. & Connor, J. (2001). Physiological and structural evidence for hippocampal involvement in persistent seizure susceptibility after traumatic brain injury. *Journal of Neuroscience*, **21**, 8523–8537.

Gorman, L., Fu, K., Hovda, D., Murray, M. & Traystman, R. (1996). Effects of traumatic brain injury on the cholinergic system in the rat. *Journal of Neurotrauma*, **13**, 457–463.

Greenough, W. T., Volkmar, F. R. & Juraska, J. M. (1973). Effects of rearing complexity on dendritic branching in frontolateral and temporal cortex of the rat. *Experimental Neurology*, **41**, 371–378.

Grundl, P. D., Biagas, K. V., Kochanek, P. M., Schiding, J. K., Barmada, M. A. & Nemoto, E. M. (1994). Early cerebrovascular response to head injury in immature and mature rats. *Journal of Neurotrauma*, **11**, 135–148.

Gsell, W., Burke, M., Wiedermann, D. *et al.* (2006). Differential effects of NMDA and AMPA glutamate receptors on functional magnetic resonance imaging signals and evoked neuronal activity during forepaw stimulation of the rat. *Journal of Neuroscience*, **26**, 8409–8416.

Gumbiner, B., Wendel, J. A. & McDermott, M. P. (1996). Effects of diet composition and ketosis on glycemia during very-low-energy-diet therapy in obese patients with non-insulin-dependent diabetes mellitus. *American Journal of Clinical Nutrition*, **63**, 110–115.

Gurkoff, G. G., Giza, C. C. & Hovda, D. A. (2006). Lateral fluid percussion injury in the developing rat causes an acute, mild behavioral dysfunction in the absence of significant cell death. *Brain Research*, **1077**, 24–36.

Hall, E. D., Andrus, P. K. & Yonkers, P. A. (1993). Brain hydroxyl radical generation in acute experimental head injury. *Journal of Neurochemistry*, **60**, 588–594.

Hardingham, G. E. & Bading, H. (2002). Coupling of extrasynaptic NMDA receptors to a CREB shut-off pathway is developmentally regulated. *Biochimica et Biophysica Acta*, **1600**, 148–153.

Hardingham, G. E. & Bading, H. (2003). The Yin and Yang of NMDA receptor signalling. *Trends in Neuroscience*, **26**, 81–89.

Hawkins, R. A., Williamson, D. H. & Krebs, H. A. (1971). Ketone-body utilization by adult and suckling rat brain in vivo. *Biochemical Journal*, **122**, 13–18.

Hensch, T., Fagiolini, M., Mataga, N., Stryker, M., Baekkeskov, S. & Kash, S. (1998). Local GABA circuit control of experience-dependent plasticity in developing visual cortex. *Science*, **282**, 1504–1508.

Himwich, H. E. (1973). Early studies of the developing brain. In Himwich, W., ed. *Biochemistry of the Developing Brain* Volume 1. New York, NY: Marcel Dekker Inc, pp. 2–20.

Hovda, D. A. (1996). In R. K. Narayan, J. E. Wilberger & J. T. Povlishock, ed. *Metabolic Dysfunction in Neurotrauma*, New York: McGraw-Hill Inc, pp. 1459–1478.

Hovda, D. A., Le, H. M., Lifshitz, J. *et al.* (1994). Long-term changes in metabolic rates for glucose following mild, moderate and severe concussive head injuries in adult rats. *Journal of Neuroscience*, **20**, 845.

Ikonomidou, C. & Turski, L. (2002). Why did NMDA receptor antagonists fail clinical trials for stroke and traumatic brain injury? *Lancet Neurology*, **1**, 383–386.

Ikonomidou, C., Bosch, F., Miksa, M. *et al.* (1999). Blockade of NMDA receptors and apoptotic neurodegeneration in the developing brain. *Science*, **283**, 70–74.

Ip, E. Y., Giza, C. C., Griesbach, G. S. & Hovda, D. A. (2002). Effects of enriched environment and fluid percussion injury on dendritic arborization within the cerebral cortex of the developing rat. *Journal of Neurotrauma*, **19**, 573–585.

Ip, E. Y., Zanier, E. R., Moore, A. H., Lee, S. M. & Hovda, D. A. (2003). Metabolic, neurochemical, and histological responses to vibrissa motor cortex stimulation after traumatic brain injury. *Journal of Cerebral Blood Flow and Metabolism*, **23**, 900–910.

Ishitani, R., Tanaka, M., Sunaga, K., Katsube, N. & Chuang, D. M. (1998). Nuclear localization of overexpressed glyceraldehyde-3-phosphate dehydrogenase in cultured cerebellar neurons undergoing apoptosis. *Molecular Pharmacology*, **53**, 701–707.

Jevtovic-Todorovic, V., Hartman, R. E., Izumi, Y. *et al.* (2003). Early exposure to common anesthetic agents causes widespread neurodegeneration in the developing rat brain and persistent learning deficits. *The Journal of Neuroscience*, **23**, 876–882.

Kaindl, A. M., Asimiadou, S., Manthey, D., Hagen, M. V., Turski, L. & Ikonomidou, C. (2006). Antiepileptic drugs and the developing brain. *Cellular and Molecular Life Sciences*, **63**, 399–413.

Katayama, Y., Becker, D. P., Tamura, T. & Hovda, D. A. (1990). Massive increases in extracellular potassium and the indiscriminate release of glutamate following concussive brain injury. *Journal of Neurosurgery*, **73**, 889–900.

Kawamata, T., Katayama, Y., Hovda, D. A., Yohino, A. & Becker, D. P. (1992). Administration of excitatory amino acid antagonists via microdialysis attenuates the increase in glucose utilization seen following concussive brain injury. *Journal of Cerebral Blood Flow and Metabolism*, **12**, 12–24.

Kim, C. I., Lee, S. H., Seong, G. J., Kim, Y. H. & Lee, M. Y. (2006). Nuclear translocation and overexpression of GAPDH by the hyper-pressure in retinal ganglion cell. *Biochemical and Biophysical Research Communications*, **341**, 1237–1243.

Kroppenstedt, S. N., Schneider, G. H., Thomale, U. W. & Unterberg, A. W. (1998). Protective effects of aptiganel HCl (Cerestat) following controlled cortical impact injury in the rat. *Journal of Neurotrauma*, **15**, 191–197.

Kumar, A., Zou, L., Yuan, X., Long, Y. & Yang, K. (2002). N-methyl-D-aspartate receptors: transient loss of NR1/NR2A/ NR2B subunits after traumatic brain injury in a rodent model. *Journal of Neuroscience Research*, **67**, 781–786.

LaPlaca, M. C., Raghupathi, R., Verma, A. *et al.* (1999). Temporal patterns of poly (ADP-Ribose) polymerase activation in the cortex following experimental brain injury in the rat. *Journal of Neurochemistry*, **73**, 205–213.

Leong, S. F. & Clark, J. B. (1984). Regional enzyme development in rat brain. Enzymes associated with glucose utilization. *Biochemical Journal*, **218**, 131–138.

Li, Q., Spigelman, I., Hovda, D. A. & Giza, C. C. (2005). Decreased NMDA receptor mediated synaptic currents in CA1 neurons following fluid percussion injury in developing rats. *Journal of Neurotrauma*, **20** (10), 1249 (abstract).

Liu, D., Diorio, J., Day, J. C., Francis, D. D. & Meaney, M. J. (2000). Maternal care, hippocampal synaptogenesis and cognitive development in rats. *Nature Neuroscience*, **3**, 799–806.

Lotze, M., Grodd, W., Rodden, F. A. *et al.* (2006). Neuroimaging patterns associated with motor control in traumatic brain injury. *Neurorehabilitation and Neural Repair*, **20**, 14–23.

Lowenstein, D. H., Thomas, M. J., Smith, D. H. & McIntosh, T. K. (1992). Selective vulnerability of dentate hilar neurons following traumatic brain injury: a potential mechanistic link between head trauma and disorders of the hippocampus. *Journal of Neuroscience*, **12**, 4846–4853.

Marklund, N., Clausen, F., Lewander, T. & Hillered, L. (2001). Monitoring of reactive oxygen species production after traumatic brain injury in rats with microdialysis and the 4-hydroxygenzoic acid trapping methods. *Journal of Neurotrauma*, **18**, 1217–1227.

Maset, A. L., Marmarou, A., Ward, J. *et al.* (1987). Pressure–volume index in head injury. *Journal of Neurosurgery*, **67**, 832–840.

McAllister, T. W., Saykin, A. J., Flashman, L. A. *et al.* (1999). Brain activation during working memory 1 month after mild traumatic brain injury: a functional MRI study. *Neurology*, **53**, 1300–1308.

McAllister, T. W., Sparling, M. B., Flashman, L. A., Guerin, S. J., Mamourian, A. C. & Saykin, A. J. (2001). Differential working memory load effects after mild traumatic brain injury. *Neuroimage*, **14**, 1004–1012.

McIntosh, T. K., Vink, R., Soares, H., Hayes, R. & Simon, R. (1989). Effects of the N-methyl-D-aspartate receptor blocker MK-801 on neurologic function after experimental brain injury. *Journal of Neurotrauma*, **6**, 247–259.

Miller, L., Lyeth, B., Jenkins, L. *et al.* (1990). Excitatory amino acid receptor subtype binding following traumatic brain injury. *Brain Research*, **526**, 103–107.

Molteni, R., Ying, Z. & Gomez-Pinilla, F. (2002). Differential effects of acute and chronic exercise on plasticity-related genes in the rat hippocampus revealed by microarray. *European Journal of Neuroscience*, **16**, 1107–1116.

Muizelaar, J., Marmarou, A., DeSalles, A. *et al.* (1989). Cerebral blood flow and metabolism in severely head injured children.1. Relationship with GCS score, outcome, ICPA and PVI. *Journal of Neurosurgery*, **71**, 63–71.

Nakamura, T., Yoshihara, D., Ohmori, T., Yanai, M. & Takeshita, Y. (1994). Effects of diet high in medium-chain triglyceride on plasma ketone, glucose and insulin concentrations in enterectomized and normal rats. *Journal of Nutritional Science and Vitaminology*, **40**, 147–159.

Nehlig, A., Pereira de Vasconcelos, A. & Boyet, S. (1987). Quantitative autoradiographic measurement of local cerebral glucose utilization in freely moving rats during postnatal development. *Journal of Neuroscience*, **8**, 2321–2333.

Nehlig, A., Pereira de Vasconcelos, A. & Boye, S. (1989). Postnatal changes in local cerebral blood flow measured by the quantitative autoradiographic ^{14}cIodoantipyrine technique in freely moving rats. *Journal of Cerebral Blood Flow and Metabolism*, **9**, 579–588.

Nehlig, A., Boyet, S. & Pereira de Vasconcelos, A. (1991). Autoradiographic measurements of local cerebral B-hydroxybutyrate uptake in the rat during postnatal development. *Neuroscience*, **40**(3), 871–878.

Olney, J. W., Young, C., Wozniak, D. F., Jevtovic-Todorovic, V. & Ikonomidou, C. (2004). Do pediatric drugs cause developing neurons to commit suicide? *Trends in Pharmacological Sciences*, **25**, 135–139.

Osteen, C. L., Moore, A. H., Prins, M. L. & Hovda, D. A. (2001). Age-dependency of ^{45}calcium accumulation following lateral fluid percussion: acute and delayed patterns. *Journal of Neurotrauma*, **18**, 141–162.

Osteen, C., Giza, C. & Hovda, D. (2004). Injury-induced alterations in *N*-methyl-D-aspartate receptor subunit composition contribute to prolonged 45calcium accumulation following lateral fluid percussion. *Neuroscience*, **128**, 305–322.

Owen, O. E., Morgan, A. P., Kemp, H. G., Sullivan, J. M., Herrera, M. G. & Cahill, G. F. J. (1967). Brain metabolism during fasting. *The Journal of Clinical Investigation*, **46**, 1589–1595.

Passineau, M. J., Zhao, W., Busto, R. *et al.* (2000). Chronic metabolic sequelae of traumatic brain injury: prolonged suppression of somatosensory activation. *American Journal of Physiology Heart Circulatory Physiology*, **279**, H924–931.

Paus, T., Zijdenbos, A., Worsley, K. *et al.* (1999). Structural maturation of neural pathways in children and adolescents: in vivo study. *Science*, **283**, 1908–1911.

Prince, D. A., Parada, I., Scalise, K., Graber, K., Jin, X. & Shen, F. (2009). Epilepsy following cortical injury: cellular and molecular mechanisms as targets for potential prophylaxis. *Epilepsia*, **50** Suppl 2, 30–40.

Prins, M. L. & Da, H. (2001). Mapping cerebral glucose metabolism during spatial learning: interactions of development and traumatic brain injury. *Journal of Neurotrauma*, **18**, 31–46.

Prins, M. L. & Hovda, D. A. (1998). Traumatic brain injury in the developing rat: effects of maturation on Morris water maze acquisition. *Journal of Neurotrauma*, **15**, 799–811.

Prins, M. L. & Hovda, D. A. (2009). The effects of age and ketogenic diet on local cerebral metabolic rates of glucose after controlled cortical impact injury in rats. *Journal of Neurotrauma*, **26**(7), 1083–1093.

Prins, M. L., Lee, S. M., Cheng, C. L. Y., Becker, D. P. & Hovda, D. A. (1996). Fluid percussion brain injury in the developing and adult rat: a comparative study of mortality, morphology, intracranial pressure and mean arterial blood pressure. *Developmental Brain Research*, **95**, 272–282.

Prins, M. L., Povlishock, J. T. & Phillips, L. L. (2003). The effects of combined fluid percussion traumatic brain injury and unilateral entorhinal deafferentation on the juvenile rat brain. *Developmental Brain Research*, **140**, 93–104.

Prins, M. L., Lee, S. M., Fujima, L. & Hovda, D. A. (2004). Increased cerebral uptake and oxidation of exogenous betaHB improves ATP following traumatic brain injury in adult rats. *Journal of Neurochemistry*, **90**, 666–672.

Prins, M. L., Fujima, L. S. & Hovda, D. A. (2005). Age-dependent reduction of cortical contusion volume by ketones after traumatic brain injury. *Journal of Neuroscience Research*, **82**, 413–420.

Quinlan, E. M., Olstein, D. H. & Bear, M. F. (1999). Bidirectional, experience-dependent regulation of *N*-methyl-D-aspartate receptor subunit composition in the rat visual cortex during postnatal development. *Proceedings of the National Academy of Sciences, USA*, **96**, 12876–12880.

Quinlan, E. M., Philpot, B. D., Huganir, R. L. & Bear, M. F. (1999). Rapid, experience-dependent expression of synaptic NMDA receptors in visual cortex in vivo [see comments]. *Nature Neuroscience*, **2**, 352–357.

Rao, V. L., Dogan, A., Todd, K. G., Bowen, K. K. & Dempsey, R. J. (2001). Neuroprotection by memantine, a non-competitive NMDA receptor antagonist after traumatic brain injury in rats. *Brain Research*, **911**, 96–100.

Reger, M. L., Gurkoff, G. G., Hovda, D. A. & Giza, C. C. (2005). The novel object recognition task detects a transient cognitive deficit after developmental TBI. *Journal of Neurotrauma*, **20** (10), 1206 (abstract).

Ritter, A. M., Robertson, C. S., Goodman, J. C., Contant, C. F. & Grossman, R. G. (1996). Evaluation of carbohydrate free diet for patients with severe head injury. *Journal of Neurotrauma*, **13**, 473–485.

Riva, M. A., Tascedda, F., Molteni, R. & Racagni, G. (1994). Regulation of NMDA receptor subunit mRNA expression in the rat brain during postnatal development. *Brain Research Molecular Brain Research*, **25**, 209–216.

Roberts, E. B. & Ramoa, A. S. (1999). Enhanced NR2A subunit expression and decreased NMDA receptor decay time at the onset of ocular dominance plasticity in the ferret. *Journal of Neurophysiology*, **81**, 2587–2591.

Robertson, C. S., Goodman, J. C., Narayan, R. K., Contant, C. F. & Grossman, R. G. (1991). The effect of glucose admnistration on carbohydrate metabolism after head injury. *Journal of Neurosurgery*, **74**, 43–50.

Rosenzweig, M. R. & Bennett, E. L. (1996). Psychobiology of plasticity: effects of training and experience on brain and behavior. *Behavioural Brain Research*, **78**, 57–65.

Rudy, J. W., Stadler-Morris, S. & Albert, P. (1987). Ontogeny of spatial navigation behaviors in the rat: dissociation of "proximal" and "distal" cue based behaviors. *Behavioral Neuroscience*, **101**, 62–73.

Satchell, M. A., Zhang, X., Kochanek, P. *et al.* (2003). A dual role for poly-ADP-ribosylation in spatial memory acquisition after traumatic brain injury in mice involving NAD+ depletion and ribosylation of 14–3–3. *Journal of Neurochemistry*, **85**, 697–708.

Shao, L., Ciallella, J., Yan, H. *et al.* (1999). Differential effects of traumatic brain injury on vesicular acetylcholine transporter and M2 muscarinic receptor mRNA and protein in rat. *Journal of Neurotrauma*, **16**, 555–566.

Sharples, P., Stuart, A., D., M., Aynsley-Green, A. & Eyre, J. (1995). Glasgow coma score, outcome, intracranial pressure and time after injury. *Journal of Neurology, Neurosurgery, and Psychiatry*, **58**, 145–152.

Sheline, C. T., Behrens, M. M. & Choi, D. W. (2000). Zinc-induced cortical neuronal death: contribution of energy failure attributable to loss of NAD+ and inhibition of glycolysis. *Journal of Neuroscience*, **20**, 3139–3146.

Sihver, S., Marklund, N., Hillered, L., Långström, B., Watanabe, Y. & Bergström, M. (2001). Changes in mACh, NMDA and GABA(A) receptor binding after lateral fluid-percussion injury: in vitro autoradiography of rat brain frozen sections. *Journal of Neurochemistry*, **78**, 417–423.

Skippen, P., Seear, M., Poskitt, K. *et al.* (1997). Effect of hyperventilation on regional cerebral blood flow in head injured children. *Critical Care Medicine*, **25**, 1402–1409.

Sutton, R. L., Hovda, D. A., Adelson, P. D., Benzel, E. C. & Becker, D. P. (1994).

Metabolic changes following coritcal contusion: relationship to edema and morphological changes. *Acta Neurochirurgica,* **60** Suppl, 446–448.

Takahashi, T., Feldmeyer, D., Suzuki, N. *et al.* (1996). Functional correlation of NMDA receptor epsilon subunits expression with the properties of single-channel and synaptic currents in the developing cerebellum. *Journal of Neuroscience,* **16**, 4376–4382.

Tanaka, R., Mochizuki, H., Suzuki, A. *et al.* (2002). Induction of glyceraldehyde-3-phosphate dehydrogenase (GAPDH) expression in rat brain after focal ischemia/reperfusion. *Journal of Cerebral Blood Flow and Metabolism,* **22**, 280–288.

Thomas, S., Prins, M. L., Samii, M. & Hovda, D. A. (2000). Cerebral metabolic response to traumatic brain injury sustained early in development: a 2-deoxy-D-glucose autoradiographic study. *Journal of Neurotrauma,* **17**, 649–665.

Toga, A., Thompson, P. & Sowell, E. (2006). Mapping brain maturation. *Trends in Neuroscience,* **29**, 148–159.

Toth, Z., Hollrigel, G. S., Gorcs, T. & Soltesz, I. (1997). Instantaneous perturbation of dentate interneuronal networks by a pressure wave-transient delivered to the neocortex. *Journal of Neuroscience,* **17**, 8106–8117.

Tovar, K. R. & Westbrook, G. L. (1999). The incorporation of NMDA receptors with a distinct subunit composition at nascent hippocampal synapses in vitro. *The Journal of Neuroscience,* **19**, 4180–4188.

Udomphorn, Y., Armstead, W. M. & Vavilala, M. S. (2008). Cerebral blood flow and autoregulation after pediatric traumatic brain injury. *Pediatric Neurology,* **38**, 225–234.

Vannucci, S. J. & Simpson, I. A. (2003). Developmental switch in brain nutrient transporter expression in the rat. *American Journal of Physiology,* **285**, E1127–E1134.

Vavilala, M. S., Muangman, S., Tontisirin, N. *et al.* (2006). Impaired cerebral autoregulation and 6-month outcome in children with severe traumatic brain injury: preliminary findings. *Developmental Neuroscience,* **28**(4–5), 348–353.

Wilder, R. T., Flick, R. P., Sprung, J. *et al.* (2009). Early exposure to anesthesia and learning disabilities in a population-based birth cohort. *Anesthesiology,* **110**, 796–804.

Ying, W., Gernier, P. & Swanson, R. A. (2003). NAD+ repletion prevents PARP-1 induced glycolytic blockade and cell death in cultured mouse astrocytes. *Biochemical and Biophysical Research Communications,* **308**, 809–813.

Yoshino, A., Hovda, D. A., Kawamata, T., Katayama, Y. & Becker, D. P. (1991). Dynamic changes in local cerebral glucose utilization following cerebral concussion in rats: evidence of a hyper- and subsequent hypometabolic state. *Brain Research,* **561**, 106–119.

Zwienenberg, M. & Muizelaar, J. P. (1999). Severe pediatric head injury: the role of hyperemia revisited. *Journal of Neurotrauma,* **16**(10), 937–943.

Chapter

3

Using serum biomarkers to diagnose, assess, treat, and predict outcome after pediatric TBI

Rachel P. Berger, Ronald L. Hayes, Kevin K.W. Wang, and Patrick Kochanek

A biomarker is an objectively measured and evaluated characteristic which is an indicator of normal biologic processes, pathogenic processes, or pharmacologic responses to a therapeutic intervention (Group, 2001). Physicians in clinical practice routinely use biomarkers to diagnose and assess disease severity, assist in disease prognosis, and evaluate treatment efficacy. Generally, injury and/or cell death results in increased concentrations of a given biomarker, either due to the release of that biomarker from the injured cell (e.g. creatine phosphokinase (CPK) in patients with myocardial infarction) or the lack of excretion of a normally excreted chemical which results in its accumulation (e.g. blood urea nitrogen in patients with renal failure). In some cases, however, a decrease in biomarker concentrations indicates pathology (e.g. haptoglobin in patients with hemolytic anemia).

Development of a clinically acceptable "brain" biomarker has proven much more difficult than the development of biomarkers for other organs. The difficulty is likely due to a combination of anatomic, physiologic, and technical issues. The complexity of the brain and the concomitant complexity of its response to injury have been barriers to development of sensitive and specific brain biomarkers. The presence of the blood–brain barrier which limits the amount and size of the biomarkers that can cross into the serum has also been an important issue. Until recently, technical difficulties had hindered the ability to identify novel candidate biomarkers using proteomics and, as a result, the number of potential biomarkers has been limited. The potential impact of the relatively new field of neuroproteomics on the ability to identify brain biomarkers is significant and is likely to change the biomarker landscape for both adults and children with TBI. It is important to consider, however, that in addition to the scientific barriers discussed above, there is another barrier which has limited the ability to bring brain biomarkers to clinical practice and which may end up being the last barrier to overcome: the barrier of unrealistic expectations. The biomarkers which are currently in clinical use for organs other than the brain, such as liver function tests are no more sensitive or specific for injury to those organs than many of the biomarkers discussed below are for the brain. The state of medicine in 2009, however, is markedly different than the state of medicine in the 1950s when many of these other biomarkers, such as liver function tests, were introduced into clinical practice. It is important for the reader to keep this barrier in mind, particularly throughout the next section which reviews the current state of the field of brain biomarkers and how the field reached this point (Table 3.1).

Pediatric Traumatic Brain Injury: New Frontiers in Clinical and Translational Research, ed. V. Anderson and K. O. Yeates. Published by Cambridge University Press. © Cambridge University Press 2010.

Table 3.1 Characteristics of the most commonly studied biomarkers

Biochemical marker	Abbreviation	Location	Serum half-life
Creatine phosphokinase – brain-specific isoform	CPK-BB	Brain, lungs	<1 hour
Myelin-basic protein	MBP	Myelin	12 hours
Neuron-specific enolase	NSE	Neurons, platelets, red blood cells, neuroendocrine cells	24 hours
S100β	NA	Astrocytes, chondrocytes, adipocytes	<100 minutes
Glial fibrillary acidic protein	GFAP	Glial cells	~1 week
Cleaved tau	c-tau	Axons of central nervous system neurons, proteolytically cleaved after release to form c-tau	Unknown
α-II spectrin/spectrin breakdown degradation products 120, 145 and 150	SBDP 120, 145 and 150	Cortical membrane cytoskeletal protein breakdown products generated by calpain or caspase	Unknown
Hyperphosphorylated neurofilament heavy chain	pNFH	Axons	Unknown

Candidate biomarkers of brain injury: a 30-year odyssey continues

The first reports of serum biomarkers of brain injury were in the late 1970s (Harwood *et al.*, 1978; Thomas *et al.*, 1978) These early biomarkers were identified because changes in their concentration were found to correlate with severity of injury and/or predict findings on neuroimaging. The biochemical mechanisms which produced the biomarker changes after TBI were not, and in some cases are still not, well understood. As a result, these biomarkers are essentially surrogate markers of TBI rather than true biochemical markers.

Myelin-basic protein (MBP), one of the two most abundant proteins in myelin, was one of the earliest brain biomarkers evaluated (Thomas *et al.*, 1978; Thomas *et al.*, 1984). The few clinical studies of serum MBP (Thomas *et al.*, 1978; Thomas *et al.*, 1984; Yamazaki *et al.*, 1995) suggest that serum MBP increases only with severe TBI and/or intracranial hemorrhage. In addition, unlike other biomarker concentrations which begin to rise immediately after injury and quickly decrease, serum MBP concentrations do not begin to increase until 24–48 hours after injury and remain increased for up to 2 weeks (Thomas *et al.*, 1978). The late increase is likely related to the association of MBP with traumatic axonal injury: although axonal injury occurs at the time of TBI, the Wallerian degeneration of the axon and release of MBP takes several days. As a result of its specificity for severe TBI and intracranial hemorrhage and its unusual time course, MBP is no longer being actively pursued as a general biomarker of brain injury. It is still being evaluated, however, for use in one specific clinical scenario. Because of the late rise and prolonged presence in the serum, MBP might be useful in identifying non-acute intracranial hemorrhage in asymptomatic or mildly symptomatic infants with inflicted TBI (e.g. shaken baby syndrome) in whom the concentrations of other biomarkers have already decreased (Berger et al., 2005). Interestingly, because its concentrations do not seem to be contaminated by a large initial increase, MBP might also be able to be used to monitor treatment effects although this use is not currently being pursued.

As interest in MBP waned for the reasons discussed above, focus turned to the brain-specific fraction of CPK (CPK-BB). Serum and CSF concentrations of CPK-BB were found to be increased after both TBI and cardiac arrest in both animal models (Vaagenes et al., 1988) and in humans (Hans et al., 1983; Karpman et al., 1981; Rabow & Hedman, 1985; Skogseid et al., 1992; Vaagenes et al., 1994) and to correlate with outcome in both (Vaagenes et al., 1988, 1994). After the mid-1990s, however, CPK was essentially abandoned as a possible brain biomarker, despite the studies which suggested that its sensitivity, specificity, and predictive value could be clinically relevant. One of the reasons for the sudden end to research involving CPK was the emergence of two other brain biomarkers: neuron-specific enolase (NSE) and S100β. Most of the literature since that time has focused on these two markers. NSE is a glycolytic enzyme localized primarily in neuronal cytoplasm and is involved in regulating intracellular chloride levels. NSE has a relatively high specificity for brain tissue, but its presence in low concentrations in platelets and red blood cells has limited its clinical utility. The inability to consistently correlate NSE concentrations with outcome or injury severity has also contributed to waning interest in NSE (Bandyopadhyay et al., 2005; Berger et al., 2005; Karkela et al., 1993; Ross et al., 1996; Skogseid et al., 1992; Vazquez et al., 1995; Yamazaki et al., 1995).

S100β, the major low affinity calcium binding protein in astrocytes (Xiong et al., 2000), is the most well-studied brain biomarker. It is released by astrocytes, which die or are irreversibly injured. Since the serum half-life of S100β is less than 100 min, increases in serum S100β after TBI are transient. Although S100β is sensitive to brain injury, one of its most important limitations is its lack of specificity. Increases in S100β can be seen with shock as well as with non-cranial injuries including fractures (Anderson et al., 2001; Pelinka et al., 2003; Romner & Ingebrigtsen, 2001; Rothoerl & Woertgen, 2001). Another limitation of S100β is its high normative concentrations in children, particularly those less than two years of age (Gazzolo et al., 2003; Portela et al., 2002). As a result of these high baseline concentrations, a single value of S100β can not be interpreted in young children, although serial concentrations in the same patient may be able to provide important information about progression and/or severity of injury (Berger et al., 2006a). At this time, S100β is most likely to be clinically useful because of high sensitivity and associated high negative predictive value; in adults with mild TBI and a Glasgow Coma Scale (GCS) score of 15, the negative predictive value of a normal S100β concentration is close to 99% (Biberthaler et al., 2006; Ingebrigtsen et al., 2000; Muller et al., 2007; Mussack et al., 2002). In Germany, S100β is currently used in clinical practice to assess the need for head CT after mild TBI; patients with a normal S100β do not undergo head CT (Peter Biberthaler, MD, personal communication). The pediatric literature related to S100β is limited to a few small studies which have confirmed its sensitivity as well as its lack of specificity (Berger et al., 2005; Piazza et al., 2007).

Because of the lack of specificity of S100β, there has been interest in a related marker of astroglial cell injury: glial fibrillary acidic protein (GFAP). A proteomic analysis of rat hippocampus after controlled cortical impact suggested that markers of astrocyte proliferation such as GFAP and vimentin represent highly sensitive markers of brain injury (Kochanek et al., 2006). Two human studies which have evaluated serum GFAP concentrations after severe TBI in adults also demonstrated that higher GFAP concentrations are associated with worse outcome (Pelinka *et al.*, 2004a; Vos *et al.*, 2004). A single study by Pelinka and colleagues suggests that, unlike S100β, GFAP is not affected by multiorgan trauma (Pelinka *et al.*, 2004b). Additional studies will need to be performed in children and in patients with mild and moderate TBI to assess whether there is a possible clinical role for GFAP in these populations.

While there is still ongoing evaluation of the markers described above, there is a new focus on a set of biomarkers which are structural markers of axonal injury. Tau, a microtubule-associated structural protein localized to axons of the central nervous system, was the first of the axonal markers to be evaluated. After axonal injury, tau is released and proteolytically cleaved to c-tau, which is detectable in the serum. Although increases in c-tau concentrations seem to specific for TBI (Shaw *et al.*, 2002), there does not appear to be a correlation between c-tau concentrations and outcome after TBI (Bazarian *et al.*, 2006; Chatfield *et al.*, 2002; Ma *et al.*, 2008). More recently, interest has shifted to a related set of axonal markers: α-II spectrin and its degradation products, spectrin breakdown products (SBDP) 120, 145 and 150. At this time, data are promising, but are limited to animal studies (Pike *et al.*, 1998, 2001, 2004, Ringger *et al.*, 2004) and two small studies in humans with severe TBI in whom CSF concentrations were measured (Cardali & Maugeri, 2006; Pineda *et al.*, 2007). There are currently no peer-reviewed publications related to serum concentrations of these markers, but a preliminary study showing elevation of the SBDPs in serum from TBI patients has been presented (Oli *et al.*, 2007; Robicsek *et al.*, 2007). Finally, recent abstracts suggest that CSF and serum concentrations of ubiquitin carboxyl hydrolase-1 (UCHL-1), a biomarker expressed exclusively in the cell bodies of neurons, and hyperphosphorylated neurofilament heavy chain (pNFH) might be useful biomarkers (Blyth *et al.*, 2008; Liu *et al.*, 2007; Papa *et al.*, 2008).

Neuroproteomics

The biomarkers discussed above have been pursued as potential markers of brain injury because their concentrations were increased after TBI and could be easily measured using an enzyme-linked immunoassay (ELISA). Proteomics and specifically neuroproteomics allows for the entire proteome to be screened and for candidate proteins to be identified. While one would expect some, if not all, of the proteins discussed above to be identified using proteomics, it is likely that proteomics will identify multiple additional biomarkers which are more sensitive and/or specific for TBI. Since approximately 90% of the proteome is composed of just 10–12 different proteins including albumin and immunoglobulins, the signal from this background noise was high. Until recently, discovery of low-abundant TBI markers in serum was almost impossible, and thus neuroproteomic studies for both TBI and other non-traumatic neurological insults has to be carried out in CSF rather than in blood (Conti *et al.*, 2004; Ekegren *et al.*, 2008; Gao *et al.*, 2007; Zhang *et al.*, 2008). When proteomic studies are performed in CSF, the goal is to identify potential biomarkers and then to use techniques such as immunoprecipitation and/or ELISA to quantify serum biomarker concentrations. An alternative approach is to perform differential antibody array- and mass spectrometry-based proteomic studies comparing brain tissue from normal rats compared to those subjected to experimental TBI (Kobeissy *et al.*, 2006; Liu *et al.*, 2006). Details about the techniques used in neuroproteomics are beyond the scope of this chapter, but the interested reader is referred to two excellent review articles on the topic (Wang et al., 2005; Ottens et al., 2007).

Novel proteomic techniques, though technically difficult and markedly expensive, are revolutionizing the ability to directly identify potential biomarkers of brain injury in serum. In a recently published feasibility study, Haqqani and colleagues (2007) used gel-free proteomics to identify 95 uniquely expressed proteins in six children with severe TBI compared to healthy adult controls. The majority of the differentially expressed proteins identified are involved in inflammation, innate immunity, and the early stress/defense response. Not surprisingly, several of the differentially expressed proteins were ones which have been previously evaluated, such as S100β.

The potential clinical roles of serum brain biomarkers

Over the next 10 years, growth in the field of neuroproteomics will likely result in a marked increase in the number of potential brain biomarkers. The potential clinical uses of these biomarkers, however, will likely remain fairly stable. For purposes of discussion, it is helpful to divide the potential roles of biomarkers in pediatric TBI into five categories: (1) diagnosis; (2) identification of intracranial injury; (3) assessment of injury severity/outcome prediction; (4) identification of injury mechanisms/development of treatment interventions; and (5) evaluation of treatment efficacy. This choice of categories is somewhat arbitrary and the categories overlap considerably. Furthermore, studies which may focus on one specific role of biomarkers may have implications for future research and/or clinical care in a different category. It is important to recognize that the biomarker or the panel of biomarkers and perhaps the timing of biomarker measurement may be different depending on the clinical context in which the biomarkers are being used. The next section of the chapter will focus on how biomarkers might be used in each of these clinical roles. Because of the dearth of pediatric data, it is necessary to reference both the pediatric and adult literature.

Diagnosis of TBI

When used in the context of TBI diagnosis, biomarkers would serve as "point to the brain" tests, much the same way that liver function tests "point to the liver" as the possible source of a patient's symptoms. Infants and young children who present for medical care with non-specific clinical symptoms such as vomiting or irritability would be the population in whom a "point to the brain" test would be most useful. In the vast majority of cases, these symptoms do not have a neurologic cause and are due to common pediatric issues such as gastro-esophageal reflux, gastritis or colic. In some cases, however, the symptoms are due to TBI or to another non-traumatic neurologic insult. In the absence of a history of head trauma and/or physical examination findings which might indicate trauma such as a bruise or soft tissue swelling, it is unlikely that a physician would consider a diagnosis of TBI in a vomiting infant, for example. The difficulty identifying TBI in this context has been well described as has the high morbidity and mortality when cases of inflicted TBI (TBI due to child abuse) are not properly identified (Alexander et al., 1990; Jenny et al., 1999; Laskey, 1998; Rubin et al., 2003). The high rate of re-abuse after misdiagnosis demonstrates the critical importance of accurate and timely diagnosis. Two studies by Berger and colleagues have suggested that biomarkers have the potential to be useful in the context of TBI diagnosis (Berger et al., 2006b, 2009). In a 2006 study, NSE and MBP concentrations were measured in 98 infants who presented for evaluation of non-specific clinical symptoms.

A head CT was performed if the treating physician ordered it as part of clinical care. All subjects were followed until 1 year of age to assess for subsequent abuse. Of the 98 infants, 74 did not have TBI identified at the time of initial evaluation and were not victims of abuse at any time during the follow-up period, 14 were identified as having inflicted TBI at the time of enrollment, five were identified as having a brain injury not due to trauma (e.g. hydrocephalus) at the time of enrollment, and five did not have TBI identified at the time of the initial evaluation, but were victims of abuse at some point during the follow-up period. Using previously derived cut-offs for abnormal biomarker concentrations (Berger *et al.*, 2005), NSE was 76% sensitive and 66% specific and MBP was 36% sensitive and 100% specific for TBI. A combination of NSE and MBP was 79% sensitive and 70% specific for TBI. Of the five subjects who were subsequently identified as victims of abuse, four had had an increased serum NSE concentration at enrollment, suggesting that these may have been missed cases of inflicted TBI. The enrollment of five subjects with non-traumatic neurologic diseases highlights the fact that if biomarkers were used in this context, they would not provide information about the type of injury (e.g. traumatic vs. non-traumatic) or the etiology of injury (e.g. abuse vs. not abuse), but would only suggest that the brain may be the source of a patient's symptoms and that the treating physician should consider this in his/her diagnostic evaluation.

Identification of intracranial injury in children with mild TBI

Using biomarkers to identify intracranial injury in patients with mild TBI has been an area of active research for almost a decade. The potential use of biomarkers to identify intracranial injury initially focused on addressing a very specific clinical problem: how to differentiate adults with acute alcohol intoxication from those with alcohol intoxication and intracranial injury without needing to perform a head CT in all of them. In one of the first studies to address this specific clinical problem, Mussack and colleagues (2002) enrolled 139 subjects during the Munich Oktoberfest in 2000. All subjects underwent head CT and had serum NSE and S100β concentrations measured. S100β, but not NSE, concentrations, were significantly higher in patients with intracranial injury compared to those without. It was possible to identify a cut-off value of S100β which provided 100% sensitivity and 50% specificity for identification of patients with intracranial injury. Virtually all of the studies performed after this initial one have focused exclusively on S100β (Biberthaler *et al.*, 2001, 2006; Muller *et al.*, 2007; Mussack *et al.*, 2000, 2002; Nygren De Boussard *et al.*, 2004; Romner *et al.*, 2000; Savola *et al.*, 2004). A recent multi-center study by the same research team in Germany enrolled 1309 adults with mild TBI, defined as a history of TBI, a GCS score of 13 to 15 and one or more clinical risk factors such as vomiting, intoxication, and severe headache. All subjects underwent head CT. S100β identified the subset with 99% sensitivity and 30% specificity using the previously derived cut-off for S100β (Biberthaler *et al.*, 2006). The authors concluded that the negative predictive value of an undetectable S100β serum level was 99%, meaning that there was 99% probability that a patient with a normal S100β did not have intracranial injury. The authors also concluded that use of S100β in this context could result in a 30% decrease in the use of head CT without missing any cases of intracranial injury. As a result of this study and several others with similar findings, S100β is currently used in clinical practice in Germany to assess the need for head CT after mild TBI; adults with a normal S100β do not undergo head CT (Peter Biberthaler, M.D., personal communication).

Although the initial impetus for the research related to the use of S100β to identify intracranial injury was a combination of cost and resource allocation, increasing recognition of the radiation risk from head CT, particularly in young children (Brenner et al., 2001; Brody et al., 2007; Kirpalani & Nahmias, 2008), has brought this potential role of serum biomarkers to the forefront in the pediatric population. Surprisingly, there is only a single published pediatric study which specifically addressed this issue. The study, published in 2000 by Fridriksson and colleagues (2000) reported on 50 children aged 0–18 years with TBI. Forty-five percent of these children had intracranial injury. In this population, an increased serum NSE concentration was 77% sensitive and 52% specific for intracranial injury. S100β was not evaluated in the study, the authors did not report on the specificity of NSE at a sensitivity of 100%, and no follow-up study has been published.

There are several reasons why pediatric-specific studies are essential. Perhaps most importantly, S100β, the most well-studied biomarker for identification of intracranial injury cannot be used in young children. In children less than two years of age, S100β concentrations are high in a significant proportion of neurologically normal children (Berger et al., 2006b; Portela et al., 2002). In addition, the role of a serum biomarker in patients with mild TBI is slightly different in children compared with adults. In adults, biomarkers are needed to identify intracranial injury. In children, however, it is also important to identify skull fractures. Identification of a skull fracture is important in order to properly follow and assess for development of a leptomeningeal cyst, a rare, but potentially life-threatening complication of a skull fracture which is unique to young children (Scarfo et al., 1989). In addition, the type of skull fracture and/or the location and type of intracranial injury may be the only clue to the physician that the history of injury provided by the caretaker may not be consistent with the injuries identified and that the child may need additional evaluation for possible child abuse. There are currently no biomarkers which have been identified as markers of skull fracture in children or adults.

Assessment of injury severity/outcome prediction after TBI

Accurate assessment of injury severity is critical in order to properly predict outcome. Outcome prediction after TBI is important for family counseling, for selection of patients who are most likely to benefit from rehabilitation services, and for decision making, particularly as it relates to the extent of care to provide and whether to continue or withdraw care. After mild TBI, outcome prediction is important for identification of patients who are at highest risk of having sequelae from their injury and in whom early rehabilitation would be most helpful. Since only 10%–15% of patients with mild TBI have sequelae, it is neither possible nor appropriate to offer rehabilitation to all mild TBI patients.

The adult literature related to biomarkers and outcome prediction is extensive and the interested reader is referred to a review article on the subject (Berger, 2006). Very briefly, numerous markers have been assessed including NSE (Lima et al., 2004; Vos et al., 2004), S100β (Pelinka et al., 2004a; Petzold et al., 2002), MBP (Thomas et al., 1978) GFAP (Pelinka et al., 2004a; Vos et al., 2004), and c-tau (Bazarian et al., 2006; Chatfield et al., 2002; Ma et al., 2008). With the exception of c-tau, the data demonstrate that higher serum biomarker concentrations are correlated with worse outcome. There has not, however, been a comprehensive assessment of whether the correlation between biomarker concentrations and outcome as assessed by the Glasgow Outcome Scale (GOS) score is stronger than the correlation between GCS and GOS.

Furthermore, the majority of the literature has focused on using a single biomarker at a single time point to predict outcome, although serial measurements of multiple biomarkers are more likely to be accurate predictors of outcome.

Biomarkers may play a particularly important role in predicting outcome after pediatric TBI because of the weak correlation between GCS and GOS, in young children. This relationship is weakest in the youngest children in whom GCS is not an accurate assessment of injury severity (Durham *et al.*, 2000) and in whom GOS is difficult to assess in an age-appropriate way. The pediatric literature related to biomarkers and their relationship to outcome is limited (Table 3.2). In the largest pediatric study to date, NSE, S100β and MBP concentrations were measured in 153 children with TBI. Biomarkers were measured at the time of presentation and then every 12 hours as long as intravenous access was available. Outcome was assessed up to 12 months after injury using the GOS score. Initial and peak biomarker concentrations were calculated for NSE, S100β and MBP. "Length of time in hours NSE was abnormal" was also calculated. Abnormal concentrations of each marker were defined based on previously published pediatric data (Berger *et al.*, 2005). For all biomarkers and at all time points, higher biomarker concentrations were associated with worse outcome. Overall, peak biomarker concentrations were more strongly correlated with outcome than initial concentrations and biomarker concentrations showed a stronger association with outcome when the time between discharge and outcome assessment was shorter (e.g. 3 mo after injury vs. 12 mo after injury). The strongest predictor of outcome was "length of time NSE was abnormal" (Berger *et al.*, 2007).

Overall, pediatric studies related to outcome prediction are limited by small sample sizes, evaluation of a limited number of biomarkers at a limited number of time points, and use of gross outcome measures such as the GOS. Significantly more research is needed in both children and adults before biomarkers could be used as outcome predictors in clinical practice.

Development of treatment interventions

Despite numerous improvements in pediatric intensive care over the past 20 years, the mortality from pediatric TBI has remained virtually unchanged (Pfenninger & Santi, 2002) and pharmacologic therapies that are currently available for the treatment of pediatric or adult TBI primarily target brain edema and intracranial hypertension. Novel neuroprotective agents are needed. One of the earliest recognized uses of biomarkers was to help define the mechanisms and pathophysiology of the response of the brain to TBI with the hope of using this information to develop effective interventions. These early studies used CSF drained from extra-ventricular drains placed for treatment of intracranial hypertension. The results were instrumental in helping to define the evolution of secondary brain injury after severe TBI and highlighted the important contributions of post-traumatic ischemia, excitotoxicity, energy failure, cerebral swelling, axonal injury, and inflammation to outcome (Kochanek *et al.*, 2000). Although numerous clinical trials which have been designed based on our improved understanding of the pathophysiology of TBI have failed to result in clinical improvement (Narayan *et al.*, 2002), the reasons are likely multi-factorial and not a reflection of the lack of potential success of this approach. For example, the demonstration of increased CSF glutamate concentrations after TBI (Bullock *et al.*, 1998; Ruppel *et al.*, 2001) and the recognition that excitotoxicity plays an important role in the secondary injury after TBI contributed to the testing of excitatory amino acid inhibitors as a potential therapy. These trials were successful in animal models (McIntosh, 1993), but failed in humans

Table 3.2 Serum biomarkers and outcome after pediatric TBI

Author (year)	Measured outcome and when	Conclusions	Significant strengths	Significant weaknesses
Spinella et al. (2003)	Dichotomous PCPC score at discharge and 6 mo	Sig. difference in S100β between poor and good outcome groups	First pediatric study	Sample size ($n = 27$), single marker, gross outcome measure
Bandyopadhyay et al. (2005)	GOS at hospital discharge	Sig. difference in NSE between good and poor outcome groups	Larger study ($n = 86$)	Single marker, gross outcome measure
Beers et al. (2007)	GOS, VABS, IQ 6 mo after injury	Peak NSE and MBP and time to peak NSE inversely correlated with GOS, VABS, IQ; Time to peak S100β inversely correlated with IQ, VABS	More refined outcome criteria, multiple markers/time points	Small sample ($n = 30$)
Berger et al. (2007)	GOS, GOS-E Peds 0–3 mo, 4–6 mo and 7–12 mo after injury	Peak NSE, S100β and MBP inversely correlated with outcome, peak levels more strongly correlated than initial levels, earlier outcome more strongly correlated than late outcome assessment	Large sample ($n = 152$), multiple time points/ biomarkers	Gross outcome measures
Piazza et al. (2007)	GOS-E 6 mo after injury	S100β concentrations do not correlate with outcome	None	Sample size ($n = 15$), outcome performed based on a phone call

Abbreviations: PCPC: pediatric cerebral performance category; NSE: neuron-specific enolase; GOS: Glasgow Outcome Scale; MBP: myelin-basic protein; VABS: Vineland Adaptive Behavior Score; GOS-E Peds: GOS extended-pediatric; GOS-E: GOS extended.

(Morris *et al.*, 1999). The reasons for failure are more likely to be related to an inadequate understanding of the complexity of the secondary response to the TBI rather than to a flaw in the approach to using biomarkers to develop new pharmacologic therapies.

Evaluation of treatment efficacy

Because of the lack of effective pharmacologic therapies, current clinical trials in TBI are focused on non-pharmacologic therapies such as hypothermia, decompressive craniectomy, osmotherapy, and controlled hyperventilation. Outcome in treated and untreated groups in these trials has generally been assessed using only gross measures of outcome (e.g. survival vs. mortality or the GOS score) which are evaluated a short time after the intervention (e.g. at hospital discharge) (Adelson *et al.*, 2005; Kochanek & Safar, 2003; McIntyre *et al.*, 2003). The use of gross outcome measures to assess the effect of a treatment such as hypothermia which affects multiple aspects of the pathophysiologic response of the brain to injury is overly simplistic. Measurement of outcome so quickly after the intervention is particularly problematic in children since even significant disabilities and functional deficits may not be apparent for years after injury. Finally, the well-established outcome measures, such as the GOS, are adult oriented. A return to pre-injury status, for example, is not relevant in children in whom expectations and developmental milestones are constantly changing. Biomarkers may be able to address at least some of these difficulties by serving as a surrogate for treatment efficacy and allowing for early assessment of clinical response to an intervention. A study of adults after cardiac arrest, for example, demonstrated decreased serum NSE, but not S100β, concentrations immediately after injury in subjects treated with hypothermia compared with normothermia, suggesting decreased neuronal death in these patients (Tiainen *et al.*, 2003). Several recent studies have begun to assess the effect of therapeutic hypothermia on a variety of CSF biomarkers including cytokines (Buttram *et al.*, 2007) and markers of oxidative stress (Bayir *et al.*, 2009). Serum biomarkers have not yet been used to assess treatment efficacy in any clinical TBI trial and therefore its use in this context is currently more theoretical than practical.

Other issues in the field of biomarkers and pediatric TBI

Biomarker sensitivity

The gold standard for identification of intracranial injury after TBI is the head CT. Since the late 1990s there has been evidence to suggest that S100β might be more sensitive for intracranial injury than the head CT (Akhtar *et al.*, 2003; Berger, 2003; Ingebrigtsen & Romner, 1996; Ingebrigtsen *et al.*, 1999; Romner *et al.*, 2000). In a study by Ingebrigtsen and colleagues of 50 adults with concussions and normal CT scans, 14 subjects (28%) had abnormal concentrations of serum S100β. Of these 14 patients, 4 had brain contusions visualized on MRI (Ingebrigtsen *et al.*, 1999). The high sensitivity of serum markers would not be unique to brain injury; serum biomarkers are currently the reference standard for diagnosis of cardiac injury, for example (Lewandrowski *et al.*, 2002). As with heart or liver, the threshold for cellular brain injury is likely well below the threshold of imaging. Future studies are needed to assess biomarker sensitivity and determine whether increases in serum biomarkers after mild TBI, for example, should warrant consideration of more sensitive neuroimaging either after head CT or instead of a head CT. At least one study evaluating sensitive, serial imaging techniques combined with very sensitive outcome measures is already underway in adults. It is also possible that the combination of serum biomarkers and imaging techniques such as magnetic resonance imaging, magnetic resonance spectroscopy, or diffusion tensor imaging may provide the ideal combination of sensitivity and specificity (Ashwal, 2006).

Single biomarkers vs. biomarker panels

The literature related to biomarkers and TBI has focused on identifying the perfect biomarker, which can serve all of the clinical roles discussed above. As a result, almost all of the studies have evaluated a single biomarker. Given the heterogeneity and complexity of TBI, it is highly unlikely that a single biomarker or even group of two or three markers will be able to accomplish all clinical roles for adults and children with TBI of all severities. It is more likely that several different panels of biomarkers with varying kinetics and specificities for different parts of the brain and different aspects of the secondary response will be needed. The strategy of using a panel of markers is being employed in adults to identify stroke (Lynch *et al.*, 2004; Reynolds *et al.*, 2003; Sotgiu *et al.*, 2006) and cardiac disease (McCann *et al.*, 2009).

The first peer-reviewed study to evaluate the use of a biomarker panel approach to detect pediatric TBI was recently published (Berger *et al.*, 2009). In this study, multiplex bead technology was used to simultaneously screen 44 different serum biomarkers. Biomarker concentrations were compared between infants with mild inflicted TBI and infants without brain injury. There were significant group differences in the concentrations of 9 of the 44 markers screened: vascular cellular adhesion molecule, interleukin-12, matrix metallopeptidase-9, intracellular adhesion molecule, eotaxin, hepatocyte growth factor, tumor necrosis factor receptor 2, interleukin-6, and fibrinogen. Using interleukin-6 and vascular cellular adhesion molecule – the two markers with the most significant group differences – cases and controls were separated using three mathematical algorithms: linear classification, five nearest neighbors, and tree classification. Only two markers were evaluated in order to avoid over-fitting with this small, sample. The classification using only these two biomarkers discriminated children with and without brain injury with a sensitivity of 87% and a specificity of 90%.

Developmental changes in the brain and its response to injury

As we are all aware, children with brain injury are very different from adults with brain injury. Even within the pediatric population, biomarkers which are sensitive and/or specific for brain injury in one age group may not be sensitive or specific in another. The inability to use S100β, the most sensitive serum biomarker, to screen for intracranial injury in infants and young children (Berger *et al.*, 2006b), is just one example of how biomarkers which work in one population may not work in another. Even within the pediatric age range, it is likely that there will be multiple differences in the biomarkers which will be useful in the different clinical contexts described above. For these reasons, it is important that clinical studies include children of all ages and age-match cases and controls, particularly in neuroproteomic studies.

Clinical research in a pediatric population

Given the morbidity and mortality of TBI in children, the number of clinical studies related to biomarkers after pediatric TBI is surprisingly limited. The reasons for this are likely multi-faceted ranging from the generally less extensive research infrastructure in pediatric compared to adult settings and the lack of pediatric clinical researchers. There are also specific barriers to biomarker research in pediatric TBI. There are barriers, for example, to collecting blood. In children with mild TBI, for example, blood not always collected as part of routine care. Although adding a blood draw to routine clinical care in these patients could be done if the biomarkers are found to provide important information, drawing blood as part of a research study in order to evaluate the use of serum biomarkers in this population is much more difficult. Based on the experience of one of the co-authors (RB), parents of infants and young children are very hesitant to allow their child to undergo phlebotomy as part of a research study and consent rates are low when a blood draw is required for research.

Difficulty assessing outcome, particularly in pre-verbal children, is another limitation of performing TBI research in children. If outcome cannot be accurately assessed, any correlation between biomarkers concentration and outcome is difficult to interpret. The fact that inflicted TBI is an important cause of TBI in infants and young children is an additional barrier since these children are more difficult to enroll in research studies, particularly ones in which long-term tracking is needed. In addition, Institutional Review Boards are often hesitant to approve protocols involving victims of child abuse. Although we can use some of the adult biomarker data to advance the pediatric field, a significant amount of research will need to be performed in children and the barriers listed above will need to be addressed.

Conclusions and future directions

The use of biomarkers after TBI has been an area of clinical interest and research for almost 30 years. Pediatric-specific research in this field is remarkably limited given the morbidity and mortality associated with pediatric TBI and the numerous potential clinical uses in this age group. But what is perhaps most striking about the work in field of biomarkers and TBI is how far we have come without any significant integration of brain biomarkers into clinical practice. When liver function tests became part of clinical practice several decades ago, for example, the number of patients who had been studied was significantly less than the number who have been enrolled in TBI studies and our understanding of the sensitivity and specificity of the liver function test was significantly less mature than our understanding of many of the brain biomarkers. Perhaps more importantly, the expectations for what liver function tests could provide from a clinical perspective were significantly lower than the expectations for brain markers. Though their sensitivity and specificity for liver injury are far from perfect, they have nonetheless had a significant impact on clinical care and it is likely that brain biomarkers could have a similar impact on clinical care. It is important to recognize that the role of the US Food & Drug Administration (FDA) in changing clinical practice is significantly different today than what it was at the time liver function tests were introduced. Decisions about whether or not to secure FDA approval, the cost of the process necessary to obtain this approval, and how much FDA approval would facilitate clinical acceptance of brain biomarkers must all be taken into consideration. There is clearly a need for more research in the field of brain biomarkers and particularly the emerging field of neuroproteomics. The technology needed to measure biomarkers in a point-of-care fashion has existed for several years though it may be several years until FDA approval of any specific device occurs. Nevertheless it may be time to begin to integrate brain biomarkers into clinical practice, while recognizing their limitations in the same way we recognize the limitations of liver function tests. Neither the pursuit of the perfect markers nor the lack of FDA approval should be barriers to the integration of brain biomarkers into clinical practice.

References

Adelson, P. D., Ragheb, J., Kanev, P. et al. (2005). Phase II clinical trial of moderate hypothermia after severe traumatic brain injury in children. Neurosurgery, 56, 740–754: discussion 755–756.

Akhtar, J. I., Spear, R. M., Senac, M. O., Peterson, B. M. & Diaz, S. M. (2003). Detection of traumatic brain injury with magnetic resonance imaging and S-100B protein in children, despite normal computed tomography of the brain.

Pediatric Critical Care Medicine, **4**, 322–326.

Alexander, R., Crabbe, L., Sato, Y., Smith, W. & Bennett, T. (1990). Serial abuse in children who are shaken. *American Journal of Diseases in Children*, **144**, 58–60.

Anderson, R. E., Hansson, L. O., Nilsson, O., Dijlai-Merzoug, R. & Settergren, G. (2001). High serum S100β levels for trauma patients without head injuries. *Neurosurgery*, **48**, 1255–1258: discussion 1258–1260.

Bandyopadhyay, S., Hennes, H., Gorelick, M. H., Wells, R. G. & Walsh-Kelly, C. M. (2005). Serum neuron-specific enolase as a predictor of short-term outcome in children with closed traumatic brain injury. *Academic Emergency Medicine*, **12**, 732–738.

Bayir, H., Adelson, P., Wisnivesky, S. *et al.* (2009). Therapeutic hypothermia preserves antioxidant defenses after severe traumatic brain injury in infants and children. *Critical Care Medicine, in press.*

Bazarian, J. J. 1R01HD0518650–01A2 – Detecting axonal damage after mild TBI.

Bazarian, J. J., Zemlan, F. P., Mookerjee, S. & Stigbrand, T. (2006). Serum S-100B and cleaved-tau are poor predictors of long-term outcome after mild traumatic brain injury. *Brain Injury*, **20**, 759–765.

Beers, S. R., Berger, R. P. & Adelson, P. D. (2007). Neurocognitive outcome and serum biomarkers in inflicted versus non-inflicted traumatic brain injury in young children. *Journal of Neurotrauma*, **24**, 97–105.

Berger, R. (2003). Biomarkers or neuroimaging in central nervous system injury: will the real "gold standard" please stand up? *Pediatrics Critical Care Medicine*, **4**, 391–392.

Berger, R. P. (2006). The use of serum biomarkers to predict outcome after traumatic brain injury in adults and children. *Journal of Head Trauma Rehabilitation*, **21**, 315–333.

Berger, R. P., Adelson, P. D., Pierce, M. C., Dulani, T., Cassidy, L. D. & Kochanek, P. M. (2005). Serum neuron-specific enolase, S100β, and myelin basic protein concentrations after inflicted and noninflicted traumatic brain injury in children. *Journal of Neurosurgery*, **103**, 61–68.

Berger, R. P., Adelson, P. D., Richichi, R. & Kochanek, P. M. (2006a). Serum biomarkers after traumatic and hypoxemic brain injuries: insight into the biochemical response of the pediatric brain to inflicted brain injury. *Developmental Neuroscience*, **28**, 327–335.

Berger, R. P., Dulani, T., Adelson, P. D., Leventhal, J. M., Richichi, R. & Kochanek, P. M. (2006b). Identification of inflicted traumatic brain injury in well-appearing infants using serum and cerebrospinal markers: a possible screening tool. *Pediatrics*, **117**, 325–332.

Berger, R. P., Beers, S. R., Richichi, R., Wiesman, D. & Adelson, P. D. (2007). Serum biomarker concentrations and outcome after pediatric traumatic brain injury. *Journal of Neurotrauma*, **24**, 1793–1801.

Berger, R. P., Ta'Asan, S., Rand, A., Lokshin, A. & Kochanek, P. (2009). Multiplex assessment of serum biomarker concentrations in well-appearing children with inflicted traumatic brain injury. *Pediatric Research*, **65**, 97–102.

Biberthaler, P., Mussack, T. & Wiedemann, E. (2001). Elevated serum levels of S-100B reflect the extent of brain injury in alcohol intoxicated patients after mild head trauma. *Shock*, **16**, 97–101.

Biberthaler, P., Linsenmeier, U. & Pfeifer, K. J. (2006). Serum S-100B concentration provides additional information for the indication of computed tomography in patients after minor head injury: a prospective multicenter study. *Shock*, **25**, 446–453.

Blyth, B., Bazarian, J. & Shaw, G. (2008). Differential patterns of release of UCHL-1 and PNFH into serum after severe traumatic brain injury. *Journal of Neurotrauma*, **25**, 862.

Brenner, D., Elliston, C., Hall, E. & Berdon, W. (2001). Estimated risks of radiation-induced fatal cancer from pediatric CT. *American Journal of Roentgenology*, **176**, 289–296.

Brody, A. S., Frush, D. P., Huda, W. & Brent, R. L. (2007). Radiation risk to children from computed tomography. *Pediatrics*, **120**, 677–682.

Bullock, R., Zauner, A., Woodward, J. J. *et al.* (1998). Factors affecting excitatory amino acid release following severe human head injury. *Journal of Neurosurgery*, **89**, 507–518.

Buttram, S. D., Wisniewski, S. R., Jackson, E. K. *et al.* (2007). Multiplex assessment of cytokine and chemokine levels in cerebrospinal fluid following severe pediatric traumatic brain injury: effects of moderate hypothermia. *Journal of Neurotrauma*, **24**, 1707–1718.

Cardali, S. & Maugeri, R. (2006). Detection of aII-spectrin and breakdown products in humans after severe traumatic brain injury. *Journal of Neurosurgical Science*, **50**, 25–31.

Chatfield, D. A., Zemlan, F. P., Day, D. J. & Menon, D. K. (2002). Discordant temporal patterns of S100beta and cleaved tau protein elevation after head injury: a pilot study. *British Journal of Neurosurgery*, **16**, 471–476.

Conti, A., Sanchez-Ruiz, Y., Bachi, A. *et al.* (2004). Proteome study of human cerebrospinal fluid following traumatic brain injury indicates fibrin(ogen) degradation products as trauma-associated markers. *Journal of Neurotrauma*, **21**, 854–863.

Durham, S. R., Clancy, R. R., Leuthardt, E. (2000). CHOP Infant Coma Scale ("Infant Face Scale"): a novel coma scale for children less than two years of age. *Journal of Neurotrauma*, **17**, 729–737.

Ekegren, T., Hanrieder, J. & Bergquist, J. (2008). Clinical perspectives of high-resolution mass spectrometry-based proteomics in neuroscience: exemplified in amyotrophic lateral sclerosis biomarker discovery research. *Journal of Mass Spectrometry*, **43**, 559–571.

Fridriksson, T., Kini, N., Walsh-Kelly, C. & Hennes, H. (2000). Serum neuron-specific enolase as a predictor of intracranial lesions in children with head trauma: a pilot study. *Academic Emergency Medicine*, **7**, 816–820.

Gao, W. M., Chadha, M. S., Berger, R. P. *et al.* (2007). Biomarkers and diagnosis; a gel-based proteomic comparison of human cerebrospinal fluid between inflicted and non-inflicted pediatric traumatic brain injury. *Journal of Neurotrauma*, **24**, 43–53.

Gazzolo, D., Michetti, F., Bruschettini, M. *et al.* (2003). Pediatric concentrations of S100β protein in blood: age- and sex-related changes. *Clinical Chemistry*, **49**, 967–970.

Group, B. D. W. (2001). Biomarkers and surrogate endpoints: preferred definitions and conceptual framework. *Clinical Pharmacological Therapy*, **69**, 89–95.

Hans, P., Born, J. D., Chapelle, J. P. & Milbouw, G. (1983). Creatine kinase isoenzymes in severe head injury. *Journal of Neurosurgery*, **58**, 689–692.

Haqqani, A. S., Hutchison, J. S., Ward, R. & Stanimirovic, D. B. (2007). Biomarkers and diagnosis: protein biomarkers in serum of pediatric patients with severe traumatic brain injury identified by ICAT-LC-MS/MS. *Journal of Neurotrauma*, **24**, 54–74.

Harwood, S. J., Catrou, P. G. & Cole, G. W. (1978). Creatine phosphokinase isoenzyme fractions in the serum of a patient struck by lightning. *Archives of Internal Medicine*, **138**, 645–646.

Ingebrigtsen, T. & Romner, B. (1996). Serial S-100 protein serum measurements related to early magnetic resonance imaging after minor head injury. Case report. *Journal of Neurosurgery*, **85**, 945–948.

Ingebrigtsen, T., Waterloo, K., Jacobsen, E. A., Langbakk, B. & Romber, B. (1999). Traumatic brain damage in minor head injury: relation of serum S-100 protein measurements to magnetic resonance imaging and neurobehavioral outcome. *Neurosurgery*, **45**, 468–475; discussion 475–476.

Ingebrigtsen, T., Romner, B., Marup-Jensen, S. *et al.* (2000). The clinical value of serum S-100 protein measurements in minor head injury: a Scandinavian multicentre study. *Brain Injury*, **14**, 1047–1055.

Jenny, C., Hymel, K. P., Ritzen, A., Reinert, S. E. & Hay, T. C. (1999). Analysis of missed cases of abusive head trauma. *Journal of the American Medical Association*, **281**, 621–626.

Karkela, J., Bock, E. & Kaukinen, S. (1993). CSF and serum brain-specific creatine kinase isoenzyme (CK-BB), neuron-specific enolase (NSE) and neural cell adhesion molecule (NCAM) as prognostic markers for hypoxic brain injury after cardiac arrest in man. *Journal of Neurological Science*, **116**, 100–109.

Karpman, R. R., Weinstein, P. R., Finley, P. R. & Karst-Sabin, B. (1981). Serum CPK isoenzyme BB as an indicator of brain tissue damage following head injury. *Journal of Trauma*, **21**, 148–151.

Kirpalani, H. & Nahmias, C. (2008). Radiation risk to children from computed tomography. *Pediatrics*, **121**, 449–450.

Kobeissy, F., Ottens, A., Zhang, Z. *et al.* (2006). Differential proteomic analysis of traumatic brain injury biomarker study using CAX-PAGE/RPLC-MSMS method. *Cellular Proteomics*, **5**, 1887–1898.

Kochanek, P. M. & Safar, P. J. (2003). Therapeutic hypothermia for severe traumatic brain injury. *Journal of the American Medical Association*, **289**, 3007–3009.

Kochanek, P. M., Clark, R. S., Ruppel, R. A. *et al.* (2000). Biochemical, cellular, and molecular mechanisms in the evolution of secondary damage after severe traumatic brain injury in infants and children: lessons learned from the bedside. *Pediatric Critical Care Medicine,* **1**, 4–19.

Kochanek, A. R., Kline, A. E., Gao, W. M. *et al.* (2006). Gel-based hippocampal proteomic analysis 2 weeks following traumatic brain injury to immature rats using controlled cortical impact. *Developmental Neuroscience*, **28**, 410–419.

Laskey, A. (1998). Shaken baby syndrome: a missed diagnosis. *1998 National Shaken Baby Conference*, Salt Lake City.

Lewandrowski, K., Chen, A. & Januzzi, J. (2002). Cardiac markers for myocardial infarction. A brief review. *American Journal of Clinical Pathology*, **118** Suppl, S93–S99.

Lima, J. E., Takayanagui, O. M., Garcia, L. V. & Leite, J. P. (2004). Use of neuron-specific enolase for assessing the severity and outcome in patients with neurological disorders. *Brazilian Journal of Medical and Biological Research*, **37**, 19–26.

Liu, M. C., Akle, V., Zheng, W. *et al.* (2006). Comparing calpain- and caspase-3-mediated degradation patterns in traumatic brain injury by differential proteome analysis. *Biochemical Journal*, **394**, 715–725.

Liu, M., Zheng, W., Akinyi, L. *et al.* (2007). Ubiquitin-c-terminal hydrolase as a biomarker for ischemic and traumatic brain injury. *The 25th Annual National Neurotrauma Society Symposium*, Kansas City, MO.

Lynch, J. R., Blessing, R., White, W. D., Grocott, H. P., Newman, M. F. & Laskowitz, D. T. (2004). Novel diagnostic test for acute stroke. *Stroke*, **35**, 57–63.

Ma, M., Lindsell, C. J., Rosenberry, C. M., Shaw, G. J. & Zemlan, F. P. (2008). Serum cleaved tau does not predict postconcussion syndrome after mild traumatic brain injury. *American Journal of Emergency Medicine*, **26**, 763–768.

McCann, C. J., Glover, B. M., Menown, I. B. *et al.* (2009). Prognostic value of a multimarker approach for patients presenting to hospital with acute chest pain. *American Journal of Cardiology*, **103**, 22–28.

McIntosh, T. (1993). Novel pharmacologic therapies in the treatment of experimental traumatic brain injury. *Journal of Neurotrauma*, **10**, 215–261.

McIntyre, L. A., Fergusson, D. A., Herbert, P. C., Moher, D. & Hutchison, J. S. (2003). Prolonged therapeutic hypothermia after traumatic brain injury in adults: a systematic review. *JAMA*, **289**, 2992–2999.

Morris, G. F., Bullock, R., Marshall, S. B., Marmarou, A., Maas, A. & Marshall, L. F. (1999). Failure of the competitive N-methyl-D-aspartate antagonist Selfotel (CGS 19755) in the treatment of severe head injury: results of two phase III clinical trials. The Selfotel Investigators. *Journal of Neurosurgery*, **91**, 737–743.

Muller, K., Townend, W., Biasca, N. *et al.* (2007). S100β serum level predicts computed tomography findings after minor head injury. *Journal of Trauma*, **62**, 1452–1456.

Mussack, T., Biberthaler, P., Wiedemann, E. *et al.* (2000). S-100b as a screening marker of the severity of minor head trauma (MHT) – a pilot study. *Acta Neurochirurgica,* **76** Suppl, 393–396.

Mussack, T., Biberthaler, P., Kanz, K. G. *et al.* (2002). Immediate S-100B and neuron-specific enolase plasma measurements for rapid evaluation of primary brain damage in alcohol-intoxicated, minor head-injured patients. *Shock*, **18**, 395–400.

Narayan, R. K., Michel, M. E., Ansell, B. *et al.* (2002). Clinical trials in head injury. *Journal of Neurotrauma*, **19**, 503–557.

Nygren De Boussard, C., Fredman, P., Lundin, A., Andersson, K., Edman, G. & Borg, J. (2004). S100 in mild traumatic brain injury. *Brain Injury*, **18**, 671–683.

Oli, M., Akinyi, L., Mo, J. *et al.* (2007). *Development and Validation of Novel Brain Biomarker Assays*. St. Pete Beach: Advanced Technology for Combat Casualty Care (ATACCC).

Ottens, A. K., Kobeissy, F. H., Fuller, B. F. *et al.* (2007). Novel neuroproteomic approaches to studying traumatic brain injury. *Progress in Brain Research*, **161**, 401–418.

Papa, L., Oli, M., Akinyi, L. *et al.* (2008). Levels of UCH-L1 in human CSF and outcome following severe traumatic brain injury. *Journal of Neurotrauma*, **25**, 854–935.

Pelinka, L. E., Toegel, E., Mauritz, W. & Redl, H. (2003). Serum S 100 B: a marker of brain damage in traumatic brain injury with and without multiple trauma. *Shock*, **19**, 195–200.

Pelinka, L. E., Kroepfl, A., Leixnering, M., Buchinger, W., Raabe, A. & Redl, H. (2004a). GFAP versus S100β in serum after traumatic brain injury: relationship to brain damage and outcome. *Journal of Neurotrauma*, **21**, 1553–1561.

Pelinka, L. E., Kroepfl, A., Schmidhammer, R. *et al.* (2004b). Glial fibrillary acidic protein in serum after traumatic brain injury and multiple trauma. *Journal of Trauma*, **57**, 1006–1012.

Petzold, A., Green, A. J., Keir, G. *et al.* (2002). Role of serum S100β as an early predictor of high intracranial pressure and mortality in brain injury: a pilot study. *Critical Care Medicine*, **30**, 2705–2710.

Pfenninger, J. & Santi, A. (2002). Severe traumatic brain injury in children – are the results improving? *Swiss Medical Weekly*, **132**, 116–120.

Piazza, O., Storti, M. P., Cotena, S. *et al.* (2007). S100β is not a reliable prognostic index in paediatric TBI. *Pediatric Neurosurgery*, **43**, 258–264.

Pike, B. R., Zhao, X., Newcomb, J. K., Posmantur, R. M., Wang, K. K. & Hayes, R. L. (1998). Regional calpain and caspase-3 proteolysis of alpha-spectrin after traumatic brain injury. *Neuroreport*, **9**, 2437–2442.

Pike, B. R., Flint, J., Dutta, S., Johnson, E., Wang, K. K. & Hayes, R. L. (2001). Accumulation of non-erythroid alpha II-spectrin and calpain-cleaved alpha II-spectrin breakdown products in cerebrospinal fluid after traumatic brain injury in rats. *Journal of Neurochemistry*, **78**, 1297–1306.

Pike, B. R., Flint, J., Dave, J. R. *et al.* (2004). Accumulation of calpain and caspase-3 proteolytic fragments of brain-derived alphaII-spectrin in cerebral spinal fluid after middle cerebral artery occlusion in rats. *Journal of Cerebral Blood Flow Metabolism*, **24**, 98–106.

Pineda, J. A., Lewis, S. B., Valadka, A. B. *et al.* (2007). Clinical significance of alphaII-spectrin breakdown products in cerebrospinal fluid after severe traumatic brain injury. *Journal of Neurotrauma*, **24**, 354–366.

Portela, L. V., Tort, A. B., Schaf, D. V. *et al.* (2002). The serum S100β concentration is age dependent. *Clinical Chemistry*, **48**, 950–952.

Rabow, L. & Hedman, G. (1985). Creatine kinaseBB-activity after head trauma related to outcome. *Acta Neurochirurgica (Wien)*, **76**, 137–139.

Reynolds, M. A., Kirchich, H. J., Dahlen, J. R. *et al.* (2003). Early biomarkers of stroke. *Clinical Chemistry*, **49**, 1733–1739.

Ringger, N. C., O'Steen, B. E., Brabham, J. G. et al. (2004). A novel marker for traumatic brain injury: CSF alphaII-spectrin breakdown product levels. *Journal of Neurotrauma*, **21**, 1443–1456.

Robicsek, S., Gabrielli, A., Layon, A. et al. (2007). BANDITS: a novel clinical platform to validate the utility of potential brain injury biomarkers. *Journal of Neurotrauma*, **24**, 1234.

Romner, B. & Ingebrigtsen, T. (2001). High serum S100β levels for trauma patients without head injuries. *Neurosurgery*, **49**, 1490: author reply 1492–1493.

Romner, B., Ingebrigtsen, T., Kongstad, P. & Borgesen, S. E. (2000). Traumatic brain damage: serum S-100 protein measurements related to neuroradiological findings. *Journal of Neurotrauma*, **17**, 641–647.

Ross, S. A., Cunningham, R. T., Johnston, C. F. & Rowlands, B. J. (1996). Neuron-specific enolase as an aid to outcome prediction in head injury. *British Journal of Neurosurgery*, **10**, 471–476.

Rothoerl, R. D. & Woertgen, C. (2001). High serum S100β levels for trauma patients without head injuries. *Neurosurgery*, **49**, 1490–1491: author reply 1492–1493.

Rubin, D. M., Christian, C. W., Bilaniuk, L. T., Zazyczny, K. A. & Durbin, D. R. (2003). Occult head injury in high-risk abused children. *Pediatrics*, **111**, 1382–1386.

Ruppel, R. A., Kochanek, P. M., Adelson, P. D. et al. (2001). Excitatory amino acid concentrations in ventricular cerebrospinal fluid after severe traumatic brain injury in infants and children: the role of child abuse. *Journal of Pediatrics*, **138**, 18–25.

Savola, O., Pyhtinen, J., Leino, T. K., Siitonen, S., Niemela, O. & Hillbom, M. (2004). Effects of head and extracranial injuries on serum protein S100β levels in trauma patients. *Journal of Trauma*, **56**, 1229–1234: discussion 1234.

Scarfo, G. B., Mariottini, A., Tomaccini, D. & Palma, L. (1989). Growing skull fractures: progressive evolution of brain damage and effectiveness of surgical treatment. *Childs Nervous System*, **5**, 163–167.

Shaw, G. J., Jauch, E. C. & Zemlan, F. P. (2002). Serum cleaved tau protein levels and clinical outcome in adult patients with closed head injury. *Annals of Emergency Medicine*, **39**, 254–257.

Skogseid, I. M., Nordby, H. K., Urdal, P., Paus, E. & Lilleaas, F. (1992). Increased serum creatine kinase BB and neuron specific enolase following head injury indicates brain damage. *Acta Neurochirurgica (Wien)*, **115**, 106–111.

Sotgiu, S., Zanda, B., Marchetti, B. et al. (2006). Inflammatory biomarkers in blood of patients with acute brain ischemia. *European Journal of Neurology*, **13**, 505–513.

Spinella, P. C., Dominguez, T., Drott, H. R. et al. (2003). S-100beta protein-serum levels in healthy children and its association with outcome in pediatric traumatic brain injury. *Critical Care Medicine*, **31**, 939–945.

Thomas, D. G., Palfreyman, J. W. & Ratcliffe, J. G. (1978). Serum-myelin-basic-protein assay in diagnosis and prognosis of patients with head injury. *Lancet*, **1**, 113–115.

Thomas, D. G., Hoyle, N. R. & Seeldrayers, P. (1984). Myelin basic protein immunoreactivity in serum of neurosurgical patients. *Journal of Neurology, Neurosurgery and Psychiatry*, **47**, 173–175.

Tiainen, M., Roine, R. O., Pettila, V. & Takkunen, O. (2003). Serum neuron-specific enolase and S-100B protein in cardiac arrest patients treated with hypothermia. *Stroke*, **34**, 2881–2886.

Vaagenes, P., Safar, P., Diven, W. et al. (1988). Brain enzyme levels in CSF after cardiac arrest and resuscitation in dogs: markers of damage and predictors of outcome. *Journal of Cerebral Blood Flow Metabolism*, **8**, 262–275.

Vaagenes, P., Mullie, A., Fodstad, D. T., Abramson, N. & Safar, P. (1994). The use of cytosolic enzyme increase in cerebrospinal fluid of patients resuscitated after cardiac arrest. Brain Resuscitation

Clinical Trial I Study Group. *American Journal of Emergency Medicine*, **12**, 621–624.

Vazquez, M. D., Sanchez-Rodriguez, F., Osuna, E. *et al.* (1995). Creatine kinase BB and neuron-specific enolase in cerebrospinal fluid in the diagnosis of brain insult. *American Journal of Forensic Medical Pathology*, **16**, 210–214.

Vos, P. E., Lamers, K. J., Hendriks, J. C. *et al.* (2004). Glial and neuronal proteins in serum predict outcome after severe traumatic brain injury. *Neurology*, **62**, 1303–1310.

Wang, K. K., Ottens, A. K., Liu, M. C. *et al.* (2005). Proteomic identification of biomarkers of traumatic brain injury. *Expert Reviews in Proteomics*, **2**, 603–614.

Xiong, Z., O'Hanlon, D., Becker, L. E., Roder, J., MacDonald, J. F. & Marks, A. (2000). Enhanced calcium transients in glial cells in neonatal cerebellar cultures derived from S100β null mice. *Experimental Cell Research,* **257**, 281–289.

Yamazaki, Y., Yada, K., Morii, S., Kitahara, T. & Ohwada, T. (1995). Diagnostic significance of serum neuron-specific enolase and myelin basic protein assay in patients with acute head injury. *Surgical Neurology,* **43**, 267–270: discussion 270–271.

Zhang, J., Sokal, I., Peskind, E. R. *et al.* (2008). CSF multianalyte profile distinguishes Alzheimer and Parkinson diseases. *American Journal of Clinical Pathology*, **129**, 526–529.

Chapter

4

Clinical trials for pediatric TBI

P. David Adelson

Introduction

Trauma and, in particular, traumatic brain injury (TBI) remain the leading causes of death and disability in children in the United States and around the world. Despite multiple preventive measures and educational programs, (i.e. Think First, Safe Kids, etc.) the mortality from trauma is greater than all other pediatric diseases combined (Arias *et al.*, 2002). TBI specifically is the leading contributor to death and disability in this traumatically injured population and of those children that suffer TBI, approximately 10%–15% are considered "severe." These patients unfortunately go on to have permanent brain damage and deficits and, in many instances, will require long-term supportive care. As well, what is unclear in TBI is those children that have suffered only "mild" or "moderate" injuries, many of whom are also frequently disabled with neurocognitive, executive function, and/or behavior deficits that impact on activities of daily living, scholastic performance, and eventually vocational choice. Unfortunately, little is known of the mechanisms contributing to these deficits as well as therapeutic interventions to try and minimize or mitigate the damage and improve outcome. This lack of understanding is a direct result of the lack of scientific studies and ultimately of clinical trials for children following TBI.

It is clear that to move forward with research in the area of TBI particularly in the pediatric population it is important to identify the status of the field and understand the extent of research and knowledge in the present day. Once we understand the problem(s), it then becomes important to identify key areas of future investigation in designing clinical trials that will provide the answers necessary to change the standard of care. Lastly, especially as we move forward with a time of limited resources of funding, it is important to optimize each study with a high-quality approach and reporting so that the "new" understanding can be directly translated into clinical practice.

Epidemiology

With regards to the magnitude of the problem, this disease and its residua are not just limited to pediatrics, but are also adult problems as well. It is now estimated that every 21 seconds a person in the United States suffers a TBI and that there are upwards of 5.3 million Americans who are currently living with disabilities resulting from their TBI. There are approximately 1.5 million Americans who sustain a TBI each year, of which upwards of 50 000–60 000 will die from their TBI (US Census Bureau estimate 3/31/98;

Pediatric Traumatic Brain Injury: New Frontiers in Clinical and Translational Research, ed. V. Anderson and K. O. Yeates. Published by Cambridge University Press. © Cambridge University Press 2010.

www.census.gov/population/estimates). These numbers are staggering in consideration that TBI far exceeds the number of cases of breast cancer, HIV/AIDS, spinal cord injuries, and brain cancer. Despite this being a significant and major public health problem in the United States and around the world, it continues to be surprising that research and particularly research funding is proportionately less for TBI and trauma from the National Institute of Health. Additionally, if one looks just at the pediatric population, of those 1.5 million Americans who sustain a TBI each year, 45% of those are children and young adults. Comparisons to other diseases in children are illuminating. There are approximately 1000 new pediatric spinal cord injuries per year. Of those due to either the spinal cord injury and/or multiple traumas, there is an annual mortality of approximately 10% or 100 patients. Spinal cord injury though receives funding of approximately $90 million from the NIH on an annual basis. HIV/AIDS has approximately 4000 new pediatric cases annually of which the annual mortality is approximately also 10% or 400 patients. The funding for HIV/AIDS though is upwards of $2.7 billion. Childhood cancer, with an annual incidence of 12 500 and an annual mortality of 2000, of which 2200 are CNS tumors with an annual mortality of only 500, receives $70 million annually in NIH funding. For TBI, there are approximately 600 000 new pediatric cases each year with an estimated annual mortality of 9000–10 000, yet only $80 million in total NIH funding is allocated across both adult and pediatric TBI. One could venture that less than $5 million annually goes to pediatric specific-TBI research. As a result, it is easy to conclude that TBI remains the most under-addressed pediatric health problem in the United States.

Traumatic brain injury guidelines

The evidence-based guidelines for the management of (adult) severe traumatic brain injury (Bullock *et al.*, 2007) were exceptionally well received by a large audience of physicians, paramedical personnel, administrators, and all allied health. These were the first guidelines developed for the central nervous system and provided the basis for all other future guideline initiatives through the last decade. The guidelines were developed with a panel of experts reviewing and grading each of the papers and studies that were obtained through a broad literature search and applying rigorous evidence-based medicine methods to arrive at the published recommendations. These recommendations then further provided a framework and treatment protocol for the management of TBI in adult patients. A number of studies in the interim have shown improved outcomes in patients managed under a protocol based on the guidelines.

Unfortunately, the evidentiary foundation upon which these guidelines were based did not address the pediatric population and, in fact, was specifically exclusive. If we are to agree that it is not true that "children are not just little adults," then it is incumbent not to generalize from the adult literature to the pediatric population in the management of the injured child. For that reason the Pediatric TBI Guidelines (Adelson *et al.*, 2003) were published following the same rigorous review of the evidence and literature as were the adult guidelines. The Pediatric TBI Guidelines were meant to serve as a companion to the adult guidelines, as they applied to children and TBI care that was unique to, or different in, the pediatric population. Many chapters from the Pediatric Guidelines were based on the original adult guidelines, though there were extra chapters included, unique to the pediatric guidelines' initiative (i.e. Temperature Regulation). Additionally, a new subsection was included in each chapter to provide guidance from the expert panel with regards to potential "*Key Areas for Future Investigation.*" Unfortunately, when constructing these guidelines, it was obvious from review of the literature that there are very few high-quality studies in the pediatric field and that much of the available evidence is of low class resulting in limited and low levels of recommendation. Of significance, there were few if any clinical trials or even well-designed studies in pediatric TBI.

Similar to previous guidelines and using standard evidence-based methodology, the evidentiary support for the pediatric guidelines utilized three classes of evidence: Class I studies are good-quality randomized control trials (RCT), and are considered the gold standard; Class II levels of evidence include moderate-quality RCT, prospective clinical studies with good-quality data, a good-quality cohort, and/or a good-quality case control study; Class III evidence is, for the most part, all other studies and included moderate- or poor-quality cohorts, or case control studies' retrospectively collected data, as well as clinical and case series, databases, case reviews and reports, registries, and/or expert opinions/consensus statements. The final levels of recommendation reflect the level of evidence that is provided, so that a Level I recommendation or "Standard" can be established as an accepted principle of patient management with a high degree of clinical certainty and is generally based on Class I evidence though possibly strong Class II evidence. A Level II recommendation or "Guideline" includes a particular strategy or a range of management strategies reflecting a moderate clinical certainty usually based on Class II evidence or a preponderance of Class III evidence. Lastly, Level III recommendations or "Options" are those remaining strategies for patient management where there is unclear clinical certainty and is usually based on Class III evidence. This level of recommendation is often much less useful, except for educational purposes and for guiding future studies.

The Pediatric TBI Guidelines included only minimal literature with regards to pediatric-specific trials. There were only three recommendations that had any high level of certainty and these included the avoidance of propofol as a continuous infusion, the avoidance of hyperventilation chronically for the management of intracranial pressure, and lastly the prophylactic use of antiepileptic medication for the treatment of late post-traumatic seizures was not recommended. Unique at the time to the guidelines process was the inclusion of a clinical pathway or suggested treatment algorithm that was based on "cumulative data and expert opinion" (Figs. 4.1 and 4.2). This, though, should only be considered Class III data (expert opinion), but provides a framework for future investigation.

Clinical trials in pediatric traumatic brain injury

As was highlighted by the Pediatric TBI Guidelines, there were very few clinical studies and particularly clinical trials that involved children. As a result, the recommendations were most often Level III that provide only limited certainty with regards to optimal manage-ment. In a recent review of clinical trials in pediatric TBI (Natale *et al.*, 2006) there were only 21 reports of randomized clinical trials in children following TBI in the modern literature. Of those, only 14 studies were exclusively in children, and only one study was multi-center (Adelson *et al.*, 2005). The total number of child-based studies was approxi-mately 900, with the maximum number of children in any one study being 103.

Based on this review and the published Pediatric TBI Guidelines, the present knowledge base in the pediatric management of severe pediatric TBI includes: (1) supportive care/the avoidance of second insults; (2) management of intracranial hypertension/a reactive response to the secondary injury; and (3) surgical intervention for evacuation of

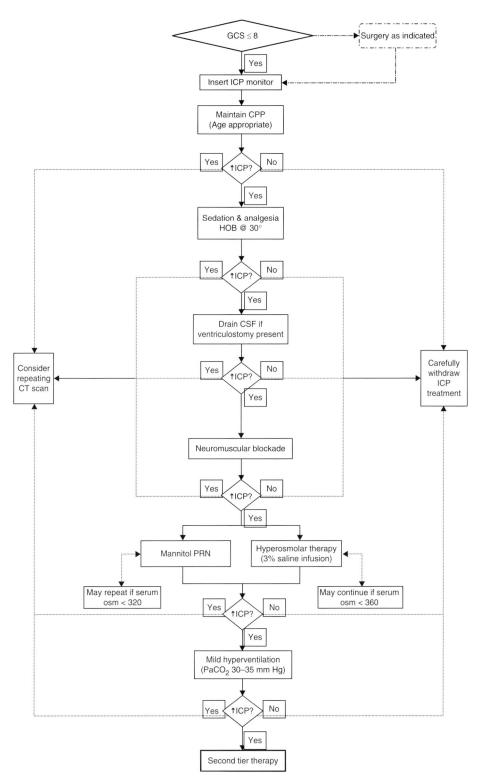

Fig. 4.1. First tier therapy as recommended in the Pediatric Traumatic Brain Injury Guidelines (Adelson *et al.*, 2003).

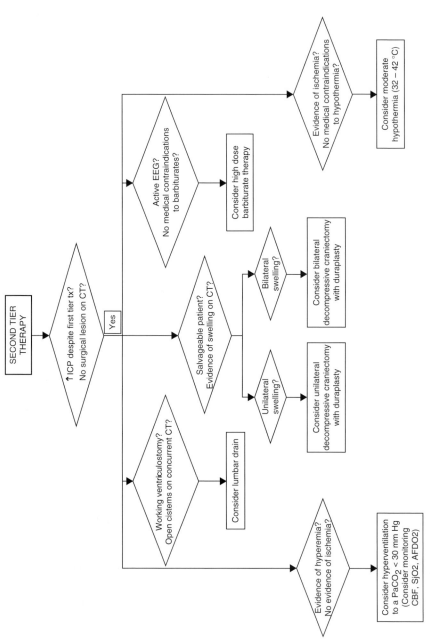

Fig. 4.2. Second tier therapy as recommended in the Pediatric Traumatic Brain Injury Guidelines (Adelson *et al*, 2003).

hematomas, epidural, subdural, and intracerebral, as well as decompressive surgery for diffuse swelling/the avoidance of second insults and a reactive response to the secondary injury, respectively. Unfortunately, none of the recommendations from the guidelines are mechanisms directed at the secondary injury response nor provide any significant new finding toward improving outcome in children.

Mechanistically, there remains a lack of understanding of the impact of the injury to the developing brain and the optimal management for this patient population. This is particularly highlighted with regards to the concept of temperature regulation and hypothermia in the management of pediatric TBI. While there are a multitude of experimental studies and adult models of TBI that have demonstrated the likely multi-factorial positive effects of hypothermia as a treatment modality including reduced excitotoxicity, inflammation, oxidative stress, cell death, etc., its role in the mechanisms for the beneficial effect clinically and its role in the treatment management is unknown. Unfortunately, few studies of temperature regulation in pediatric experimental models have been conducted to date, providing little pre-clinical basis. Even less is known as to potential use of hypothermia in the management and treatment of children clinically, with some findings contradictory to widely held beliefs as to hypothermia's optimal impact. Lastly, there are very few clinical studies that lend support to the use of hypothermia for TBI in children. Until recently, there were only three studies of the use of hypothermia for TBI in children; one from the 1950s (Hendrick, 1959) and another from the 1970s (Grushiwiecz, 1973) that showed some potential for hypothermia as a treatment option. Another study, not in the guidelines, failed to show improved outcome, probably due to small numbers, but did show reduced intracranial hypertension and safety (Biswas *et al.*, 2002). The recent multi-center RCT mentioned earlier (Adelson *et al.*, 2005), is the only published RCT for children following TBI, was a Phase II study examining safety and performance. This study confirmed safety of hypothermia in children and also provided preliminary data for a Phase III RCT based on a trend toward reduced mortality, decreased intracranial hypertension, and positive neuropsychological outcome. A multi-center Phase III RCT in the US utilizing moderate hypothermia following severe TBI in children is now enrolling patients (P.D. Adelson, personal communication).

Development of quality clinical research and clinical trials in pediatric TBI

In order to develop good-quality clinical trials it is important for us to identify the problems that have weakened published studies in the past and make recommendations that would be necessary for future studies. The two important and significant general areas that have impacted on the development of good-quality clinical trials are: clinical and logistical. The *clinical* challenges unique to pediatric TBI and its management include: (1) aspects of the developing brain and age issues; (2) inconsistency in terminology used for the different injuries; (3) lack of valid and reliable measures of the severity of these children on arrival/ initial assessment; and similarly, (4) lack of valid and reliable measures of outcome such that we lack good endpoints for ascribing efficacy of clinical trials and therapies. The second general area of deficiency has been *logistical*. This includes: (1) difficulties in obtaining adequate patient numbers; (2) developing quality centers with little intercenter variability; (3) ethical barriers raised by Institutional Review Boards for pediatric research; and (4) the poor level of funding of pediatric trauma and TBI.

Clinical issues – development

There are a number of different concepts that need to be taken into consideration when looking at aspects of TBI care that make children unique from the adult population. This is not just limited to the pediatric population, but is also an issue for adults when viewing the entire age gamut and full spectrum of adult TBI. The brain throughout life goes through innumerous changes and differences through natural aging. While the immature brain of the child cannot easily be compared to the young or older adult, similarly the young adult cannot easily be compared to the octogenarian. These age-related differences reflect the normal neurobiology of the brain and the systemic changes that occur first in the developing child and then onward in the aging adult. They have an impact on our interpretation of pre-clinical data and clinical measures and highlight that any comparisons must be considered as relative to normal age-appropriate expectations whether neuroanatomic, physiologic, biochemical, etc. Secondly, there are age-related differences in the types of injuries incurred (primary mechanisms) (Arias, 2003). For example, it is unusual for an infant to be the victim of an unrestrained motor vehicle collision, yet the syndrome of shaken impact or shaken baby is unique to children under the age of two to three years and a non-entity after that age. Third, there are age-related differences in the pathobiology and response to injury. These secondary injury mechanisms also may differ based on unique age-related differences in the neurobiology, i.e. differential expression of N-methyl-D-aspartate (NMDA) receptors and their subunits differ during different ages of development and may be more sensitive to excitotoxicity due to these differences. Fourth, there are age-related differences in response to treatment and it has been suggested that pediatric-specific approaches to treatment may need to be developed that may differ from the present algorithm. Treatment strategies developed for the mature brain may not be effective in the immature brain and may even be detrimental. For example, NMDA antagonism in experimental models in mature animals is beneficial to reduce post-traumatic excitoxicity and outcome. In contrast, NMDA antagonism in the developing brain worsens outcome both behaviorally and anatomically (Pohl *et al.*, 1999). Lastly, we need to take into consideration the age-related differences in response to recovery and rehabilitation (see Kolb & Gibb, Chapter 12). Again, there may be unique aspects to the pediatric brain, particularly during critical periods of development and upward, that make differences with regards to the optimal rehabilitation capability and timing of the initiation of rehabilitation that may necessitate the development of age-specific rehabilitative strategies and protocols in order to optimize outcome.

Clinical issues – terminology

One of the problems that has led to confusion in the literature is the mixing and blurring of the terminology and definitions of injury and insult. Because of this lack of clarity with regards to terminology, there is often confusion in treatment and management. It is therefore important at the outset for those involved in TBI to begin to define standard terminology so that all future literature, proposals, and studies do not continue this confusion and can be comparable.

The terms "mechanism," "injury," and "insults" require definition and standardization particularly as they relate to TBI. The terms that have been used invariably that should be used consistently have included: "primary mechanism," "primary injury," "second insult," and "secondary mechanism." The primary mechanism is the etiology or mode of trauma that leads to the primary injury (i.e. motor vehicle collision, recreational, etc.). The primary mechanism may impart different forces such as linear or rotational acceleration that when applied to the brain result in different types of tissue injury. The primary injury is defined as the tissue injury that occurs at the time of the impact or trauma as a result of the primary mechanism and unique forces from that impact. A second insult is an additional insult that follows the primary injury that may be either directly or indirectly as a result of that injury (i.e. hypotension, hypoxia, hematoma formation, etc.). The secondary injury or mechanism is the pathophysiologic response following the primary injury and includes excitotoxicity, inflammation, dysautoregulation, and delayed cell death that leads to further injury or damage. The secondary injury mechanism differs from the second insult as it is the secondary response of the brain to the primary injury. Second insults in contrast are not mechanistic but rather external events that may negatively impact on the secondary injury response leading to worsening in the tissue damage and outcome. It is here that the terminology has often been blurred, but it is important to make this distinction because second insults are preventable and avoidable. Much of our present management is directed at reducing or avoiding second insults, but do not directly address the mechanisms incurred in the secondary injury phase. For example, maintaining oxygenation and blood pressure, evacuation of hematoma, anti-epileptic medication in the acute period, and temperature regulation but not limiting excitotoxicity directly. Our present management does not include any of the secondary mechanism treatment in the realm of treatment for these patients.

Clinical issues – initial assessment

Another contributing factor that may have impacted on the reporting of clinical trials in children is the lack of valid and reliable assessments of the initial severity of injury particularly in younger children. For the most part, the Glasgow Coma Score (GCS) (Teasdale et al., 1979) has been the gold standard in the assessment of initial injury severity both in children and adults. While much of the TBI literature in children has utilized the GCS as an initial injury severity assessment, the GCS does not take into account developmental differences from infancy through adolescence. Originally developed for adults in the 1970s, the GCS has never truly been validated for children, since the scale includes verbalization and eye opening, which may not be adequately measured in the young injured child. As a result, when the GCS is used as an index of injury severity across a wide age range, comparably injured populations may not be being studied. There have been some pediatric assessment scales developed to assess acute state, including the Adelaide Coma Scale, (a modified GCS for children); the Infant Face Scale (Durham et al., 2000), (a scale that takes into account the unique developmental issues in infants and young toddlers), and the Relative Head Injury Severity Scale (RHISS) (Cuff et al., 2007) that uses ICD-9 codes and does not really measure severity directly. None of these "new" scales have been validated or used reliably in pediatric TBI studies.

Clinical issues – outcome assessment

Outcome assessment is another area that is unique and difficult in the pediatric population and has served as a problematic part of the literature because of the variability and lack of validity for outcome measures in children specifically following TBI. Outcome assessments can be grouped into either mortality or morbidity. Mortality is fairly easy to assess and has shown a percent decline in children following TBI from the mid twentieth century to the present. Because of this significant decline due to what is believed to be better and more aggressive treatment management paradigms, there is an increased burden on clinical trials with regards to larger patient numbers needed to show significant improvement in outcomes if mortality is used as a primary outcome measure. Unfortunately, mortality has had to be used as the primary outcome measure in children following TBI because of the lack of other valid and reliable outcome assessments and measures of morbidity in children.

Morbidity, in contrast, is more difficult to assess due to the large spectrum of post-TBI pathology in children following injury, and relies on the gamut of neurologic and cognitive measures. Because of the lack of baseline understanding of morbidity following pediatric TBI and the lack of any scale or assessment tool that has been validated for TBI, published studies and trials to date have been difficult to interpret and often have not shown efficacy. Because of lack of valid assessments, the testing of treatment paradigms and potential improvements in outcome cannot be truly defined. The lack of adequate, reliable, valid, objective outcome assessments has truly created a difficult and significant impediment to moving forward with clinical trials for children following TBI and will need to be corrected if there are to be any further advances in pediatric TBI.

Morbidity or outcomes assessment for pediatric TBI can be divided into two functional domains. Global function is most often measured presently using mortality, the Glasgow Outcome Score (GOS), versus the Glasgow Outcome Score – Extended (GOS-E) (Hudak et al., 2005; Pettigrew et al., 2003), and the more recent revision (for children), the GOS-E Peds (Beers et al., 2005). While likely useful tools, all of these outcome scores based on the original GOS remain untested with respect to their reliability and validity in children. The GOS-E Peds is pediatric-specific but requires further validity and reliability confirmation prior to its widespread utilization.

"Neuropsychological outcome" is a very broad topic and not easily defined, which has made it difficult to confirm reliability and validity in the post-injured child. Most would agree that neuropsychological evaluations encompass the seven different domains of function that are categorized into: (1) intelligence; (2) language; (3) memory and learning; (4) attention and executive function; (5) visuospatial; (6) motor and psycho-motor function; and (7) behavior. Though there may be other areas not included, these have lesser impact with regard to understanding of outcomes specific to childhood TBI. Additionally, investigators need to further define neuropsychological and/or other cognitive measures taking into account the variability of: the different types of assessments, the different ages at application following injury, the different domains of measure, and the multitude of other variables that have made the literature very complex. Similarly, consensus as to the optimal outcome assessments has been complicated by the range of factors associated with injury and recovery including: the primary mechanism of injury, the age at injury, the differing developmental stages or time within the critical period of development, the changing developmental age during the recovery phase, the lack of normative data in some of the assessments for the different aged children, and the aging out or cross-exam comparisons between different ages, to name just a few. Lastly, because of the complexity of the neurocognitive outcomes and the lack of an agreed battery, other measures of outcome success have been sought to infer improved outcome including: the effect of therapy on intracranial pressure/intracranial hypertension and cerebral perfusion pressure, the intensity or level of therapy, the use of serum and/or CSF biomarkers, and the use of imaging modalities, both anatomic and functional imaging. As a result, the literature in the assessment of outcomes in children to date has not provided guidance toward a valid and reliable "scale" for the assessment of pediatric "outcome" and needs to be further addressed if the results of clinical trials in pediatric TBI are going to progress.

Logistical

"Logistical" refers to the difficulties in conducting a clinical trial due to unique aspects of pediatric trauma or even pediatric disease as a whole. The first and likely most significant of these difficulties is the need for large sample sizes in order to reach conclusions in severe TBI and even mild–moderate TBI. Often, there are small and inadequate numbers of children at any one center that preclude a single center from being able to develop conclusions general-izeable to the pediatric population. There are likely a number of different and variable contributors that will need to be evaluated and accounted for in future trials including: broad categories of variability of injury, recruitment and consent, and improvements in the care and management of injured children. With regard to variability of injury, TBI is quite variable and complex due to the multiple mechanisms of injury, both primary and secondary, i.e. non-accidental vs. accidental trauma; extra-axial (epidural vs. subdural) vs. intracerebral hematoma; contusive vs. diffuse swelling and or diffuse axonal injury; timing of injury; potential impact of genetic predisposition; etc. These children are most often not categorized based on the types of injury they suffer but on the Glasgow Coma Scale, which in, and of, itself has not been validated for young children. Recruitment and consent are also issues in attempting to have adequate numbers for the sample size in a clinical trial. Since often there is referral of pediatric patients to tertiary and quaternary care centers, there can be mixed populations of time to evaluation and initiation of treatment; ability to get parental or guardian consent; and the capability to get emergency waiver of consent in pediatric patients. Lastly, as mentioned earlier, because of the decline in mortality, and/or the lack of valid and reliable neurocognitive outcome assessment tools, as well as the need to take into account behavioral interventions and treatments during the rehabilitative phase during the time period that outcomes are being measured, it is likely that large sample sizes and recruitment numbers will be necessary for neurotrauma, and particularly for TBI. As a result, future studies in children will require a consortium of centers in order to achieve adequate recruitment numbers to meet sample size requirements.

Quality centers and intercenter variability

As the concept of a pediatric TBI consortium and the need for adequate recruitment is developed, it is important that study centers be of high quality with high levels of expertise with regards to clinical neurosurgery, specifically pediatric neurotrauma, and clinical trial implementation, and can recruit samples representative with respect to key outcome predictors, including both injury-related and environmental factors (e.g. socioeconomic status, ethnicity). The options will likely depend on the study but considerations will need to include: (1) size of center – large academic centers vs. community centers; (2) number of sites – few large centers vs. many smaller centers; (3) developed network – reliability of patient referral from surrounding community and communication so that there is a high percentage of recruitment vs. the intermittent patient referred; (4) expertise with clinical trials – experience in pediatric TBI clinical management. It is important that the centers have little intercenter variability with regards to clinical management in order to conform to an agreed practice management algorithm. This allows for the potential for general-izeability as long as a particular algorithm or treatment paradigm is followed and allows for practice variation in different community situations and environments.

Informed versus emergency waiver of consent

The issue of informed consent is important as it pertains to clinical medical research in our society particularly with the utilization of pediatric patients. Research though following acute injury has its own particular issues. Because of the unexpected timing of injury and the need to institute therapy immediately to likely have the best outcome, the use of emergency waiver and waiver of consent have been successfully utilized for TBI and other acute emergency situations. With the unknown impact of age, the results from adult studies have not translated well to children, but raise ethical as well as complex societal issues. In pediatric research, third-party consent of the parent is already a necessity, but what is the optimal approach when children are often transported long distances to higher level facilities and family members are not immediately available? Emergency waiver allows for the initiation of the research study prior to the parent or guardian arrival with the permission to continue or stop the research upon their availability. It would seem optimal to waiver consent in that no permission from parent or guardian is necessary. There are well-delineated regulations for the institution of emergency waiver for adult and pediatric patients who have suffered an emergency-type disease requiring acute intervention that still allow for the input of the parental or family as well as community interests, concerns, and ethical issues of the involvement of children in clinical research, though these can often be addressed at the local level in an appropriate and ethical manner. For pediatric patients, it is clear that, to date, there has been minimal to no use of the emergency waiver option, but trauma is uniquely suited such that the emergency waiver rule must be taken into consideration if indeed speed of treatment intervention is necessary.

Pediatric trauma-specific funding

Presently, there is a relative lack of funding for the most common cause of death and disability in children, trauma. This has led to a lack of experimental studies in pediatric, immature models with regards to understanding the pediatric response to injury leading to the lack of pediatric-specific therapies for TBI both in the acute and chronic phases. This dearth of pre-clinical data has led to minimal progress in the translation to the bedside and clinical research initiatives. While one could argue that the lack of good science or interest has led to the lack of sufficiently strong proposals, interest and dedication are often aligned with the potential and existence of funding. If pediatric trauma-specific funding were to be developed, there would be a need for both pre-clinical experimental paradigms that have some potential for translational research and then clinical research. The opportunity to expand on the concept of the "bench-to-the-bedside" is necessary, but needs to be balanced at this early time with support for the observations of the bedside and with the need to take these back to the pre-clinical setting in order to develop potential novel therapeutic opportunities and interventions. At the present time, there is a significant time lag from concept to trial, and until the studies begin, it is likely that pediatric-specific therapeutic interventions will be lacking unless these concepts and studies can be pushed forward. The impetus will be pediatric trauma and neurotrauma-specific funding.

Quality clinical trials

It is clear that good-quality studies and particularly randomized controlled trials are necessary in order to begin to change the standards of care and the types of interventions for the pediatric population. There have been a multitude of studies, reviews, and literature defining different standards of criteria for good clinical trials that can be applied to pediatric studies to ensure and optimize the scoring being published. The types of quality criteria that should be applied in all studies include: adequate random assignment methods, allocation concealment, similar groups at baseline, adequate sample size, intention-to-treat analysis, blinded outcome assessors, follow-up rate of greater than 85%, no differential loss to follow-up, and maintenance of comparable groups particularly with regards to follow-up. Having each of these criteria as part of the clinical trial design at the outset will lead to the greater likelihood of a quality study at the outcome providing potential Class I level of evidence and finally a Level I recommendation for treatment management. Because of the lack of clinical trials in any area of pediatric TBI, there is a golden opportunity at the outset of moving the field forward to define and demand high-quality studies and trials in this era of evidence-based medicine.

With a more stringent approach to trial design and implementation, the reporting of clinical trials in future literature should include stringent criteria for those reviewing studies in order to ensure that the data presented are objective, unbiased, and reflect the highest level of evidence possible. In the reporting of clinical studies, especially as treatment decisions are based on the evidence in the medical literature, it is important that all the relevant trial results are available. They must be easily identified in the manuscript, and they must be consistent. It is common in submitted and published studies to have trouble identifying the study hypothesis, the research questions, the clinical design of the trial, and the type of analysis used and its justification, and even the number of participants in therapeutic groups. As a result, it is often impossible to know whether the conclusions drawn by the authors are justified by their data. This problem has been recognized for a while and measures have now been suggested to correct these deficits in the medical literature.

The evolution in the reporting of clinical trials was initially in 1994 with the publication of the Standards of Reporting Trials (SORT) recommendations (The Standards of Reporting Trials Group, 1994). One year later an attempt was made to put the SORT recommendations into practice in the literature with individual studies (Williams, Jr. *et al.*, 1995). Following review and critique by numerous authors the Consolidated SORT (CONSORT) recommendations were developed (Begg, 1996) which were also opened to critique and review. This occurred over the next two years and these recommendations were later published (Moher, 1998). These critiques often detailed the poor manner in which clinical trials were still being reported, stressing the importance of the CONSORT as an improving and evolving tool. The benefit of the CONSORT is that it provides a checklist of items to include when reporting a clinical trial, such as those listed above, as well as the necessity to provide a flow diagram so that the reviewers and readers can more easily understand the patient flow and decision making for the randomization and management of the patients in the study. To retain credibility, the CONSORT authors felt it important to maintain transparency in the reporting of the criteria checklist, acknowledging that these criteria were not meant to be rigid and unchanging, but rather provide a framework and guideline for authors as they were writing their clinical study for publication: CONSORT has developed as a first tool in evolution to make aware the reviewers, editors, authors, and readers the criteria at least at this point in time of a good clinical trial. It was expected that these criteria would evolve through further discussion and experimentation but that it would lead to decreased interpretation of the results by physician readers, and decrease the variability of the interpretation of the results by physician readers avoiding any sense of bias in reporting results due to preconceived scientific notions or commercial influence.

Summary, conclusions, recommendations

In conclusion, there is an overwhelming shortage of Class I and II data in the pediatric TBI literature; this though, provides countless opportunities for researchers. At this point, every well-designed and well-reported clinical trial or study focused on pediatric TBI would have major impact and significant importance in defining the field. The Pediatric Guidelines provide an excellent starting point in developing these ideas and strategies for future studies. The "Key Areas of Investigation" cited in each of the chapters are consensus statements developed by the multiple experts in this area, highlighting the most relevant and pertinent ideas and the needs for developing new ideas and strategies for future studies. It is absolutely clear that further studies and trials are warranted and needed because the understanding of the optimal therapeutic treatment in children following TBI is lacking. There is also a need to translate clinical research from bench science and this will depend only on the quality of science arising from the laboratory and being translated to the clinical arena.

What is problematic at least at this time is that the assessment instruments, both the initial assessment and outcomes need to be improved and standardized in order to better stratify the individual patient groups and direct the optimal management strategies, and will need to address issues of age at injury, types of injury, and resultant pathology. There is truly a need to develop good-quality clinical trials at the outset in order to insure that the findings provide adequate recommendations and that the reporting of those recommendations remain transparent. It is through the stringent review of studies as they come for review prior to implementation, as well as in the reporting of these studies at the publication process, that appropriate recommendations of clinical management based on the data can be developed.

Finally, similar to other pediatric specialties, it will be important to consider the development of a pediatric TBI/neurotrauma consortium, specific for pediatric injury in order to run multiple and concurrent studies. It is through these multiple concurrent and often ancillary studies of ongoing trials that the knowledge base and translation to the clinical arena will be advanced and in a timely manner.

References

Adelson, P. D. (1999). Animal models of traumatic brain injury in the immature: a review. *Experimental and Toxicologic Pathology*, **51**, 130–136.

Adelson, P. D., Bratton, S. L., Carney, N. A. *et al.* (2003). Guidelines for the acute medical management of severe traumatic brain injury in infants, children, and adolescents. *Pediatric Critical Care Medicine*, **4**(3) Suppl., S1–S75.

Adelson, P. D., Ragheb, J., Muizelaar, J. P. *et al.* (2005). Phase II clinical trial of moderate hypothermia following severe traumatic brain injury in children. *Neurosurgery*, **56**(4), 740–754.

Arias, E., MacDorman, M. F., Strobino, D. M. & Guyer, B. (2003). Annual summary of vital statistics – 2002. *Pediatrics*, **112**, 1215–1230.

Beers, S. R., Hahner, T. P. & Adelson, P. D. (2005). Validity of a pediatric version of the Glasgow outcome scale-extended (GOS-E PEDS). *Journal of Neurotrauma*, **22**(10), 1224.

Begg, C., Cho, M., Eastwood, S. *et al.* (1996). Improving the quality of reporting of randomized controlled trials. The CONSORT Statement. *Journal of the American Medical Association*, **276**, 637–639.

Biswas, A. K., Bruce, D. A., Sklar, F. H., Bokovoy, J. L. & Sommerauer, J. F. (2002). Treatment of acute traumatic brain injury in children with moderate hypothermia improves intracranial hypertension. *Critical Care Medicine*, **30**(12), 2742–2751.

Bullock, R., Chesnut, R. & Clifton, G. L. (2007). Guidelines for the management of severe head injury. *Journal of Neurotrauma*, Suppl. **24**.

Cuff, S., DiRusso, S., Sullivan, T. *et al.* (2007). Validation of a relative head injury severity scale for pediatric trauma. *Journal of Trauma*, **63**(1), 172–177.

Durham, S. R., Clancy, R. R., Leuthardt, E. *et al.* (2000). CHOP Infant Coma Scale ("Infant Face Scale"): a novel coma scale for children less than two years of age. *Journal of Neurotrauma*, **17**(9), 729–737.

Gruszhiewicz, J., Doron, Y. & Peyser, E. (1973). Recovery from severe craniocerebral injury with brain stem lesions in childhood. *Surgical Neurology*, **1**, 197–201.

Hendrick, E. B. (1959). The use of hypothermia in severe head injuries in childhood. *American Medical Association Archives Surgical*, **79**(3), 362–364.

Hudak, A. M., Caesar, R. R. & Frol, A. B. (2005). Functional outcome scales in traumatic brain injury: a comparison of the Glasgow Outcome Scale (Extended) and the Functional Status Examination. *Journal of Neurotrauma*, **22**(11), 1319–1326.

Moher, D. (1998). CONSORT: an evolving tool to help improve the quality of reports of randomized controlled trials. Consolidated Standards of Reporting Trials. *Journal of the American Medical Association*, **279**(18), 1489–1491.

Natale, J. E., Joseph, J. G., Pretzlaff, R. K., Silber, T. J. & Guerguerian, A. M. (2006). Clinical trials in pediatric traumatic brain injury: unique challenges and potential responses. *Developmental Neuroscience*, **28**(4–5), 276–290.

Pettigrew, L. E., Wilson, J. T. & Teasdale, G. M. (2003). Reliability of ratings on the Glasgow Outcome Scales from in-person and telephone structured interviews. *Journal of Head Trauma Rehabilitation*, **18**(3), 252–258.

Pohl, D., Bittigau, P., Ishimaru, M. J. *et al.* (1999). N-Methyl-D-aspartate antagonists and apoptotic cell death triggered by head trauma in developing rat brain. *Proceedings of the National Academy of Sciences, USA*, **96**(5), 2508–2513.

Teasdale, G., Murray, G., Parker, L. & Jennett, B. (1979). Adding up the Glasgow Coma Score. *Acta Neurochirurgica (Wien)*, **28**(1) Suppl., 13–16.

The Standards of Reporting Trials Group. (1994). A proposal for structured reporting of randomized controlled trials. *Journal of the American Medical Association*, **272**, 1926–1931.

Williams, Jr., J. W., Holleman, Jr., D. R., Samsa, G. P. & Simel, D. L. (1995). Randomized controlled trial of 3 vs 10 days of trimethoprim/sulfame thoxazole for acute maxillary sinusitis. *Journal of the American Medical Association*, **273**, 1015–1021.

Advanced neuroimaging techniques in children with traumatic brain injury

Stephen Ashwal, Karen A. Tong, Andre Obenaus, and Barbara A. Holshouser

Pediatric traumatic brain injury remains a major public health problem. Fortunately, the advent of several neuroimaging techniques has improved our ability to better diagnose and treat affected children. Because intensive care therapy has resulted in lowered mortality and morbidity, attention is also focusing on issues related to brain recovery and reorganization. It is likely that, in the future, imaging may better define the relation between structural and functional deficits and approaches will be developed to guide treatment paradigms. In this review, we examine four imaging methods that are increasingly used for the assessment of pediatric brain injury. *Susceptibility weighted imaging* is a 3-D high-resolution magnetic resonance imaging technique that is more sensitive than conventional imaging in detecting hemorrhagic lesions that are often associated with diffuse axonal injury. *Magnetic resonance spectroscopy* acquires metabolite information reflecting neuronal integrity and functions from multiple brain regions and provides sensitive, non-invasive assessment of neurochemical alterations that offers early prognostic information regarding outcome. *Diffusion weighted imaging* is based on differences in diffusion of water molecules within the brain and is sensitive in the early detection of ischemic injury. *Diffusion tensor imaging* is a form of diffusion weighted imaging and allows better evaluation of white matter fiber tracts by taking advantage of the intrinsic directionality (anisotropy) of water diffusion in human brain and is useful in identifying white matter abnormalities after diffuse axonal injury. An important aspect of these advanced methods is that they demonstrate that "normal-appearing" brain in many instances is not normal, i.e. there is evidence of significant undetected injury that may underlie a child's clinical status. Availability and integration of these advanced imaging methods will lead to better treatment and change the standard of care for use of neuroimaging to evaluate children with traumatic brain injury.

Introduction

Advances in neuroimaging over the past two decades have greatly helped in the clinical care and management of children with traumatic brain injury (TBI) (Blackman *et al.*, 2003; Grados *et al.*, 2001). Immediately after injury, computed tomography (CT) is important for the rapid detection of extra-axial hemorrhage (e.g. subdural or epidural hematomas), acute hydrocephalus, fractures or other intracranial lesions that may require acute neurosurgical intervention (Sigmund *et al.*, 2007). Magnetic resonance imaging (MRI) appears to be very

Pediatric Traumatic Brain Injury: New Frontiers in Clinical and Translational Research, ed. V. Anderson and K. O. Yeates. Published by Cambridge University Press. © Cambridge University Press 2010.

sensitive for intraparenchymal lesion detection in TBI patients but frequently is not easily obtainable acutely after injury.

The advent of newer and more sensitive imaging techniques is now being used to better characterize the nature and evolution of injury and the underlying mechanisms that lead to progressive neurodegeneration, recovery, or subsequent plasticity. These advanced imaging techniques have also begun to demonstrate that in many patients, "normal-appearing" brain as examined with computed tomographic (CT) scanning or with conventional magnetic resonance imaging (MRI), may not adequately depict brain injury (Sigmund *et al.*, 2007).

This review will describe four advanced MRI techniques as related to their use in TBI. They include susceptibility weighted imaging (SWI), magnetic resonance spectroscopy (MRS) and magnetic resonance spectroscopic imaging (MRSI), diffusion weighted imaging (DWI) and diffusion tensor imaging (DTI). These techniques were selected as they are of value in the acute period after injury in contrast to functional MRI (fMRI) that has been used for long-term evaluation. Several of these methods appear particularly useful for the assessment of diffuse axonal injury (DAI) that is responsible for a wide range of motor and cognitive impairments. However, before describing these four methods, we will review data comparing the prognostic yield of standardized CT vs. MRI in assessment of children with TBI.

Comparison of CT and MRI for outcome prediction

In a recent study of 40 children with TBI, we assessed several imaging methods including CT, T2-weighted magnetic resonance imaging (MRI), fluid-attenuated inversion recovery (FLAIR) MRI, and SWI to determine which were most valuable in predicting 6–12-month outcomes after injury (Sigmund *et al.*, 2007). T2 and fluid-attenuated inversion recovery (FLAIR) are common sequences in MRI evaluation of TBI patients. T2 is a more standard technique, generally able to detect a wide range of intraparenchymal lesions including edema, infarction, demyelination, moderate to large hemorrhages, and other parenchymal lesions. FLAIR is a more recent technique that may be more sensitive in detecting some lesions within the parenchyma including edema, particularly near the cortex or ventricles. It is unknown whether there is any significance of intraparenchymal edema leading to more adverse outcomes when compared with hemorrhage. Susceptibility weighted imaging (SWI) is also very useful in detecting hemorrhagic lesions associated with diffuse axonal injury (DAI) (Tong *et al.*, 2008). T2, FLAIR, and SWI showed no significant difference in lesion volume between normal and mild outcome groups, but did show significant differences between normal and poor, as well as mild and poor outcome groups. CT showed no significant differences in lesion volume between any groups. Our findings suggested that T2, FLAIR, and SWI MRI sequences provide a more accurate assessment of injury severity and detection of outcome-influencing lesions than CT in children with TBI. However, although CT was inconsistent at lesion detection/outcome prediction, it remains an essential part of the acute TBI workup to assess the need for neurosurgical intervention.

Susceptibility weighted imaging

Susceptibility weighted imaging (SWI) is a high spatial resolution 3-D gradient echo MRI technique with phase-subtraction post-processing that accentuates the paramagnetic properties of blood products and is very sensitive for detection of intravascular venous deoxygenated blood as well as extravascular blood products (Haacke *et al.*, 2004). It was originally referred to as HRBV – high-resolution BOLD (blood oxygen level dependent) venography, but because of its broader application than evaluating venous structures, it is now referred to as SWI (Haacke *et al.*, 2004). In the past decade, the clinical value of SWI in adults with neurological disorders has been reported (Sehgal *et al.*, 2005). SWI has been used in studies of arterial venous malformations, occult venous disease, multiple sclerosis, trauma, tumors and functional brain imaging. SWI has been used at our institution since 2001 and in a recent review we described its role in providing additional imaging information in neonates, infants, and children with a wide variety of neurological conditions (Tong *et al.*, 2008).

Principles of SWI

SWI exploits the loss of signal created by disturbance of a homogeneous magnetic field. These disturbances can be caused by various paramagnetic or ferromagnetic substances as well as markedly different tissue interfaces such as air/bone adjacent to brain parenchyma. As spins encounter heterogeneity in the local magnetic field, they precess at different rates and cause overall signal loss in $T2^*$-weighted (i.e. gradient echo) images. Sensitivity to susceptibility effects increase as one progresses from fast spin echo to routine spin echo to gradient echo techniques, from T1 to T2 to $T2^*$ weighting, from short to long echo times, and from lower to higher field strengths.

Application of a magnetic field to the brain generates an induced field that depends on the applied magnetic field and on the magnetic susceptibility of molecules. Magnetic susceptibility variations are higher at the interface of two regions and signal changes are also dependent on the delay between symptom onset and scanning and other factors including hematocrit, deoxyhemoglobin concentration, red blood cell integrity, clot structure, diffusion, pH, temperature, field strength, voxel size, previous contrast material use, blood flow, and vessel orientation. A detailed explanation of the underlying radiological and mathematical principles is beyond the scope of this clinical review. Several recent publications describe this information in depth (Haacke *et al.*, 2004; Sehgal *et al.*, 2005).

Clinical application of SWI in pediatric TBI

As in adults, SWI has been found to be helpful in evaluating children with traumatic brain injury, cerebrovascular malformations, venous shunting, infarction with increased oxygen extraction, intracranial hemorrhage, coagulopathy associated strokes and sinovenous thrombosis, complications of central nervous system infections, and degenerative/neuro-metabolic disorders associated with intracranial calcifications (e.g. Fahr's disease, panto-thenic kinase deficiency) (Tong *et al.*, 2008).

SWI has been shown to be much more sensitive in detecting hemorrhagic DAI lesions after TBI in children compared to conventional MRI. In a previous study, we examined seven children with TBI (age 14 ± 4 years; SWI obtained 5 ± 3 days after injury) and demonstrated that the number of hemorrhagic DAI lesions seen on SWI was six times greater than on conventional $T2^*$-weighted 2-D-gradient-recalled echo (GRE) imaging, and that the volume of hemorrhage was approximately two fold greater (Tong *et al.*, 2003). A comparison of SWI with 2D-GRE in a TBI patient is seen in Fig. 5.1. SWI can visualize smaller and thus more numerous hemorrhages than previous MRI, and by inference much more than CT.

In an expanded SWI study, 40 children and adolescents with mild to severe TBI and DAI (mean age 12 years; SWI 7 ± 4 days after injury) were examined (Tong *et al.*, 2004). The number and volume of hemorrhagic lesions were compared to long-term neurologic outcome assessed using the Pediatric Cerebral Performance Category Scale (PCPCS) score which is modified from the Glasgow Outcome Scale (GOS) score and quantifies the overall

(a)

(b)

(c)

(d)

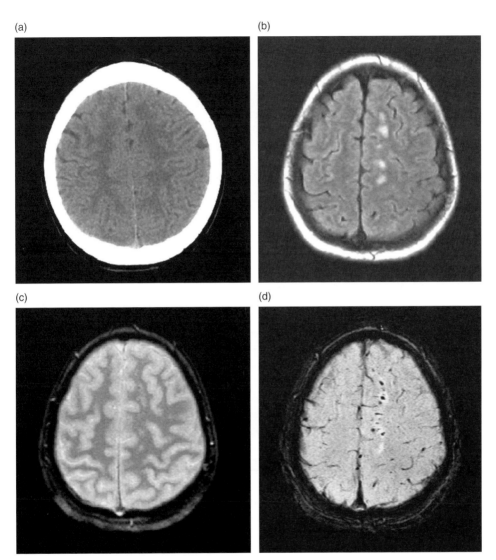

Fig. 5.1. Improved detection of small hemorrhages using SWI. Axial CT (a) image is normal. Corresponding Fluid-Attenuated Inversion Recovery (FLAIR) image (b) shows small hyperintense lesions in the left frontal white matter. Conventional GRE (c) (fast imaging with steady-state precession, TR/TE = 500/18, 15° flip angle, 78 Hz per pixel, two signals acquired, 4 mm thick sections) image shows faint matching hyperintensity. However, the SWI (d) (three-dimensional fast low-angle shot, TR/TE = 57/40, 20° flip angle, 78 Hz per pixel, 64 partitions, one signal acquired, 2 mm thick sections reconstructed over 4 mm) image demonstrates multiple tiny hypointense foci consistent with small hemorrhages within the area of injury. (Courtesy of Dr. Karen Tong, Loma Linda University School of Medicine).

functional neurologic morbidity and cognitive impairment of infants and children. We found that children with lower Glasgow Coma Scale (GCS) scores (≤ 8, $n = 30$) or prolonged coma (>4 days, $n = 20$) had a significantly greater average number and volume of hemorrhagic lesions. Also children with normal outcomes or mild neurologic disability at 6–12 months after injury had significantly fewer number and volume of hemorrhagic DAI lesions than those who were moderately or severely disabled or in a vegetative state (Fig. 5.2). We also determined that there were regional differences in DAI injury. Over 90%

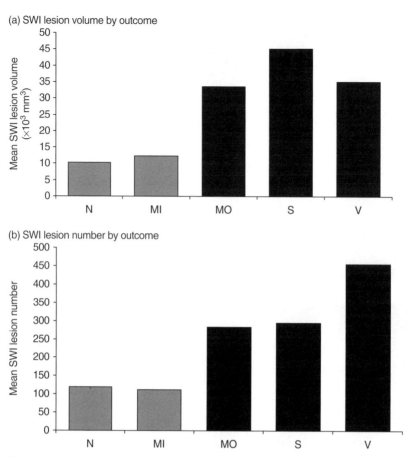

(a) SWI lesion volume by outcome

(b) SWI lesion number by outcome

Fig. 5.2. Extent of hemorrhagic lesions within individual outcome groups. The mean volume (a) and number (b) of hemorrhagic lesions tend to increase with worsening severity of outcomes. N = normal ($n = 14$); MI = mild disability ($n = 16$); MO = moderate disability ($n = 7$); S = severe disability ($n = 2$); V = vegetative state ($n = 1$). When the outcome groups were dichotomized, the mean volume and number of lesions were also significantly higher in the poor outcome group (black bars) compared to the good outcome group (gray bars). Data based on Tong et al., 2004. (Courtesy of Dr. Karen Tong, Loma Linda University School of Medicine).

of patients had lesions in the parieto-temporal-occipital gray matter (PTOG), parieto-temporal-occipital white matter (PTOW), and frontal white matter (FWM). Four regions were less commonly affected (i.e. < 65% of patients): thalamus, brainstem (BS), cerebellum, basal ganglia. Twelve of 40 patients (30%) had lesions in all nine of the brain regions examined. Forty-two percent of these patients had poor outcomes. There were 14 patients who had lesions in six or fewer regions and all had good outcomes at 6–12 months. Only patients with involvement of seven or more regions had poor outcomes. In Fig. 5.3 we show examples of hemorrhagic DAI lesions detected in TBI patients that illustrate that SWI allows better detection of these lesions, even in brain close to the skull and in regions such as the brainstem, which are not as well visualized with conventional MRI. Because SWI is much more sensitive in detecting hemorrhagic DAI, more accurate data can be obtained to objectively assess the severity of acute injury and the extent of detected hemorrhage can provide long-term neurological and neuropsychological prognostic information.

(a) (b)

(c) (d)

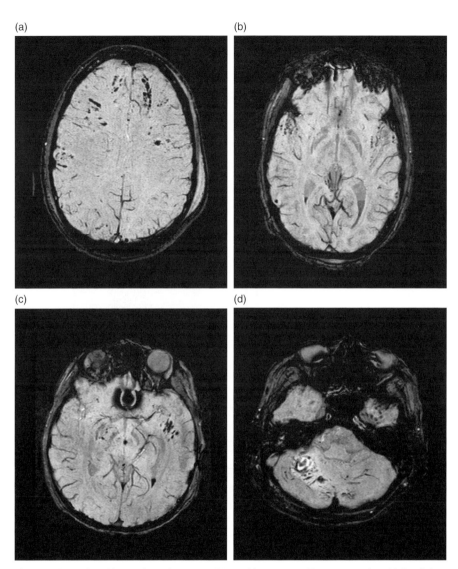

Fig. 5.3. Examples of hemorrhagic lesions on SWI, visible as areas of hypointense foci. (a) Small shearing injuries at the gray/white matter junction of the frontal lobes. (b) Small hemorrhages associated with contusions in the anterior temporal lobes. (c) Brainstem lesions, usually indicative of more severe injury, as well as shearing injuries in the left temporal white matter. (d) Shearing injuries in the cerebellum. The majority of these lesions are not seen or are much smaller on conventional MRI. (Courtesy of Dr. Karen Tong, Loma Linda University School of Medicine).

Magnetic resonance spectroscopy (MRS)

Magnetic resonance spectroscopy (MRS) is a non-invasive neuroimaging tool that allows in vivo analysis of neurochemicals and their metabolites in humans. MRI uses the strong signals from proton nuclei of water and their spatial location to reconstruct anatomical images. In contrast, ^{1}H-MRS focuses on protons located on neurochemicals other than

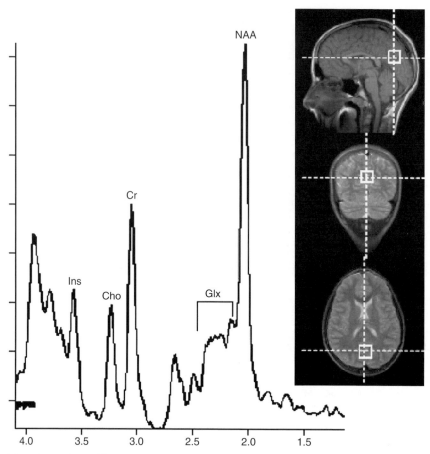

Fig. 5.4. Single voxel ^{1}H-MR spectrum (STEAM; TR/TE/TM = 3000/20/13 msec) from occipital gray matter of a normal 12-year-old male. NAA = N-acetylaspartate; Glx = glutamate/glutamine; Cr = creatine/phosphocreatine; Cho = choline; Ins = myoinositol. (Courtesy of Dr. Barbara Holshouser, Loma Linda University School of Medicine).

water that are present in much lower concentrations within tissues and thus necessitates the use of water suppression techniques and reduced spatial resolution compared to imaging in order to measure them. ^{1}H-MRS is the most widely used application of in-vivo MRS in humans and will be discussed in this review, but other atoms that are used include ^{31}P, ^{13}C, ^{14}N, ^{19}F, and ^{23}Na.

Principles of MRS

Several key brain metabolites are measured with ^{1}H-MRS using both short (i.e. TE = 20–40 ms) and intermediate to long (i.e. TE = 135–270 ms) echo time MRS techniques. Each metabolite resonates at a particular frequency, dependent on the structure of the molecule and the strength of interaction between the nucleus and the electronic cloud within the particular molecule. The size of the change in frequency is known as the chemical shift (measured in ppm). After Fourier analysis, the plot of signal amplitude versus frequency in ppm is known as the MR spectrum (Fig. 5.4). N-acetylaspartate (NAA; 2.01 ppm), an amino acid synthesized in mitochondria, is a neuronal and axonal marker that decreases with neuronal loss or dysfunction (Danielsen & Ross, 1999). In white matter, the NAA peak includes a greater contribution from N-acetylaspartylglutamate (NAAG) than in gray matter. Total creatine (Cr; 3.0 ppm) composed of phosphocreatine and its precursor creatine are markers for intact brain energy metabolism. Total choline (Cho; 3.02 ppm) primarily consisting of phosphoryl and glycerophosphoryl choline is a marker for membrane synthesis or repair, inflammation, or demyelination. Lactate (Lac; 1.33 ppm) accumulates as a result of anaerobic glycolysis and in the setting of TBI may be a response to release of glutamate (Alessandri et al., 2000). Short echo time acquisitions allow for measurement of additional metabolites not seen with long echo time acquisitions because the metabolites have short T2 relaxation times. Specifically, glutamate and immediately formed glutamine (Glx; 2.1–2.4 ppm) are excitatory amino acid neurotransmitters released to the extracellular space after brain injury and play a major role in neuronal death (Bullock et al., 1998). Myoinositol (Ins; 3.56 ppm), an organic osmolyte located in astrocytes, increases as a result of glial proliferation (Garnett et al., 2000).

Several techniques are commonly used to acquire spectroscopic data. Single voxel spectroscopy (SVS) allows acquisition of a single spectrum from one volume element (voxel) typically 8cc or more, whereas two- or three-dimensional magnetic resonance spectroscopic imaging (2-D-MRSI/3-D-MRSI), also called chemical shift imaging, allows simultaneous acquisition of multiple spectra from smaller adjacent voxels through multiple sections of the brain. MRSI has an inherent advantage over SVS because it is better able to evaluate regional distributions of neurochemical alterations. A complication for all MRSI studies of the brain, however, is the contributions to metabolite signal arising from both gray and white matter within the same voxel, as well as cerebrospinal fluid within voxels that mimics signal loss. However, segmentation (McLean et al., 2000) and linear regression (Schuff et al., 2001) techniques using MRI to estimate contributions from various tissues contained in MRS/MRSI voxels have been employed to account for partial volume problems. An additional complication of any short echo time MRS study of the brain is accounting for lipid signal arising from the skull. This is particularly challenging for MRSI studies that sample near the brain surface and moreso in infants and neonates with small brain sizes. Investigators have reported acquisition of spectra with little lipid contamination by using outer volume suppression pulses that saturate subcutaneous lipid tissue (McLean et al., 2000) or by using lipid nulling and k-space extrapolation (Schuff et al., 2001; Soher et al., 2000).

Following acquisition, spectral processing identifies metabolites according to their chemical shift resonance, measures the area under each peak corresponding to their concentration, and reports the findings as peak area metabolite ratios such as NAA/Cr or Cho/Cr. The distribution of metabolite levels or ratios acquired with MRSI displayed as signal intensities are known as metabolite maps or images. Previously, it was thought that Cr is maintained at a constant level in the brain and was therefore used in many early studies as an internal standard. Although it is known that Cr levels can change in certain conditions, ratios continue to be useful for reporting and comparing serial measurements or data between institutions using similar acquisition techniques. Methods to quantitate metabolite levels are being used routinely and use water as an internal reference (Barker et al., 1993) or phantoms containing known metabolite concentrations to quantify peak areas and report absolute or relative metabolite concentrations rather than ratios (Danielsen et al., 1995; Provencher, 1993).

MRS and development

Metabolite levels vary by anatomic region (Frahm *et al.*, 1989) and change rapidly as the brain develops (Fig. 5.5) (Kreis *et al.*, 1993) requiring the use of normal age-matched reference data for interpreting MR spectra from children. During early brain development, NAA reflects active myelination and is expressed early in the thalamus and later in parieto-occipital and periventricular white matter (Cady *et al.*, 1996; Huppi, 2001). Metabolite concentrations in babies change non-linearly with age, with changes occurring most rapidly in premature newborns. Detailed assessments of the normal distribution of metabolites in pre-term and term neonates report significant spectral differences between anatomic locations and post-conceptual age, with premature neonates showing lower NAA/Cho and NAA/Cr ratios in the thalami and basal ganglia than term neonates (Vigneron *et al.*, 2001). Other studies have found that the absolute brain metabolite content in premature neonates at term was not substantially different from neonates born at term suggesting that prematurity did not substantially affect biochemical brain maturation (Kreis *et al.*, 2002). Metabolite changes associated with brain maturation continue rapidly through the first year of life (Holshouser *et al.*, 1997; Pouwels *et al.*, 1999) and continue to a lesser degree through adolescence (Horska *et al.*, 2002; McLean *et al.*, 2000).

MRS in the evaluation of TBI

MRS provides a sensitive, non-invasive assessment of neurochemical alterations after brain injury and has shown potential for providing early prognostic information regarding clinical outcome in pediatric patients with head injury (Ashwal *et al.*, 2000; Brenner *et al.*, 2003; Holshouser *et al.*, 1997). Several MRS studies have shown its utility in detecting DAI. Elevated choline (Cho) detected in white matter may be a breakdown product after shearing of myelin and cellular membranes and reduced NAA likely results from neuronal or axonal injury (Ross *et al.*, 1998). Increased Cho following TBI may be an indication of cell membrane shearing injury or astrocytosis (Garnett *et al.*, 2001). Studies specifically looking at the splenium of the corpus callosum in brain-injured patients showed decreased NAA (Cecil *et al.*, 1998; Sinson *et al.*, 2001).

MRS has been used to study children with accidental and non-accidental trauma (Ashwal *et al.*, 2000). Short echo SVS from normal-appearing occipital gray matter and parietal white matter measured at a mean of 5 ± 3 days post injury in 26 infants (1–18 months) and 8 ± 6 days post injury in 28 children (≥ 18 months) found lower NAA/Cr or NAA/Cho and higher Cho/Cr in poor outcome patients. Lactate was present in 91% of infants and 80% of children with poor outcomes; none of the good outcome patients had lactate. Using a logistic regression model, clinical variables alone predicted outcome in 77% of infants and 86% of children whereas lactate presence alone predicted outcome in 96% of infants and children. These findings showed that MRS acquired early after injury was more accurate than clinical variables in predicting outcome. The strong correlation between lactate and outcome was primarily in infants who had non-accidental trauma rather than after accidental trauma. Of great interest was that spectra from brain areas that did not appear visibly injured showed altered metabolite ratios that correlated with injury.

Quantitation of short echo time MRS using a time-domain fitting routine (LCModel) (Provencher, 1993) was performed in one study in children and facilitated the measurement of Ins and Glx levels along with NAA, Cr, Cho and Lac. In this study of 38 children

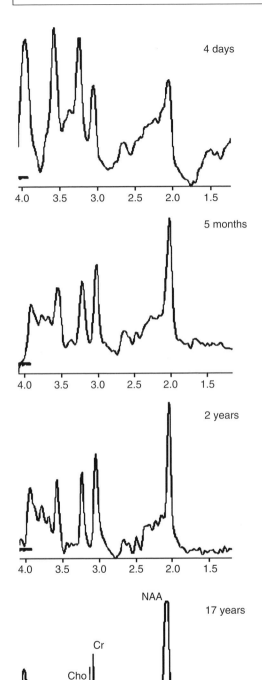

Fig. 5.5. Spectra illustrating rapid metabolite changes that occur during normal brain maturation from birth through adolescence. All spectra were acquired with single voxel 1H-MRS (STEAM; TR/TE/TM = 3000/20/13 msec) from occipital gray matter (Courtesy of Dr. Barbara Holshouser, Loma Linda University School of Medicine). (From Ashwal, Babikian *et al.*, 2006).

(MRS at 7 ± 4 days after injury), Ins levels from occipital gray matter were increased in children with TBI (Ashwal *et al.*, 2004a). Patients with poor outcomes had higher Ins levels compared to patients with good outcomes. It was postulated that increased Ins in TBI patients with poor long-term neurologic outcome might be due to astrogliosis or to a disturbance in osmotic function. In addition, Glx from occipital gray matter was significantly increased in children with TBI compared to controls but there was no difference between children with good compared to poor outcomes (Ashwal *et al.*, 2004b). This finding was attributed by the authors to the delay from the time of injury to imaging in severe TBI patients compared to mild–moderate, for the former to be medically stabilized for transport to the scanner. According to the literature, Glx levels most likely peak early after injury and fall rapidly (Schumann *et al.*, 2000; Zhang *et al.*, 2001), therefore, Glx differences may have been comparable between outcome groups if the timing of the measurements were controlled.

Other investigators have used 2-D-MRSI to study TBI. Macmillan and colleagues studied normal and abnormal areas of brain as seen on T2-weighted images in patients with TBI with and without subarachnoid hemorrhage (SAH) and found low NAA levels in both areas compared to controls (Macmillan *et al.*, 2002). They also found higher Cho and Cr levels in patients with SAH but no lactate (Lac) that would have suggested ischemic neurochemical changes. Another study demonstrated a uniform global reduction of NAA in head injured patients that returned to normal values in those patients who made a good recovery (Signoretti *et al.*, 2002). A recent publication using volumetric 3-D-MRSI to study 14 subjects with mild TBI found significant reductions in NAA/Cr and NAA/Cho and increases in Cho/Cr ratios compared to controls in brain regions that appeared normal on conventional MRI, further illustrating the high sensitivity of non-invasive MRS for evaluating diffuse brain injury (Govindaraju *et al.*, 2004).

Multi-voxel MRSI has also been used to study TBI in children. In one study 2-D-MRSI in normal-appearing occipital and frontal regions of school-aged children six weeks after TBI showed that NAA/Cho ratios were lower in TBI patients than in control subjects, but no group differences were present for Cho or Cr (Hunter *et al.*, 2005). In a recent study we used 2-D-MRSI in children to examine whether metabolite ratios from visibly injured (lesions seen on SWI) or from normal-appearing brain (no abnormalities on SWI or MRI) were more accurate in predicting long-term outcome and to examine regional differences in injury between TBI patients and controls (Holshouser *et al.*, 2005). Proton MRSI in 40 pediatric TBI patients was acquired in a transverse plane through the level of the corpus callosum within 1–16 days after injury. T2-weighted, FLAIR, and SWI were used to identify voxels as normal-appearing or with non-hemorrhagic or hemorrhagic injury. Metabolite ratios for global (all voxels included), normal-appearing, and hemorrhagic brain were compared and used in a logistic regression model to predict long-term neurologic outcome. A significant decrease in NAA/Cr and increase in Cho/Cr (evidence of DAI) was observed in normal-appearing and visibly injured (hemorrhagic) brain compared to controls. NAA/Cr was decreased more in normal-appearing brain for poor outcome patients compared to patients with good outcomes or controls, whereas ratios were altered similarly for all TBI patients in visibly injured brain. Reduction of NAA in visibly injured brain is most likely caused by the primary impact, whereas reduction of NAA in normal-appearing brain may reflect DAI and Wallerian degeneration (Garnett *et al.*, 2000). Ratios from normal-appearing brain predicted outcome with 85% accuracy compared to 67% using ratios from visibly injured brain.

Shown in Fig. 5.6 are examples of SWI and MRSI in a patient from this study (see legend for detailed description). These figures show the exquisite localization that can be accomplished with these techniques, the superior sensitivity of SWI in detecting hemorrhagic DAI lesions, and that a spectrum from normal-appearing brain has decreased NAA, which indicates neuronal injury or dysfunction.

These findings emphasize that additional information is detected by MRSI that is not seen by current conventional neuroimaging or SWI. To estimate this quantitatively, we analyzed MRSI voxel data from TBI patients in the above study (Holshouser *et al.*, 2005). In patients with good outcomes, an average of 8.2% of the voxels contained hemorrhagic lesions and 1.6% contained non-hemorrhagic DAI lesions. This is compared with patients with poor outcomes in which a larger percentage contained hemorrhagic (27.6%) and non-hemorrhagic lesions (2.2%). We also determined the percentage of voxels from normal-appearing brain in which NAA/Cr ratios were below two standard deviations of normal for age in each patient. Fig. 5.7 is a plot of these percentages grouped by neurologic outcome assessed at 6–12 months after injury. Approximately 60% of voxels from normal-appearing brain taken at the level of the corpus callosum in children who have normal or mild long-term outcomes have decreased NAA/Cr ratios early after injury. The percentage of abnormal voxels from normal-appearing brain increases with increasing severity of outcome. This demonstrates that proton MRSI is extremely sensitive for detecting neuronal injury in brain that appears normal on neuroimaging. This is also an excellent demonstration of the diffuse nature of TBI and helps explain why global neuropsychological deficits are often seen in patients with normal imaging findings.

Using currently available MRI sequences such as T2-weighted and FLAIR with SWI and MRSI should allow clinicians to categorize DAI into two radiographic groups, "visibly-injured" and "normal-appearing" brain. Visibly injured brain consists of the hemorrhagic lesions that we can more sensitively detect with SWI as well as the non- hemorrhagic lesions seen with T2 and FLAIR. Normal-appearing brain consists of those areas that appear normal on MRI but in which we see evidence of abnormal MRSI metabolites (e.g. reduced NAA, increased Cho). Developing a much more sensitive method to detect DAI and to identify the brain regions involved, has the potential of being extremely important clinically. It should allow us to identify lesions that are currently being undetected. This has significant implications for the care of children with TBI especially if we can continue to correlate areas of injury with functional outcomes. A much better estimation of the location and severity of injury will allow better implementation of focused treatment strategies that are likely to be studied and used in the future.

Diffusion weighted imaging

DWI has allowed exploration of the function and physiology of the brain (Huisman, 2003), and its general use in infants and children has been reviewed (Beaulieu *et al.*, 1999). Because DWI uses fast (echo-planar) imaging technology, it is highly resistant to patient motion and imaging time ranges from a few seconds to 2 minutes (Schaefer *et al.*, 2000).

Diffusion represents the random thermal movement of molecules (i.e. Brownian motion) and is determined by several variables including the nature of the molecules present in the local tissue environment, temperature, and the local structural architecture in which diffusion takes place (Hou *et al.*, 2007). Image contrast on DWI is related to differences in the diffusion rate of water molecules rather than to changes in total tissue

(a)

(b)

(c)

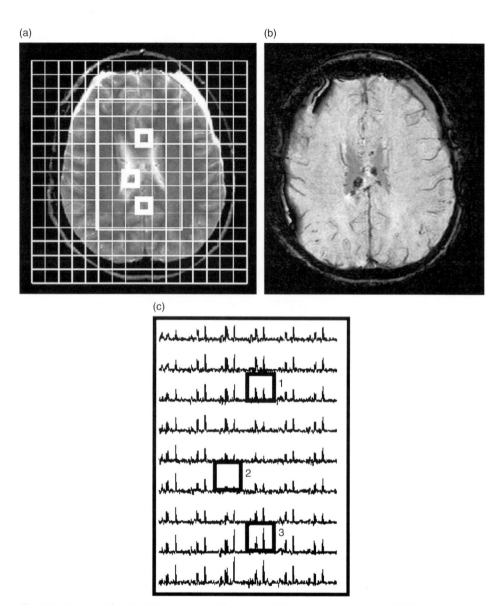

Fig. 5.6. 15-year-old female adolescent ejected from a car. Patient had a good outcome (GOS score = 1, normal) at 12 months after injury. (a) T2-weighted MR image and corresponding SWI (b) show hemorrhagic lesions in the body of the corpus callosum (CC) and bifrontal extra-axial collections. (a) with grid overlay shows the 160 mm field of view (FOV) and 54 (6 × 9) voxel volume of interest (rectangle). Boxes indicate corresponding voxels in c. (c) Spectral map from 54 voxels in the volume of interest shows a (1) spectrum from normal-appearing brain in the anterior CC with decreased NAA (2.0 ppm), (2) a spectrum with reduced metabolite signal intensity due to a small hemorrhagic lesion in the mid CC, and (3) a spectrum from parietal white matter with normal metabolite ratios (From Holshouser *et al.*, 2005). (Courtesy of Dr. Barbara Holshouser, Loma Linda University School of Medicine).

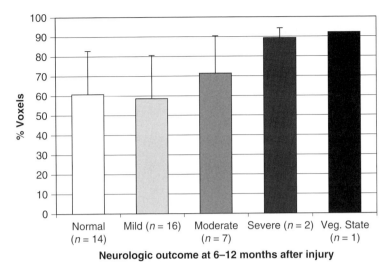

Fig. 5.7. Plot of percentages of voxels from normal-appearing brain in which NAA/Cr ratios were below 2 standard deviations of normal for age in 40 pediatric TBI patients in whom MRSI (PRESS, TR/TE = 3000/144 msec) was acquired from a 10 mm thick slab through the level of the corpus callosum within 1–16 days after injury (From Ashwal *et al.*, 2006a). (Courtesy of Dr. Barbara Holshouser, Loma Linda University School of Medicine).

water. DWI can differentiate between lesions with decreased and increased diffusion compared to normal brain tissue. Restricted diffusion is believed to reflect cytotoxic edema in contrast to increased diffusion that typically occurs with vasogenic edema. DWI has proven to be sensitive in the early detection of acute cerebral ischemia and seems promising in the evaluation of TBI, potentially revealing pathology when conventional MRI is normal. Technical aspects of DWI are beyond the scope of this review but have been described by Huisman (2003) and by Schaefer and colleagues (2000).

DWI and TBI

Experimental studies in rodents and piglets and human clinical studies have demonstrated that DWI is useful and sensitive in detecting lesions due to TBI, although the results are variable. An example of DWI in a child with TBI and DAI is shown in Fig. 5.8.

DWI can be used to show shearing injuries not visible on T2-weighted FLAIR images but is less sensitive than T2* imaging to detect hemorrhagic lesions (Huisman, 2003). The potential usefulness of DWI was analyzed in a study by Hergan and colleagues (2002). DWI was obtained in 98 adult TBI/DAI patients and lesions were classified into three categories depending on their DWI and ADC signal characteristics (Hergan *et al.*, 2002). *Type 1* lesions were DWI and ADC hyperintense, most likely representing lesions with vasogenic edema. *Type 2* lesions were DWI hyperintense and ADC hypointense, likely reflecting cytotoxic edema. *Type 3* lesions were central hemorrhagic lesions surrounded by an area of increased diffusion. In addition, lesions were classified according to the size and extent of lesions into three groups: *group A*, focal injury; *group B*, regional/confluent injury; and *group C*, extensive/diffuse injury. This was a retrospective review that did not evaluate time-dependent changes or correlation with outcomes.

(a)

(b)

(c)

(d)

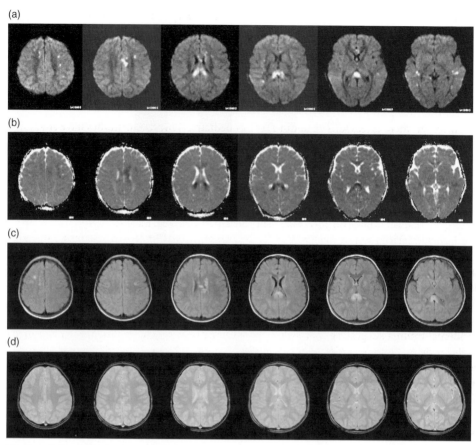

Fig. 5.8. Diffusion weighted imaging in acute TBI. DWI images (a) show multiple small foci of hyperintensity scattered throughout the hemispheric white matter and particularly prominent in the splenium of the corpus callosum, in areas that are typically involved in diffuse axonal injury. The corresponding ADC maps (b) show hypointensity within these lesions, suggestive of cytotoxic edema. These lesions are also hyperintense on FLAIR images (c) but not visible on conventional T2* GRE images (d). (Courtesy of Dr. Karen Tong, Loma Linda University School of Medicine).

Another study by Huisman and colleagues of 25 adult patients with TBI/DAI, found that the ADC values of DWI hyperintense lesions were reduced in 64% of lesions, were elevated in 24%, and were similar to the ADCs of normal brain tissue in 12% (Huisman *et al.*, 2003).

As reviewed by Hergan and colleagues (2002), cytotoxic and vasogenic edema have been observed in multiple studies involving experimental and clinical TBI, although the time course may differ. In addition, associated conditions such as hypoxia or ischemia may worsen development of cytotoxic edema. Restriction of water diffusion associated with cytotoxic edema is most likely related to a graded failure of energy metabolism that results in membrane pump failure, and then a net translocation of water from the extracellular space to the intracellular compartment, where water mobility is relatively more restricted (Hergan *et al.*, 2002). Cell swelling also results in a reduction of the volume of the extracellular space, increased tortuosity of the extracellular space, and is believed to contribute to restricted diffusion (Sykova, 2004).

Some studies have reported that DWI identifies the largest number of overall lesions as well as the largest volume of trauma-related signal abnormalities in DAI compared with conventional MRI sequences that include T2-weighted fast spin echo, fluid-attenuated inversion recovery, and T2*-weighted gradient echo sequences (Huisman *et al.*, 2003). The total volume of DWI signal abnormalities encountered in DAI correlates better than other imaging variables with the acute Glasgow Coma Scale score and the subacute Rankin Scale score (Schaefer *et al.*, 2004).

Although there is less known about DWI in pediatric TBI, recent studies have suggested that DWI may be a sensitive indicator of TBI particularly in the setting of non-accidental trauma (Field *et al.*, 2003). In one study 89% of 18 children with presumed non-accidental trauma showed abnormalities on DWI and ADC maps, and in 81% of the positive cases DWI revealed more extensive injury than conventional MRI or showed injuries when MRI appeared normal (Biousse *et al.*, 2002; Suh *et al.*, 2001). Studies by Geddes, Hackshaw, and colleagues (2001a) and Geddes, Vowles, and colleagues (2001b) have suggested that hypoxia and ischemia are common mechanisms of intraparenchymal injury in children with non-accidental trauma and this may be due to reactive vasospasm adjacent to hemorrhagic lesions, strangulation, cervicomedullary injuries, and apnea. All of these mechanisms alone or in combination could likely cause cerebral ischemic injury that would be manifest by changes in DWI.

Other case reports have also demonstrated DWI changes in white matter after non-accidental trauma suggesting that DWI is more sensitive than conventional MRI and more likely to detect lesions earlier in the evolution of injury (Chan *et al.*, 2003; Parizel *et al.*, 2003). These reports also noted large areas of dramatic diffusion restriction, which support the belief that ischemia is a major component of brain injury in non-accidental trauma, probably more so than diffuse axonal injury.

In a recent study, we evaluated the role of DWI and ADC for outcome prediction after pediatric TBI ($n = 37$ TBI, $n = 10$ controls) (Galloway *et al.*, 2008). Fifteen regions of interest (ROIs) were manually drawn on ADC maps that were grouped for analysis into peripheral gray matter, peripheral white matter, deep gray and white matter, and posterior fossa. All ROIs excluded areas that appeared abnormal on T2-weighted images. Acute injury severity was measured using the Glasgow Coma Scale score and 6–12 month outcomes were assessed using the Pediatric Cerebral Performance Category Scale score. Patients were categorized into five groups: (1) controls; (2) all TBI patients; (3) mild/moderate TBI with good outcomes; (4) severe TBI with good outcomes; and (5) severe TBI with poor outcomes. ADC values in the peripheral white matter were significantly reduced in children with severe TBI with poor outcomes ($72.8 \pm 14.4 \times 10^{-3}$ mm^2/s) compared to those with severe TBI and good outcomes ($82.5 \pm 3.8 \times 10^{-3}$ mm^2/s; $P < 0.05$). We also found that the average total brain ADC value alone had the greatest ability to predict outcome and could correctly predict outcome in 84% of cases. This study demonstrated that assessment of DWI and ADC values in pediatric TBI was useful in evaluating injury particularly in brain regions that appear normal on conventional imaging.

Diffusion tensor imaging

DTI allows evaluation of white matter fiber tracts by taking advantage of the intrinsic directionality of water diffusion in human brain and has been helpful in studying myelination during maturation (McGraw *et al.*, 2002). In adults, it is being used to evaluate neurological disorders including multiple sclerosis, epilepsy, Alzheimer's disease, and brain tumors. Although less studied, several reports have described DTI in adult and pediatric patients with TBI.

Principles underlying DTI

DWI and DTI incorporate pulsed magnetic field gradients into a standard MRI sequence resulting in images that are sensitive to the small displacements of water molecules (Rugg-Gunn *et al.*, 2001). DTI is a more complex form of DWI for which the resulting diffusion parameters, including a quantitative measure of anisotropy, are insensitive to subject positioning and fiber-tract alignment within the diffusion gradients of the scanner.

Diffusion is considered *isotropic* when motion is equal and unconstrained in all directions. Brain tissue forms physical boundaries that restrict diffusion and in white-matter tracts, diffusion of water mobility is more restricted perpendicular rather than parallel to the fiber tracts. This form of diffusion restriction is termed *anisotropic* diffusion (Klingberg *et al.*, 1999).

As described by Sundgren and colleagues (2004), diffusion anisotropy can be measured in several ways. A common way to summarize diffusion measurements is to calculate parameters for overall diffusivity and anisotropy. The ADC serves for overall diffusivity and is derived from the trace of the diffusion tensor, while anisotropy is represented by *fractional anisotropy* (FA), *relative anisotropy* (RA), volume ratio (VR), or lattice index (LI). Fractional anisotropy is a measure of the portion of the diffusion tensor due to anisotropy. The relative anisotropy is derived from a ratio between the anisotropic and isotropic portions of the diffusion tensor. The volume ratio expresses the relation between the diffusion ellipsoid volume and that of a sphere or radius. The lattice index characterizes the anisotropy of the fiber structure (Arfanakis *et al.*, 2002). Technical aspects are beyond the scope of this article and are considered in several recent papers (Mukherjee *et al.*, 2002; Sundgren *et al.*, 2004).

In fiber tractography or fiber tracking, white-matter tract directions are mapped on the assumption that, in each voxel, a measure of the local fiber orientation is obtained using DTI. Because fiber tractography requires more extensive computer calculations and manpower than DWI or DTI, it remains more of a research tool and so far has limited application (Sundgren *et al.*, 2004). As technology improves, use of tractography will be more feasible in child neurology, particularly in the study of acquired brain injuries that result in disorders such as cerebral palsy and in the study of congenital and genetic disorders that affect white matter development.

DTI and development

DWI, particularly DTI, has been applied to assess myelination in the developing nervous system (Bydder *et al.*, 2001; McGraw *et al.*, 2002; Prayer & Prayer, 2003) and can demonstrate changes associated with white matter maturation from pre-myelination to post-myelination stages. It is also of use to assess the function of developing white-matter tracts and the sequelae of disruption of white-matter tracts after injury (McKinstry *et al.*, 2002). These features are demonstrated in the results of one study that examined 30 children ranging in age from 1 day to 17 years and reported that apparent anisotropy in compact white matter was higher than that in the non-compact white matter structures of the corona radiata and centrum semiovale (Morriss *et al.*, 1999). There were also age-related increases in anisotropy in all white matter structures, with adult values reached by three years of age. Numerous other reports have described the regional and temporal course of myelin development.

DTI studies in children have shown that the diffusion tensor ($\bar{D}$) decreases with age in gray and white matter and that spatial anisotropy (i.e. Aσ) increases with age, especially in white matter (Morriss et al., 1999; Mukherjee et al., 2002; Neil et al., 1998). Lower FA values have also been found in neonates compared to adults (Sundgren et al., 2004). As reviewed by Mukherjee and colleagues (2002), the presumed mechanisms of these maturational changes in water diffusivity are a decrease in brain water content; the formation of new barriers to water mobility, such as cell membranes associated with the outgrowth of axons and dendrites as well as glial processes; and white matter myelination. Several studies have examined the regional maturational changes in pre-term infants as young as 28 weeks' gestation as they matured to term (Huppi et al., 1998). It has been suggested that the diffusion tensor ($\bar{D}$) values reflect overall brain water content whereas the A$_\sigma$ values are more sensitive to tissue microstructure associated with white matter packing and myelination (Neil et al., 1998).

DTI and TBI

Most DTI studies in TBI have focused on the adult population. Huisman and colleagues (2004) studied 20 adults within 7 days and found that FA was reduced in the internal capsule and splenium of the corpus callosum, and correlated better with the GCS and Rankin scores (measures of injury severity) than ADC values. As DAI most commonly affects white matter, it was suggested that DTI could serve as a sensitive marker of early white matter injury and that changes seen with DTI most likely represented changes in axonal microstructure. Examples of DTI in children with TBI are shown in Figs. 5.9 and 5.10.

Ptak and colleagues (2003) evaluated 15 patients within the first 7 days after TBI and developed a composed score (i.e. C-FAST score) based on measurements of FA from six white matter regions. They found good correlation between the C-FAST score and death, hospital stay greater than 10 days, and intensive care unit stay greater than 5 days. Also the correlation with discharge to a rehabilitation facility was good when adjusted for age and sex. The GCS score, revised trauma score, and Abbreviated Injury Scale also showed good correlation as predictors of a critical C-FAST. This study, which incorporated measurement FA from multiple areas, was interesting and unique in that the authors assumed that focal injury affects function throughout the entire axon and that inclusion of the injury site was not required. Because focal injuries affect membrane function of the entire axon, altered anisotropy should be apparent throughout the entire axon and therefore, the white matter region measured need not necessarily include the injured site.

In another study, DTI data were acquired in five adult TBI patients with traumatic focal contusions or hematomas (Jones et al., 2000). A reduction in mean diffusivity in gray and white matter without an associated increase in T2-weighted signal intensity was observed in four patients. This change was interpreted as indicating either a partial redistribution of water from the extra- to intracellular compartment, or a reduction in the diffusivity of water in the intracellular or cytosolic environment. These diffusion changes with normal T2-weighted characteristics can be found early after ischemia, suggesting that such regions could represent salvageable tissues.

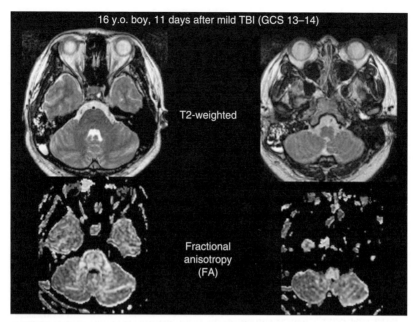

Fig. 5.9. Diffusion tensor imaging of cerebellar white matter injury after mild head trauma. Axial T2-weighted images of the posterior fossa (top row) demonstrate only fluid within the right mastoid sinuses due to temporal bone fracture. No cerebellar abnormality is identified. However, fractional anisotropy images derived from DTI (bottom row) show asymmetrically reduced anisotropy in the white matter of the right cerebellar hemisphere. Note that the images are displayed using radiological convention, where the right side of the patient corresponds to the left side of the image. (Figure courtesy of Dr. Pratik Mukhergee, University of California, San Francisco).

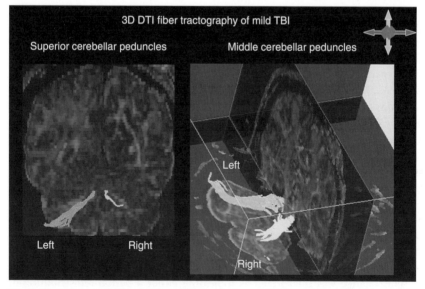

Fig. 5.10. 3-D coronal (left) and oblique (right) projections of DTI fiber tractography of the superior cerebellar peduncles (left) and the middle cerebellar peduncles (right) show decreased number and length of tracks extending into the right cerebellar hemisphere, compared to the left. The fiber tracks are overlaid on a directionally encoded color FA map, where red indicates left–right fiber orientation, green indicates anteroposterior, and blue indicates up–down (see color compass at top right). (Figure courtesy of Dr. Pratik Mukhergee, University of California, San Francisco). See color plate section.

In two recent studies of DTI in patients with TBI, diffusion anisotropy was found to be decreased in normal-appearing cerebral white matter on conventional MR images, whereas mean diffusivity was described as either normal (Arfanakis *et al.*, 2002) or increased (Rugg-Gunn *et al.*, 2001). Several mechanisms were suggested to explain the DTI changes including axoplasmic transport impairment or axolemmal disruption, misalignment, or increased permeability.

In the study by Arfanakis and colleagues (2002), DTI was acquired in five patients (mean age 35.6 yrs) within the first 24 hours after mild TBI. In all patients, images of diffusion anisotropy (FA, LI) revealed regions of reduced anisotropy compared with contralateral brain regions as well as control subjects. These regions differed from lesions associated with hemorrhage or edema and did not show abnormalities on other MR images. Reduction in diffusion anisotropy was less evident one month after injury in several patients. The mechanism of reduced anisotropy was attributed to misalignment of the cytoskeletal network, which is believed to be an early neuropathological abnormality seen with DAI (Arfanakis *et al.*, 2002). Misalignment of axonal membranes were believed to increase restriction in diffusion parallel to the main axis of the neurons as well increase diffusion in directions perpendicular to the axons. The overall effect of this misalignment of the axonal membranes in DAI could be responsible for reductions of anisotropy. As described by these authors, a second phase of DAI that includes impaired axoplasmic transport, local accumulation of organelles, and local swelling and expansion of the axonal cylinder could increase diffusion restriction parallel to the main axis of the fibers and decrease local diffusion anisotropy. As neurons further degenerate, further diffusion restriction along directions perpendicular to the axon may occur, reducing anisotropy. Also, for moderate and severe traumatic brain injuries, an increase of permeability may also take place in injured axons. This may increase diffusivity in directions perpendicular to axons and reduce anisotropy.

In the second report, two adult patients were studied 11 and 18 months after injury (Rugg-Gunn *et al.*, 2001). Both patients, despite having a normal non-acute MRI, showed regions of significantly increased mean diffusivity as well as other regions of decreased anisotropy. In contrast to the patients reported by Arfanakis and colleagues (2002), these two patients had suffered severe TBI. When the DTI studies were done, the first patient had mild pyramidal signs and sensory loss affecting the right arm and leg and mild frontal lobe dysfunction. The second patient had only moderately increased left lower limb reflexes but severe frontal lobe dysfunction and personality change. The findings of increased mean diffusivity suggested that there was an expansion of the extracellular space, caused by neuronal or glial cell loss, which was not identified by conventional MRI. In addition, the reduction of anisotropy in the internal capsule of the second patient suggested that there was structural disorganization and a loss of the parallel fiber arrangement of major white matter-tracts within the internal capsule. Serial DTI and fiber tracking (at 4 days, 24 days, 2 months) have been reported in one adult patient after TBI and have documented changes in the evolution of axonal injury over time (Naganawa *et al.*, 2004).

Several studies have presented data on DTI in children after TBI. The first publication was a case report of a 14-month-old male infant with suspected non-accidental trauma who underwent DTI within 24 hours of injury. DTI within 24 hours of hospitalization revealed transient changes in relatively large areas of cortical and subcortical right hemisphere with markedly increased anisotropy. Mildly increased mean diffusivity in regions of the right frontal, temporal, parietal, and occipital lobes. These findings correlated with clinical symptoms of left focal seizures and hemiparesis and a follow-up MRI (at 135 hrs) that showed diffuse right hemisphere swelling with DWI and ADC maps that revealed markedly restricted diffusion throughout most of the right hemisphere. The mechanisms for the DTI changes in this infant were considered to possibly be related to development over different time courses of cytotoxic and vasogenic edema. Cytotoxic edema has been associated with reduced mean diffusivity, possibly due to shrinking and increased tortuosity of the extra-cellular space engendered by water shifting from extra- to intracellular compartments (van der Toorn et al., 1996). Vasogenic edema has been shown to increase mean diffusivity and to decrease anisotropy (Mukherjee et al., 2001).

More recent investigations have demonstrated the value of DTI after pediatric TBI in larger groups of children. In a series of papers from the Baylor group spearheaded by the lifelong work of Harvey Levin and colleagues, the value of DTI in early imaging assessment as a predictor of long-term neuropsychological outcomes is becoming better established. Wilde and colleagues first demonstrated that the anterior commissure, like the corpus callosum, was vulnerable to white matter degenerative changes after TBI (Wilde et al., 2006a). A companion study in 16 children demonstrated that higher FA values in the corpus callosum correlated with increased cognitive processing speed, faster interference resolution on an inhibition task, and better functional outcome as measured by the Glasgow Outcome Scale score (Wilde et al., 2006b). A third study in ten adolescents with mild TBI (GCS score of 15 and negative CT) found increased FA values, decreased ADCs, and radial diffusivity and more intense postconcussion symptoms and emotional distress compared to the control group (Wilde et al., 2008).

Two other groups of investigators have also reported DTI in pediatric TBI. One study compared 14 TBI children with 14 controls and found that the TBI group had lower FA values in three WM regions (inferior frontal, superior frontal, and supracallosal) as well as slower processing speed, working memory, executive deficits, and greater behavioral dysregulation (Wozniak et al., 2007). FA values in the frontal and supracallosal regions correlated with executive functioning whereas supracallosal FA was also correlated with motor speed and behavior rating scales. The second group examined FA values in 9 children with TBI and 12 controls and found lower FA values in the TBI group in the genu of the corpus callosum, posterior limb of internal capsule, superior longitudinal fasciculus, superior fronto-occipital fasciculus, and centrum semiovale (Yuan et al., 2007). GCS scores correlated with the FA values in these brain regions.

Conclusions

We have entered a new era in how we can begin to apply many of the newer imaging techniques to evaluate children with TBI. This should provide new understanding of how the pediatric brain responds to injury across development and also improve our under-standing of the correlation between specific regional injuries and neuropsychological outcomes. Hopefully, this knowledge will translate to improved outcomes and quality of life for children suffering from such devastating injuries.

Acknowledgments

Portions of this chapter were taken from previous publications of the author as cited in the text and, in particular, Ashwal, Holshouser & Tong, 2006b.

Condition 1 vs 3

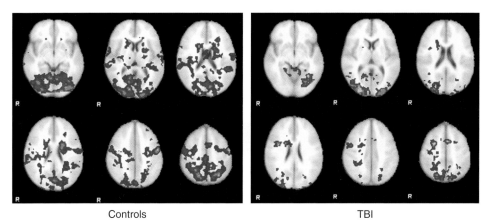

Controls   TBI

Fig. 2.5. Functional MRI activation maps during a non-verbal working memory task in adolescents. Control subjects show blood oxygen level dependent (BOLD) signal activation in a widespread bilateral fronto-temporo-parietal network that appears markedly attenuated in adolescents 3–6 months after moderate-severe TBI (Cazalis *et al.*, 2007).

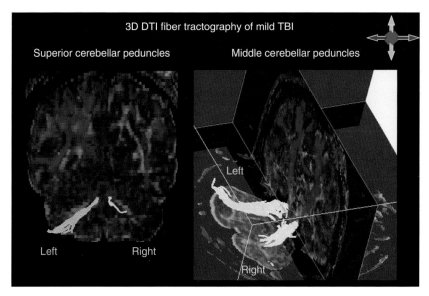

Fig. 5.10. 3-D coronal (left) and oblique (right) projections of DTI fiber tractography of the superior cerebellar peduncles (left) and the middle cerebellar peduncles (right) show decreased number and length of tracks extending into the right cerebellar hemisphere, compared to the left. The fiber tracks are overlaid on a directionally encoded color FA map, where red indicates left-right fiber orientation, green indicates anteroposterior, and blue indicates up–down (see color compass at top right). (Figure courtesy of Dr. Pratik Mukhergee, University of California, San Francisco.)

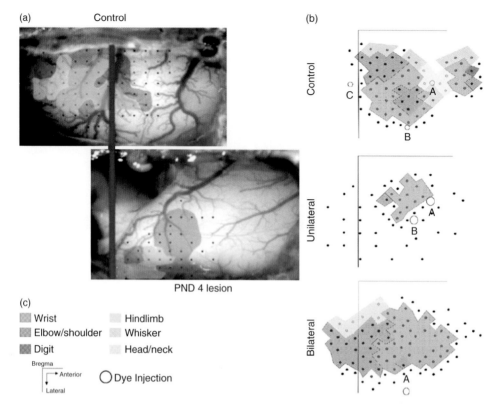

Fig. 12.2. Motor maps after perinatal cortical lesions. (a) Removal of motor cortex on postnatal day 2 caused the map to shift posterior into the posterior parietal region (J. Kleim & B. Kolb, unpublished photograph). (b) Unilateral medial prefrontal lesions that do not invade the motor cortex still alter the motor maps. Unilateral lesions lead to very small maps on the ipsilateral side whereas bilateral lesions produce large maps that have no rostral forelimb area. (After Williams *et al.*, 2006.)

References

Alessandri, B., Samsam, R., Corwin, F., Fatouros, P., Young, H. F. & Bucclock, R. M. (2000). Acute and late changes in N-acetyl-aspartate following diffuse axonal injury in rats: an MRI spectroscopy and microdialysis study. *Neurological Research*, **22**, 705–712.

Arfanakis, K., Haughton, V. M., Carew, J. D., Rogers, B. P., Dempsey, R. J. & Meyerand, M. E. (2002). Diffusion tensor MR imaging in diffuse axonal injury. *American Journal of Neuroradiology*, **23**, 794–802.

Ashwal, S., Holshouser, B. A., Shu, S. K. *et al.* (2000). Predictive value of proton magnetic resonance spectroscopy in pediatric closed head injury. *Pediatric Neurology*, **23**, 114–125.

Ashwal, S., Holshouser, B., Tong, K. *et al.* (2004a). Proton spectroscopy detected myoinositol in children with traumatic brain injury. *Pediatric Research*, **56**, 630–638.

Ashwal, S., Holshouser, B. A., Tong, K. *et al.* (2004b). Proton MR spectroscopy detected glutamate/glutamine is increased in children with traumatic brain injury. *Journal of Neurotrauma*, **21**, 1539–1552.

Ashwal, S., Babikian, T., Gardner-Nichols, J., Freier, M. C., Tong, K. A., & Holshouser, B. A. (2006a). Susceptibility-weighted imaging and proton magnetic resonance spectroscopy in assessment of outcome after pediatric traumatic brain injury. *Archives Physical and Medical Rehabilitation*, **87**(12), Suppl. 2, S50–S58.

Ashwal, S., Holshouser, B. A. & Tong, K. A. (2006b). Use of advanced neuroimaging techniques in the evaluation of pediatric traumatic brain injury. *Developmental Neuroscience*, **28**(4–5), 309–326.

Barker, P. B., Soher, B. J., Blackband, S. J., Chatham, J. C., Mathews, V. P. & Bryan, R. N. (1993). Quantitation of proton NMR spectra of the human brain using tissue water as an internal concentration reference. *NMR Biomedicine*, **6**, 89–94.

Beaulieu, C., D'arcueil, H., Hedehus, M., de Crepigny, A., Kastrup, A. & Moseley, M. E. (1999). Diffusion-weighted magnetic resonance imaging: theory and potential applications to child neurology. *Seminars in Pediatrics*, **6**, 87–100.

Biousse, V., Suh, D. Y., Newman, N. J., Davis, P. C., Mapstone, T. & Lambert, S. R. (2002). Diffusion-weighted magnetic resonance imaging in shaken baby syndrome. *American Journal of Ophthalmology*, **133**, 249–255.

Blackman, J. A., Rice, S. A., Matsumoto, J. A. *et al.* (2003). Brain imaging as a predictor of early functional outcome following traumatic brain injury in children, adolescents, and young adults. *Journal of Head Trauma Rehabilitation*, **18**, 493–503.

Brenner, T., Freier, M. C., Holshouser, B. A., Burley, T. & Ashwal, S. (2003). Predicting neuropsychologic outcome after traumatic brain injury in children. *Pediatric Neurology*, **28**, 104–114.

Bullock, R., Zauner, A., Woodward, J. J. *et al.* (1998). Factors affecting excitatory amino acid release following severe head injury. *Journal of Neurosurgery*, **89**, 507–518.

Bydder, G. M., Rutherford, M. A. & Cowan, F. M. (2001). Diffusion-weighted imaging in neonates. *Childs Nervous System*, **17**, 190–194.

Cady, E. B., Penrice, J., Amess, P. N. *et al.* (1996). Lactate, *N*-acetylaspartate, choline and creatine concentrations and spin-spin relation in thalamic and occipito-parietal regions of developing human brain. *Magnetic Resonance Medicine*, **36**, 878–886.

Cecil, K. M., Hills, E. C., Sandel, M. E. *et al.* (1998). Proton magnetic resonance spectroscopy for detection of axonal injury in the splenium of the corpus callosum of brain-injured patients. *Journal of Neurosurgery*, **88**, 795–801.

Chan, Y. L., Chu, W. C., Wong, G. W. & Yeung, D. K. (2003). Diffusion-weighted MRI in shaken baby syndrome. *Pediatric Radiology*, **33**, 574–547.

Danielsen, E. R., Michaelis, T. & Ross, B. D. (1995). Three methods of calibration in quantitative proton MR spectroscopy. *Journal of Magnetic Resonance*, **106**, 287–291.

Danielsen, E. R. & Ross, B. (1999). *Magnetic Resonance Spectroscopy Diagnosis of*

Neurological Diseases. New York: Marcel Dekker.

Field, A. S., Hasan, K., Jellison, B. J., Arfanakis, K. & Alexander, A. L. (2003). Diffusion tensor imaging in an infant with traumatic brain swelling. *American Journal of Neuroradiology*, **24**, 1461–1464.

Frahm, J., Bruhn, H., Gyngell, M. L., Merboldt, K. D., Hanicke, W. & Sauter, R. (1989). Localized NMR spectroscopy in different regions of the human brain in vivo: relaxation times and concentration of cerebral metabolites. *Magnetic Resonance Medicine*, **11**, 47–63.

Galloway, N. R., Tong, K. A., Ashwal, S., Oyoyo, U. & Obenaus, A. (2008). Diffusion-weighted imaging improves outcome prediction in pediatric traumatic brain injury. *Journal of Neurotrauma*, **25**, 1153–1162.

Garnett, M. R., Blamire, A. M., Corkill, R. G., Cadoux-Hudson, T. A., Rajagopalan, B. & Stylet, P. (2000). Early proton magnetic resonance spectroscopy in normal-appearing brain correlates with outcome in patients following traumatic brain injury. *Brain*, **123**, 2046–2054.

Garnett, M. R., Corkill, R. G., Blamire, A. M. *et al.* (2001). Altered cellular metabolism following traumatic brain injury: a magnetic resonance spectroscopy study. *Journal of Neurotrauma*, **18**, 231–240.

Geddes, J. F., Hackshaw, A. K., Vowles, G. H., Nickols, C. D. & Whitwell, H. L. (2001a). Neuropathology of inflicted head injury in children. I. Pattern of brain damage. *Brain*, **124**, 1290–1298.

Geddes, J. F., Vowles, G. H., Hackshaw, A. K., Nickols, C. D., Scott, I. S. & Whitwell, H. L. (2001b). Neuropathology of inflicted head injury in children. II. Microscopic brain injury in infants. *Brain*, **124**, 1299–1306.

Govindaraju, V., Gauger, G. E., Manley, G. T., Ebel, A., Meeker, M. & Maudsley, A. A. (2004). Volumetric proton spectroscopic imaging of mild traumatic brain injury. *American Journal of Neuroradiology*, **25**, 730–737.

Grados, M. A., Slomine, B. S., Gerring, J. P., Vasa, R., Bryan, N. & Denckla, M. B. (2001).

Depth of lesion model in children and adolescents with moderate to severe traumatic brain injury: use of SPGR MRI to predict severity and outcome. *Journal of Neurology, Neurosurgery, and Psychiatry*, **70**, 350–358.

Haacke, E. M., Xu, Y., Cheng, Y. C. & Reichenbach, J. R. (2004). Susceptibility weighted imaging (SWI), *Magnetic Resonance Medicine*, **52**, 612–618.

Hergan, K., Schaefer, P. W., Sorensen, A. G., Gonzalez, R. G. & Huisman, T. A. G. M. (2002). Diffusion-weighted MRI in diffuse axonal injury of the brain. *European Radiology*, **12**, 2536–2541.

Holshouser, B. A., Ashwal, S., Luh, G. Y. *et al.* (1997). Proton MR spectroscopy after acute central nervous system injury: outcome prediction in neonates, infants, and children. *Radiology*, **202**, 487–496.

Holshouser, B. A., Ashwal, S. & Tong, K. A. (2005). Proton MR spectroscopic imaging depicts diffuse axonal injury in children with traumatic brain injury. *American Journal of Neuroradiology*, **26**, 1276–1285.

Horska, A., Kaufmann, W., Brant, L. J., Naidu, S., Harris, J. C. & Barker, P. B. (2002). In vivo quantitative proton MRSI study of brain development from childhood to adolescence. *Journal of Magnetic Resonance Imaging*, **15**, 137–143.

Hou, D. J., Tong, K. A., Ashwal, S. *et al.* (2007). Diffusion-weighted magnetic resonance imaging improves outcome prediction in adult traumatic brain injury. *Journal of Neurotrauma*, **24**, 1558–1569.

Huisman, T. A. (2003). Diffusion-weighted imaging: basic concepts and application in cerebral stroke and head trauma. *European Radiology*, **13**, 2283–2297.

Huisman, T. A., Sorensen, A. G., Hergan, K., Gonzalez, R. G. & Schaefer, P. W. (2003). Diffusion-weighted imaging for the evaluation of diffuse axonal injury in closed head injury. *Journal of Computer Assisted Tomography*, **27**, 5–11.

Huisman, T. A., Schwamm, L. H., Schaefer, P. W. *et al.* (2004). Diffusion tensor imaging as potential biomarker of white matter injury in diffuse axonal injury. *American Journal of Neuroradiology*, **25**, 370–376.

Hunter, J. V., Thornton, R. J., Wang, Z. J. *et al.* (2005). Late proton MR spectroscopy in children after traumatic brain injury: correlation with cognitive outcomes. *American Journal of Neuroradiology*, **26**, 482–488.

Huppi, P. S. (2001). MR imaging and spectroscopy of brain development. In A. James Barkovich, A. Robert and R. A. Zimmerman, eds. *Pediatric MR Neuroimaging, Magnetic Resonance Imaging Clinics of North America*, pp. 1–18.

Huppi, P. S., Maier, S. E., Peled, S., Zientara, G. P., Barnes, P. D. & Jolesz, F. A. (1998). Microstructural development of human newborn cerebral white matter assessed in vivo by diffusion tensor magnetic resonance imaging. *Pediatric Research*, **44**, 584–590.

Jones, D. K., Dardis, R., Ervine, M. *et al.* (2000). Cluster analysis of diffusion tensor magnetic resonance images in human head injury. *Neurosurgery*, **47**, 306–317.

Klingberg, T., Vaidya, C. J., Gabrieli, J. D., Moseley, M. E. & Hedehus, M. (1999). Myelination and organization of the frontal white matter in children: a diffusion tensor MRI study. *Neuroreport*, **10**, 2817–2821.

Kreis, R., Ernst, T. & Ross, B. D. (1993). Development of the human brain: in vivo quantification of metabolite and water content with proton magnetic resonance spectroscopy. *Magnetic Resonance Medicine*, **30**, 424–437.

Kreis, R., Hofmann, L., Kuhlmann, B., Boesch, C., Bossi, E. & Huppi, P. S. (2002). Brain metabolite composition during early human brain development as measured by quantitative in vivo ^{1}H magnetic resonance spectroscopy. *Magnetic Resonance Medicine*, **48**, 949–958.

Macmillan, C. S., Wild, J. M., Wardlaw, J. M., Andrews, P. J., Marshall, I. & Easton, V. J. (2002). Traumatic brain injury and subarachnoid hemorrhage: in vivo occult pathology demonstrated by magnetic resonance spectroscopy may not be "ischaemic." A primary study and review of the literature. *Acta Neurochirurgica (Wien)*, **144**, 853–862.

McGraw, P., Liang, L. & Provenzale, J. M. (2002). Evaluation of normal age-related changes in anisotropy during infancy and childhood as shown by diffusion tensor imaging. *American Journal of Roentgenology*, **179**, 1515–1522.

McKinstry, R. C., Miller, J. H., Snyder, A. Z. *et al.* (2002). A prospective, longitudinal diffusion tensor imaging study of brain injury in newborns. *Neurology*, **59**, 824–833.

McLean, M. A., Woermann, F. G., Barker, G. J. & Duncan, J. S. (2000). Quantitative analysis of short echo time ^{1}H-MRSI of cerebral gray and white matter. *Magnetic Research Medicine*, **44**, 401–411.

Morriss, M. C., Zimmerman, R. A., Bilaniuk, L. T., Hunter, J. V. & Hasselgrove, J. C. (1999). Changes in brain water diffusion during childhood. *Neuroradiology*, **41**, 929–934.

Mukherjee, P. & McKinstry, R. C. (2001). Reversible posterior leukoencephalopathy syndrome: evaluation with diffusion tensor MR imaging. *Radiology*, **219**, 756–765.

Mukherjee, P., Miller, J. H., Shimony, J. S. *et al.* (2002). Diffusion-tensor MR imaging of gray and white matter development during normal human brain maturation. *American Journal of Neuroradiology*, **23**, 1445–1456.

Naganawa, S., Sato, C., Ishihra, S. *et al.* (2004). Serial evaluation of diffusion tensor brain fiber tracking in a patient with severe diffuse axonal injury. *American Journal of Neuroradiology*, **25**, 1553–1536.

Neil, J. J., Shiran, S. I., McKinstry, R. C. *et al.* (1998). Normal brain in human newborns: apparent diffusion coefficient and diffusion anisotropy measured by using diffusion tensor MR imaging. *Radiology*, **209**, 57–66.

Parizel, P. M., Ceulemans, B., Laridon, A., Ozsarlak, O., Van Goethem, J. W. & Jorens, P. G. (2003). Cortical hypoxic-ischemic brain damage in shaken-baby (shaken impact) syndrome: value of diffusion-weighted MRI. *Pediatric Radiology*, **33**, 868–871.

Pouwels, P. J., Brockmann, K., Kruise, B. *et al.* (1999). Regional age-dependence of human brain metabolites form infancy to adulthood as detected by quantitative localized proton MRS. *Pediatric Research*, **46**, 474–485.

Prayer, D. & Prayer, L. (2003). Diffusion-weighted magnetic resonance imaging of cerebral white matter development. *European Journal of Radiology*, **45**, 235–243.

Provencher, S. W. (1993). Estimation of metabolite concentrations from localized in vivo proton NMR spectra. *Magnetic Resonance Medicine*, **30**, 672–679.

Ptak, T., Sheridan, R. L., Rhea, J. T. *et al.* (2003). Cerebral fractional anisotropy score in trauma patients: a new indicator of white matter injury after trauma. *American Journal of Roentgenology*, **181**, 1401–1407.

Ross, B. D., Ernst, T., Kreis, R. *et al.* (1998). ¹H MRS in acute traumatic brain injury. *Journal of Magnetic Resonance Imaging*, **8**, 829–840.

Rugg-Gunn, F. J., Symms, M. R., Barker, G. J., Greenwood, R. & Duncan, J. S. (2001). Diffusion imaging shows abnormalities after blunt head trauma when conventional magnetic resonance imaging is normal. *Journal of Neurology, Neurosurgery, and Psychiatry*, **70**, 530–533.

Schaefer, P. W., Grant, P. E. & Gonzalez, R. G. (2000). Diffusion-weighted MR imaging of the brain. *Radiology*, **217**, 331–345.

Schaefer, P. W., Huisman, T. A., Sorensen, A. G., Gonzalez, R. G. & Schwamm, L. H. (2004). Diffusion-weighted MR imaging in closed head injury: high correlation with initial Glasgow coma scale score and score on modified Rankin scale at discharge. *Radiology*, **233**, 58–66.

Schuff, N., Ezekiel, F., Gamst, A. C. *et al.* (2001). Region and tissue differences of metabolites in normally aged brain using multislice ¹H magnetic resonance spectroscopic imaging. *Magnetic Resonance Medicine*, **45**, 899–907.

Schumann, M. U., Stiller, D., Thomas, B., Brinker, T. & Samii, M. (2000). ¹H-MR spectroscopic monitoring of post-traumatic metabolism following controlled cortical impact injury: pilot study. *Acta Neurochirurgica*, **76** Suppl., 3–7.

Sehgal, V., Delproposto, Z., Haacke, E. M. *et al.* (2005). Clinical applications of neuroimaging with susceptibility-weighted imaging. *Journal of Magnetic Resonance Imaging*, **22**, 439–450.

Sigmund, G. A., Tong, K. A., Nickerson, J. P., Wall, C. J., Oyoyo, U. & Ashwal, S. (2007). Multimodality comparison of neuroimaging in pediatric traumatic brain injury. *Pediatric Neurology*, **36**, 217–226.

Signoretti, S., Marmarou, A., Fatouros, P. *et al.* (2002). Application of chemical shift imaging for measurement of NAA in head injured patients. *Acta Neurochirurgica*, **81** Suppl., 373–375.

Sinson, G., Bagley, L. J., Cecil, K. M. *et al.* (2001). Magnetization transfer imaging and proton MR spectroscopy in the evaluation of axonal injury: correlation with clinical outcome after traumatic brain injury. *American Journal of Neuroradiology*, **22**, 143–151.

Soher, B. J., Vermathen, P., Schuff, N. *et al.* (2000). Short TE in vivo (1)H MR spectroscopic imaging at 1.5 T: acquisition and automated spectral analysis. *Magnetic Resonance Imaging*, **18**, 1159–1165.

Suh, D. Y., Davis, P. C., Hopkins, K. L., Fajman, N. N. & Mapstone, T. B. (2001). Nonaccidental pediatric head injury: diffusion-weighted imaging findings. *Neurosurgery*, **49**, 309–318.

Sundgren, P. C., Dong, Q., Gomez-Hassan, D., Mukherji, S. K., Maly, P. & Welsh, R. (2004). Diffusion tensor imaging of the brain: review of clinical applications. *Neuroradiology*, **46**, 339–350.

Sykova, E. (2004). Extrasynaptic volume transmission and diffusion parameters of the extracellular space. *Neuroscience*, **129**, 861–876.

Tong, K. A., Ashwal, S., Holshouser, B. A. *et al.* (2003). Hemorrhagic shearing lesions in children and adolescents with post-traumatic diffuse axonal injury: improved detection and initial results. *Radiology*, **227**, 332–339.

Tong, K. A., Ashwal, S., Holshouser, B. A. *et al.* (2004). Diffuse axonal injury in children:

clinical correlation with hemorrhagic lesions. *Annals of Neurology*, **56**, 36–50.

Tong, K. A., Ashwal, S., Obenaus, A., Nickerson, J. P., Kido, D. & Haacke, E. M. (2008). Susceptibility-weighted MR imaging: a review of clinical applications in children. *American Journal of Neuroradiology*, **29**, 9–17.

van der Toorn, A., Sykova, E., Dijkhuizen, R. M. *et al.* (1996). Dynamic changes in water ADC, energy metabolism, extracellular space volume, and tortuosity in neonatal rat brain during global ischemia. *Magnetic Resonance Medicine*, **36**, 52–60.

Vigneron, D. B., Barkovich, A. J., Noworolski, S. M. *et al.* (2001). Three-dimensional proton MR spectroscopic imaging of premature and term neonates. *American Journal of Neuroradiology*, **22**, 1424–1433.

Wilde, E. A., Bigler, E. D., Haider, J. M. *et al.* (2006a). Vulnerability of the anterior commissure in moderate to severe pediatric traumatic brain injury. *Journal of Child Neurology*, **21**, 769–776.

Wilde, E. A., Chu, Z., Bigler, E. D. *et al.* (2006b). Diffusion tensor imaging in the corpus callosum in children after moderate to severe traumatic brain injury. *Journal of Neurotrauma*, **23**, 1412–1426.

Wilde, E. A., McCauley, S. R., Hunter, J. V. *et al.* (2008). Diffusion tensor imaging of acute mild traumatic brain injury in adolescents. *Neurology*, **70**, 948–955.

Wozniak, J. R., Krach, L., Ward, E. *et al.* (2007). Neurocognitive and neuroimaging correlates of pediatric traumatic brain injury: a diffusion tensor imaging (DTI) study. *Archives in Clinical Neuropsychology*, **22**, 555–568.

Yuan, W., Holland, S. K., Schmithorst, V. J. *et al.* (2007). Diffusion tensor MR imaging reveals persistent white matter alteration after traumatic brain injury experienced during early childhood. *American Journal of Neuroradiology*, **28**, 1919–1925.

Zhang, H., Zhang, X., Zhang, T. & Chen, L. (2001). Excitatory amino acids in cerebrospinal fluid of patients with acute head injuries. *Clinical Chemistry*, **47**, 1458–1462.

Chapter

6

Neurobehavioral outcomes of pediatric mild traumatic brain injury

Michael W. Kirkwood and Keith Owen Yeates

In the United States, approximately 475 000 children between the ages of 0 and 14 years are treated annually for traumatic brain injury (TBI) in hospital settings. Of these, 435 000 (91.5%) receive care and are released from the emergency department (Langlois *et al.*, 2006). These data correspond to other estimates indicating that mild injuries account for 80% to 90% of all treated pediatric TBI (Cassidy *et al.*, 2004). Rates of mild TBI are likely even higher than these numbers suggest, as many milder injuries go unreported entirely or are treated in outpatient settings and remain unaccounted for in hospital-based estimates (Sosin *et al.*, 1996). Because severe TBI causes the vast majority of mortality and the most significant morbidity, it has attracted much of the scientific attention to date. However, given the sheer frequency of mild TBI and its potential for disruptive effects, these injuries clearly warrant scientific interest and investigation in their own right. The present chapter will focus on the neurobehavioral outcomes of mild TBI in childhood, highlighting relevant cross-disciplinary, translational research and collaborative opportunities.

Summary of neurobehavioral research findings

Ancient medical tracts, myths, legends, biblical texts, plays, and poems all indicate that mild TBI has been recognized since antiquity as a distinct type of head injury (Shaw, 2002). Nonetheless, for much of recorded history, the neurobehavioral outcomes of mild TBI were largely ignored scientifically, because mild TBI was assumed to produce transient functional impairment, not associated with underlying brain damage or lasting problems. For children, these assumptions changed most dramatically in the 1980s after several studies and reviews drew widespread attention to the idea that pediatric mild TBI might lead to long-lasting cognitive, behavioral, somatic, and educational problems. This early work helped raise awareness about the importance of studying mild TBI, even though many of these initial concerns were based on flawed data from studies that lacked methodological rigor (Satz *et al.*, 1997).

In the last two decades, considerable progress has been made in understanding the neurobehavioral impact of pediatric mild TBI. Nevertheless, well-designed prospective studies remain relatively rare, and thus, the natural clinical history of mild TBI is not yet completely characterized. Existing quality research has mostly confirmed that the effects of a single mild TBI are likely to be self-limiting and fairly benign in the short-term for the majority of school-age children. At the same time, neurobehavioral outcomes of mild TBI are apt to be more complex than assumed historically and are almost certainly influenced by

Pediatric Traumatic Brain Injury: New Frontiers in Clinical and Translational Research, ed. V. Anderson and K. O. Yeates. Published by Cambridge University Press. © Cambridge University Press 2010.

multiple injury and non-injury related variables. The severity of the mild TBI and the method by which post-injury change is measured are but two factors that more recent research indicates may play an important role in determining the effects of mild TBI.

The presence of intracranial abnormalities on conventional neuroimaging has been identified as one marker of severity that influences neurobehavioral outcome after mild TBI. In adult populations, a number of studies have found that visible intracranial pathology after mild TBI increases the risks for select neuropsychological problems during the initial months post-injury, as well as for more persistent functional difficulties (Iverson, 2006; Kashluba et al., 2008; Kurca et al., 2006; Sadowski-Cron et al., 2006; Williams et al., 1990). These injuries are now thought to be similar to moderate TBI in their functional outcomes and are generally classified as such or referred to as "complicated" mild TBI. Distinguishing between complicated and uncomplicated mild TBI has received less attention in pediatric populations, though available data support this intuitively sensible distinction. For example, a recent prospective longitudinal study by Levin and colleagues (2008) examined outcomes over 12 months post-injury between groups of children with mild TBI associated with intracranial pathology on computed tomography (CT) versus those without. Children who had intracranial abnormalities performed worse in multiple cognitive and academic domains when compared with those who had normal CT findings or only a linear skull fracture.

After mild TBI, empirical work indicates that, during the initial hours and days post-injury, a constellation of neurobehavioral changes can be seen in children, not unlike those apparent in adult populations. These changes can include a combination of somatic, cognitive, and emotional/behavioral difficulties. How long and why postconcussive problems last after an uncomplicated injury has been the subject of a great deal of scientific controversy. Methodologically rigorous studies indicate that, by two to three months post-injury, and oftentimes much sooner, deficits are not apparent when measured in group analyses using standardized performance-based neurocognitive or academic tests (Carroll et al., 2004b; Satz et al., 1997; Satz, 2001). These results correspond with the general conclusions of several meta-analytic studies focused on the neuropsychological outcomes of mild TBI in adults (Belanger et al., 2005; Binder et al., 1997; Schretlen & Shapiro, 2003).

Many fewer studies have systematically examined outcomes using postconcussive symptom reports from parents or children, though available research suggests that a minority of pediatric patients may display more persistent problems than might be expected if examining test-based results alone (Yeates & Taylor et al., 2005b; Yeates et al., 2009). As Table 6.1 highlights, understanding the nature of subjectively reported postconcussive symptomatology is complicated by the fact that the symptoms are non-specific and can be seen for multiple reasons aside from brain injury (Asarnow et al., 1991). Premorbid problems, the emotional or physical effects of trauma more generally, post-injury difficulties unrelated to the trauma, and particular fears and expectations associated with cerebral injury can all produce problems that may be mistaken for neurologically based postconcussive symptoms (Asarnow et al., 1995; Bijur et al., 1990; Goldstrohm & Arffa, 2005; Mittenberg et al., 1997; Nacajauskaite et al., 2006).

That postconcussive symptoms are non-specific, however, does not rule out the potential explanatory power of injury-related or neurogenic variables in some cases. A recent prospective controlled study by Yeates, Taylor, and colleagues (2009) found that, after accounting for numerous non-injury variables, parents of children with mild TBI were more likely than parents of children with orthopedic injuries to report high levels of acute postconcussive symptoms that persisted over 12 months post-injury, especially in the presence of clinical features indicating more significant mild TBI (e.g. loss of consciousness,

Table 6.1 Potential explanations for symptoms seen after mild TBI

Relationship between symptoms and TBI	Example
(1) Symptoms predate TBI	* Poor concentration seen post-injury reflects a premorbid learning or attentional disorder.
(2) TBI exacerbates pre-existing condition	* Premorbid sleep problems are worsened by TBI.
(3) TBI triggers symptoms in a predisposed individual	* Dizziness is first seen after TBI in an individual with an underlying Chiari malformation.
(4) Symptoms result directly from TBI	* De novo headaches develop after TBI.
(5) Symptoms are a secondary effect of trauma or TBI	* Irritability reflects a post-traumatic stress response to injury circumstances or pain from orthopedic injury. * Initial memory problems after TBI are continued for secondary gain.
(6) Symptoms appear after trauma but are unrelated to TBI	* Personality change is due to coinciding familial dysfunction or social stressors.

Glasgow Coma Scale score <15). On the other hand, similar proportions of children who suffered mild TBI and those who suffered orthopedic injuries displayed a moderate increase in symptoms after injury that persisted over time, highlighting the fact that "postconcussive" symptoms are indeed non-specific and will occur and persist for different reasons in different children. Regardless of the exact etiology, the existence of post-injury symptomatology (for children sustaining both brain injuries and orthopedic injuries) may have functional consequences, including increasing family burden and parental distress within the first few months of injury (Ganesalingam *et al.*, 2008).

Ultimately, in any given study, the documented neurobehavioral impact of mild TBI will depend not only on whether the complicated vs. uncomplicated distinction is recognized and whether multi-dimensional neurobehavioral assessments are conducted, but also on how researchers handle the many other methodological and conceptual issues that arise when studying this population. Many of these issues can be appreciated through consideration of the six "W" questions.

Methodological and conceptual issues for research
Who is the population?
The focus of research on pediatric mild TBI is the still actively developing child. The number of published mild TBI studies involving children pales in comparison to those conducted with adults, with a particular dearth of studies focused on infants and toddlers. Although much of the extant pediatric outcome literature parallels that seen in adults, conclusions based on adult studies cannot be assumed to generalize necessarily to younger populations. Moreover, given the rapidity and complexity of change that occurs throughout childhood, data based on one developmental epoch may not match that of another.

The mechanisms that commonly produce TBI vary by age at injury, and hence will influence the type and severity of the biomechanical force responsible for injury and could lead to different pathological effects and outcomes. In pediatric populations, inflicted trauma is most common in infancy; falls are heavily represented in the toddler and preschool years; sport- and motor vehicle-related TBI increases in middle childhood; and TBI from motor vehicle-related trauma and assaults peaks during older adolescence (Keenan & Bratton, 2006). Because the compositional and mechanical properties of the head and brain differ between developing and mature organisms, the specific effects of the applied forces may be age-dependent as well. Developmental factors such as brain water content, cerebral blood volume, degree of myelination, skull geometry, and suture elasticity undoubtedly affect the biomechanics of mild TBI, although exactly how remains largely undetermined (Bauer & Fritz, 2004; Gefen et al., 2003; Prins & Hovda, 2003; Thibault & Margulies, 1998). Once injury occurs, the immature brain may respond less well in some respects. For example, in comparison to adults, children and adolescents are more likely to experience cerebral edema after minor head injury, though this outcome is rare overall (Bruce, 1984; McCrory & Berkovic, 1998; Snoek et al., 1984).

Neurobehaviorally, multiple studies have shown that more severe TBI during the infancy and preschool years is associated with worse outcomes than injury occurring in later childhood or adolescence and that skills not yet developed or currently in development may be particularly susceptible to injury (Anderson et al., 2005; Catroppa et al., 2007; Ewing-Cobbs et al., 2004). Initial work suggests the same could be true after mild TBI (Gronwall et al., 1997). Based on these data, a reasonable hypothesis is that worse neurobehavioral outcomes may occur in very young children after mild TBI, though the lack of quality data to evaluate this idea renders it largely speculative at present.

What is mild TBI?

A fundamental challenge confronting all TBI researchers is defining exactly what is meant by "mild" injury. Inconsistencies and scientific disagreement have resulted in varying definitions over the years (see Table 6.2). When examining the literature, two definitional complexities stand out. First, TBI severity can be characterized on a number of injury-related dimensions, any of which may conflict with judgments based on data from another dimension. Although several studies have focused on determining which injury character-istics are most important to predicting outcomes after more severe TBI (Massagli et al., 1996; McDonald et al., 1994), the clinical features that should be used to define pediatric mild TBI remain more uncertain empirically. The second challenge is that a broad spectrum of injuries has been classified traditionally under the rubric of mild TBI. For instance, a child who loses consciousness for 15 minutes and the child who bumps his or her head and is dazed and dizzy for a matter of minutes are likely to both be considered to have sustained a mild TBI. To address this variability, a number of more specific classification schemes have been proposed to grade severity within the spectrum of mild TBI (Esselman & Uomoto, 1995); however, the value of these classification attempts has not yet been investi-gated seriously in child populations.

Across studies, the Glasgow Coma Scale (GCS) is by far the most common means to determine TBI severity. The scale was originally designed to predict mortality and morbid-ity after more severe injury by gauging the depth of impaired consciousness and coma; it or similar scales have been used for decades with management and prognostic benefit after more severe pediatric TBI. The insensitivity and limitations of the GCS after mild TBI, defined by scores from 13 to 15, are well recognized, even by its developers (Jennett, 1989). Duration of post-traumatic amnesia (PTA) and loss of consciousness (LOC) have

Table 6.2 Definitions of mild TBI and related constructs

Professional group	Term of use	Definitional criteria
American Congress of Rehabilitation Medicine Mild TBI Committee (1993)	Mild TBI	Traumatically induced physiological disruption manifested by at least one: • LOC < 30 minutes • loss of memory or alteration in mental state around time of accident (PTA < 24 hours) • transient or intransient focal neurological deficit (GCS 13–15 after 30 minutes)
American Academy of Neurology (Kelly & Rosenberg, 1997)	Concussion	Trauma-induced alteration in mental status that may or may not involve LOC. Confusion and amnesia are hallmarks, occurring immediately after injury or several minutes later. *Grade I* • transient confusion; no LOC; symptoms or mental status abnormalities resolve in less than 15 minutes *Grade II* • transient confusion; no LOC; symptoms or mental status abnormalities last more than 15 minutes *Grade III* • any LOC
American Academy of Pediatrics (1999)	Minor closed head injury	• normal mental status on initial examination • no abnormal or focal neurological findings • no evidence of skull fracture • LOC <1 minute • may have had a seizure, vomited, or may exhibit other signs or symptoms (e.g. headache, lethargy)

| World Health Organization Collaborating Centre Task Force on Mild TBI (Carroll et al., 2004a) | Mild TBI | Acute brain injury resulting from mechanical energy to the head from external physical forces. Includes one or more of the following:
• confusion or disorientation, LOC < 30 minutes, PTA < 24 hours, and/or transient neurological abnormalities such as focal signs, seizure, intracranial lesion not requiring surgery (GSC 13–15 after 30 minutes) |
| Concussion in Sport Group (McCrory et al., 2005) | Sports Concussion | Complex pathophysiological process affecting the brain, induced by traumatic biomechanical forces. Common features include:
• typically results in rapid onset of short lived neurological impairment
• may result in neuropathological changes, but symptoms largely reflect functional disturbance
• results in graded set of clinical syndromes that may or may not involve LOC; symptom resolution typically follows sequential course
• typically associated with grossly normal structural neuroimaging studies |

Notes: LOC = loss of consciousness; PTA = post-traumatic amnesia; GCS = Glasgow Coma Scale.

also been used to define mild TBI, albeit less frequently and operationally much less consistently than the GCS. Lengthier periods of PTA and LOC are clearly related to neurobehavioral outcome after more severe injury (Yeates, 2000). Greater than five minutes of LOC or PTA has also been found to predict intracranial pathology after milder head injury (Dunning et al., 2004; Dunning et al., 2006). Less research has examined the predictive validity of PTA and LOC at a neurobehavioral level after mild TBI in children. In adult mild TBI trauma patients and concussed athletes, PTA is generally the better of the two predictors, at least when examining short-term neuropsychological outcomes (Iverson et al., 2007a).

Because of the insensitivity of the GCS, PTA, and LOC to the upper limit of mild TBI, multiple other signs and symptoms are also commonly used alone or in combination to define such injury, including headache, dizziness, vomiting, feeling dazed, disorientation, and focal neurological deficits. The type, severity, and number of these signs and symptoms that warrant a mild TBI diagnosis has not been determined scientifically. The fact that many of these acute characteristics are non-specific and have multiple causes aside from brain injury also obscures the diagnostic process. For instance, one of the most common post-concussive symptoms is headache; however, headache can have multiple causes aside from brain injury (e.g. neck strain) and differentiating headache as a symptom of mild TBI from headache as a distinct clinical entity can be challenging. Many other classic features of mild TBI (e.g. appearing stunned or dazed) are equally non-specific and in some cases may be attributable to psychological factors such as intense anxiety or pain associated with the injury-producing event. In practice, without evidence of more significant injury, underlying neurological and psychological disruption are often indistinguishable behaviorally. As such, definitive diagnosis of brain injury at the mildest end of the spectrum will most likely depend on associated evidence of pathophysiological disruption. To date, a "gold standard" pathophysiologic diagnostic tool remains elusive, despite impressive advancements in recent years in neuroimaging and biomarker technology.

In the end, much of the available research on pediatric mild TBI can be criticized for failing to precisely state and rigorously apply well-specified selection criteria. Future studies will also need to move away from arbitrary cut-points used to stratify injury severity toward a multi-dimensional severity continuum, empirically linking any posited thresholds to documentable pathophysiological disruption and neurobehavioral or medical outcomes.

When are data collected?

Given the rapid recovery trajectory seen after most mild TBI, the timing of post-injury assessment can make a considerable difference to a study's findings. In general, the most notable neurocognitive change following an uncomplicated mild TBI can be expected to be seen in the initial hours and days after injury. When examining sport-related concussion data from adolescent and older athletes, cognitive changes essentially dissipate by 7–10 days post-injury (Belanger & Vanderploeg, 2005). Although more variability may be seen when examining outcomes in younger children or injuries caused by a broader array of mechanisms, these data suggest that to detect neurocognitive effects via performance-based tests, contact within hours or days of injury is apt to be most fruitful. Early contact post-injury is also important to ensure the accurate collection of injury-related and premorbid information. Self-report of whether or not a mild TBI was even sustained can become unreliable when reported retrospectively months or years post-injury (Valovich McLeod et al., 2008).

Gathering information about the post-acute recovery course, as well as estimates of premorbid symptomatology and functioning, can also be expected to become less reliable with increasing time after injury.

Although early contact is important, past studies can also be faulted for failing to follow children for sufficient periods after an injury has occurred. After mild TBI, postconcussive symptoms may persist in a minority of children. Assessments that follow children for months or even years after injury will be necessary to more fully appreciate the course and functional consequences of these difficulties (see Chapter 7). The idea that children will "grow into a deficit" after mild TBI as the demands increase in later years seems unlikely after an injury with initially transient effects, though further research will be needed to test the scientific merit of this hypothesis. Longer term assessments will also be necessary to document the relative contributions of injury characteristics and non-injury-related factors as predictors of persistent postconcussive symptoms. In adult studies, injury-related variables account for more variance in the initial post-injury presentation and non-injury-related variables explain more variance in subsequent periods (Iverson *et al.*, 2007b).

Where is the sample identified and recruited?

Although mild TBI patients are often treated equivalently regardless of recruitment setting, injury- and non-injury-related characteristics may vary by the source of enrollment. At the broadest level, cultural context has been found to influence expectations after mild TBI in adults. In turn, what an individual simply expects to happen following a mild head injury has been shown to independently affect neurobehavioral outcomes (Mittenberg *et al.*, 1992; Suhr & Gunstad, 2002, 2005). In an interesting cross-cultural study, Ferrari and colleagues (2002) compared the type and duration of postconcussive symptoms that a group of Canadians and a group of Lithuanians expected to experience following an imagined mild TBI. Both groups reported a pattern of acute symptoms that closely resembled what is commonly reported after actual injury. However, many Canadian subjects anticipated that these symptoms would last months or years, whereas relatively few Lithuanians shared this expectation for persistent symptoms. These findings highlight the potentially important role of broader societal or demographic variables in influencing a child's or parent's attention to symptoms and symptom expectation after mild TBI, a topic that has thus far received very little study.

The specific referral setting may also affect the nature of the injury, type of patient, or timing of post-injury contact likely to come under study. In contrast to the wide majority of children with more severe TBI who present soon after injury to hospital settings, mild TBI patients present in a much less predictable fashion. We lack empirical data to determine how this variability might affect the characteristics of a sample. Nonetheless, differences would not be unexpected when recruitment occurs in settings as diverse as an inpatient hospital, emergency department, pediatrician's office, specialty outpatient healthcare clinic, school, or athletic setting. Until these differences are examined directly, researchers will need to provide sufficient detail about a study's recruitment procedure and sample to allow judgments to be made about the representativeness of the sample and generalizability of any findings.

As one example of how referral setting may influence sample characteristics, Table 6.3 presents data comparing 186 mild TBI patients enrolled from an emergency department (Yeates *et al.*, 2009) and 658 concussed high school and college athletes described by

Table 6.3 Acute injury characteristics of samples from an emergency department vs. athletic setting

	Emergency department sample (Yeates et al., 2009)	Athletic sample (McCrea, 2008)
LOC	40%	10%
PTA	32%	23%
Headache	76%	80–85%
Nausea	41%	40%
Vomiting	44%	<5%
Dizziness	26%	75–80%

Notes: LOC = loss of consciousness; PTA = post-traumatic amnesia.

McCrea (2008). Although these samples differ in a number of respects (e.g. age at injury) and need to be compared cautiously, the data support the logical idea that a mild TBI sample drawn from an emergency department may include what appear to be more severe or different types of injuries than one drawn strictly from an athletic setting. For instance, 40% of the hospital sample had a loss of consciousness and 44% presented with emesis, whereas these signs were relatively uncommon in the sport-based setting. Though far from conclusive, these results suggest that rigorous data collection across a variety of settings will be important when attempting to chart the underlying natural history of pediatric mild TBI.

Why are the patients being seen?

In adult samples, the purpose of contact following mild TBI has been shown to affect neurobehavioral outcomes. This is especially true in examining data from individuals who are seen under adversarial circumstances (e.g. post-injury litigation), where secondary gain issues are prominent. In this context, effort (or the lack thereof) can have powerful effects on neuropsychological performance (Binder & Rohling, 1996).

Previous research on mild TBI in child populations can be faulted for failing to systematically evaluate the presence of secondary gain, effort, response bias, and symptom exaggeration. Because children are rarely involved directly in litigation, rates of suboptimal effort after mild TBI are likely to be lower than in adult populations. However, different types of secondary gain contexts are commonly seen in pediatric populations (e.g. getting out of school), and children are clearly capable of deception, symptom magnification, and poor test effort (Faust et al., 1988a; Lu & Boone, 2002; Oldershaw & Bagby, 1997; Peebles et al., 2005). Examiner judgment alone is unlikely to be consistently effective in identifying reduced effort or impression management in children (Faust et al., 1988a,b). Thus, similar to what has become accepted practice in studies of adult mild TBI, future pediatric research needs to formally measure and control for effort-related variables. Research focused on how to measure response bias in children is relatively sparse, although several measures of symptom validity have demonstrated utility in younger populations, including the Word Memory Test (Courtney et al., 2003; Green & Flaro, 2003), Medical Symptom Validity Test (Green, 2004), Computerized Assessment of Response Bias (Courtney et al., 2003), and Test of Memory Malingering (Constantinou & McCaffrey, 2003; Donders 2005).

Table 6.4 Commonly examined postconcussive symptoms

Physical	Cognitive	Emotional/Behavioral
Headache	Poor concentration	Sadness
Fatigue	Forgetfulness	Nervousness
Balance problems/dizziness	Mental slowing	Irritability
Nausea or vomiting	Fogginess	Lack of initiation
Light or noise sensitivity		Personality change
Sleep disturbance		

How are data collected and analyzed?

Mild TBI produces non-specific effects that are less robust and less persistent than those seen after moderate or severe injury. Because children are still actively developing, recovery in pediatric populations is also occurring against the backdrop of ongoing change. Given these complexities, how mild TBI data are collected and analyzed becomes especially important to ensuring that effects can be detected, tracked over time, and disentangled from natural development and non-injury-related variables.

As discussed previously, comprehensive evaluation of the neurobehavioral outcomes of mild TBI will require examination of both postconcussive symptomatology and neuro-psychological data. Youth are generally able to report postconcussive symptoms reliably (Mailer, 2008), though research has yet to examine how gathering symptom data using different methodologies (e.g. structured interview vs. self-completed scales; dichotomous vs. graded symptom ratings) affects child (and parent) responses. Studies with adults have established that postconcussive symptoms exist across several dimensions (e.g. cognitive, somatic, and emotional). Recent factor analytic work has also identified similar dimensions in children (Ayr *et al.*, 2009). Nevertheless, no specific set of postconcussive symptoms has been widely validated after pediatric injury, even though there is considerable overlap in symptoms examined across studies (see Table 6.4).

When objectively evaluating post-injury cognitive change, neuropsychological tests that tap dynamic processes such as speeded processing, learning and memory, and attention/executive control are likely to be more sensitive than those that tap automatized infor-mation or functioning (e.g. academic skills). Regardless of domain, however, the effects of uncomplicated mild TBI on performance-based cognitive tests can be expected to be relatively small and transient. No particular battery of tests has been shown to be more or less sensitive or valid. In recent years, claims have been made about the superiority of computerized batteries over paper-and-pencil measures when identifying post-injury change, especially after sport-related concussions. Computerized tests do have a number of inherent advantages, including easily measuring reaction time and allowing for the testing of multiple subjects simultaneously. Nonetheless, computerized tests have received very little investigation in pediatric populations specifically and have not been shown to be any more sensitive than conventional measures in high school and older athletes (Belanger & Vanderploeg, 2005). A number of psychometric questions also remain about the instru-ments marketed for athletic purposes, illustrated by a recent study examining the test–retest reliability of the three most common commercially sold batteries (Broglio *et al.*, 2007).

The average intraclass correlation coefficient over 45 days for each battery was below 0.50, no higher than estimates from many paper-and-pencil measures (Barr, 2003) and far below what most would consider to be a minimum acceptable standard to reliably detect neurocognitive change.

Methodologically, the cross-sectional design of many existing mild TBI studies has allowed for the generation of hypotheses about outcomes, though simply detecting effects can be difficult if a cross-sectional study is not timed appropriately and limited conclusions about causation and recovery can be drawn from these designs. To gain a fuller appreciation of the clinical history of mild TBI, prospective, longitudinal investigations will be required, preferably using a developmental approach when modeling outcomes. As highlighted by Yeates and Taylor and colleagues (2005b), development in children is continuous and individually determined, so longitudinal studies that incorporate change as a major focus of study will be needed to adequately characterize the developmental effects. Growth curve modeling and other newer statistical approaches should permit such analysis, as they will allow for the rate of development, changes in that rate over time, and the eventual level of outcome to be considered simultaneously (Francis et al., 1991).

Nearly all studies of the outcomes of mild TBI are focused on group data, and do not focus on variations in outcome at the individual level. Because the focus in clinical work is the single patient, analyses of individual or subgroup outcomes are especially relevant to clinical decision making. Future research on mild TBI will benefit from examination of individual outcomes in relation to particular risk factors, a task made possible by recent statistical advances. Random slopes regression, in which regression coefficients vary systematically across individuals, and mixture modeling, which can be used to identify latent classes of individuals based in part on variations in background factors, should allow a more sophisticated examination of factors related to individual outcomes (Yeates & Taylor et al., 2005b).

To contribute to the available literature, future studies must also explore a broader range of injury and non-injury-related risk factors to better predict neurobehavioral outcomes. With regard to injury-related variables, previous pediatric studies have almost exclusively examined injury severity as the variable of interest. Other injury variables could be informative as well, such as the causal mechanism or the constellation of acute injury characteristics, either of which could help to identify whether mild TBI subtypes exist that may differentially affect outcome. More careful examination of non-injury-related factors should also be incorporated into future work. After moderate-severe TBI, family-related variables have been shown to be a more significant predictor of persistent emotional and behavioral symptomatology than injury severity (Yeates et al., 2001). Other non-injury-related variables that may be worth considering include post-injury expectations for recovery, co-occurring psychiatric conditions, and pain level, all of which have been shown to play a role in the outcomes after mild TBI in adults (Iverson et al., 2007b).

Premorbid child variables warrant attention as well. The role of a child's "cerebral reserve" at the time of injury has demonstrated conceptual value in understanding risk and outcomes after significant pediatric brain injury (Dennis et al., 2006). In adult populations, a history of moderate-severe TBI is one measure of decreased reserve that has been found to hasten the clinical expression of dementia, presumably because of diminished ability to compensate for age-related neurodegeneration (Guo et al., 2000). In professional American football players, one preliminary study using retrospective survey data has suggested that multiple concussions may also serve to increase the risk for dementia-related problems later in life (Guskiewicz et al., 2005). How a previous history of one or more concussions affecting a child's neurobiological reserve and development are virtually unknown at this point and will need to be investigated as a potential premorbid risk factor in future studies.

Past research has clearly shown that children who sustain TBI and other types of injury have a history of increased developmental and behavioral problems (Bijur *et al.*, 1988). As such, pre-injury behavioral and psychiatric status must be examined carefully in all studies of pediatric TBI. A comparison group of children with injuries not involving the head is now recognized as an important methodological control for these premorbid differences. Much of the early research on mild TBI did not include control groups or only included non-injured, demographically matched controls. These studies had no means to account for the acute trauma experience of the patient with mild TBI, nor to control for the behaviors that put the child at increased risk for injury to begin with. The importance of using control groups with injuries not involving the head was nicely illustrated in a large study of mild head injury from UCLA (Asarnow *et al.*, 1995). In a prospective design, the mild head injury group had elevated scores on the total behavior problem scale of the Child Behavior Checklist (CBCL) at 12 months post-injury as compared to a non-injury control group. Conclusions based on this result would have been that head injury produced elevated rates of behavior problems. However, children in the head injury group had elevated rates of behavior problems prior to the injury and the behavioral problems did not differ between the head injury and the other injury group. A similar picture emerged when examining the post-injury neurocognitive status of the mild head injury group as well.

Children's cognitive functioning prior to mild TBI also may be an important moderator of outcomes. A recent study examined cognitive ability as a potential moderator of the effects of mild TBI in children on postconcussive symptoms (Fay *et al.*, in press). The sample included children with complicated mild TBI, uncomplicated mild TBI, and orthopedic injuries. Cognitive ability did not differ among the groups, but did play an important moderating role in both parent and child reports of postconcussive symptoms. Specifically, children with lower cognitive ability who had a complicated mild TBI showed acute increases and persistent levels of postconcussive symptoms as compared to children with orthopedic injuries. Differences were less pronounced for children with low cognitive ability and uncomplicated mild TBI. Among children with higher cognitive ability, group differences in postconcussive symptoms were not significant.

Integration with research in other domains

Neurobehavioral outcome research is most useful when integrated with cross-disciplinary lines of study. At a biomechanical level, an exciting topic in recent years has been testing the historic idea that a common g-force threshold exists above which an individual will sustain injury to the brain (McCrea, 2008). American football provides an ideal research opportunity in this regard, as predictable high impact forces and concussive injury occur at the high school, college, and professional levels. With the advent of accelerometers that can be inserted into players' helmets, researchers are now able to examine real-time head acceleration data while tracking behavioral effects. Findings so far indicate that individuals sustain concussions from impacts that range widely in magnitude and location, and that a concussion threshold is unlikely to be shared universally but will depend upon multiple individual and injury determined variables (Guskiewicz *et al.*, 2007; McCaffrey *et al.*, 2007; Mihalik *et al.*, 2007; Schnebel *et al.*, 2007). Future biomechanical studies, combined with neurophysiologic and neurobehavioral data, will allow for a better specification of these variables, and for the measurement of the effects of repeated head trauma that does not cause behavioral evidence of brain injury (i.e. "subconcussive" blows). Because most of this research has so far been conducted in older athletes, much work remains to apply these concepts to the unique biomechanical properties and circumstances associated with childhood TBI.

From a neuropathologic perspective, non-human animal research indicates that sufficient mechanical force to the head sets in motion a complex, multi-layered pathophysiological response, which has been summarized in detail on multiple occasions (Giza & Hovda, 2001; Iverson et al., 2007a; Shaw, 2002). This physiologic disruption can include unchecked ionic shifts, abrupt neuronal depolarization, widespread release of excitatory neurotransmitters, alteration in glucose metabolism, reduced cerebral blood flow, and disturbed axonal function. Experimental work suggests that the pathophysiological effects of mild TBI most often result in temporary cellular and neural system dysfunction, rather than permanent cell damage or destruction. Thus, after a milder injury, dynamic restoration over time is typically allowed as the system re-regulates. Of course, injury at the cellular level is on a continuum, and as injury becomes more severe, the expectation for slow or incomplete recovery or cell death increases.

In humans, a variety of technologies have been used to capture the pathological effects of TBI. Conventional computed tomography (CT) and magnetic resonance imaging (MRI) have received the most attention and remain the only technologies that are widely accepted for clinical use. MRI is more sensitive than CT in detecting most intracranial pathology; however, CT is generally preferred as the initial choice clinically because of its ease of use, cheap cost, and effectiveness in detecting surgically significant lesions. Approximately 5% of individuals presenting to hospital settings with a GCS score of 15 have intracranial abnormalities identified by CT scan, with percentages considerably higher if the GCS score is 13 or 14 or MRI is utilized (Borg et al., 2004a). Findings on imaging have long been linked to neurobehavioral outcome after more severe pediatric TBI and serve as the basis of the previously discussed distinction between complicated and uncomplicated mild TBI.

Because the majority of individuals who sustain mild TBI do not display abnormalities identifiable by conventional CT or MRI, newer technologies are receiving growing scientific attention. In adult populations, a number of these technologies, such as susceptibility weighted and diffusion tensor imaging, have demonstrated greater sensitivity to the effects of mild TBI than conventional techniques (Belanger et al., 2007). The specificity, duration, and clinical meaning of such findings remain much less clear. Relatively few studies have examined these newer technologies after pediatric mild TBI, and existing studies are generally characterized by small sample size, mixed TBI severity samples, and other methodological limitations that restrict conclusions and clinical application at present (see Chapter 5).

Several small studies have compared traditional CT to single photon emission computed tomography (SPECT) after pediatric TBI. Researchers have reported that SPECT may be more sensitive than CT in detecting abnormality and predicting outcomes after mild TBI and may also help to identify children who are at risk for persistent problems (Agrawal et al., 2005; Emanuelson et al., 1997; Gowda et al., 2006). Several recent studies have investigated the potential sensitivity of MRI technologies as well. Diffusion tensor imaging (DTI) has been utilized in two identified studies. One of these compared ten adolescents with mild TBI (GCS 15 and negative CT) with ten uninjured controls and found that the mild TBI group displayed increased fractional anisotropy and decreased diffusivity on DTI within six days of injury (Wilde *et al.*, 2008). Another study using DTI compared 14 older children and adolescents with TBI (six with mild TBI; eight with moderate TBI) and 14 uninjured controls 6 to 12 months post-injury (Wozniak *et al.*, 2007). As a group, the TBI patients showed lower fractional anisotropy in three white matter regions, though differences between the mild TBI group and controls were only found in one of these regions. The value of functional MRI (fMRI) was also investigated recently in 28 concussed teenage and young adult athletes (aged 13 to 24 years) and 13 uninjured controls. Athletes who displayed an initial hyperactivation on fMRI were reported to be more likely to display a lengthier clinical recovery course (Lovell *et al.*, 2007).

The value of biomarkers after pediatric mild TBI has also been examined. In two small studies, serum and urine S100β levels were found to be sensitive to the effects of mild TBI (Piazza *et al.*, 2007; Pickering *et al.*, 2008). However, concentration levels were also elevated after extracranial trauma in both studies, highlighting the known lack of specificity of S100β to cerebral injury. In the largest existing study of biomarkers for pediatric TBI, the sensitivity of serum S100β, neuron-specific enolase (NSE), and myelin basic protein (MBP) were all examined (Berger *et al.*, 2007). The sample consisted of 152 children who sustained mixed severity TBI, the majority of which were classified as mild (though all children were admitted to a level I trauma center suggesting more severe mild injury). Higher biomarker concentrations were associated with worse outcome as measured by the Glasgow Outcome Scale. The negative predictive power of a normal biomarker concentration was quite high ($> 95\%$), whereas the positive predictive values were lower, ranging from 33% to 77% depending on the time of outcome measurement. These data suggest that biochemical markers may have value in identifying children at low risk of displaying a poor outcome after TBI but will likely classify a significant portion of children who will not develop problems as being at risk.

In comparison to research focused on the biomechanics or pathology of mild TBI, considerably less work has focused on intervention. Most of the research thus far has been conducted at the psychological level with adults. Early intervention focused on the provision of education, advice, and reassurance has the strongest empirical support of any medical or psychological treatment for mild TBI (Borg *et al.*, 2004b; Comper *et al.*, 2005; Mittenberg *et al.*, 2001; Ponsford, 2005; Snell *et al.*, 2008). In a pediatric population, Ponsford and colleagues (2001) documented improved outcomes three months post-injury after providing a child-friendly educational booklet soon after injury. Limited single-session treatment in adult populations within several weeks of injury has been found to be as effective as more intensive interventions (Paniak *et al.*, 1998, 2000).

Current and potential translational applications of neurobehavioral research

Neurobehavioral research on mild TBI has numerous potential translational applications. Traditionally, in many emergency department and primary care settings, post-injury cognitive status has been evaluated with a non-standardized mental status exam, which is unlikely to be consistently sensitive to the effects of mild TBI (Maddocks *et al.*, 1995; McCrea, 2001). Incorporating some of the tools used in neurobehavioral research to study cognitive and other postconcussive disruption may be helpful in documenting the acute post-injury presentation of injured children. The Standardized Assessment of Concussion

(SAC) is one such instrument and has been used with benefit in ED settings with adults (Naunheim *et al.*, 2008). Its value in children in a hospital setting remains to be established, though normative data exist down to six years of age (McCrea *et al.*, 2000).

Because neurobehavioral research suggests that acute postconcussive symptoms can be differentiable from neurocognitive status, an adequate post-injury evaluation in any health-care setting should also include ratings of postconcussive symptoms. These ratings should be collected from both children and parents, as their reports can be expected to differ to some extent. Research is clear in documenting that postconcussive symptoms are non-specific and many individuals report or display these types of symptoms in the absence of mild TBI. Consequently, another important role of the acute healthcare provider could be to record ratings of pre-injury symptoms for later reference.

Multiple studies suggest that mild TBI severity and a number of non-injury-related factors such as poorer family functioning, child psychiatric problems, and history of previous TBI may play a role in predicting outcomes, at least for some children (Goldstrohm & Arffa, 2005; Ponsford *et al.*, 1999; Yeates *et al.*, 2009). One potential application of these data in the healthcare setting would be to ensure that children exhibiting such risk factors receive more acute attention and are monitored more closely during follow-up to facilitate appropriate intervention. More generally, as already discussed, research with adults and one pediatric study suggest that the provision of education and reassurance soon after mild TBI may help to reduce morbidity. Healthcare personnel could therefore take steps to provide such intervention. No pediatric studies of which we are aware have investigated interventions aimed specifically at reducing persistent postconcussive symptomatology. However, cognitive-behavioral techniques would seem to have significant potential application, as they have shown beneficial effects in adult populations with mild TBI (Snell *et al.*, 2008) as well as in children without mild TBI who exhibit common postconcussive complaints such as headache and sleep problems (Gurr & Coetzer, 2005; Holden *et al.*, 1999; Sadeh, 2005).

Because no proven treatment for mild TBI exists, prevention efforts are clearly indicated. Neurobehavioral research has identified certain children who are known to be at risk for sustaining TBI. For example, children with attention-deficit/hyperactivity disorder (ADHD) are at more than twice the risk for sustaining TBI than their peers (Levin *et al.*, 2007; Max *et al.*, 2005; Schachar *et al.*, 2004; Yeates *et al.*, 2005a, b). Implementing TBI prevention programs for high-risk populations such as this may be particularly worthwhile. Sport-based research has also suggested that athletes who have sustained one concussion may be more likely to sustain future concussions, perhaps especially soon after the first injury (Guskiewicz *et al.*, 2000, 2003). Accordingly, healthcare practitioners should consider restricting pediatric athletes from play for a period of time after a concussion. Research does not provide an empirical answer as to exactly how long a young athlete should be restricted, but most consensus guidelines would recommend a restriction from high-risk sports at least until the athlete is asymptomatic and neuroimaging and neurological examination are unremarkable (Kirkwood *et al.*, 2006).

Obstacles to collaborative research efforts

Collaborative, cross-disciplinary research on mild TBI is not without obstacles. One fundamental hurdle is that bench scientists and clinicians operate from different paradigms. Basic science is reductionistic and focuses on accumulating knowledge from well-controlled experimentation. Clinical work is focused on the big picture of the whole child, who functions in an infinitely complex real world environment. Despite some notable exceptions, scientists and practitioners concerned with pediatric TBI have historically paid insufficient attention to making their findings relevant to those in other disciplines to allow for a bridging of this paradigmatic gap. Another challenge to any research involving clinicians is that many operate in settings focused on cost control, with substantial clinical demands. Unidirectional communication can result, whereby bench scientists publish their work but practitioners are too busy to digest it or too busy to publish their own observations and findings to close the bidirectional communication loop that underpins truly translational investigation.

Another obstacle to collaborative research is simply identifying children who have sustained mild TBI. A hefty percentage of patients who suffer such injury never seek medical care and so are unlikely to come to the attention of researchers in a manner that would allow for rigorous investigation. Collaborating with community healthcare professionals, athletic personnel, or school personnel to identify children who might not be brought to an academic medical center can be logistically daunting. Even in settings that readily support research, case detection is confounded by the lack of consensus in defining mild TBI, by poor ascertainment when using diagnostic codes retrospectively (Bazarian et al., 2006), and by the potential failure of acute care personnel to consistently recognize and document mild TBI (Powell et al., 2008).

Much of the research studying the physics and pathology of mild TBI has stemmed from non-human animals. Substantial cross-species differences in brain architecture, physiology, and behavior raise significant questions about the generalizability of these findings to humans. As many of these experimental studies involve injuring or sacrificing animals, ethical questions arise from this practice as well. Using dummy models to study biomechanics is without ethical problems, although precise modeling of young children's heads and brains lags behind models for adults. Using newer biomechanical methods such as real-time accelerometers to study pediatric mild TBI is also associated with challenges, because concussive injuries are less predictable in younger children and therefore less practically studied in this fashion.

Available techniques to study the pathophysiology of mild TBI in children are associated with their own set of problems. At this point, the primary means to obtain biomarkers is to collect either blood or cerebrospinal fluid; however, neither of these substances is collected during the routine clinical care of most patients with mild TBI. The study of biochemical markers through non-invasive means (e.g. MR spectroscopy) is complicated by the fact that many markers are exquisitely time sensitive, leaving little window for error in coordinating data acquisition. Though CT and MRI technologies are commonly used clinically after mild TBI, their use in research is less straightforward. CT, SPECT, and positron emission tomography (PET) scans are associated with small doses of radiation. Because children are more sensitive to radiation than adults and have a greater opportunity for expressing radiation damage over their lifetime, even the remote potential for developing radiation-related cancers needs serious attention when studies are conducted exclusively for research purposes. While MRI technologies are not associated with radiation exposure, they do require the subject to be very still in the confined space of a scanner, which limits their use in children who are particularly young, anxious, or have difficulty regulating their behavior.

As neuroscientific technologies become ever more powerful, incidental or unexpected findings will undoubtedly become more common. Current technologies used to study mild TBI allow for analysis of genes, neurochemistry, structural neuropathology, brain functioning, and behavior. How to handle findings that are not the focus of a mild TBI study, especially when those results have uncertain clinical significance, remains unclear. For example, a not insignificant number of healthy children will have incidental abnormalities on brain MRI (Kumra *et al.*, 2006). Whether to provide information about these results to families and, if so, how, is not yet settled. This situation is exacerbated when researchers from one discipline use tools from another without having experts available to interpret unexpected findings, making an interdisciplinary research team all the more valuable.

Finally, a number of unique obstacles arise because of the relatively small effect sizes and transience of many mild TBI-related problems. When attempting to measure outcomes, the sensitivity of many newer instruments is apt to outpace the specificity of the findings, leading to relatively high false positive rates and potentially unnecessary concern or resource expenditure if applied clinically. Some of the newer technologies will almost certainly contribute to the development of evidence-based criteria for documenting the effects of mild TBI. However, at present, most of the techniques remain investigational, and the eventual value of these tools will only be realized as they are coupled with data carefully tracking the natural recovery of mild TBI and are shown to add diagnostic or prognostic value unavailable from current sources.

Recommendations for promoting integrative and translational research

Mild TBI remains one of the most common and controversial of all medical and psychological conditions. Though much work is still needed, neurobehavioral and neuropsychological research has contributed substantially to understanding the expected outcomes of mild TBI in children. Available research suggests that complicated mild TBI (i.e. mild TBI associated with identifiable intracranial pathology) increases the risks for a variety of post-injury problems. After an uncomplicated mild TBI, most methodologically rigorous studies have found that neuropsychological outcomes are quite positive when measured by performance-based tests. When measuring postconcussive change via subjective symptom report, a minority of pediatric patients have been found to display persistent problems; the prevalence, incidence, and etiology of these difficulties remain poorly understood.

To further clarify the short- and long-term risks of mild TBI, researchers need to more clearly operationalize the defining features of mild TBI along multiple dimensions, including developing a terminology that can be shared across disciplines and specifying both the upper and lower threshold of mild injury. To optimize prevention efforts, more work will be needed to identify children most at risk for sustaining mild TBI, delineating risky behaviors and traits, and how pre-injury factors such as genetic status and cerebral reserve may influence outcomes and susceptibility to injury. Further exploration of the mechanisms by which injury and non-injury variables serve as risk or protective factors will also be necessary, and this work should be especially valuable in allowing for effective early identification and intervention for those youth and families at greatest risk. Evaluating the consequences of mild TBI in infancy and early childhood should be considered a pressing need, given the potential but as yet uncertain increased risks associated with injury early in development. In the virtual absence of randomized controlled trials examining mild TBI-related interventions in children, future behavioral and physiological research aimed at speeding recovery and reducing morbidity should also be prioritized.

To capture the often subtle and non-specific effects of mild TBI in children, study design and analyses will be crucial. Recruiting children soon after injury and following them prospectively over lengthier post-injury periods will be most helpful, as will the use of more recent statistical methods to model change over time and analyze outcomes at the level of the individual. Future research should also include control groups comprised of children sustaining equivalent injuries not involving the head, and incorporate measures of symptom validity to formally evaluate effort and response bias. Multi-dimensional assessment will be required when examining neurobehavioral outcomes as well, to account for differences that arise when examining results from performance-based tests as opposed to symptom reports. The functional effect of mild TBI and postconcussive symptoms warrants more attention, including the potential impact on school performance, family functioning, and healthcare utilization.

In the end, to add appreciably to the scientific knowledge base, future research will require a sophisticated conceptualization of mild TBI that recognizes that both the injury and post-injury problems occur in a dynamic, biopsychosocial context. Collaborative multidisciplinary studies integrating neurobehavioral outcome data with data from other levels of analysis (e.g. biomechanics, physiology) will undoubtedly advance the science of mild TBI much more readily than studies focused on any single injury dimension or any single discipline's perspective.

References

Agrawal, D., Gowda, N. K., Bal, C. S., Pant, M. & Mahapatra, A. K. (2005). Is medial temporal injury responsible for pediatric postconcussion syndrome? A prospective controlled study with single-photon emission computerized tomography. *Journal of Neurosurgery*, **102**, 167–171.

American Academy of Pediatrics (1999). The management of minor closed head injury in children. Committee on Quality Improvement, American Academy of Pediatrics. Commission on Clinical Policies and Research, American Academy of Family Physicians. *Pediatrics*, **104**, 407–415.

American Congress of Rehabilitation Medicine (1993). Definition of mild traumatic brain injury. Developed by the Mild Traumatic Brain Injury Committee of the Head Injury Interdisciplinary Special Interest Group of the American Congress of Rehabilitation Medicine. *Journal of Head Trauma Rehabilitation*, **8**, 86–87.

Anderson, V., Catroppa, C., Morse, S., Haritou, F. & Rosenfeld, J. (2005). Functional plasticity or vulnerability after early brain injury? *Pediatrics*, **116**, 1374–1382.

Asarnow, R. F., Satz, P., Light, R., Lewis, R. & Neumann, E. (1991). Behavior problems and adaptive functioning in children with mild and severe closed head injury. *Journal of Pediatric Psychology*, **16**, 543–555.

Asarnow, R. F., Satz, P., Light, R., Zaucha, K., Lewis, R. & McCleary, C. (1995). The UCLA study of mild closed head injury in children and adolescents. In S. H. Broman & M. E. Michel, eds. *Traumatic Head Injury in Children*. New York: Oxford University Press.

Ayr, L. K., Yeates, K. O., Taylor, H. G. & Browne, M. (2009). Dimensions of postconcussive symptoms in children with mild traumatic brain injuries. *Journal of the International Neuropsychological Society*, **15**, 19–30.

Barr, W. B. (2003). Neuropsychological testing of high school athletes. Preliminary norms and test–retest indices. *Archives of Clinical Neuropsychology*, **18**, 91–101.

Bauer, R. & Fritz, H. (2004). Pathophysiology of traumatic injury in the developing brain: an introduction and short update. *Experimental and Toxicology Pathology*, **56**, 65–73.

Bazarian, J. J., Veazie, P., Mookerjee, S. & Lerner, E. B. (2006). Accuracy of mild traumatic brain injury case ascertainment using ICD-9 codes. *Academic Emergency Medicine*, **13**, 31–38.

Belanger, H. G. & Vanderploeg, R. D. (2005). The neuropsychological impact of sports-related concussion: a meta-analysis. *Journal of the International Neuropsychological Society*, 11, 345–357.

Belanger, H. G., Curtiss, G., Demery, J. A., Lebowitz, B. K. & Vanderploeg, R. D. (2005). Factors moderating neuropsychological outcomes following mild traumatic brain injury: a meta-analysis. *Journal of the International Neuropsychological Society*, 11, 215–227.

Belanger, H. G., Vanderploeg, R. D., Curtiss, G. & Warden, D. L. (2007). Recent neuroimaging techniques in mild traumatic brain injury. *Journal Neuropsychiatry and Clinical Neuroscience*, 19, 5–20.

Berger, R. P., Beers, S. R., Richichi, R., Wiesman, D. & Adelson, P. D. (2007). Serum biomarker concentrations and outcome after pediatric traumatic brain injury. *Journal of Neurotrauma*, 24, 1793–1801.

Bijur, P., Golding, J., Haslum, M. & Kurzon, M. (1988). Behavioral predictors of injury in school-age children. *American Journal of Diseases in Children*, 142, 1307–1312.

Bijur, P. E., Haslum, M. & Golding, J. (1990). Cognitive and behavioral sequelae of mild head injury in children. *Pediatrics*, 86, 337–344.

Binder, L. M. & Rohling, M. L. (1996). Money matters: a meta-analytic review of the effects of financial incentives on recovery after closed-head injury. *American Journal of Psychiatry*, 153, 7–10.

Binder, L. M., Rohling, M. L. & Larrabee, J. (1997). A review of mild head trauma. Part I: meta-analytic review of neuropsychological studies. *Journal of Clinical Experimental Neuropsychology*, 19, 421–431.

Borg, J., Holm, L., Cassidy, J. D., *et al.* (2004a). Diagnostic procedures in mild traumatic brain injury: results of the WHO Collaborating Centre Task Force on Mild Traumatic Brain Injury. *Journal of Rehabilitation Medicine*, 43, 61–75.

Borg, J., Holm, L., Peloso, P. M. *et al.* (2004b). Non-surgical intervention and cost for mild traumatic brain injury: results of the WHO Collaborating Centre Task Force on Mild Traumatic Brain Injury. *Journal of Rehabilitation Medicine*, 43, 76–83.

Broglio, S. P., Ferrara, M. S., Macciocchi, S. N., Baumgartner, T. A. & Elliott, R. (2007). Test–retest reliability of computerized concussion assessment programs. *Journal of Athletic Training*, 42, 509–514.

Bruce, D. A. (1984). Delayed deterioration of consciousness after trivial head injury in childhood. *British Medical Journal (Clinical Research Education)*, 289, 715–716.

Carroll, L. J., Cassidy, J. D., Holm, L., Kraus, J. & Coronado, V. G. (2004a). Methodological issues and research recommendations for mild traumatic brain injury: the WHO Collaborating Centre Task Force on Mild Traumatic Brain Injury. *Journal of Rehabilitation Medicine*, 43, 113–125.

Carroll, L. J., Cassidy, J. D., Peloso, P. M. *et al.* (2004b). Prognosis for mild traumatic brain injury: results of the WHO Collaborating Centre Task Force on Mild Traumatic Brain Injury. *Journal of Rehabilitation Medicine*, 43, 84–105.

Cassidy, J. D., Carroll, L. J., Peloso, P. M. *et al.* (2004). Incidence, risk factors and prevention of mild traumatic brain injury: results of the WHO Collaborating Centre Task Force on Mild Traumatic Brain Injury. *Journal of Rehabilitation Medicine*, 43, 28–60.

Catroppa, C., Anderson, V. A., Morse, S. A., Haritou, F. & Rosenfeld, J. V. (2007). Children's attentional skills 5 years post-TBI. *Journal of Pediatric Psychology*, 32, 354–369.

Comper, P., Bisschop, S. M., Carnide, N. & Tricco, A. (2005). A systematic review of treatments for mild traumatic brain injury. *Brain Injury*, 19, 863–880.

Constantinou, M. & McCaffrey, R. J. (2003). Using the TOMM for evaluating children's effort to perform optimally on neuropsychological measures. *Child Neuropsychology*, 9, 81–90.

Courtney, J. C., Dinkins, J. P., Allen, L. M., III & Kuroski, K. (2003). Age related effects in children taking the computerized assessment of response bias and word memory test. *Child Neuropsychology*, **9**, 109–116.

Dennis, M., Yeates, K. O., Taylor, H. G. & Fletcher, J. M. (2006). Brain reserve capacity, cognitive reserve capacity, and age-based functional plasticity after congenital and acquired brain injury in children. In Stern, Y., ed. *Cognitive Reserve: Theory and Applications.* New York: Taylor and Francis.

Donders, J. (2005). Performance on the test of memory malingering in a mixed pediatric sample. *Child Neuropsychology*, **11**, 221–227.

Dunning, J., Batchelor, J., Stratford-Smith, P. *et al.* (2004). A meta-analysis of variables that predict significant intracranial injury in minor head trauma. *Archives of Disease in Childhood*, **89**, 653–659.

Dunning, J., Daly, J. P., Lomas, J. P., Lecky, F., Batchelor, J. & Mackway-Jones, K. (2006). Derivation of the children's head injury algorithm for the prediction of important clinical events decision rule for head injury in children. *Archives of Disease in Childhood*, **91**, 885–891.

Emanuelson, I. M., Von Wendt, L., Bjure, J., Wiklund, L. M. & Uvebrant, P. (1997). Computed tomography and single-photon emission computed tomography as diagnostic tools in acquired brain injury among children and adolescents. *Developmental Medicine and Child Neurology*, **39**, 502–507.

Esselman, P. C. & Uomoto, J. M. (1995). Classification of the spectrum of mild traumatic brain injury. *Brain Injury*, **9**, 417–424.

Ewing-Cobbs, L., Prasad, M. R., Landry, S. H., Kramer, L. & Deleon, R. (2004). Executive functions following traumatic brain injury in young children: a preliminary analysis. *Developmental Neuropsychology*, **26**, 487–512.

Faust, D., Guilmette, T. J., Hart, K., Arkes, H. R., Fishburne, F. J. & Davey, L. (1988a). Neuropsychologists' training, experience, and judgment accuracy. *Archives of Clinical Neuropsychology*, **3**, 145–163.

Faust, D., Hart, K. & Guilmette, T. J. (1988b). Pediatric malingering: the capacity of children to fake believable deficits on neuropsychological testing. *Journal of Consulting and Clinical Psychology*, **56**, 578–82.

Fay, T. B., Yeates, K. O., Taylor, H. G. Bangert, B., Dietach, A., Nuss, K. E., Rusin, J., & Wright, M. (in press). Cognitive reserve as a moderator of post-concussive symptoms in children with complicated and uncomplicated mild traumatic brain injury. *Journal of the International Neuropsychological Society.*

Ferrari, R., Obelieniene, D., Russell, A., Darlington, P., Gervais, R. & Green, P. (2002). Laypersons' expectation of the sequelae of whiplash injury. A cross-cultural comparative study between Canada and Lithuania. *Medical Science Monitor*, **8**, CR728–CR734.

Francis, D. J., Fletcher, J. M., Stuebing, K. K., Davidson, K. C. & Thompson, N. M. (1991). Analysis of change: modeling individual growth. *Journal of Consulting and Clinical Psychology*, **59**, 27–37.

Ganesalingam, K., Yeates, K. O., Ginn, M. S. (2008). Family burden and parental distress following mild traumatic brain injury in children and its relationship to post-concussive symptoms. *Journal of Pediatric Psychology*, **33**, 621–629.

Gefen, A., Gefen, N., Zhu, Q., Raghupathi, R. & Margulies, S. S. (2003). Age-dependent changes in material properties of the brain and braincase of the rat. *Journal of Neurotrauma*, **20**, 1163–1177.

Giza, C. C. & Hovda, D. A. (2001). The neurometabolic cascade of concussion. *Journal of Athletic Training*, **36**, 228–235.

Goldstrohm, S. L. & Arffa, S. (2005). Preschool children with mild to moderate traumatic brain injury: an exploration of immediate and post-acute morbidity. *Archives of Clinical Neuropsychology*, **20**, 675–695.

Gowda, N. K., Agrawal, D., Bal, C. *et al.* (2006). Technetium Tc-99m ethyl cysteinate dimer brain single-photon emission CT in mild traumatic brain injury: a prospective study. *American Journal of Neuroradiology*, **27**, 447–451.

Green, P. (2004). *Manual for the Medical Symptom Validity Test.* Edmonton: Green's Publishing.

Green, P. & Flaro, L. (2003). Word memory test performance in children. *Child Neuropsychology*, **9**, 189–207.

Gronwall, D., Wrightson, P. & McGinn, V. (1997). Effect of mild head injury during the preschool years. *Journal of the International Neuropsychological Society*, **3**, 592–597.

Guo, Z., Cupples, L. A., Kurz, A. *et al.* (2000). Head injury and the risk of AD in the MIRAGE study. *Neurology*, **54**, 1316–1323.

Gurr, B. & Coetzer, B. R. (2005). The effectiveness of cognitive-behavioural therapy for post-traumatic headaches. *Brain Injury*, **19**, 481–491.

Guskiewicz, K. M., Weaver, N. L., Padua, D. A. & Garrett, W. E., Jr. (2000). Epidemiology of concussion in collegiate and high school football players. *American Journal of Sports Medicine*, **28**, 643–650.

Guskiewicz, K. M., McCrea, M., Marshall, S. W. *et al.* (2003). Cumulative effects associated with recurrent concussion in collegiate football players: the NCAA Concussion Study. *Journal of the American Medical Association*, **290**, 2549–2555.

Guskiewicz, K. M., Marshall, S. W., Bailes, J. *et al.* (2005). Association between recurrent concussion and late-life cognitive impairment in retired professional football players. *Neurosurgery*, **57**, 719–726: discussion 719–726.

Guskiewicz, K. M., Mihalik, J. P., Shankar, V. *et al.* (2007). Measurement of head impacts in collegiate football players: relationship between head impact biomechanics and acute clinical outcome after concussion. *Neurosurgery*, **61**, 1244–1252: discussion 1252–1253.

Holden, E. W., Deichmann, M. M. & Levy, J. D. (1999). Empirically supported treatments in pediatric psychology: recurrent pediatric headache. *Journal of Pediatric Psychology*, **24**, 91–109.

Iverson, G. L. (2006). Complicated vs uncomplicated mild traumatic brain injury: acute neuropsychological outcome. *Brain Injury*, **20**, 1335–1344.

Iverson, G. L., Lange, R. T., Gaetz, M. & Zasler, N. D. (2007a). Mild TBI.

In N. D. Zasler, D. I. Katz & R. D. Zafonte, eds. *Brain Injury Medicine*. New York: Demos, 333–371.

Iverson, G. L., Zasler, N. D. & Lange, R. T. (2007b). Post-concussive disorder. In N. D. Zasler, D. I. Katz & R. D. Zafonte, eds. *Brain Injury Medicine*. New York: Demos, 373–403.

Jennett, B. (1989). Some international comparisons. In H. S. Levin, H. M. Eisenberg & A. L. Benton, eds. *Mild Head Injury*. New York: Oxford, 22–34.

Kashluba, S., Hanks, R. A., Casey, J. E. & Millis, S. R. (2008). Neuropsychologic and functional outcome after complicated mild traumatic brain injury. *Archives of Physical Medicine and Rehabilitation*, **89**, 904–911.

Keenan, H. T. & Bratton, S. L. (2006). Epidemiology and outcomes of pediatric traumatic brain injury. *Developmental Neuroscience*, **28**, 256–263.

Kelly, J. P. & Rosenberg, J. H. (1997). Diagnosis and management of concussion in sports. *Neurology*, **48**, 575–580.

Kirkwood, M. W., Yeates, K. O. & Wilson, P. E. (2006). Pediatric sport-related concussion: a review of the clinical management of an oft-neglected population. *Pediatrics*, **117**, 1359–1371.

Kumra, S., Ashtari, M., Anderson, B., Cervellione, K. L. & Kan, L. (2006). Ethical and practical considerations in the management of incidental findings in pediatric MRI studies. *Journal of the American Academy of Child and Adolescent Psychiatry*, **45**, 1000–1006.

Kurca, E., Sivak, S. & Kucera, P. (2006). Impaired cognitive functions in mild traumatic brain injury patients with normal and pathologic magnetic resonance imaging. *Neuroradiology*, **48**, 661–669.

Langlois, J. A., Rutland-Brown, W. & Thomas, K. E. (2006). *Traumatic Brain Injury in the United States: Emergency Department Visits, Hospitalizations, and Deaths*. Atlanta: Centers for Disease Control and Prevention, National Center for Injury Prevention and Control.

Levin, H. S., Hanten, G., Max, J. *et al.* (2007). Symptoms of attention-deficit/hyperactivity disorder following traumatic brain injury in children. *Journal of Developmental and Behavioral Pediatrics*, **28**, 108–118.

Levin, H. S., Hanten, G., Roberson, G. *et al.* (2008). Prediction of cognitive sequelae based on abnormal computed tomography findings in children following mild traumatic brain injury. *Journal of Neurosurgery: Pediatrics*, **1**, 461–470.

Lovell, M. R., Pardini, J. E., Welling, J. *et al.* (2007). Functional brain abnormalities are related to clinical recovery and time to return-to-play in athletes. *Neurosurgery*, **61**, 352–359: discussion 359–360.

Lu, P. H. & Boone, K. B. (2002). Suspect cognitive symptoms in a 9-year-old child: malingering by proxy? *Clinical Neuropsychology*, **16**, 90–96.

Maddocks, D. L., Dicker, G. D. & Saling, M. M. (1995). The assessment of orientation following concussion in athletes. *Clinical Journal of Sport Medicine*, **5**, 32–35.

Mailer, B. J., Valovich McLeod, T. C. & Bay, R. C. (2008). Healthy youth are reliable in reporting symptoms on a graded symptom scale. *Journal of Sport Rehabilitation*, **17**, 11–20.

Massagli, T. L., Michaud, L. J. & Rivara, F. P. (1996). Association between injury indices and outcome after severe traumatic brain injury in children. *Archives of Physical Medicine and Rehabilitation*, **77**, 125–132.

Max, J. E., Schachar, R. J., Levin, H. S. *et al.* (2005). Predictors of attention-deficit/ hyperactivity disorder within 6 months after pediatric traumatic brain injury. *Journal of the American Academy of Child and Adolescent Psychiatry*, **44**, 1032–1040.

McCaffrey, M. A., Mihalik, J. P., Crowell, D. H., Shields, E. W. & Guskiewicz, K. M. (2007). Measurement of head impacts in collegiate football players: clinical measures of concussion after high- and low-magnitude impacts. *Neurosurgery*, **61**, 1236–1243: discussion 1243.

McCrea, M. (2001). Standardized mental status assessment of sports concussion. *Clinical Journal of Sport Medicine*, **11**, 176–181.

McCrea, M., Kelly, J. & Randolph, C. (2000). Standardized Assessment of Concussion (SAC): *Manual for Administration, Scoring, and Interpretation*. Waukesha, WI: CNS Inc.

McCrea, M. A. (2008). *Mild Traumatic Brain Injury and Postconcussion Syndrome.* Oxford, UK: Oxford University Press.

McCrory, P. R. & Berkovic, S. F. (1998). Second impact syndrome. *Neurology*, **50**, 677–683.

McCrory, P., Johnston, K., Meeuwisse, W. *et al.* (2005). Summary and Agreement Statement of the 2nd International Conference on Concussion in Sport, Prague 2004. *Clinical Journal of Sport Medicine*, **15**, 48–55.

McDonald, C. M., Jaffe, K. M., Fay, G. C. *et al.* (1994). Comparison of indices of traumatic brain injury severity as predictors of neurobehavioral outcome in children. *Archives of Physical Medicine and Rehabilitation*, **75**, 328–337.

Mihalik, J. P., Bell, D. R., Marshall, S. W. & Guskiewicz, K. M. (2007). Measurement of head impacts in collegiate football players: an investigation of positional and event-type differences. *Neurosurgery*, **61**, 1229–1235: discussion 1235.

Mittenberg, W., Digiulio, D. V., Perrin, S. & Bass, A. E. (1992). Symptoms following mild head injury: expectation as aetiology. *Journal of Neurology, Neurosurgery, and Psychiatry*, **55**, 200–204.

Mittenberg, W., Wittner, M. S. & Miller, L. J. (1997). Postconcussion syndrome occurs in children. *Neuropsychology*, **11**, 447–452.

Mittenberg, W., Canyock, E. M., Condit, D. & Patton, C. (2001). Treatment of post-concussion syndrome following mild head injury. *Journal of Clinical and Experimental Neuropsychology*, **23**, 829–836.

Nacajauskaite, O., Endziniene, M., Jureniene, K. & Schrader, H. (2006). The validity of post-concussion syndrome in children: a controlled historical cohort study. *Brain and Development*, **28**, 507–514.

Naunheim, R. S., Matero, D. & Fucetola, R. (2008). Assessment of patients with mild concussion in the emergency department.

Journal of Head Trauma Rehabilitation, **23**, 116–122.

Oldershaw, L. & Bagby, R. M. (1997). Children and deception. In Rogers, R., ed. *Clinical Assessment of Malingering and Deception.* New York: The Guilford Press, 153–166.

Paniak, C., Toller-Lobe, G., Durand, A. & Nagy, J. (1998). A randomized trial of two treatments for mild traumatic brain injury. *Brain Injury*, **12**, 1011–1023.

Paniak, C., Toller-Lobe, G., Reynolds, S., Melnyk, A. & Nagy, J. (2000). A randomized trial of two treatments for mild traumatic brain injury: 1 year follow-up. *Brain Injury*, **14**, 219–226.

Peebles, R., Sabella, C., Franco, K. & Goldfarb, J. (2005). Factitious disorder and malingering in adolescent girls: case series and literature review. *Clinical Pediatrics (Philadelphia)*, **44**, 237–243.

Piazza, O., Storti, M. P., Cotena, S. *et al.* (2007). S100β is not a reliable prognostic index in paediatric TBI. *Pediatric Neurosurgery*, **43**, 258–264.

Pickering, A., Carter, J., Hanning, I. & Townend, W. (2008). Emergency department measurement of urinary S100β in children following head injury: can extracranial injury confound findings? *Emergency Medical Journal*, **25**, 88–89.

Ponsford, J. (2005). Rehabilitation interventions after mild head injury. *Current Opinion in Neurology*, **18**, 692–7.

Ponsford, J., Willmott, C., Rothwell, A. *et al.* (1999). Cognitive and behavioral outcome following mild traumatic head injury in children. *Journal of Head Trauma Rehabilitation*, **14**, 360–372.

Ponsford, J., Willmott, C., Rothwell, A. *et al.* (2001). Impact of early intervention on outcome after mild traumatic brain injury in children. *Pediatrics*, **108**, 1297–1303.

Powell, J. M., Ferraro, J. V., Dikmen, S. S., Temkin, N. R. & Bell, K. R. (2008). Accuracy of mild traumatic brain injury diagnosis. *Archives in Physical Medicine Rehabilitation*, **89**(8), 1550–1555.

Prins, M. L. & Hovda, D. A. (2003). Developing experimental models to address traumatic brain injury in children. *Journal of Neurotrauma*, **20**, 123–137.

Sadeh, A. (2005). Cognitive-behavioral treatment for childhood sleep disorders. *Clinical Psychology Review*, **25**, 612–628.

Sadowski-Cron, C., Schneider, J., Senn, P., Radanov, B. P., Ballinari, P. & Zimmermann, H. (2006). Patients with mild traumatic brain injury: immediate and long-term outcome compared to intra-cranial injuries on CT scan. *Brain Injury*, **20**, 1131–1137.

Satz, P. (2001). Mild head injury in children and adolescents. *Current Directions in Psychological Science*, **10**, 106–109.

Satz, P., Zaucha, K., McCleary, C., Light, R., Asarnow, R. & Becker, D. (1997). Mild head injury in children and adolescents: a review of studies (1970–1995). *Psychological, Bulletin*, **122**, 107–131.

Schachar, R., Levin, H. S., Max, J. E., Purvis, K. & Chen, S. (2004). Attention deficit hyperactivity disorder symptoms and response inhibition after closed head injury in children: do preinjury behavior and injury severity predict outcome? *Developmental Neuropsychology*, **25**, 179–198.

Schnebel, B., Gwin, J. T., Anderson, S. & Gatlin, R. (2007). In vivo study of head impacts in football: a comparison of National Collegiate Athletic Association Division I versus high school impacts. *Neurosurgery*, **60**, 490–495: discussion 495–496.

Schretlen, D. J. & Shapiro, A. M. (2003). A quantitative review of the effects of traumatic brain injury on cognitive functioning. *International Reviews in Psychiatry*, **15**, 341–349.

Shaw, N. A. (2002). The neurophysiology of concussion. *Progress in Neurobiology*, **67**, 281–344.

Snell, D. L., Surgenor, L. J., Hay-Smith, E. J. & Siegert, R. J. (2008). A systematic review of psychological treatments for mild traumatic brain injury: an update on the evidence. *Journal of Clinical and Experimental Neuropsychology*, **31**(1), 20–38.

Snoek, J. W., Minderhoud, J. M. & Wilmink, J. T. (1984). Delayed deterioration following mild head injury in children. *Brain*, **107** (Pt 1), 15–36.

Sosin, D. M., Sniezek, J. E. & Thurman, D. J. (1996). Incidence of mild and moderate brain injury in the United States, 1991. *Brain Injury*, **10**, 47–54.

Suhr, J. A. & Gunstad, J. (2002). "Diagnosis Threat": the effect of negative expectations on cognitive performance in head injury. *Journal of Clinical and Experimental Neuropsychology*, **24**, 448–457.

Suhr, J. A. & Gunstad, J. (2005). Further exploration of the effect of "diagnosis threat" on cognitive performance in individuals with mild head injury. *Journal of the International Neuropsychological Society*, **11**, 23–29.

Thibault, K. L. & Margulies, S. S. (1998). Age-dependent material properties of the porcine cerebrum: effect on pediatric inertial head injury criteria. *Journal of Biomechanics*, **31**, 1119–1126.

Valovich McLeod, T. C., Bay, R. C., Heil, J. & McVeigh, S. D. (2008). Identification of sport and recreational activity concussion history through the preparticipation screening and a symptom survey in young athletes. *Clinical Journal of Sport Medicine*, **18**, 235–240.

Wilde, E. A., McCauley, S. R., Hunter, J. V. *et al.* (2008). Diffusion tensor imaging of acute mild traumatic brain injury in adolescents. *Neurology*, **70**, 948–955.

Williams, D. H., Levin, H. S. & Eisenberg, H. M. (1990). Mild head injury classification. *Neurosurgery*, **27**, 422–428.

Wozniak, J. R., Krach, L., Ward, E. *et al.* (2007). Neurocognitive and neuroimaging correlates of pediatric traumatic brain injury: a diffusion tensor imaging (DTI) study. *Archives of Clinical Neuropsychology*, **22**, 555–568.

Yeates, K. O. (2000). Closed-head injury. In K. O. Yeates, M. D. Ris & H. G. Taylor, eds. *Pediatric Neuropsychology: Research, Theory, and Practice*. New York: The Guilford Press, 92–116.

Yeates, K. O., Taylor, H., Barry, C., Drotar, D., Wade, S. & Stancin, T. (2001). Neurobehavioral symptoms in childhood closed-head injuries: changes in prevalence and correlates during the first year postinjury. *Journal of Pediatric Psychology*, **26**, 79–91.

Yeates, K. O., Armstrong, K., Janusz, J. *et al.* (2005a). Long-term attention problems in children with traumatic brain injury. *Journal of the American Academy of Child and Adolescent Psychiatry*, **44**, 574–584.

Yeates, K. O. & Taylor, H. G. *et al.* (2005b). Neurobehavioural outcomes of mild head injury in children and adolescents. *Pediatric Rehabilitation*, **8**, 5–16.

Yeates, K. O., Taylor, H. G., Rusin, J. *et al.* (2009). Longitudinal trajectories of postconcussive symptoms in children with mild traumatic brain injuries and their relationship to acute clinical status. *Pediatrics*, **123**, 735–743.

Chapter

7

Very long-term neuropsychological and behavioral consequences of mild and complicated mild TBI: increased impact of pediatric versus adult TBI

Erik Hessen

This chapter is based on three recently published papers (Hessen *et al.*, 2006b; 2007; 2008) that describe different aspects of a 23-year follow-up of primarily mild traumatic brain injury (mTBI) of children and adults in Norway. There are two main purposes of this chapter: first to discuss possible long-term neuropsychological and behavioral consequences of pediatric and adult mild and complicated mTBI; and second to suggest areas of research that might increase our knowledge about neurobehavioral consequences and rehabilitation after pediatric complicated mTBI.

Introduction

Different studies suggest that the annual prevalence of mTBI ranges from 100 to 550 per 100 000 (Andersson *et al.*, 2003; Duus *et al.*, 1991; Evans, 1992; Thornhill *et al.*, 2000). Approximately 80% of all TBI are classified as mild (Kraus & Nourjah, 1988). Regarding pediatric TBI estimates of incidence vary from 185 per 100 000 (Kraus & Rock, 1989) per year to over 300 per 100 000 (British Society of Rehabilitation Medicine, 1988; House of Commons Select Committee on Health, 2001). Most of pediatric cases (81%–86%) are mTBI, about 8% are moderate, 6% are severe, and 5% are fatal (Kraus *et al.*, 1986; 1990). Even after mTBI, it is common to suffer acute cognitive problems, but most persons recover fully within three months (Dikmen *et al.*, 1986; Levin *et al.*, 1987; Rutherford *et al.*, 1978). However, there is a group of patients who continue to experience cognitive, behavioral, and neurological symptoms long after sustaining their injury (Dikmen *et al.*, 1989; Hartlage *et al.*, 2001). This group of symptoms is often referred to as postconcussive syndrome and characteristic symptoms are headache, fatigue, dizziness, depression, anxiety, irritability, and problems with concentration and memory. Occurrence of postconcussive syndrome varies across studies from 7%–8% (Binder *et al.*, 1997) to about 15% (Alexander, 1995). The etiology of this syndrome is uncertain and both organic (Hayes & Dixon, 1994; Miller 1996) and psychological causes (Bryant & Harvey, 1999; Lishman, 1988) have been suggested.

There is convincing evidence that mTBI causes acute disturbance of brain function. Functional MRI (fMRI) one month after injury commonly shows different patterns of

Pediatric Traumatic Brain Injury: New Frontiers in Clinical and Translational Research, ed. V. Anderson and K. O. Yeates. Published by Cambridge University Press. © Cambridge University Press 2010.

regional brain activation in response to working memory loads in patients with mTBI compared with controls (McAllister *et al.*, 1999). Likewise positron emission tomography (PET) within one month after injury shows abnormalities related to the injury (Bergsneider *et al.*, 2000). A troublesome question is whether these brain disturbances recover or if they persist over time post-injury. The cortical and global PET abnormalities that may be evident one month after mTBI are, for instance, not present in chronic post-concussional syndrome in which fronto-temporal hypometabolism is seen (Ruff *et al.*, 1994). This is a pattern that is not unique to brain injury and more frequently is seen in depression (Dolan *et al.*, 1994).

Long-term outcome after mTBI – previous studies

Whether neuropsychological dysfunction can endure after the acute recovery phase is also a topic for continued debate. Several review papers have been published on neuropsychological outcomes after mTBI. One meta-analytic paper by Binder *et al.* (1997) included eight studies at least three months after mTBI. A history of TBI rather than having symptoms was an important inclusion criterion in the reviewed papers. Only tests of attention were found to have an effect size greater than zero. An analysis by Zakzanis *et al.* (1999) that included 12 studies found moderate to large effect sizes for all seven cognitive domains included. The largest effect size was found for tests of abstraction/flexibility. This study included both clinic-based and unselected samples of participants, and did not specify time since injury. Thus, the larger effect sizes may reflect inclusion of clinic-based samples and subjects in the acute recovery phase. More recently, Belanger *et al.* (2005) published an analysis based on 39 studies to evaluate the impact of mTBI within nine neuropsychological domains. In prospective or unselected samples, the general analysis revealed no evidence of remaining neuropsychological dysfunction by three months after head injury. Interestingly, they found that patient-based samples and samples including subjects in litigation were associated with poorer cognitive function after mTBI.

Regarding children and adolescents, Satz *et al.* (1997) published a comprehensive review of studies (1970–1995) of mTBI. Based on a detailed analysis, they found no convincing evidence for adverse effects on academic or psychosocial outcome across the spectrum of mTBI. Neither did their analysis reveal clear indication of neuropsychological or cognitive impairments as a consequence of pediatric mTBI. However, in studies that included some-what greater injury severity, increasing variability in neuropsychological outcome was seen.

More recent studies also confirm findings of variable neuropsychological outcome after pediatric mTBI. Anderson *et al.* (2000b) found that children with mTBI had normal memory performance both in the acute and long-term phases of recovery. However, in 2001 the same group (2001) reported failure to make progress on tests of verbal fluency and story recall at 30 months follow-up after mTBI in childhood. A study by Roncadine *et al.* (2004) found poor performance on working memory tests three years after moderate and severe brain injuries in children, while the scores in the mTBI group were normal. Levin *et al.* (2004) examined working memory after mild, moderate, and severe TBI in children at 3, 6, 12, and 24 months after TBI. All the patients improved their working memory during the first year after injury regardless of age and severity of brain injury. Performance on working memory tasks worsened between 12 and 24 months in children with severe TBI. This pattern was not found in the mild to moderately injured children who continued to show improvement in working memory. In another, prospective longitudinal study, scores of academic achievement were registered from children 5–15 years of age from baseline to five years after mild to severe TBI

(Ewing-Cobbs *et al.*, 2004). Continual deficits were evident on all achievement scores in the children with severe brain injury compared with children with mild–moderate brain injury. Age-related differences in outcome were evident as the increase in arithmetic and reading scores was greater for the children injured at an older age, while deceleration in growth curves was evident for the younger children with both mild–moderate and severe brain injury. The authors consider that this result gives support to the hypothesis that early brain injury may disrupt the acquisition of certain academic skills.

A recent study tested the assumption that early TBI can have a more profound impact on development than injuries later in childhood (Anderson *et al.*, 2005). In a prospective longitudinal study, 122 children with TBI were divided according to age and injury severity. They were evaluated at 12 and 30 months post-injury. Additionally another group of children injured before 3 years of age was compared with these groups with respect to global intellectual ability. The study found a clear relationship between injury severity and cognitive function. For children with severe TBI, young age was associated with minimal recovery, and more favorable outcomes were observed among older children. Age was not related to outcome for children with mild or moderate TBI. However, infants (between 0 and 2.11 years) with moderate brain injuries showed poorer outcomes than older children with injuries of similar severity. The authors of this study concluded that children sustaining moderate or severe head injuries in infancy and early childhood are particularly vulnerable to lasting cognitive dysfunction.

Very few studies report on long-term outcome after mTBI. Vanderploeg *et al.* (2005) assessed long-term cognitive outcomes of self-reported mTBI eight years post-injury in a non-clinical community dwelling group of 254 male veterans. In this study no differences were found between the TBI group and any of two control groups on a standard cognitive test battery. Compared with control groups the TBI group had slight problems with attention in: (i) their lower rate of continuation to completion on Paced Auditory Serial Addition Test (PASAT); and (ii) in excessive proactive interference on the California Verbal Learning Test. The authors concluded that mTBI can have negative long-term cognitive outcomes on subtle aspects of attention and working memory.

Previously, only one study has reported on very long-term consequences (23 years) after mainly mTBI in children (Klonoff *et al.*, 1993). In this study severity of head injury was determined by the following variables: unconsciousness, neurological status, skull fracture, EEG, post-traumatic seizures, and a composite measure. The outcome was measured by physical complaints, subjective experience of intellectual function, and psychological/psychiatric problems. The study found that the severity of the TBI measured by a composite measure of these neurological variables was the best predictor of long-term sequelae. Measures of IQ in the post-acute phase were also found to be predictive of long-term outcome. Subjective sequelae specified as related to the TBI within the mentioned categories were reported by 31% of the study sample.

Very long-term neuropsychological and behavioral outcome after pediatric mTBI

Three recent papers have focused on very long-term neuropsychological and behavioral outcome 23 years after pediatric and adult mTBI (Hessen *et al.*, 2006b; 2007; 2008). These papers were based on a study conducted in Norway by Nestvold and Lundar (Nestvold *et al.*, 1988) in 1974/1975.

For a 12-month period Nestvold and Lundar (1988) conducted a prospective study of all patients referred to Akershus University Hospital due to injuries to the head, face, and neck. The study took place before the introduction of the Glasgow Coma Scale (Jennet & Bond, 1975). Therefore, severity of the head injuries was primarily classified according to length of post-traumatic amnesia (PTA). In addition, a comprehensive standardized form was completed by the surgeon on duty for each patient on arrival to the hospital: data were collected about the accident, transport to the hospital, and the clinical condition of the patient with special emphasis on questions regarding loss of consciousness and PTA. Also, within the first 24 hours all the patients underwent a neurological examination (Nestvold *et al.*, 1988). Before discharge from the hospital more information was collected from the patient and relatives regarding education, work, family and social relations, previous hospitalization, accidents, and illness. Information was also collected from the National Insurance about previous sick leave and previous diagnoses. Additional information that was recorded in standardized format included: intracranial hematomas, X-ray of the skull, face and cervical-columna, results from standard EEG recorded within the first 24 hours, and length of hospitalization. Based on the definition that mTBI is characterized by PTA < 24 hours Esselman & Uomoto, 1995, approximately 92% of the patients in the original sample had suffered mTBI.

Twenty-three years after the initial TBI, all patients still living in the counties of Oslo and Akershus ($n = 170$) were invited to take part in a neuropsychological and behavioral follow-up study. They received a letter explaining the purpose of the study and 70% (119 patients) accepted the invitation. The patients did not receive any payment or any kind of benefits for taking part other than undergoing a thorough neuropsychological/behavioral and neurological examination. The group of patients had previously never been assessed with neuropsychological tests except for sporadic psychological testing. At the time of the 23-year follow-up, none of the participants were seeking compensation in relation to their TBI. In addition to extensive neuropsychological and behavioral assessment, data were also collected about possible confounding post-injury factors, including somatic and mental health and highest level of education and current work status. With regard to pre-injury risk factors, supplementary data reported retrospectively by the pediatric patients were also included in the analysis: one patient (2.4%) was born with poor vision; three patients (7.3%) reported concentration problems at school; and three (7.3%) had problems with reading or writing prior to the head injury. Also, two of the patients (4.9%) had learning problems at school pre-injury. None of the patients was diagnosed with a pre-injury diagnosis of ADHD or conduct disorder. Baseline characteristics of the study patients are shown in Table 7.1.

Neuropsychological assessment

All the patients underwent conventional neuropsychological assessment. Intellectual ability was tested by six subtests from the Norwegian edition of the Wechsler Adult Intelligence Scale (Engvik *et al.*, 1978; Wechsler, 1955): information, similarities, digit span, picture arrangement, block design, and digit symbol. Data about attention and memory were obtained from eight subtests from the Norwegian edition of the Wechsler Memory Scale – Revised (Gimse, 1995; Wechsler, 1987): digit span forward and backward, visual memory span forward and backward, logical memory I and II, and visual reproduction I and II. Additional neuropsychological functions were assessed by six subtests from the Halstead–Reitan Neuropsychological Test Battery (Reitan & Wolfson, 1985): category test, trail making test, seashore rhythm test, finger tapping test, grooved pegboard test, and dynamometer test.

Table 7.1 Baseline characteristics of study patients

Demographic variables	All patients (n = 119)	Injury >15 yrs (n = 74)	Injury <15 yrs (n = 45)
Age at injury M (SD)	21.9(14.4)	29.8(12.8)	8.9(3.4)
Age at testing M (SD)	45.2(14.6)	53.2(13.0)	32.2(3.4)
Female n (%)	47(39)	26(35)	21(47)
Education (yrs) M (SD)	12.1(3.3)	11.3(3.3)	13.3(3.0)
Disability benefit n (%)	5(4)	3(4)	2(4)
Head injury variables			
PTA >½ hour n (%)	40(34)	25(34)	15(33)
PTA >6 hours n (%)	14(12)	10(14)	4(9)
PTA >24 hours (%)	9(8)	6(8)	3(7)
Skull fracture n (%)	10(8)	5(7)	5(11)
Path. neurol. signs >3 first 24 hrs n (%)	27(23)	15(20)	12(27)
EEG pathology first 24 hours n (%)	60(50)	36(49)	24(53)
PTA >½ hour + EEG pathology n (%)	27(23)	17(23)	10(22)
Headache first 24 hours n (%)	50(42)	27(37)	23(51)
Pre-traumatic risk factors			
Concussion n (%)	14(12)	9(12)	5(11)
Psychological or somatic illness n (%)	39(33)	30(41)	9(20)
Period with sick leave within 2 years before injury n (%)	27(23)	16(22)	11(24)
Post-traumatic risk factors			
Concussion n (%)	6(5)	2(3)	4(9)
No psychological/somatic illness n (%)	67(56)	35(47)	32(71)

Normative data

Normative data by Heaton *et al.* (1991) were used to score the tests of intelligence and neuropsychological function from the Wechsler Adult Intelligence Scale and from the Halstead–Reitan Neuropsychological Test Battery. The original normative data for the Wechsler Memory Scale – Revised (Wechsler, 1987) were used to score the memory tests used in this study. All test results were converted to T-scores, a normally distributed scale with a mean score of 50 and standard deviation (SD) of 10.

Behavioral assessment

Previous research indicates that postconcussive symptoms are more common after mTBI than persistent cognitive deficits. To study very long-term behavioral outcome and potential postconcussive symptoms after pediatric mTBI, the patients were assessed with the

Minnesota Multiphasic Personality Inventory-2. The MMPI/MMPI-2 is a standardized and widely used inventory for assessment of subjective experience of emotional, behavioral, and somatic symptoms (Butcher *et al.*, 1989). The inventory has shown potential for use in diagnostic assessment and rehabilitation planning of patients with brain injuries (Greene, 2000; Mark, 1979). Characteristic MMPI-2 findings in primarily mTBI patients are elevation of the subscales Hypochondriasis (Hs) and Hysteria (Hy) (Greiffenstein & Baker, 2001; Warriner *et al.*, 2003). Clear elevations on these scales is commonly seen in patients with actual physical disabilities and physical illness or in patients excessively concerned about physical symptoms (Greene, 2000). In studies of patients with a variety of TBI severity both Chervinsky *et al.* (1998) and Dearth *et al.* (2005) found that the Hypochondriasis (Hs), the Schizophrenia (Sc), and the Depression (Dep) scale were most likely to be elevated. High elevation of the Sc-scale may reflect difficulties in logic and concentration, which are symptoms frequently reported by brain-injured individuals (Greene, 2000).

The described findings indicate that MMPI-2 profiles in TBI may reflect typical post-concussive symptoms. Therefore, behavioral function was evaluated with the Norwegian Edition of *The Minnesota Multiphasic Personality Inventory–2* (MMPI-2) (Butcher *et al.*, 1989; 2004). Norwegian normative data were used to score data from the MMPI-2 (Butcher *et al.*, 2004). All test results were converted to T-scores. In addition to the ten standard clinical scales, the other MMPI-2 scales used in this study were chosen with special emphasis on typical postconcussive symptoms like depression, anxiety, and somatic complaints (Content scales and Harris–Lingoes subscales) (Butcher *et al.*, 1989).

Neuropsychological Deficit Index

A Neuropsychological Deficit Index was developed using all 24 subtests in the cognitive/neuropsychological test battery. Where participants achieved a T-score of 39 or below, they were given a score of 1 and, where T-scores were above 39, a score of 0 was allocated. This resulted in a deficit index score ranging from 0 to 24 for each patient. Thus a higher index score reflect greater neuropsychological impairment.

Testing and scoring procedures

An experienced specialist in clinical neuropsychology conducted the testing. In order to prevent biases in administration and scoring the examiner was blind to TBI characteristics until after examination and scoring were completed. Two experienced specialists in clinical neuropsychology, also blinded to patient characteristics, checked the test protocols independently to make certain correctness in scoring procedures.

Summary of results

In the first paper (Hessen *et al.*, 2006b) follow-up data 23 years after TBI were reported for the group of patients that were children or adolescents at the time of injury. All the patients with age 15 years or less at the time of TBI and still living in the counties of Oslo and Akershus (n = 62) were invited to take part in the follow-up study. Sixty-nine percent (45 patients) from this group consented to participate. The main purpose of the study was to investigate very long-term neuropsychological outcome after sustaining mainly mild pediatric TBI, and to analyze outcome in relation to different head injury variables and in relation to other risk factors for neuropsychological dysfunction.

Average length of education in the patient group was found to match the normal population mean in Norway for persons between 30 and 39 years. On the basis of both sets of normative data, the mean T-scores for all the 24 neuropsychological tests were in the normal range. The only neuropsychological measure with a borderline result, possibly indicating impairment from the normative mean, was the Category Test, which is a test of abstraction and concept formation. The group as a whole achieved a mean T-score close to 40. The finding of a borderline Category score is in line with the claim that higher cognitive function is more at risk after brain lesion than any single measure at lower levels (Reitan & Wolfson, 1985). However, the poor Category score did not correlate with any of the TBI severity measures. Thus, the results from this study are in agreement with most studies on long-term consequences of mTBI in children (Satz et al., 1997) in that no definite adverse effects were found with regard to neuropsychological and academic function.

Neuropsychological function in relation to various TBI variables, or in combination with variables, revealed interesting patterns. The occurrence of PTA for more than 30 minutes was the single most important diagnostic risk factor for poor scores in tests of attention and memory (Table 7.2). For the other TBI variables only sporadic relations were found with current neuropsychological function. Presence of several TBI variables combined may indicate a more complicated and severe head injury than presence of only one variable. This assumption was supported by fairly strong and significant findings of impaired neuropsychological function especially related to the combination of PTA above 30 minutes and pathological EEG within the first 24 hours after TBI (Table 7.2 and Fig. 7.1).

Pre- and post-injury risk factors for neuropsychological dysfunction in the patient group have been described above, but analysis revealed no significant influence of these factors on present neuropsychological function.

Most of the head injuries in this study were originally diagnosed as mild injuries. The diagnostic criteria for mTBI include a spectrum of severity from uncomplicated injuries with no signs of neurological damage to more complicated injuries with both PTA, loss of consciousness, EEG abnormalities, pathological reflexes, and fractures. The results from the described study suggest that complicated mild TBI in children and adolescents may cause persistent mild neuropsychological dysfunction.

In the second paper (Hessen et al., 2007) a total of 119 patients were included in the analysis. Seventy-four of these were above 15 years of age at the time of head injury. In addition, the 45 patients described in the Hessen et al. (2006b) study that sustained head injuries as children and adolescents, were included. On the basis of previous research about neuropsychological consequences of mild pediatric and adult head injuries, the following hypotheses were proposed: (i) that the group would show normal neuropsychological function; (ii) that TBI variables indicating complicated mild and moderate head injuries could be related to poorer neuropsychological outcome with emphasis of attention, learning, and memory; and (iii) that children sustaining mild and moderate head injuries would be more vulnerable to long-term neuropsychological problems than adults sustaining similar head injuries.

The main findings of this study were that pediatric mTBI variables (PTA >30 minutes or a combination of PTA >30 minutes and pathological EEG within 24 hours) could significantly predict poor neuropsychological outcome after 23 years while similar adult head injury variables could not predict poor neuropsychological outcome (Table 7.3 and Fig. 7.2). Second, that no pre- or post-injury risk factors for neuropsychological impairment could explain neuropsychological function in the total sample or in any of the two age

Table 7.2 Test results for the total study population expressed as T-scores and as Index scores

Tests	Total Group (N = 119) M(SD)	>3 neurol. signs (n = 27) No/Yes	Path. EEG 24 hrs post-injury (n = 60) No/Yes	Skull fracture (n = 10) No/Yes	PTA >30 min (n = 40) No/Yes	PTA >30 min + path. EEG (n = 27) No/Yes
Wechsler Adult Intelligence Scale (WAIS)						
Information	45.4(9.6)	46.3(9.1) / 44.1(9.3)	46.4(8.3) / 45.1(10.3)	45.6(9.2) / 48.6(10.0)	46.0(9.9) / 44.2(8.8)	45.7(10.0) / 43.9(7.9)
Similarities	52.7(13.2)	52.9(12.3) / 52.8(12.5)	52.6(11.5) / 52.8(14.0)	51.9(12.8) / 56.9(13.3)	53.1(13.5) / 51.8(12.5)	52.5(13.8) / 52.6(10.2)
Picture arrangement	51.7(10.6)	50.8(10.4) / 53.1(10.7)	51.6(9.8) / 51.5(11.1)	51.8(10.6) / 51.8(10.3)	51.2(10.6) / 52.7(10.6)	51.4(10.8) / 53.0(10.0)
Block design	51.6(11.4)	51.7(11.5) / 52.2(11.4)	51.9(11.0) / 51.6(12.3)	51.9(11.2) / 48.9(15.6)	52.1(10.5) / 50.5(13.1)	51.9(11.1) / 49.9(12.6)
Digit Span	45.0(7.3)	45.1(7.7) / 45.6(8.1)	46.1(8.2) / 44.5(6.4)	45.7(7.29) / 41.0(3.9)	45.7(7.4) / 43.8(7.1)	45.2(7.7) / 44.5(5.7)
Digit symbol	48.2(10.7)	48.1(11.1) / 47.7(11.3)	49.9(11.5) / 46.8(10.0)	48.1(10.9) / 49.8(9.5)	48.4(10.1) / 47.7(12.0)	49.3(10.9) / 44.5(10.1)*
Wechsler Memory Scale – Revised (WMS-R)						
Digit span: F	44.5(12.8)	44.8(14.5) / 46.3(9.9)	43.9(14.9) / 45.4(10.4)	45.2(12.5) / 41.0(12.0)	46.0(12.0) / 41.6(13.8)	44.0(13.5) / 46.0(9.9)
Digit span: B	46.9(11.8)	47.1(11.3) / 47.0(14.4)	48.1(12.2) / 46.2(11.8)	47.5(11.6) / 45.1(7.9)	47.9(11.2) / 44.9(12.8)	46.7(12.6) / 47.3(8.3)
Visual mem. span: F	49.9(9.8)	49.5(11.6) / 50.5(8.6)	50.3(9.4) / 49.8(10.7)	50.2(10.1) / 48.9(7.9)	50.9(9.4) / 47.9(10.5)	50.1(8.9) / 48.9(13.1)
Visual mem. span: B	50.9(9.8)	51.1(7.6) / 51.8(11.4)	52.1(10.3) / 49.6(8.9)	51.2(9.7) / 49.6(9.1)	51.9(10.7) / 48.8(7.2)	51.2(9.9) / 50.1(9.1)

Table 7.2 (cont.)

Tests	Total Group (N = 119) M(SD)	>3 neurol. signs (n = 27) No/Yes	Path. EEG 24 hrs post-injury (n = 60) No/Yes	Skull fracture (n = 10) No/Yes	PTA >30 min (n = 40) No/Yes	PTA >30 min + path. EEG (n = 27) No/Yes
Logical memory I	51.0(9.9)	52.2(9.5) 50.9(9.4)	51.2(9.1) 50.7(10.7)	51.1(9.4) 52.1(10.3)	51.4(10.0) 50.1(10.4)	50.9(10.0) 51.0(9.8)
Logical memory II	50.9(9.5)	51.8(9.4) 50.7(8.7)	51.9(8.3) 49.9(10.2)	51.2(9.1) 50.5(8.8)	51.4(10.0) 50.0(8.5)	51.1(9.8) 50.0(8.2)
Visual reproduct I	49.7(10.3)	48.3(10.1) 53.2(9.2)*	50.6(11.1) 49.7(9.6)	50.0(10.6) 50.8(7.9)	50.8(10.7) 47.6(9.4)	49.8(10.7) 48.6(8.3)
Visual reproduct II	47.7(10.3)	47.7(10.2) 50.1(8.6)	49.0(11.0) 46.6(9.6)	47.9(11.2) 46.3(10.2)	48.9(10.3) 45.4(10.1)	47.9(10.4) 46.6(10.0)
Halstead–Reitan Neuropsychological Test Battery (HRNB)						
Category test	41.0(9.1)	40.0(9.8) 41.8(7.7)	40.9(8.1) 40.7(9.7)	40.4(9.1) 45.8(7.8)	42.2(9.0) 38.9(8.9)	41.5(8.8) 38.3(9.1)
TMT-A	45.5(10.2)	46.0(10.3) 47.0(10.1)	47.5(11.1) 43.5(9.0)*	45.7(10.1) 45.5(7.2)	45.5(10.0) 45.4(10.9)	46.2(10.4) 42.9(9.4)
TMT-B	44.5(10.3)	44.3(10.9) 45.9(10.3)	45.8(11.1) 43.4(9.9)	44.3(10.0) 48.0(11.8)	45.0(10.1) 43.7(10.7)	44.5(10.6) 44.0(8.9)
Seashore rhythm	49.1(11.9)	49.5(12.7) 50.7(12.4)	48.8(11.8) 49.5(12.6)	49.8(12.2) 47.2(8.2)	49.9(12.1) 47.7(11.6)	44.8(11.9) 50.7(12.3)
Finger tapping D	53.1(10.6)	52.7(9.1) 54.6(13.3)	53.6(11.0) 53.3(9.8)	53.1(11.0) 55.0(9.1)	52.1(10.5) 54.9(10.7)	53.5(11.0) 51.0(9.3)
Finger tapping ND	54.6(11.3)	55.4(11.2) 53.8(13.9)	56.9(12.1) 53.4(9.5)	54.6(11.9) 56.3(8.9)	53.8(11.6) 56.4(10.7)	55.3(11.9) 51.8(8.7)

Dynamomet. D	51.0(9.1)	50.3(8.2)	49.8(8.0)	51.2(9.1)	51.7(9.1)	51.7(8.6)
		50.4(11.0)	51.2(9.2)	44.5(7.2)*	49.7(9.1)	47.9(10.5)
Dynamomet. ND	53.1(9.1)	52.4(6.8)	52.4(7.3)	53.8(9.4)	53.6(9.0)	53.6(8.8)
		54.3(12.6)	53.6(9.9)	47.3(6.3)*	52.0(9.3)	50.3(10.0)
Grooved Pegboard D	48.0(11.0)	47.4(11.4)	49.8(11.0)	48.6(10.9)	48.1(10.7)	48.8(11.4)
		48.7(10.1)	46.8(11.1)	47.7(10.8)	47.9(11.8)	45.0(9.3)
Grooved Pegboard ND	46.4(11.1)	45.9(11.3)	48.2(11.0)	47.6(10.7)	46.8(11.1)	46.7(11.6)
		48.1(10.1)	45.2(11.2)	42.3(9.6)	45.6(11.3)	44.6(9.0)
Neuropsychological Deficit Index. Range: 0–24						
Index score	4.3(3.9)	4.2(4.0)	3.9(3.7)	4.1(3.7)	4.0(3.7)	4.2(4.0)
		4.1(4.0)	4.6(4.1)	4.4(3.7)	4.8(4.2)	4.7(3.4)

Notes: *$P < 0.05$; **$P < 0.01$.

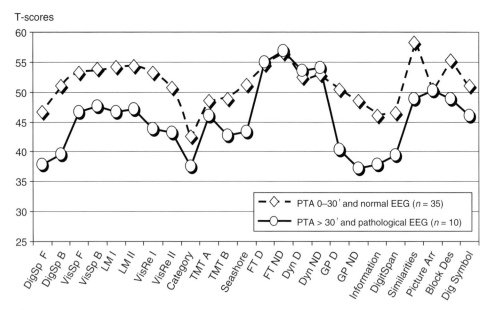

Fig. 7.1. PTA/pathological EEG – pediatric group.

categories, and finally that patients having sustained mild pediatric and adult TBI 23 years ago had normal neuropsychological function, average length of education, and lower percentage of subjects on disability benefit than normally expected for age-matched Norwegians (Table 7.2).

Our view was that the results support the notion of potentially differential impact of uncomplicated versus complicated mild traumatic brain injury. Furthermore, the results indicate that children sustaining complicated mild traumatic brain injury should be regarded as at potential risk of developing chronic mild neuropsychological dysfunction. These children may need to be monitored during childhood and adolescence about potential problems that should be addressed for optimal development. Based on the findings in the described study functions like attention, learning, and memory may be at particular risk of subnormal development.

In the third paper (Hessen *et al.*, 2008) 23-year follow-up data was based on the MMPI-2 profiles of patients 15 years or less at the time of TBI. Forty-one patients (66%) still living in the counties of Oslo and Akershus agreed to take part in the study and to answer the comprehensive MMPI-2 inventory. On the basis of previous research indicating that post-concussive symptoms are more common after mTBI than persistent cognitive deficits, and on the basis of the results described in the two previous papers on very long-term outcome after pediatric mTBI, our assumptions were: (i) that mild TBI would be associated with mean MMPI-2 scores in the normal range; and (ii) that participants with complicated mTBI would report increased symptoms compatible with postconcussive syndrome compared with the patients with less severe mTBI.

The main findings were that pediatric mTBI variables (skull fracture and a combination of PTA >30 minutes and pathological EEG within 24 hours) were associated with significantly elevated subscales on the MMPI-2 after 23 years (Tables 7.4 and 7.5 and

Table 7.3 Test results for adult and pediatric patients expressed as T-scores and as Index scores

	Injury >15 yrs (n = 74) M(SD)	PTA >30m. (n = 25) No/Yes	PTA >30 m. + path. EEG (n = 17) No/Yes	Injury <15 yrs (n = 45) M(SD)	PTA >30 m. (n = 15) No/Yes	PTA >30 m. + path. EEG (n = 10) No/Yes
Wechsler Adult Intelligence Scale (WAIS)						
Information	46.0(9.8)	46.1(11.2) / 45.8(6.3)	46.1(10.6) / 45.7(6.2)	44.3(9.2)	45.6(7.5) / 41.5(11.7)	46.1(7.5) / 37.8(11.8)**
Similarities	50.6(13.6)	50.4(15.0) / 51.0(10.2)	50.4(14.7) / 51.2(9.0)	56.1(11.9)	57.6(9.2) / 53.1(15.9)	58.2(9.2) / 48.9(17.2)*
Picture arrangement	52.6(11.2)	51.6(11.8) / 54.6(9.7)	52.2(11.7) / 54.0(9.4)	50.3(9.4)	50.7(8.3) / 49.7(11.6)	50.4(8.1) / 50.2(13.6)
Block design	50.2(9.2)	49.8(8.3) / 50.9(10.8)	50.0(8.0) / 50.7(12.9)	53.9(14.1)	56.0(12.4) / 49.8(16.6)	55.3(13.1) / 48.9(16.76)
Digit span	45.1(6.0)	45.0(6.5) / 45.4(4.9)	44.9(6.3) / 46.0(5.0)	44.9(9.2)	46.7(8.7) / 41.2(9.3)	46.5(8.6) / 39.4(9.2)*
Digit symbol	47.1(9.7)	47.0(8.4) / 47.3(12.2)	48.1(9.6) / 43.6(9.5)	49.9(12.1)	50.6(12.4) / 48.3(11.8)	51.0(12.2) / 46.0(11.4)
Wechsler Memory Scale – Revised (WMS-R)						
Digit span: F	44.3(11.6)	45.1(10.3) / 42.8(13.9)	43.7(11.9) / 46.5(10.5)	44.7(14.6)	47.3(14.5) / 39.5(14.0)	46.7(13.9) / 37.8(15.8)
Digit span: B	45.8(9.9)	45.4(10.9) / 46.8(7.7)	45.5(10.4) / 47.0(8.3)	48.5(14.3)	51.9(10.7) / 41.7(18.3)*	51.1(10.8) / 39.6(21.2)*
Visual mem. span: F	48.8(8.7)	48.8(9.4) / 48.6(7.1)	48.3(9.0) / 50.2(7.4)	51.8(11.3)	54.3(8.3) / 46.7(14.7)*	53.2(8.3) / 46.7(18.1)
Visual mem. span: B	49.9(9.3)	50.2(10.4) / 49.3(6.8)	50.0(9.7) / 49.6(7.9)	52.5(11.4)	54.8(9.3) / 48.0(8.1)*	53.9(10.3) / 47.6(9.6)

Table 7.3 (cont.)

	Injury >15 yrs (n = 74) M(SD)	PTA >30 m. (n = 25) No/Yes	PTA >30 m. + path. EEG (n = 17) No/Yes	Injury <15 yrs (n = 45) M(SD)	PTA >30 m. (n = 15) No/Yes	PTA >30 m. + path. EEG (n = 10) No/Yes
Logical memory I	50.0(9.4)	49.4(9.4) / 51.2(9.6)	49.9(9.2) / 50.4(10.4)	52.6(10.6)	54.8 (9.3) / 48.2(11.8)*	54.3(9.4) / 46.6(12.6)*
Logical memory II	49.8(9.2)	49.4(9.9) / 50.7(7.7)	49.9(9.6) / 49.6(8.2)	52.8(9.8)	54.8(9.2) / 48.9(10.0)	54.4(8.9) / 47.2(11.1)*
Visual Reproduct. I	48.9(10.5)	49.2(11.2) / 48.2(9.4)	49.0(11.0) / 48.6(9.2)	51.2(10.0)	53.5(9.4) / 46.5(9.7)*	53.3(9.5) / 43.8(7.9)**
Visual Reproduct. II	46.9(10.1)	47.3(10.3) / 46.1(9.9)	47.3(10.4) / 45.7(9.2)	49.0(10.6)	51.4(9.9) / 44.3(10.6)*	50.7(9.9) / 43.2(11.5)*
Halstead–Reitan Neuropsychological Test Battery (HRNB)						
Category test	40.8(9.2)	41.9(9.2) / 38.5(8.9)	41.4(9.4) / 38.5(8.4)	41.5(9.0)	42.5(8.8) / 39.5(9.2)	42.6(8.3) / 37.6(10.6)
TMT-A	44.0(9.1)	44.2(9.3) / 43.5(8.7)	44.6(9.3) / 41.7(7.9)	48.0(11.6)	47.8(10.7) / 48.4(13.6)	48.6(10.7) / 46.0(14.9)
TMT-B	42.7(9.2)	42.4(9.2) / 43.4(9.3)	42.6(9.7) / 42.9(7.5)	47.5(11.3)	49.2(10.2) / 44.1(13.1)	48.9(10.0) / 42.8(14.8)
Seashore rhythm	48.9(12.2)	48.5(12.4) / 49.8(11.9)	47.9(12.0) / 52.4(12.4)	49.4(11.6)	52.1(11.2) / 44.1(10.6)*	51.2(10.8) / 43.4(12.7)
Finger tapping D	52.1(11.0)	51.1(11.7) / 53.9(9.7)	52.4(11.6) / 50.9(9.2)	54.7(9.8)	53.8(8.2) / 56.2(12.4)	54.7(9.0) / 54.9(12.8)
Finger tapping ND	53.5(12.6)	52.5(13.0) / 55.4(11.7)	54.0(13.4) / 51.8(9.7)	56.6(8.6)	55.9(8.5) / 58.1(8.7)	56.5(8.7) / 56.9(8.6)

Dynamometer D	50.0(9.2)	51.2(9.4)	47.7(8.4)	50.4(9.0)	48.7(9.7)	52.6(9.0)	52.4(8.9)	53.0(9.5)	52.4(8.4)	53.5(11.3)
Dynamometer ND	53.0(10.0)	54.2(9.9)	50.4(9.8)	53.4(9.7)	51.3(11.2)	53.2(7.6)	52.6(7.4)	54.5(8.1)	53.0(7.4)	54.1(8.6)
Grooved pegboard D	47.9(10.3)	47.1(10.6)	49.4(9.8)	47.8(10.9)	48.2(8.4)	48.3(12.3)	49.7(11.0)	45.4(14.5)	50.5(11.6)	40.4(11.9)*
Grooved pegboard ND	46.6(10.9)	46.1(11.2)	47.6(10.3)	46.6(11.3)	46.5(9.7)	46.0(11.6)	47.9(11.0)	42.2(12.4)	48.5(11.4)	37.2(7.5)**
Neuropsychological Deficit Index. Range: 0–24										
Index score	4.4(3.6)	4.6(3.3)	4.0(2.9)	4.5(3.8)	4.0(3.1)	4.1(4.4)	3.0(3.0)	6.1(5.7)*	3.0(2.9)	7.5(6.4)**

Notes: *$P < 0.05$; **$P < 0.01$.

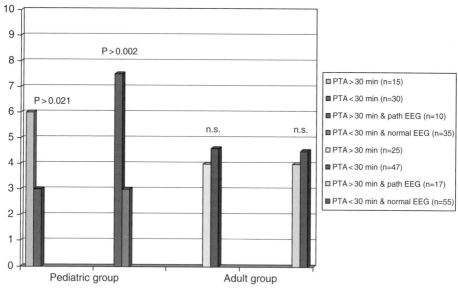

Fig. 7.2. Number of tests out of 24 in the impaired range (T-score ≤ 39).

Figs 7.3 and 7.4). Most of the elevated subscales measure somatic complaints, fatigue, worry about health problems, and negative experience of work capability. Second we found that no pre- or post-injury risk factors for neuropsychological impairment or postconcussional symptoms could explain the results on the MMPI-2, and third that patients having sustained mild pediatric TBI 23 years previously had mean scores on the MMPI-2 very close to the normative mean.

For children with complicated mild head injuries, more pathological scores, typical for mild postconcussive syndrome were evident on the MMPI-2. The findings suggest that children and adolescents sustaining complicated mTBI may be at risk of developing subtle chronic symptoms typical for postconcussive syndrome. As with the cognitive outcomes described above, the results give support for the notion of potentially differential impact of uncomplicated versus complicated mild traumatic brain injury. The children with complicated mild TBI may therefore need to be monitored during childhood and adolescence about potential problems that should be addressed for most favorable development. Based on our findings these children and adolescents may have a slightly increased occurrence of different somatic complaints and fatigue.

Discussion

The key strengths of the 23-year follow-up study of mild TBI in children and adults are that this is a prospective study and that previous studies have not been able to systematically follow a sample of mild pediatric and adult head injuries for such a long period, and attain equally good retention rates. Additionally, no previous study has been able to demonstrate no differences between initial and follow-up samples, and no other study of very long-term outcome of mTBI has administered a comprehensive face-to-face neuropsychological battery and a comprehensive, psychometrically robust personality inventory as an outcome measure.

Table 7.4 MMPI-2 Clinical Scales for the pediatric patients (T-scores and as Index scores)

	Total sample (N = 41) M(SD)	>2 neurol. signs (n = 13) No/Yes	Path. EEG (n = 21) No/Yes	Skull fracture (n = 4) No/Yes	PTA>30 min (n = 12) No/Yes	PTA>30 min + path. EEG (n = 8) No/Yes
MMPI-2 Clinical Scales						
L	55.3(11.0)	55.6(12.3) 58.5(9.0)	50.5(10.3) 54.2(11.7)	54.4(10.9) 56.8(9.5)	55.7(10.4) 54.3(12.8)	56.3(10.8) 52.5(12.0)
F	51.7(10.8)	51.4(9.4) 46.5(5.0)	48.8(7.8) 54.4(12.6)	50.7(10.5) 55.0(10.7)	49.8(8.3) 56.2(14.9)	49.2(8.0) 61.1(16.0)**
K	51.3(10.5)	50.6(11.0) 55.4(9.4)	50.8(10.3) 51.7(10.9)	50.2(10.9) 58.3(3.2)	52.7(10.8) 47.8(9.2)	52.8(10.2) 46.0(10.9)
Hypochondriasis (Hs)	56.8(12.1)	55.7(13.7) 54.9(10.4)	52.6(11.1) 60.8(11.9)*	54.9(11.2) 69.5(13.3)**	55.5(8.8) 60.1(17.9)	55.1(10.6) 62.1(16.5)
Depression (D)	54.4(11.6)	54.6(12.6) 52.3(8.7)	51.8(11.4) 56.9(11.5)	52.9(11.3) 61.5(8.6)	53.8(11.8) 55.9(11.5)	53.3(11.6) 58.3(12.4)
Hysteria (Hy)	54.9(14.8)	54.7(16.7) 52.2(9.9)	50.6(13.3) 59.1(15.2)	51.7(12.4) 74.8(15.9)**	52.6(11.3) 60.6(20.4)	52.4(12.8) 62.6(19.5)
Psychopathic deviate (Pd)	47.9(11.2)	47.3(13.5) 46.0(7.2)	48.4(8.5) 47.5(13.4)	46.6(11.0) 57.0(11.7)	47.0(11.1) 50.2(11.6)	46.6(10.8) 51.8(12.4)
Masculinity–femininity (Mf)	46.1(10.9)	45.2(12.0) 45.5(8.8)	43.6(8.9) 48.4(12.3)	45.9(10.9) 45.5(11.4)	47.9(11.5) 41.7(8.1)	46.0(11.2) 44.0(8.0)
Paranoia (Pa)	51.4(9.6)	52.0(9.1) 48.2(9.6)	50.9(11.4) 51.9(7.7)	50.6(9.5) 54.3(9.9)	51.3(9.2) 51.6(10.8)	51.0(10.0) 52.4(8.6)

Table 7.4 (cont.)

	Total sample (N = 41) M(SD)	>2 neurol. signs (n = 13) No/Yes	Path. EEG (n = 21) No/Yes	Skull fracture (n = 4) No/Yes	PTA>30 min (n = 12) No/Yes	PTA>30 min + path. EEG (n = 8) No/Yes
Psychasthenia (Pt)	51.6(11.6)	52.5(13.1) / 47.2(6.5)	50.5(12.2) / 52.6(11.3)	50.9(11.8) / 54.5(4.5)	52.1(11.3) / 50.4(12.7)	51.0(11.3) / 52.8(13.9)
Schizophrenia (Sc)	52.3(10.2)	52.0(9.8) / 48.8(8.8)	50.6(9.4) / 54.0(10.7)	51.1(9.9) / 60.0(5.5)	52.4(9.3) / 52.1(12.4)	51.5(9.2) / 53.5(13.4)
Hypomania (Ma)	49.3(11.1)	47.8(8.5) / 46.4(7.7)	50.0(9.6) / 48.9(12.5)	50.4(11.4) / 42.3(6.9)	49.4(11.0) / 49.0(11.7)	48.2(9.2) / 49.5(12.0)
Social Introversion (Si)	48.7(9.4)	48.9(10.8) / 45.9(7.8)	47.9(10.2) / 49.4(8.9)	48.6(9.7) / 47.8(9.5)	48.9(9.6) / 48.0(9.4)	48.0(9.6) / 50.9(9.5)

Notes: $^*P < 0.05$; $^{**}P < 0.01$.

Table 7.5 MMPI-2 Harris–Lingoes Subscales for the pediatric patients (T-scores)

	Total group (N = 41) M (SD)	>2 neurol. signs (n = 13) No/Yes	Path. EEG (n = 21) No/Yes	Skull fracture (n = 4) No/Yes	PTA>30 min (n = 12) No/Yes	PTA>30 min +path. EEG (n = 8) No/Yes
MMPI-2 Harris-Lingoes Subscales						
Subjective depression (D1)	51.3(12.0)	52.5(12.9) / 46.0(7.7)	49.4(13.3) / 53.1(10.7)	50.5(12.2) / 53.3(7.4)	51.0(12.9) / 52.0(10.1)	50.0(12.3) / 54.6(10.3)
Psychomotor retardation (D2)	51.0(8.9)	50.7(8.7) / 51.1(7.7)	50.8(9.0) / 51.1(9.1)	50.1(7.8) / 52.0(10.7)	52.0(10.0) / 48.4(5.1)	51.8(9.7) / 48.0(5.1)
Physical malfunction (D3)	56.9(13.2)	57.4(13.7) / 54.2(12.2)	52.6(10.6) / 61.0(14.3)*	55.4(12.7) / 63.5(16.0)	54.3(11.9) / 63.0(14.8)	54.0(11.6) / 68.3(14.6)**
Mental dullness (D4)	54.8(11.3)	55.4(10.3) / 50.5(7.4)	52.9(11.4) / 56.5(11.1)	54.0(10.8) / 57.8(4.6)	54.9(11.1) / 54.5(12.2)	53.8(10.9) / 57.0(13.2)
Brooding (D5)	54.5(10.6)	54.8(9.9) / 50.6(8.5)	53.9(11.5) / 55.1(9.8)	54.6(10.7) / 54.0(12.4)	54.8(10.8) / 53.8(10.3)	54.4(10.5) / 54.0(11.9)
MMPI-2 Harris-Lingoes Subscales						
Lassitude – Malaise (Hy3)	54.2(13.3)	55.8(14.4) / 47.2(7.3)	51.5(11.7) / 56.8(14.5)	52.6(12.6) / 64.3(15.3)	52.1(11.6) / 59.1(16.3)	51.5(11.3) / 61.6(16.3)*
Somatic complaints (Hy4)	54.4(13.8)	52.1(12.1) / 51.2(13.4)	50.8(11.4) / 57.9(15.2)	52.9(13.9) / 64.3(8.4)	52.5(11.4) / 59.2(18.0)	51.8(11.8) / 63.4(18.1)*

Notes: *$P < 0.05$; **$P < 0.01$.

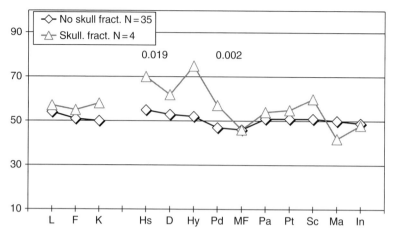

Fig. 7.3. MMPI-2 clinical scales – T-scores.

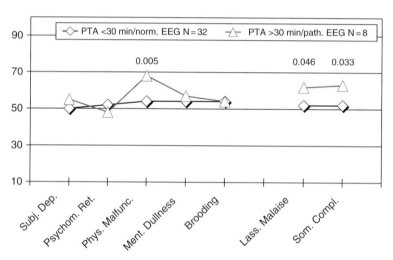

Fig. 7.4. MMPI-2 Harris–Lingoes subscales of selected somatic and depressive complaints – T-scores.

A limitation with the study is the lack of a matched control group. A substitute for this with regard to the neuropsychological part of the study is the use of standardized tests with two different sets of available normative data (Heaton *et al.*, 1991; Wechsler, 1987). These normative data are being used in ordinary clinical practice as well as in research in Norway. Several recent studies support the validity of these norms in Norway (Egeland *et al.*, 2005; 2006; Lund *et al.*, 2005). In addition, the study was also able to compare the TBI group with national data with respect to functional domains such as education, employment, and need for disability services. In this respect, it is important to note that, overall, mild TBI victims do not present differently in these domains from the normal population in the long-term post-injury. With regard to the behavioral part of the study, Norwegian normative data were used to score the results from the MMPI-2 (Butcher *et al.*, 2004).

The original prospective study was conducted before the introduction of the Glasgow Coma Scale (GCS) and head injury severity was determined by length of PTA. This may be considered a limitation because it is unclear if the sample meet the current criteria for mTBI with a GCS score of 13–15. However, whether GCS is a reliable indicator of mTBI severity may be questioned. It is generally recognized that GCS was not designed to measure the milder types of injury, and is not considered to be sensitive in mild injury (Rees, 2003). It is also of importance to note, that in mild TBI, clinical outcome has been found to correlate better with PTA than GCS (Dikmen & Levin, 1993; Van der Naalt et al., 1999a,b). On the basis of this, an extended GCS (GCS-E) has been proposed which blends amnesia with the GCS criteria in the identification of mTBI (Nell et al., 2000). In addition, others simply advocate the use of PTA as a severity measure for the milder degrees of injury (Rees, 2003).

The finding that some of the patients in the pediatric group had more neuropsychological deficits and more elevated subscales on the MMPI-2 than normally expected may suggest that this group included persons with more severe head injury than mild TBI. All the patients were part of a prospective study that involved more comprehensive assessment and diagnosis at admission to the hospital than is common in ordinary clinical practice. Only 8% were diagnosed with moderate to severe injuries, based on length of PTA. The neuropsychological function of these patients 23 years post-injury was in the normal range and was not found to differ significantly from the patients with more severe injuries within the mild spectrum (PTA between 30 minutes and 24 hours). Also, the patient group had an average length of education and a lower percentage of subjects on disability benefit than normally expected for demographically matched Norwegians. This clearly suggests that overall performance has not been compromised, providing no evidence to support a suggestion that the group consisted of cases with more severe head injuries.

Another concern might be that the pediatric group and the adult group differed in terms of pre-injury somatic and psychological conditions. This variable included a wide variety of common somatic and psychological conditions. As expected, the adult group with a mean age of 29.8 years when they sustained their TBI had experienced more of these conditions in their lives than the pediatric group with a mean age of 8.9 years. However, patients characterized by this variable in the different age groups showed no differences in neuropsychological function. Neither did this variable predict neuropsychological impairment in the total patient sample or in any of the two age categories.

The original prospective TBI study was conducted in 1973–74 before neuroimaging was available. Even today, neuroimaging is only applied clinically in a small proportion of TBI presentations. It is probable that several of the study patients would have shown some evidence of neuropathology and comparison of current neuropsychological and behavioral function with data from neuroimaging would have been of particular interest.

The described follow-up is primarily of a mild TBI group. There is a general agreement about neuropsychological and behavioral symptoms in the acute stages after mild TBI, but most studies find good recovery after a few months (Dikmen et al., 1986; Levin et al., 1987; Rutherford et al., 1978; Satz et al., 1997; Wrightson & Gronwall, 1999). Some studies suggest slight long-term neuropsychological deficits after both pediatric and adult mild TBI (Anderson et al., 2001; Ewing-Cobbs et al., 2004; Klonoff et al., 1993; Vanderploeg et al., 2005), but the long-term neuropsychological outcome of mild TBI remains a controversial issue (Lezak et al., 2004). While most patients recover from the common initial cognitive symptoms, the recovery from subjective symptoms known as postconcussive syndrome (Alexander, 1995) is more uncertain, as several studies have documented such symptoms long after injury (Anderson et al., 2000a; Binder et al., 1997; Satz et al., 1997). The results from the present study indicate that pediatric and adult mTBI in general have good long-term neuropsychological and behavioral recovery. However, mild neuro-psychological deficits in the younger sample that sustained head injuries characterized by either PTA >30 minutes or both PTA >30 minutes and pathological EEG within 24 hours, suggest that long-term neuropsychological recovery after pediatric mTBI characterized by these variables is less clear. Neither injury severity or non-injury factors could explain these group differences, as the adult and pediatric groups were very similar in both these domains. This finding suggests possible differential vulnerability after brain injury in children and adults and also raises questions about the diagnostic criteria of mild head injury, which include a rather wide spectrum of head injury severity. Clearly, elevated subscales on the MMPI-2 measuring somatic complaints, fatigue, worry about health problems, and negative experience of work capability in patients who sustained head injuries characterized by either skull fractures or a combination of both PTA >30 minutes and pathological EEG within 24 hours as children, also suggest that long-term behavioral recovery after pediatric mTBI characterized by these variables is uncertain.

A widespread belief among professionals working with brain-injured patients is that younger patients have better prognosis than older patients (Hux et al., 2000; Johnson et al., 2003). A common explanation for this belief is the idea of the "plasticity" of the young brain. However, recent research indicates that early generalized brain insult may have a profound impact on development (Anderson et al., 2000; Eslinger et al., 1992; Giedd et al., 1999). These suggestions are largely untested. One exception from this is a study by Anderson et al. (2005), where it was found that children with severe head injuries in early childhood or moderate injuries in infancy may be more vulnerable to enduring cognitive deficits than children sustaining similar injuries later in childhood. The notion of increased vulnerability to brain injury at a younger age may also have relevance for pediatric mTBI versus adult mTBI, especially with respect to the more severe head injuries within the spectrum of mild head injury. A comparison of very long-term outcome of similar pediatric and adult mTBI has not been done before this study. However, one recent study may have relevance for this topic. In a large study of "easy-to-treat" epilepsy patients who had been seizure free for two years or more, Hessen et al. (2006a) found that, in patients with idiopathic generalized epilepsy (IGE), seizure debut before 18 years of age was a powerful and significant predictor of neuropsychological impairment compared with later onset of seizures. As the seizure-free IGE patients usually have short duration of active epilepsy and have no confounding variables from cerebral lesions, this study has similarities with the present study, and does suggest that mild cerebral dysfunction IGE may have a more negative impact on neuropsychological function with early debut in childhood and adolescence than with debut in adulthood.

The diagnostic criteria of mild TBI are a key problem with regard to both short- and long-term neuropsychological and behavioral outcome. The most commonly used definition by the American Congress of Rehabilitation Medicine (Esselman & Uomoto, 1995) includes a broad range of trauma variables and severity with the possibility of inconsistent outcome: (1) any period of loss of consciousness (LOC) of <30 minutes and Glasgow Coma Scale score (GCS) of 13–15 after this period of LOC; (2) any loss of memory for events immediately before or after the accident, with PTA of <24 hours; (3) any alteration in mental state at the time of the accident (e.g. feeling dazed, disoriented, or confused); or (4) focal neurological deficit(s) that may or may not be transient. Another commonly accepted definition of mTBI is a Glasgow Coma Scale (GCS) (Jennet & Bond, 1975) score of 13–15. This is also a definition with problematic accuracy as heterogeneity in pathophysiology may occur in patients with GCS 13–15. Studies have shown development of traumatic intracranial hematoma in 15%–20% of patients with perfect GCS (Miller *et al.*, 1990) and one study even reports intracranial abnormalities evidenced by pathological CT in 31% of patients with GCS 13–15 (Tellier *et al.*, 1999). On the basis of the complexity of diagnostic criteria of mTBI, Williams *et al.* (1990) introduced a practical distinction of uncomplicated versus complicated mild head injury. The most important difference between these categories is that uncomplicated mTBI is not associated with signs of intracranial brain pathology and often has excellent recovery 1–3 months post-injury (Dikmen *et al.*, 1989) in contrast with mTBI with indication of intracranial brain pathology, which "complicates" (Williams *et al.*, 1990) the understanding of recovery from mTBI. The results in the described study with poorer long-term neuropsychological and behavioral outcome in children and adolescents with the most severe mild head injuries support the distinction between uncomplicated and complicated mild head injury.

The variables that were most significantly related to poor neuropsychological or behavioral function 23 years post-injury were skull fracture, pediatric mTBI associated with PTA >30 minutes or even more significant PTA >30 minutes in combination with pathological EEG within the first 24 hours after head injury. These brain injury variables indicate mTBI with some degree of severity, probably well matched with the category of complicated mTBI, that have been shown to be associated with poorer cognitive outcome than uncomplicated mTBI (Borgaro *et al.*, 2002). The fact that significant associations were found only in the pediatric group suggests that children and adolescents may be more vulnerable to long-term subtle neuropsychological consequences of complicated mTBI than adults sustaining similar head injuries.

To our knowledge, this is the first study to compare very long-term neuropsychological and behavioral outcome after pediatric and adult mTBI. Although there is reason to be cautious about drawing clinical implications, the results from the present study give support to the view that children sustaining complicated mTBI should be regarded at potential risk of developing subtle chronic symptoms typical for postconcussive syndrome as well as chronic mild neuropsychological dysfunction. The results provide the argument that some of these children may need to be monitored cognitively and with regard to different somatic complaints and fatigue during childhood and adolescence.

Future perspectives

The findings of clear age-related differences in outcome, suggesting that children and adolescents may be more vulnerable to complicated mTBI than adults, may be thought-provoking as they are contrary to the common conception among professionals working with brain-injured patients, that younger patients have better prognosis than older patients (Hux *et al.*, 2000; Johnson *et al.*, 2003). A logical implication of this is that many clinical professionals in the field probably give advice to patients, families, and schools that is not in accordance with the findings in this study, namely that complicated mild TBI in children are benign incidents without persistent sequelae. Our findings, suggesting the possibility of persistent neuropsychological and postconcussive symptoms after complicated mild TBI in childhood, call upon further studies for verification of the findings.

Pediatric complicated mTBI probably represents a sizeable portion of mTBI, which constitutes the vast majority of all TBI. The group of complicated pediatric mTBI has, to our knowledge, never been followed in a prospective multidisciplinary, controlled, and longitudinal study employing current diagnostic criteria of mTBI, current neuroimaging, and neurophysiological technology, in addition to relevant neurological, neuropsychological, and behavioral outcome measures. If the present findings of poorer neuropsychological and behavioural outcome in children sustaining complicated mTBI are possible to replicate in a well-controlled study, utilizing more advanced diagnostic techniques, this ought to have consequences both for diagnostic practice, and for treatment and rehabilitation of a rather large group of children: First, it should provoke a re-evaluation of the diagnostic practice of pediatric mTBI. Second, the potential verification of neurobehavioral problems in this group of children will necessitate a more vigilant monitoring of children and adolescents after complicated mTBI with regard to prevention and treatment of possible learning disabilities, cognitive dysfunctions, and behavioral problems. These children may show evidence of relatively subtle neurobehavioral problems and will probably need different, and much more available, treatment and rehabilitation than is necessary in rehabilitation of more severely brain-injured children (Braga *et al.*, 2005; Van't Hooft *et al.*, 2003). The problems that may persist after pediatric complicated mTBI, like problems with attention, learning, memory, headache, fatigue, irritability, or other behavioral problems, can after proper diagnosis probably be handled within the ordinary healthcare system, at schools, and within the family, and with less demand for specialized rehabilitation.

Based on the discussion, the following hypotheses that ought to be tested in future studies are proposed: (1) that children and adolescents with complicated mTBI will show poorer neuropsychological, academic, and behavioral outcome than a comparison group of demographically matched healthy children; (2) that the differences in outcome should necessitate a refinement or redefinition of the diagnostic category of mild pediatric TBI; and (3) that the often subtle dysfunctions exhibited by these children will require a rethinking of clinical protocols for monitoring, treating, and following up this group of children.

References

Alexander, M. P. (1995). Mild traumatic brain injury. *Neurology*, 45, 1253–1260.

Anderson, V., Catroppa, C., Morse, S., Haritou, F. & Rosenfeldt, J. (2000a). Recovery of intellectual ability following TBI in childhood: impact of injury severity and age at injury. *Pediatric Neurosurgery*, 32, 282–290.

Anderson, V., Catroppa, C. & Rosenfeld, J. (2000b). Recovery of memory function following traumatic brain injury in pre-school children. *Brain Injury*, 14, 679–692.

Anderson, V., Catroppa, C., Morse, S., Haritou, F. & Rosenfeld, J. (2001). Outcome from mild head injury in young children: a prospective study. *Journal of Clinical and Experimental Neuropsychology*, 23, 705–717.

Anderson, V., Catroppa, C., Morse, S., Haritou, F. & Rosenfeld, J. (2005). Functional plasticity or vulnerability after early brain injury? *Pediatrics*, 116, 1374–1382.

Andersson, E. H., Bjørklund, R., Emanuelson, I. & Stalhamar, D. (2003). Epidemiology of traumatic brain injury: a population based study in western Sweden. *Acta Neurologica Scandinavica*, 107, 256–259.

Belanger, H. G., Curtiss, G., Demery, J. A., Lebowitz, B. K. & Vanderploeg, R. D. (2005). Factors moderating neuropsychological outcomes following mild traumatic brain injury: a meta-analysis. *Journal of the International Neuropsychological Society*, 11, 215–227.

Bergsneider, M., Hovda, D. A., Lee, S. M. *et al.* (2000). Dissociation of cerebral glucose metabolism and level of consciousness during the period of metabolic depression following human traumatic brain injury. *Journal of Neurotrauma*, 17, 389–401.

Binder, L. M., Rohling, M. L. & Larrabe, G. J. (1997). A review of mild head trauma.

Part I: meta-analytic review of neuropsychological studies. *Journal of Clinical and Experimental Neuropsychology*, **19**, 421–431.

Borgaro, S. R., Prigatano, G. P., Kwasnica, C. & Rexer, J. L. (2002). Cognitive and affective sequelae of complicated and uncomplicated mild traumatic brain injury. *Brain Injury*, **17**, 189–198.

Braga, L. W., Da Paz, A. C. & Ylvisaker, M. (2005). Direct clinician-delivered versus indirect family-supported rehabilitation of children with traumatic brain injury: a randomised controlled trial. *Brain Injury*, **19**, 819–31.

British Society of Rehabilitation Medicine. (1998). *Rehabilitation after Traumatic Brain Injury. A Working Party Report.*

Bryant, R. A. & Harvey, A. G. (1999). Postconcussive symptoms and posttraumtic stress disorder after mild traumatic brain injury. *Journal of Nervous and Mental Disease*, **187**, 302–305.

Butcher, J. N., Dahlstrom, W. G., Graham, J. R. et al. (1989). *MMPI-2: Manual for Administration and Scoring.* Minneapolis: University of Minnesota Press.

Butcher, J. N., Dahlstrom, W. G., Graham, J. R. et al. (2004). *MMPI-2 – Norwegian Edition.* Stockholm: Psykologiförlaget AB.

Chervinsky, A. B., Ommaya, A. K., deJonge, M., Spector, J., Schwab, K. & Salazar, A. M. (1998). Motivation for Traumatic Brain Injury Rehabilitation Questionnaire (MOT-Q): reliability, factor analysis, and relationship to MMPI-2 variables. *Archives of Clinical Neuropsychology*, **13**, 433–446.

Dearth, C. S., Berry, D. T. R., Vickery, C. D. et al. (2005). Detection of feigned head injury symptoms on the MMPI-2 in head injured patients and community controls. *Archives of Clinical Neuropsychology*, **20**, 95–110.

Dikmen, S. S. & Levin, H. S. (1993). Methodological issues in the study of mild head injury. *Journal of Head Trauma Rehabilitation*, **8**, 30–37.

Dikmen, S., McLean, A. & Temkin, N. (1986). Neuropsychological and psychosocial consequences of minor head injury.

Journal of Neurology, Neurosurgery and Psychiatry, **49**, 1227–1232.

Dikmen, S., Temkin, N. & Armsden, G. (1989). Neuropsychological recovery: relationship to psychosocial functioning and postconcussional complaints. In H. S. Levin, H. M. Eisenberg & A. L. Benton, eds. *Mild Head Injury.* New York: Oxford University Press, pp. 229–241.

Dolan, R. J., Bench, C. J., Brown, R. G., Scott, L. C. & Frackowiak, R. S. (1994). Neuropsychological dysfunction in depression; the relationship to regional cerebral blood flow. *Psychological Medicine*, **24**, 847–857.

Duus, B. R., Kruse, K. V., Nielsen, K. B. & Boesen, T. (1991). Minor head injuries in a Copenhagen district. 1. *Epidemiology. Ugeskrift Læger*, **153**, 2111–2113.

Egeland, J., Sundet, K., Landro, N. I. et al. (2005). Validation of norms for translated tests of attention and memory in a representative sample of Norwegians. *Journal of the Norwegian Psychological Association*, **42**, 99–105.

Egeland, J., Landro, N. I., Tjemsland, E. & Walbaekken, K. (2006). Norwegian norms and factor-structure of phonemic and semantic word list generation. *Clinical Neuropsychology* **20**(4), 716–728.

Engvik, H., Hjerkinn, O. & Seim, S. (1978). *Wechsler Adult Intelligence Scale. Norwegian Edition.* Oslo: The Norwegian Psychological Association.

Eslinger, P., Grattan, L., Damasio, H. & Damasio, A. (1992). Developmental consequences of childhood frontal lobe damage. *Archives of Neurology*, **49**, 764–769.

Esselman, P. C. & Uomoto, J. M. (1995). Classification of the spectrum of mild traumatic brain injury. *Brain Injury*, **9**, 417–424.

Evans, R. V. (1992). The postconcussion syndrome and the sequelae of mild head injury. *Neurologic Clinics*, **10**, 815–847.

Ewing-Cobbs, L., Barnes, M., Fletcher, J. M., Levin, H., Swank, P. R. & Song, J. (2004). Modeling of longitudinal academic achievement scores after paediatric traumatic brain injury. *Developmental Neuropsychology*, 25, 107–133.

Giedd, J., Blumenthal, J., Jefferies, N. *et al.* (1999). Brain development during childhood and adolescence. A longitudinal MRI study. *Nature Neuroscience*, 2, 861–863.

Gimse, R. (1995). *Wechsler Memory Scale – Revised.* Norwegian Edition. Trondheim: University of Trondheim.

Greene, R. L. (2000). *The MMPI-2 – An Interpretive Manual.* Boston: Allyn and Bacon.

Greiffenstein, F. M. & Baker, J. W. (2001). Comparison of premorbid and postinjury MMPI-2 profiles in late postconcussion claimants. *The Clinical Neuropsychologist*, 15, 162–170.

Hartlage, L. C., Durant-Wilson, D. & Patch, P. C. (2001). Persistent neurobehavioural problems following mild traumatic brain injury. *Archives of Clinical Neuropsychology*, 16, 561–570.

Hayes, R. L. & Dixon, C. E. (1994). Neurochemical changes in mild head injury. *Seminars in Neurology*, 14, 25–31.

Heaton, R. K., Grant, I. & Matthews, C. G. (1991). *Comprehensive Norms for an Expanded Halsted–Reitan Battery: Demographic Corrections, Research Findings, and Clinical Applications.* Odessa, FL: Psychological Assessment Resources.

Hessen, E., Lossius, M., Reinvang, I. & Gjerstad, L. (2006a). Predictors of neuropsychological impairment in seizure-free epilepsy patients. *Epilepsia*, 47(11), 1870–1878.

Hessen, E., Nestvold, K. & Sundet, K. (2006b). Neuropsychological function in a group of patients 25 years after sustaining minor head injuries as children and adolescents. *Scandinavian Journal of Psychology*, 47, 245–251.

Hessen, E., Nestvold, K. & Anderson, V. (2007). Neuropsychological function 23 years after mild traumatic brain injury. A comparison of outcome after pediatric and adult head injuries. *Brain Injury*, 21, 963–979.

Hessen, E., Anderson, V. & Nestvold, K. (2008). MMPI-2 profiles 23 years after pediatric

mild traumatic brain injury. *Brain Injury*, 22, 39–50.

House of Commons Select Committee on Health (2001). *Third Report: Head Injury: Rehabilitation.* London: HM Stationery Office.

Hux, K., Rogers, T. & Mongar, K. (2000). Common perceptions about strokes. *Journal of Community Health*, 25, 47–65.

Jennet, B. & Bond, M. (1975). Assessment of outcome after severe brain damage. A practical scale. *Lancet*, *i*, 480–484.

Johnson, D. A., Rose, F. D., Brooks, B. M. & Eyers, S. (2003). Age and recovery from brain injury: legal opinions, clinical beliefs and experimental evidence. *Pediatric Rehabilitation*, 6, 103–109.

Klonoff, H., Clark, C. & Klonoff, P. S. (1993). Long-term outcome of head injuries: a 23-year follow up study of children with head injuries. *Journal of Neurology, Neurosurgery, and Psychiatry*, 56, 410–415.

Kraus, J. F. & Nourjah, P. (1988). The epidemiology of mild, uncomplicated brain injury. *Journal of Trauma*, 28, 1637–1643.

Kraus, J. F., Fife, D., Cox Pramstein, K. & Conroy C. (1986). Incidence, severity, and external causes of pediatric brain injury. *American Journal of Diseases in Children*, 140, 687–693.

Kraus, J. F., Rock, A. & Hemyari, P. (1989). Brain injuries among infants, children and adolescents. *Psychiatric Medicine*, 7, 11–16.

Kraus, J. F., Kraus, J. F., Rock, A. & Hemyari, P. (1990). Brain injuries among infants, children, adolescents, and young adults. *American Journal of Diseases in Children*, 144, 684–691.

Levin, H. S., Mattis, S., Ruff, R. M. *et al.* (1987). Neurobehavioural outcome following minor head injury: a three center study. *Journal of Neurosurgery*, 66, 234–243.

Levin, H. S., Hanten, G., Zhang, L. *et al.* (2004). Changes in working memory after traumatic brain injury in children. *Neuropsychology*, 18, 240–247.

Lezak, M. D., Howieson, D. B. & Loring, D. (2004). *Neuropsychological Assessment.* Oxford: Oxford University Press.

Lishman, W. A. (1988). Physiogenesis and psychogenesis in the "post concussional syndrome". *British Journal of Psychiatry*, **153**, 460–469.

Lund, C., Sundet, K., Tennøe, B. *et al.* (2005). Cerebral ischemic injury and cognitive impairment after off-pump and on-pump coronary artery bypass grafting surgery. *Annals in Thoracic Surgery*, **80**, 2126–2131.

Mack, J. L. (1979). The MMPI and neurological dysfunction. In Newmark, C. S., ed. *MMPI Clinical and Research Trends*. New York: Praeger Publishers, pp. 53–79.

McAllister, T. W., Saykin, A. J., Flashman, L. A. *et al.* (1999). Brain activation during working memory 1 month after mild traumatic brain injury. *Neurology*, **53**, 1300–1308.

Miller, J. D., Murray, L. S. & Teasdale, G. M. (1990). Development of a traumatic intracranial hematoma after a "minor" head injury. *Neurosurgery*, **27**, 669–673.

Miller, L. (1996). Neuropsychology and pathophysiology of mild head injury and the postconcussion syndrome: clinical and forensic considerations. *The Journal of Cognitive Rehabilitation*, **14**, 8–23.

Nell, V., Yates, D. W. & Kruger, J. (2000). An extended Glasgow Coma Scale (GCS-E) with enhanced sensitivity to mild brain injury. *Archives of Physical Medicine and Rehabilitation*, **81**, 614–617.

Nestvold, K., Lundar, T., Blikra, G. & Lønnum, A. (1988). Head injuries during one year in a Central Hospital in Norway: a prospective study. *Neuroepidemiology*, 134–144.

Rees, P. M. (2003). Contemporary issues in mild traumatic brain injury. *Archives of Physical Medicine and Rehabilitation*, **84**, 1885–1894.

Reitan, R. M. & Wolfson, D. (1985). *The Halstead–Reitan Neuropsychological Test Battery*. Tucson: Neuropsychology Press.

Roncadine, C., Guger, S., Archibald, J., Barnes, M. & Dennis, M. (2004). Working memory after mild, moderate, or severe childhood closed head injury. *Developmental Neuropsychology*, **25**, 21–36.

Ruff, R. M., Crouch, J. A., Troster, A. I. *et al.* (1994). Selected cases of poor outcome following a minor brain trauma: comparing neuropsychological and positron emmission tomography assessment. *Brain Injury*, **8**, 297–308.

Rutherford, W. H., Merret, J. D. & McDonald, J. R. (1978). Symptoms at one year following concussion from minor head injuries. *Injury*, **10**, 225–230.

Satz, P., Zaucha, K., McCleary, C., Light, R. & Asarnow, R. (1997). Mild head injury in children and adolescents: a review of studies (1970–1995). *Psychological Bulletin*, **122**, 107–131.

Tellier, A., Malva, L. C. D., Cwinn, A., Grahovac, S., Morrish, W. & Brennan-Barnes, M. (1999). Mild head injury: a misnomer. *Brain injury*, **13**, 463–475.

Thornhill, S., Teasdale, G. M., Murray, G. D., McEwen, J., Roy, C. W. & Penny, K. I. (2000). Disability in young people and adults one year after head injury: prospective cohort study. *British Medical Journal*, **320**, 1631–1635.

Van der Naalt, J., Hew, J. M., van Zomeren, A. H., Sluiter, W. J. & Minderhoud, J. M. (1999a). Computed tomography and magnetic resonance imaging in mild to moderate head injury: early and late imaging related to outcome. *Annals in Neurology*, **46**, 70–78.

Van der Naalt, J., van Zomeren, A. H., Sluiter, W. J. & Minderhoud, J. M. (1999b). One year outcome in mild to moderate head injury: the predictive value of acute injury characteristics related to complaints and return to work. *Journal of Neurology, Neurosurgery, and Psychiatry*, **66**, 207–213.

Vanderploeg, R. D., Curtiss, G. & Belanger, H. G. (2005). Long term neuropsychological outcomes following mild traumatic brain injury. *Journal of the International Neuropsychological Society*, **11**, 228–236.

Van't Hooft, I., Andersson, K., Sejersen, T., Bartfai, A. & von Wendt, L. (2003). Attention and memory training in children with acquired brain injuries. *Acta Paediatrica*, **92**, 935–940.

Warriner, E. M., Rourke, B. P., Velikonja, D. & Metham, L. (2003). Subtypes of emotional and behavioural sequelae in patients with traumatic brain injury. *Journal of Clinical and Experimental Neuropsychology*, **25**, 904–917.

Wechsler, D. (1955). *Wechsler Adult Intelligence Scale*. New York: The Psychological Corporation.

Wechsler, D. (1987). *Wechsler Memory Scale – Revised Manual*. San Antonio: The Psychological Corporation.

Williams, D., Levin, H. & Eisenberg, H. (1990). Mild head injury classification. *Neurosurgery*, **27**, 422–428.

Wrightson, P. & Gronwall, D. (1999). *Mild Head Injury*. Oxford: Oxford University Press.

Zakzanis, K. K., Leach, L. & Kaplan, E. (1999). Mild traumatic brain injury. In ed(s). *Neuropsychological Differential Diagnosis*. Exton, Pennsylvania: Swets & Zeitlinger, pp. 163–171.

Chapter

8

Neurobehavioral outcomes of pediatric traumatic brain injury

H. Gerry Taylor

Introduction

The multiple roles of neurobehavioral assessment in evaluating outcomes after TBI are to: (1) describe the effects of injury on cognitive skills, behavior, and educational progress; (2) determine how these outcomes are related to the brain insult and to any ensuing abnormalities in neural development; (3) identify environmental and psychosocial factors that add to or moderate the effects of brain pathology on these outcomes; and (4) specify the cognitive deficits that contribute to problems in behavior and scholastic achievement. Assessment is guided by existing knowledge and theory regarding TBI-related brain insults, the neuropsychological and developmental effects of these insults, other influences on children's development such as the home or school environments, and the relation of cognitive impairments to behavior and learning. By adding to this knowledge base, assessment findings can point to the need for refinements in the evaluation process and inform efforts to improve outcomes.

The primary objective of this chapter is to describe neurobehavioral outcomes of TBI in children and emphasize the need for further, methodologically sound investigation in this area. Consistent with the emphasis of this volume on "translational" research, progress in understanding the nature and determinants of injury consequences can be measured by the degree to which findings from individual cases can inform research design, as well as by the relevance of research findings to evidenced-based management of individual children. The "translational" aspect of research in this area also entails interdisciplinary work that bridges different levels of analysis, from neurobiological mechanisms and effects on neural development to the consequences of injury for cognitive, educational, and behavioral functioning and environmental influences on those same outcomes. One specific aim is to review findings on the neurobehavioral outcomes of TBI, with an emphasis on the nature and predictors of injury consequences. While referring to the more general literature, data from a longitudinal study conducted by our research group (Taylor *et al.*, 1995) will be cited to illustrate findings. After outlining the methods of our study, this chapter reviews the developmental consequences of TBI, patterns of recovery from injury, and factors that help account for variability in outcomes. Additional aims are to discuss the limitations of our existing knowledge base, identify the methodological requirements of studies in this area, and identify promising directions for future research.

Pediatric Traumatic Brain Injury: New Frontiers in Clinical and Translational Research, ed. V. Anderson and K. O. Yeates. Published by Cambridge University Press. © Cambridge University Press 2010.

The nature and predictors of outcomes following pediatric TBI

A longitudinal study of outcomes following TBI in school-age children: the Ohio Project

Study description, aims, and hypotheses

In 1990, our Ohio-based research team initiated a prospective follow-up study of school-age children hospitalized for moderate to severe TBI and their families. A comparison group of children hospitalized for orthopedic injuries not involving central nervous system injury were also followed. In collaboration with my colleagues Drs. Keith Owen Yeates, Shari Wade, Dennis Drotar, and Terry Stancin, children were recruited prospectively from admissions to four hospitals in Ohio. The rationale for limiting recruitment to children with more significant TBI was to permit study of the family consequences of injuries that were likely to result in neurocognitive and behavioral impairment. Recruitment of these children also allowed us to examine post-injury changes following these impairments and to identify injury and non-injury predictors. A comparison group of children with orthopedic injuries (OI) were recruited to control for pre-injury characteristics associated with traumatic injury. This group also helped control for the effects of other injuries and the hospitalization experience of child outcomes.

The purposes of the study were to examine the effects of TBI on the children and their families and to explore the influences of the post-injury family environment on the child's recovery. Our first hypothesis was that TBI would have more adverse consequences for the family environment and result in more parental burden and psychological distress than OI. Our second hypothesis was that more negative post-injury family characteristics would predict neuropsychological, educational, and behavioral outcomes in the TBI group. Further aims were to examine the nature of the effects of TBI on the child and to examine non-injury factors as predictors of outcome.

Participants

Children were recruited by monitoring admissions to each of the participating hospitals. Eligibility criteria included at least one night's stay for moderate to severe TBI due to blunt trauma or OI, age at injury between 6 and 12 years, the absence of evidence for child abuse or a previous neurological disorder, and residence in an English-speaking household. Children with severe TBI had a lowest Glasgow Coma Scale (GCS) (Teasdale & Jennett, 1974) score <9, and those with moderate TBI had either a lowest GCS score of 9–12, or a higher GCS score that was accompanied by an extended loss of consciousness (>15 minutes), intracranial abnormality (mass, lesion, contusion, diffuse cerebral swelling), skull fracture, or post-traumatic neurological abnormality. Many children in the TBI groups had orthopedic injuries, but the OI group consisted only of children without symptoms suggestive of central nervous system insult.

Design

The project employed a cohort/prospective design involving repeated post-injury assessment of child and family outcomes. The children and families in both the TBI and OI groups were first assessed at a baseline evaluation conducted an average of about three weeks after injury. Follow-up assessments were scheduled 6 and 12 months after the baseline, and again at an average of 4, 5, and 6 years post-injury.

Table 8.1 Sample for Ohio TBI Project at initial (baseline) assessment

Characteristic	Group		
	Severe TBI	Moderate TBI	OI
	(*n* = 53)	(*n* = 56)	(*n* = 80)
Age at injury in years, Mean (SD)	9.4(2.1)	10.0(1.9)	9.3(1.9)
No. of boys (%)	39(74%)	41(73%)	47(59%)
No. of Whites (%)	40(76%)	43(77%)	45(56%)
Days hospitalized, Mean (SD)*	13.4(10.0)	7.0(7.5)	13.8(13.7)
Glasgow Coma Scale Score, Mean (SD)*	4.8(1.9)	14.0(1.8)	
Mechanism of injury:*			
Motor vehicle	41(77%)	22(39%)	27(34%)
Sports/recreational	3(6%)	23(41%)	30(37%)
Falls	5(9%)	6(11%)	14(18%)
Assault	2(4%)	5(9%)	4(5%)
Other	2(4%)	0(0%)	5(6%)

Notes: TBI = traumatic brain injury; OI = orthopedic injury
*Significant group difference, $p < 0.01$

Methods

The project was approved by the Institution Review Boards of each of the hospitals, and families were not approached for study participation until children were medically stable. Informed consent was obtained from parents and assent from the children who were capable of assenting. As soon as consent was given, information was obtained from parents regarding pre-injury child and family characteristics by having parents complete retrospective ratings on the Family Assessment Device–General Functioning Index (FAD-GF) (Byles *et al.*, 1988) and the Child Behavior Checklist (CBCL) (Achenbach, 1991a) and by administering the Vineland Adaptive Behavior Scales (VABS) (Sparrow *et al.*, 1994) based on the child's functioning prior to injury. The children were considered eligible for neuropsychological testing after having obtained normal range scores on the Children's Amnesia and Orientation Test (COAT) (Ewing-Cobbs *et al.*, 1990) for two consecutive days.

At the initial or baseline assessment conducted an average of three weeks post-injury, we administered a short form of the Wechsler Intelligence Scale for Children – 3rd edn. (WISC-III) (Wechsler, 1991) along with tests of non-verbal problem solving, language, perceptual motor skills, memory, attention, and executive function (Taylor *et al.*, 1999). Tests of academic achievement included subtests of the Woodcock–Johnson Tests of Achievement – Revised (Woodcock & Mather, 1989) assessing reading, writing, and mathematics. To assess post-injury child behavior and school performance, the CBCL and VABS were again administered to parents, and teachers completed the Teacher's Report Form (TRF) (Achenbach, 1991b). Table 8.1 summarizes sample characteristics at the baseline assessment.

The test battery was repeated at follow-up assessments conducted 6 and 12 months after the baseline evaluation, and again for three consecutive "extended" follow-up visits at an average of 4, 5, and 6 years post-injury. Most of the same outcome measures were administered at all assessments, with only minor modifications in testing made for the extended follow-ups. At each follow-up assessment, child behavior and school performance were assessed by re-administering the CBCL and TRF, and the family environment was measured by re-evaluating sociodemographic status and by administering measures of parent stressors and resources and family functioning.

Cognitive outcomes

Studies of the cognitive sequelae of TBI document global reductions in ability as measured by IQ tests, as well as impairments in the domains of language, memory, problem solving, perceptual motor skills, and attention and executive function (Levin & Hanten, 2005; Taylor et al., 2008; Yeates, 2000). Despite the pervasiveness of these impairments, effects are especially pronounced on measures of non-verbal intelligence; verbal learning and retrieval; processing speed, verbal fluency, and other measures of executive function; and discourse processing. In contrast, lesser effects are observed on tests assessing verbal intelligence; measures of immediate, implicit, or recognition memory; and tasks providing external structure or tapping children's existing knowledge base (Anderson et al., 2005a, b; Barnes & Dennis, 2001; Catroppa & Anderson, 2005; Dennis & Barnes, 2001; Dennis et al., 2001; Donders & Giroux, 2005; Ewing-Cobbs & Barnes, 2002).

Findings of the Ohio TBI study were generally consistent with this literature. In a report of outcomes over the first year post-injury, we found differences on tests of perceptual motor skill, verbal memory, verbal (phonemic) fluency, and attention (Taylor et al., 1999). These differences were evident even when controlling for demographic and family factors and a parent rating of pre-injury academic performance. Differences in Verbal IQ but not in Performance IQ on the WISC-III likely reflected the fact that several children with severe TBI had orthopedic injuries that precluded them from taking the performance subtests. Similar group differences were evident in analyses by Yeates et al. (2002) that considered cognitive outcomes across the first four assessments (baseline, 6-month, 12-month, and first extended follow-up at four years post-injury). Again, controlling for demographic and family factors, we observed deleterious effects of severe TBI relative to OI on WISC-III Similarities and Object Assembly and on tests of naming, verbal recall, verbal fluency, and attention and executive function (specifically, speeded visual search and verbal set-shifting). Weaknesses in cognitive skills were observed for both the severe and moderate TBI groups but were more pervasive among children with severe TBI.

Educational outcomes

Children with severe TBI score more poorly than children with less severe TBI or community controls in tests of academic achievement. All core academic skills are affected, including reading, spelling, writing, and arithmetic (Barnes et al., 1999; Ewing-Cobbs et al., 1998), with differences noted both shortly after TBI and in longer term follow-ups (Anderson et al., 2006b; Ewing-Cobbs et al., 2004a; Ewing-Cobbs et al., 2006). Adverse effects of moderate TBI are also reported (Anderson et al., 2006b; Jaffe et al., 1995; Taylor et al., 1999). Some academic skills are more affected than others. For example, Barnes et al. (1999) found that reading fluency was compromised even in children who were not impaired in word decoding. Other researchers have found more pronounced effects of TBI on mathematics than on word recognition (Catroppa & Anderson, 2007; Ewing-Cobbs et al., 1998).

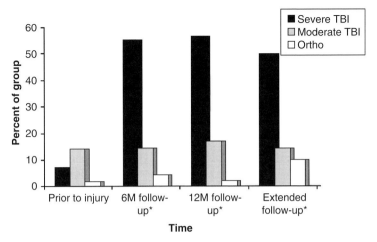

Fig. 8.1. Rates of special education placements immediately prior to injury and at each follow-up in the severe TBI, moderate TBI, and OI groups. M = month. *Significant group difference, $p < 0.01$. (Reproduced by permission of the publisher (American Psychological Association, Inc.) from Taylor *et al.*, 2003).

Difficulties in school performance after TBI can be demonstrated even in children whose core academic achievement skills are relatively intact (Ewing-Cobbs *et al.*, 2004a). Ewing-Cobbs *et al.* (1998) found that 79% of the children with severe TBI had failed a grade or received special education within two years post-injury despite average scores on achievement tests. Other studies also report high rates of special education and grade repetition or declining grades following TBI (Fay *et al.*, 1994; Kinsella *et al.*, 1995; 1997). Children's neuropsychological impairments in domains such as executive function, memory, processing speed are the likely culprits of these problems in school performance (Ewing-Cobbs *et al.*, 1998; 2004a).

In the Ohio TBI Project, children with severe TBI scored more poorly than the OI group across follow-up on the Woodcock–Johnson Writing Samples subtest (Taylor *et al.*, 2002). The severe TBI also obtained lower scores at follow-up on the Woodcock–Johnson Calculation subtest, though this difference was significant only among children from more disadvantaged environments. Problems in school performance among children with severe TBI were documented on the TRF School Performance scale. In a study of the educational interventions received by children in the sample, we found that rates of special education assistance were similar prior to injury but higher in the TBI groups at the post-injury follow-ups (Taylor *et al.*, 2003: see Fig. 8.1). The severe TBI group also had a higher rate of post-injury grade retention than the moderate TBI and OI groups.

Behavior outcomes

A substantial percentage of children with TBI have post-injury behavior problems that were not present prior to injury. Fletcher *et al.* (1996) documented behavior problems on the parent-based Personality Inventory for Children – Revised in about 30% of a sample with mild to severe TBI that had been screened for pre-existing neuropsychiatric disorders and followed to 1–2 years after injury. Based on interview measures, Brown *et al.* (1981) documented post-injury-onset behavior disorders in 52% of a sample of children with severe TBI examined one year post-injury. Other findings are consistent with these results (Bloom *et al.*, 2001).

Although behavioral disinhibition and socially inappropriate behaviors may be more common in children with TBI than in the general child population, there is no "signature" behavior impairment (Brown *et al.*, 1981). Behavior problems vary from child to child and include both internalizing and externalizing disorders. Specific disorders emerging after TBI in children include secondary (new onset) attention deficit/hyperactivity disorder (ADHD), personality change disorder, oppositional defiant disorder symptomatology, and mood and anxiety disorders (Gerring *et al.*, 1998; Luis & Mittenberg, 2002; Max *et al.*, 1998, Max *et al.*, 2005a,b). Other adverse behavioral consequences include weaknesses in adaptive functioning as measured by the Vineland Adaptive Behavior Scales (Anderson *et al.*, 2001a, b; Fletcher *et al.*, 1990; Woodward *et al.*, 1999), behavioral manifestations of weaknesses in executive function (Sesma *et al.*, 2008), neurobehavioral (i.e. post concussive) symptoms (Yeates *et al.*, 2001), and lowered health-related quality of life (McCarthy *et al.*, 2006).

Findings from the Ohio TBI Project are consistent with the general literature on behavior outcomes of TBI. Defining a post-injury behavior problem as a Total Problem T-score >63 on the CBCL (<10th percentile of normative population), we documented significantly higher rates of behavior disturbance at the 4-year follow-up in the severe and moderate TBI groups (36% and 22%) compared with the OI group (10%). Although evident in the earlier post-injury follow-ups, most of these problems were not present prior to injury. In keeping with other literature, the types of behavior problems observed in our TBI sample included internalizing and externalizing disorders. Compared with the OI group, both TBI groups had higher ratings on the CBCL Somatic Complaints and Anxious/Depressed scales at the 6- and 12-month follow-ups (Kirkwood *et al.*, 2000) and more neurobehavioral symptoms across the first year post-injury (Barry *et al.*, 1996; Yeates *et al.*, 2001). The severe TBI also had: (a) higher teacher ratings of behavior problems at the 6-month, 12-month, and 4-year follow-ups; (b) more symptoms of post-traumatic stress disorder at the 6- and 12-month follow-ups; (c) poorer adaptive functioning as measured by the VABS; (d) higher rates of mental health counseling and lower health-related quality of life at the 4-year follow-up; (e) more behavioral symptoms of executive dysfunction at the 5-year follow-up; and (f) more symptoms of persistent post-injury sleep problems (Beebe *et al.*, 2007; Levi *et al.*, 1999; Mangeot *et al.*, 2002; Stancin *et al.*, 2002; Taylor *et al.*, 1999; 2002; Yeates & Taylor, 2006).

Factors contributing to variability in outcomes
Injury-related factors
Classification of children according to TBI severity is the most commonly reported predictor of neurobehavioral outcomes of childhood TBI. Although severe TBI is frequently defined in terms of GCS scores <9, definitions based on length of post-traumatic amnesia (PTA) or duration of impaired consciousness have also been applied (Ewing-Cobbs *et al.*, 2004a). We and other investigators have defined moderate TBI in terms of a GCS score of 9–12 or a higher GCS with neurological or neuroimaging abnormalities (Anderson *et al.*, 2006b; Fletcher *et al.*, 1990; Prasad *et al.*, 2002). However, other studies have relied solely on the initial post-injury GCS score (Barnes *et al.*, 1999; Jaffe *et al.*, 1995; Wilde *et al.*, 2007) or have considered duration of impaired consciousness, time to return to a GCS score of 15, or multiple criteria (Catroppa & Anderson, 2005; Ewing-Cobbs *et al.*, 2004a). Despite general agreement that mild TBI after a blunt trauma involves some change in mental status of a lesser

severity than moderate to severe TBI, studies differ with respect to the criteria used to define mild TBI, inclusion of children with neuroimaging abnormalities, and recruitment from hospital admissions versus outpatient emergency departments (Kirkwood *et al.*, 2008).

Severe TBI has more pronounced and pervasive consequences than moderate TBI, though even the latter children have poorer outcomes relative to groups with mild TBI, OI, or non-injured controls (Anderson *et al.*, 2004; 2006b; Fay *et al.*, 1994; Taylor *et al.*, 2008). Results of studies assessing the effects of mild TBI have been inconsistent (Satz *et al.*, 1997). Some studies indicate adverse neurobehavioral outcomes (Anderson *et al.*, 2001b; Dennis & Barnes, 2001; McKinlay *et al.*, 2002), while others suggest only transient deficits, or fail to reveal group differences when background factors are taken into account (Anderson *et al.*, 2006b; Bijur & Haslum, 1995). The different findings likely relate to lack of a common definition of mild TBI or to differences in recruitment strategies (Yeates & Taylor, 2005). It seems likely, however, that at least some cases of mild TBI are associated with brain insults and persistent cognitive deficits and post concussive symptoms (Bigler, 2008; Kirkwood *et al.*, 2008; Levine *et al.*, 2008).

Injury factors besides the classification of TBI severity that predict poorer neurobehavioral outcomes in children include a lower initial GCS score, longer period of impaired consciousness, greater time to return to a GCS score of 15 or to resolution of PTA, and abnormal pupillary responses (Massagli *et al.*, 1996; Prasad *et al.*, 2002; Woodward *et al.*, 1999). Bilateral brain swelling and larger, more numerous, or more diffuse brain lesions on neuroimaging also predict poorer outcomes (Ewing-Cobbs *et al.*, 2006; Prasad *et al.*, 2002; Salorio *et al.*, 2005). Additional findings from neuroimaging associated with worse cognitive outcomes include decreased volumes of white matter, frontal lobes, or subcortical structures, increased ventricular size, abnormal metabolite ratios on proton magnetic resonance spectroscopy, and lower fractional anisotropy of white matter as measured by diffusion tensor imaging (Bonnier *et al.*, 2007; Brenner *et al.*, 2003; Levin *et al.*, 1997; Serra-Grabulosa *et al.*, 2005; Wilde *et al.*, 2006; 2007). Investigators have also found evidence for specific brain–behavior relationships, such as associations of frontal lobe lesions with impairments in executive function, adaptive behavior skills, and emotional regulation (Anderson *et al.*, 2006a; Bloom *et al.*, 2001; Levin *et al.*, 2004); and of subcortical lesions with ADHD (Gerring *et al.*, 2000).

Time since injury

Studies that have followed children after TBI document short-term recovery in cognitive outcomes. The most marked recovery occurs during the first year after injury (Jaffe *et al.*, 1995). The pattern of recovery is particularly evident for children with severe TBI on measures of non-verbal, motor, and memory skills. Further though less marked improvement in cognitive skills relative to control groups may occur well after this point. However, such recovery is incomplete and deficits remain for years after injury in both cognitive and academic skills (Anderson *et al.*, 2006b; Barlow *et al.*, 2005; Catroppa *et al.*, 2008; Ewing-Cobbs *et al.*, 2006; Jaffe *et al.*, 1995; Verger *et al.*, 2000). In younger children, these deficits can even emerge with increasing age and time since injury (Anderson *et al.*, 2000; Ewing-Cobbs *et al.*, 2004b). The adverse effects of TBI on behavior appear soon after injury and, unlike cognitive skills, show little evidence of remitting over time (Brown *et al.*, 1981; Taylor *et al.*, 2002). Some investigators have found negative effects of childhood TBI on behavior and independent functioning that extend into adulthood (Cattelani *et al.*, 1998; Jonsson *et al.*, 2004).

Age at injury

Numerous studies have found poorer cognitive and academic outcomes in children less than eight years of age compared with older children and adolescents (Taylor & Alden, 1997; Verger *et al.*, 2000). Longitudinal studies have also revealed slower recovery of cognitive and academic skills – or alternatively, more effects on post-injury development – for children injured early in life (Anderson *et al.*, 2005a; Ewing-Cobbs *et al.*, 2004a). Potential bases for this age difference include more diffuse brain insults or cerebral edema, more abnormalities in neurogenesis (e.g. due to less complete myelinization), or a greater likelihood of significant longitudinal effects related to the developmental immaturity (Anderson & Moore, 1995; Bittigau *et al.*, 1999). Findings indicating more pronounced effects of earlier TBI on expressive language and academic achievement are consistent with the special vulnerability of emerging skills (Ewing-Cobbs & Barnes, 2002). For example, Barnes *et al.* (1999) found that children injured before 6½ years of age had lower scores on a test of word decoding than children injured later, and that children injured at 9 years or earlier had lower reading comprehension scores than those injured after 9 years.

Other factors associated with poorer child outcomes

Other factors associated with poorer outcomes of childhood TBI include lower pre-injury IQ and adaptive abilities, pre-existing learning and behavior problems, and family characteristics suggestive of lower socioeconomic status (SES), such as single-parent household, public assistance, and fewer family resources (Anderson *et al.*, 2005b; Brown *et al.*, 1981; McCarthy *et al.*, 2006; Sesma *et al.*, 2008; Woodward *et al.*, 1999). While some of these findings may reflect associations that pre-existed the occurrence of TBI, prospective follow-up studies suggest that these factors predict post-injury-onset behavior problems (Brown *et al.*, 1981; Gerring *et al.*, 1998; Max *et al.*, 1998).

Additional risk factors are post-acute cognitive deficits, injuries to body areas besides the head, and the family's adjustment to the child's injury. Several studies suggest that post-acute cognitive deficits predict worse outcomes (Brown *et al.*, 1981; Kinsella *et al.*, 1995; Klonoff *et al.*, 1993). Although the cognitive consequences of TBI in children are only weakly related to behavioral outcomes (Fletcher *et al.*, 1990), associations are more robust when specific cognitive skills are related to parent ratings of analogous behaviors, as for example when measures of social cognition are correlated with parent ratings of social-behavioral regulation (Dennis *et al.*, 2001; Yeates *et al.*, 2004). With respect to the effects of injuries to body areas besides the head, McCarthy *et al.* (2006) discovered that children with TBI who sustained concomitant lower extremity fractures or spinal injuries had poorer health-related quality of life. Results from an adult study suggest that non-brain injuries can affect cognitive outcomes as well (Dacey *et al.*, 1991). Support for the relevance of parent adjustment comes from findings by Kinsella *et al.* (1999), who found that greater parental emotional distress 3 months after injury was associated with more concurrent child behavior problems. Although it is possible that parental distress was secondary to child behavior problems, rather than vice versa, this finding is consistent with post-injury environmental influences on outcomes. Finally, a study by Donders and Woodward (2003) showing more marked effects of TBI on memory in boys than girls implies a male vulnerability to TBI. While such a difference is biologically plausible (Raz *et al.*, 1995), sex differences in the effects of TBI are not widely reported. Furthermore, worse outcomes in boys could reflect a bias in TBI samples for males to have more pre-injury developmental problems than girls.

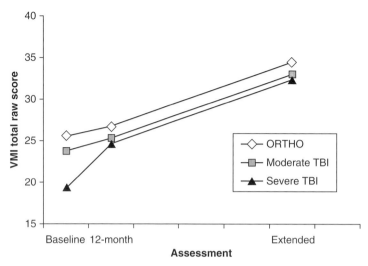

Fig. 8.2. Model estimates of group means for total raw scores on the Developmental Test of Visual Motor Integration (VMI) at the baseline, 12-month, and extended (4-year) follow-ups. Time-related effects were modeled in terms of linear change across two intervals: baseline to 12-month follow-up, and 12-month follow-up to extended follow-up. The plot illustrates more rapid growth in the severe TBI group than in the other two groups from baseline to the 12-month follow-up and stable group differences from 12-month follow-up to extended follow-up. (Reproduced by permission of the publisher (American Psychological Association, Inc.) from Yeates *et al.*, 2002).

Factors related to child outcomes in the Ohio TBI Project

Findings from the Ohio TBI Project confirm the effects of TBI severity and the longitudinal changes in outcome reported in the literature reviewed above. Deficits in cognition, achievement, and behavior were more pronounced and pervasive in the severe TBI group than in the moderate TBI group, with both groups performing worse than the OI group on some measures (Taylor *et al.*, 2002; Yeates *et al.*, 1997; 2002; 2004). As in other prospective follow-up studies, the severe TBI group showed some initial recovery in cognitive skills (Taylor *et al.*, 1999; Yeates *et al.*, 2002); and when recovery was observed it leveled off within the first year post-injury. Longer term follow-up revealed continuing improvement in skills in all groups but without further catch-up of either TBI group to the children with OI. This pattern of recovery is illustrated in Fig. 8.2, which plots growth modeling estimates of raw scores on the Developmental Test of Visual Motor Integration (VMI) (Beery, 1989) in the three groups from baseline through the 4-year follow-up. Impairments in the TBI groups persisted across the follow-up interval, with no suggestion of differences in short- or long-term outcomes related to age at injury.

Predictors of poorer cognitive and behavior outcomes for the total sample or the two TBI groups combined included pre-injury problems in behavior and school performance and more disadvantaged pre-injury family environments (Stancin *et al.*, 2002; Yeates & Taylor, 1997; Yeates *et al.*, 1997; 2001). After the injury, disadvantaged family environments also predicted poorer cognitive outcomes and more neurobehavioral symptoms (Barry *et al.*, 1996; Taylor *et al.*, 1999; 2002; Yeates *et al.*, 2002). Lower post-injury cognitive abilities also predicted psychosocial outcomes (Kirkwood *et al.*, 2000; Mangeot *et al.*, 2002; Yeates *et al.*, 2001; 2004; 2005). Additionally, children in the TBI sample with accompanying orthopedic

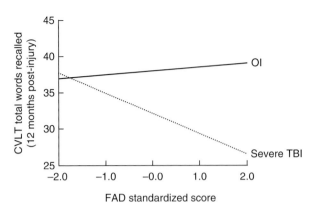

Fig. 8.3. Relationship between the pre-injury standardized score on a measure of family functioning (the Family Assessment Device – General Functioning Scale, or FAD) and total words recalled on the California Verbal Learning Test (CVLT) at 12 months post-injury in the severe TBI and OI groups. (Reproduced by permission of the publisher (Cambridge University Press) from Yeates et al., 1997).

injuries had more short-term functional impairments and that these impairments were related to lower extremity fractures (Stancin et al., 2001).

Of special interest with respect to environmental influences, several non-injury factors moderated the effects of TBI on child outcomes. Moderating effects of family factors are illustrated in Fig. 8.3, which plots differences between the severe TBI and OI group in estimated means on the California Verbal Learning Test – Children's Version (CVLT-C) (Delis et al., 1986) at the 12-month follow-up at varying levels of pre-injury family functioning as measured by the FAD-GF. As shown in the figure, the severe TBI group's deficit in memory was amplified at higher levels of family dysfunction. Similar environmental moderation of the effects of severe TBI were observed for WISC-III Verbal IQ, math skills, parent-based assessments of behavior problems and adaptive functioning, and teacher ratings of academic performance (Taylor et al., 1999; 2002; Yeates et al., 1997). Consistent with findings by Gerring et al. (1998), we also found that effects of severe TBI relative to OI on parent ratings of attention problems at the 4-year follow-up were more pronounced for children with more pre-injury attention problems (Yeates et al., 2005).

One approach to investigate predictors of adverse developmental changes after TBI is to consider only children without problems prior to injury and to identify the factors that differentiate the subsets with and without post-injury problems. Compared with children in the TBI groups without a behavior disorder either before or after injury, those with a behavior disorder at the 4-year follow-up, but not prior to injury, had more pre-injury behavior problems, greater socioeconomic disadvantage, more family burden, distress, and dysfunction, and poorer performance on a test of verbal working memory. Similarly, compared with children in the TBI groups who did not receive special education either before or after injury, those who were in special education at the 4-year follow-up, but not before injury, had more pre-injury behavior problems, poorer pre-injury school performance, greater socioeconomic disadvantage, and lower scores on tests of language and achievement at the baseline evaluation (Taylor et al., 2003). Both sets of findings confirm the multi-factorial nature of risks for adverse consequences of TBI.

Another approach is to examine risk factors that moderated effects on group differences in post-injury development. Using growth modeling methods, we discovered several instances in which effects of TBI on longitudinal change were evident only for subsets of

(a)

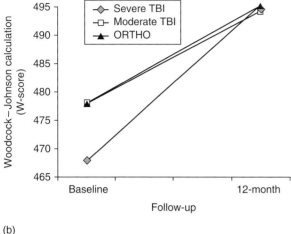

(b)

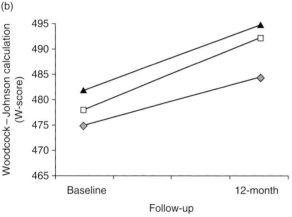

Fig. 8.4. Model estimates of group mean W scores on the Calculation subtest of the Woodcock–Johnson Tests of Achievement – Revised at the baseline and 12-month follow-up for children with (a) low and (b) high levels of family stressors as defined by scores one standard deviation below and above the sample mean. The plots show catch-up in math skills in the severe TBI group relative to the OI group but only when family stressors were low. (Reproduced by permission of the publisher (American Psychological Association, Inc.) from Taylor *et al.*, 2002).

the sample (Taylor *et al.*, 2002). Moderating effects took one of two forms, suggesting both facilitative influences of environmental advantage on recovery and a special vulnerability of children with severe TBI to environmental disadvantage. The first pattern is illustrated in Fig. 8.4, which plots gains in estimated mean scores on the Woodcock–Johnson Calculation subtest for the three groups under conditions of low and high stressors. As evident in the figure, children with severe TBI from families reporting low stressors demonstrated recovery in math skills from the baseline evaluation to the 12-month follow-up, while children from families with high stressors did not. The second pattern is illustrated in Fig. 8.5, which plots estimated mean scores on the VABS Socialization domain from the 6- to 12-month follow-ups for children from high vs. low levels of socioeconomic status (SES). In this instance, lower SES appeared to hinder or disrupt the development of socialization skills in children with TBI more so than for children with OI. A similar pattern was evident in examining teacher ratings of children's academic performance. Less evidence of environmental moderation was found in examining predictors of post-injury changes in cognitive skills, suggesting that these skills may be less subject to environmental modification (Yeates *et al.*, 2002).

(a)

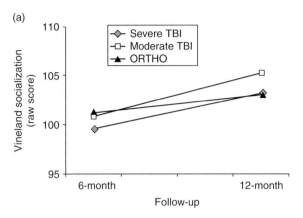

(b)

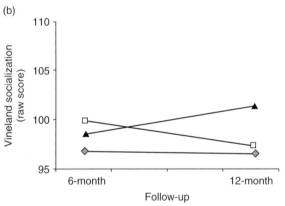

Fig. 8.5. Model estimates of group raw score means for the Socialization domain of the Vineland Adaptive Behavior Scales at the 6- and 12-month follow-ups for children with (a) high and (b) low socioeconomic status (SES) as defined by values one standard deviation above and below the sample mean on the Socioeconomic Composite Index (Yeates *et al.*, 1997). The plots show poorer development of socialization skills in the TBI group than in the OI group but only when SES was low. (Reproduced by permission of the publisher (American Psychological Association, Inc.) from Taylor *et al.*, 2002).

Research limitations and needs

Research design

Progress in understanding the effects of childhood TBI has been substantial but has been hampered by research methods that make it difficult to interpret findings or that limit sensitivity to injury effects. One common limitation in research design is a potential bias in recruiting children with TBI or in retaining them in follow-up (Natale *et al.*, 2006). Findings from studies that recruit children who are likely to be representative of hospital admissions – through methods such as contacts with the families of consecutive admissions of children meeting eligibility criteria – are more meaningful than those obtained from convenience samples or from studies that fail to specify recruitment methods.

Description of attrition rates and comparisons of drop-outs to participants remaining in follow-up on background and injury-related characteristics is also essential in detecting potential biases and interpreting results. To illustrate the magnitude of this issue, Fig. 8.6 graphs attrition rates in the Ohio TBI Project and demonstrates the challenges of maintaining the interests of families and their older children and adolescents in repeated follow-ups. To the extent that factors related to drop-out, such as SES or group, are included in data analysis, estimates of effects are unbiased. However, because of unmeasured factors associated with drop-out that may also be related to outcomes, findings may be biased and

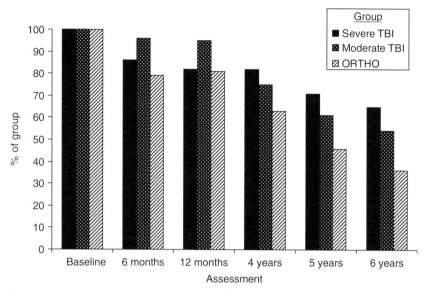

Fig. 8.6. Percentages of the severe TBI, moderate TBI, and OI groups in the Ohio TBI Project assessed across follow-up. The steady reduction in these percentages relative to baseline (100%) over the follow-up interval document increasing attrition, which was most pronounced in the OI group.

methods such as pattern-mixture analysis (Hedeker & Gibbons, 1997) are needed to examine this possibility.

Another common design limitation is failure to adequately control for potential confounds in assessing TBI consequences (Taylor & Alden, 1997). Although background differences between children with TBI and non-injured controls or between children with varying degrees of TBI severity are not universally reported, researchers need to address potential confounding of group membership with background characteristics. Examples of these approaches are to exclude children with pre-injury problems, match cases and controls on background factors, recruit comparison children with non-head injuries, and control statistically for pre-injury child and family characteristics in analysis of TBI effects. Our research team's experience has been that assessments of pre-injury child functioning based on retrospective parent reports, though admittedly susceptible to report bias, yield estimates of pre-injury status that are unrelated to group status but differ markedly from reports of children's post-injury status. In the absence of other more direct methods of pre-injury assessment, this approach appears well advised. By obtaining measures of pre-injury child status and controlling for them in analysis, any group differences are more likely to reflect the effects of TBI. Because SES and other demographic factors are associated with performance on cognitive tests, academic achievement, and behavior (Dacey *et al.*, 1991; McDermott, 1995) controlling for background factors can also improve precision in estimating TBI consequences and allows the research to examine possible moderating effects.

Measurement

Progress in understanding the effects of pediatric TBI have been further hampered by measurement limitations. Most of the existing studies have utilized relatively crude indices of brain status to determine the presence, nature, and severity of TBI. Measures of acute encephalopathy (e.g. GCS scores, duration of impaired consciousness) and results from clinical neuroimaging most frequently based on computed tomography (CT) scans are only weakly associated with outcome and fail to adequately characterize the effects of injury on the brain (Keenan & Bratton, 2006; Ruijs *et al.*, 1994). More recently developed quantitative MRI techniques have higher sensitivity to neuropathological changes after injury and can provide useful information about the loci and depth of focal insults, the extent of diffuse injury, amount and regions of post-injury volume loss, metabolite ratios, and cortical connectivity (Ashwal *et al.*, 2006; Bonnier *et al.*, 2007; Brenner *et al.*, 2003; Serra-Grabulosa *et al.*, 2005; Wilde *et al.*, 2006). Efforts to relate these more precise measures of brain pathology to outcomes are warranted to explore brain–behavior relationships and improve prediction of neurobehavioral outcomes.

Additional limitations include reliance on generic parent and teacher ratings like the Child Behavior Checklist and Teacher's Report Form to assess behavior outcomes and inadequate assessment of "real-life" social-emotional and academic functioning (Taylor & Alden, 1997). One drawback in relying on widely applied behavior ratings is that they may be insensitive to some of the behavior effects of TBI, such as increased neurobehavioral symptoms, personality changes, and internalizing disorders (Bloom *et al.*, 2001; Green *et al.*, 1998; Taylor *et al.*, 2002). Sensitivity to these effects may be enhanced through interviews and child observations, efforts to measure pre- to post-injury behavioral change, and consideration of neurobehavioral symptoms. More detailed evaluations are needed to measure children's ability to solve social problems, interact appropriately with peers, and engage appropriately in classroom activities (e.g. follow directions, answer questions, complete assignments, take tests). Knowledge of the ways in which these outcomes vary with contextual demands and supports would have direct implications for intervention.

Longitudinal consequences

Failure to assess outcomes across multiple points in time is a further obstacle to progress. Cross-sectional assessments allow us to determine how children with TBI are faring relative to controls at a given point after injury but provide little insight into recovery processes or ways in which injury may have altered developmental trajectories (Fletcher *et al.*, 1995; Taylor & Alden, 1997). TBI in children can lead to impairments in already established skills but can also impair development of to-be-acquired abilities. Moreover, these two types of effects are likely to vary depending on the child's age and developmental status at the time of injury. The distinction between effects on established versus to-be-acquired skills is illustrated in Fig. 8.7, which contrasts hypothetical recovery in skills that were present prior to injury with deleterious effects on future skill development. Skill development in children with brain injury (solid lines) is compared in the figure with the development of non-injured controls (dotted lines). Figure 8.7(a) depicts a relatively large initial deficit "a" in previously acquired skills at time t_1 in children with brain injury compared with non-injured controls. The children with brain injury then recover at rate "b" such that they have a smaller residual deficit "c" relative to controls at time t_2. This pattern is consistent with the results of several longitudinal studies demonstrating pronounced post-acute deficits followed by partial recovery (Ewing-Cobbs *et al.*, 2004a; Jaffe *et al.*, 1995; Yeates *et al.*, 2004). Figure 8.7(b) exemplifies the dampening effects of TBI on growth rates in to-be-

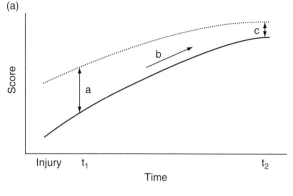

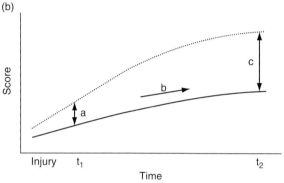

Fig. 8.7. Hypothetical developmental changes in established (1a) versus to-be-acquired (1b) skills in children with brain insults (solid line) and in unaffected children (broken line). (Reproduced by permission of the publisher (Cambridge University Press) from Taylor & Alden, 1997).

acquired skills, as evidenced by a smaller growth rate "b" in children with brain injury relative to controls and by an increasing degree of deficit from t_1 to t_2 ("c" > "a"). Empirical support for longitudinal consequences of this sort is provided by studies of postinjury development in young children with severe TBI (Anderson *et al.*, 2005a; Ewing-Cobbs *et al.*, 2004a), as well as by results from the Ohio TBI Project indicating the failure of some children with severe TBI to progress at expected rates in socialization skills and school performance (Taylor *et al.*, 2002).

Mechanisms of effect

Past research on the neurobehavioral effects of pediatric TBI has been largely descriptive (Fletcher *et al.*, 1995). Relatively few studies have been motivated by efforts to explain injury consequences in terms of underlying mechanisms of effect. For example, it is unclear why children with severe TBI display partial recovery in some cognitive skills during the first year after injury. Does recovery reflect generalized restoration of neural function, reorganization or regeneration of damaged neural systems, activation of alternative undamaged brain systems, or application by children of cognitive strategies that help them compensate for dysfunctional brain regions? Similarly, what factors contribute to post-injury-onset behavior problems? Do such problems reflect the direct effects of injury on brain systems underlying social cognition and emotions, increased vulnerability

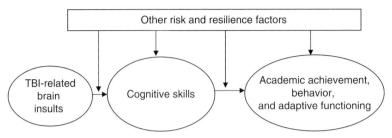

Fig. 8.8. Generic causal framework for investigation of outcomes of pediatric TBI.

to post-injury stressors, adjustment to post-injury skill deficits, or non-optimal behavior management? Furthermore, why do young children show less marked recovery than older children and what does this imply about neural systems underlying skill acquisition? Does the worsening of some outcomes over time reflect a slowed pace of development, the emergence of latent deficits, or motivational problems? Finally, what factors account for selective cognitive, academic, or behavior disorders; how do these outcomes relate to one another; and what are important determinants of variations in injury effects? Research designed to answer questions like these may shed light on processes responsible for injury effects.

Investigations of causal mechanisms can be guided by hypotheses based on: brain–behavior relationships (Levin *et al.*, 2001; Yeates *et al.*, 2007); theories as to the cognitive antecedents of clinical disorders such as ADHD and learning disabilities (Barkley, 1997; Ewing-Cobbs *et al.*, 2004; Schachar *et al.*, 2004); and developmental models of skill acquisition and behavioral change (Anderson, 1998; Pennington, 1994). Theoretically driven study of brain–behavior relationships will benefit from use of experimental paradigms to delineate core processing deficits, such as those used to investigate meta-cognition, prospective memory, and language comprehension (Dennis & Barnes, 2001; Hanten *et al.*, 2004; McCauley & Levin, 2004).

Because brain insult is only one of several influences on post-injury development, researchers also need to test broader causal frameworks that take into account influences on development in addition to TBI. The causal framework depicted in Fig. 8.8 illustrates the general form of these models. The basic assumptions entailed in the framework are that: (a) outcomes are influenced conjointly by TBI and other risk and resilience factors; (b) these other factors may have moderating as well as direct effects; and (c) neuropsychological deficits mediate the effects of TBI on achievement, behavior, and adaptive functioning. The multi-dimensional integrative model used by Yeates *et al.* (2007) to account for the effects of brain disorders on social competence exemplifies such a framework. A longitudinal application is illustrated by the Ohio TBI Project's cross-lagged path model of bidirectional influences between child and family functioning after pediatric TBI (Taylor *et al.*, 2001).

With respect to mechanisms responsible for recovery or continuing neurobehavioral impairment, further research is needed to better understand individual difference factors that buffer or exacerbate injury effects, such as constitutional-genetic variations in brain reserve and in individual capacities to compensate for acquired cognitive impairments (Dennis *et al.*, 2007).

Summary and conclusions

The neurobehavioral consequences of TBI in children are well established. Findings from the Ohio TBI Project and many other studies indicate that moderate to severe TBI results in deficits in executive function and memory and difficulties in behavioral and emotional self-regulation. These deficits may emerge as components of generalized cognitive impairment or as more selective deficiencies. Similarly, while children's academic competencies may be generally impaired, TBI may have a greater impact on mathematics than on reading decoding or may result in difficulties in functioning within the classroom despite intact basic academic skills. Post-injury-onset behavior problems frequently entail difficulties in behavioral and emotional self-regulation, with increased risks for secondary ADHD, mood and anxiety disorders, disruptive behavior problems, personality changes, and PTSD.

Severe and moderate TBI have similar effects, though some studies suggest that children with moderate TBI are less likely to sustain generalized cognitive deficits. The long-term effects of mild TBI in children are less clear. However, these children are at risk for at least transient cognitive deficits and neurobehavioral symptoms that are similar to those observed in children with more severe TBI. Recovery of cognitive abilities and a reduction in neurobehavioral symptoms over time is evident in children at all levels of severity but is far from complete in children with more severe TBI.

MRI studies of children with TBI suggest the neurobehavioral consequences are associated with focal insults to frontal regions and temporal regions, but that other types of lesions such as those involving extra-frontal regions, subcortical structures, or white matter may also be relevant in predicting outcomes (Anderson *et al.*, 2006a; Salorio *et al.*, 2005). Given the potential of blunt trauma to disrupt widely distributed neural networks, highly selective sequelae are likely to be rare occurrences. Variability in outcomes may thus be best explained by a combination of focal and non-focal lesions.

However, outcomes of TBI are highly variable, even after considering injury severity and brain status. While unmeasured variations in neuropathology no doubt explain some of the variability, non-injury factors are also relevant. Findings from the Ohio TBI Project and other studies indicate worse outcomes in children with more pre-injury learning and behavior problems, lower SES or less family resources, and greater family stress, burden, and dysfunction. Although some of these associations are likely to have been present prior to TBI, research suggests that some of the consequences of TBI may be worse in children with pre-injury developmental problems or in those from disadvantaged family environments. Children with pre-existing developmental problems may have a lower threshold for manifesting injury effects or fewer resources to compensate for injury-related impairments. Environmental disadvantage may moderate outcomes by either failing to promote recovery from TBI or by disrupting post-injury development. Additional research reveals young age at injury is another risk factor for poorer long-term cognitive outcomes.

Further investigation of multiple risk and protective factors will improve prediction of neurobehavioral outcomes and clarify the role of TBI relative to other influences. Specification of the skills most and least affected and of the associations of specific deficits to the nature of brain insult (e.g. localization and pattern of lesions) will also enhance knowledge of brain–behavior relationships. Similarly, longitudinal studies are required to assess recovery of established abilities and the effects of TBI on acquisition of new knowledge and skills. Parallel efforts to measure TBI-related changes in brain status and patterns of brain activation during cognitive tasks would shed light on the basis of neural reserve, functional recovery, and disruptive effects of TBI on post-injury development.

More generally, successful research will demand translational approaches that are informed by theory and clinical observation and that involve links between multiple levels of analysis (brain, cognition, learning and behavior, and functioning in everyday contexts). Because of the sample sizes required, potential obstacles are difficulties in establishing inter-institutional collaborations and in securing funding for recruitment and follow-up of children across these multiple sites (Natale *et al.*, 2006). A better understanding of key determinants of neurobehavioral outcomes, identification of risk and protective factors, and informed clinical assessment and intervention will more than offset these costs.

Acknowledgments

The studies by our research team sited in the chapter were funded by grant NS36335 from the National Institute of Neurological Diseases and Stroke of the National Institutes of Health, and by grant MCJ-390611, Maternal and Child Health Bureau (Title V, Social Security Act, Health Resources and Services Administration, Department of Health and Human Services). Participating hospitals were Rainbow Babies & Children's Hospital of the University Hospitals and MetroHealth Medical Center, Cleveland, Ohio; Nationwide Children's Hospital, Columbus, Ohio; and Children's Hospital Medical Center of Akron, Akron, Ohio. Co-investigators were Drs. Dennis Drotar, Susan K. Klein, Terry Stancin, George H. Thompson, Shari Wade, and Keith Owen Yeates. The author is indebted to his colleagues for their many years of active collaboration.

References

Achenbach, T. M. (1991a). *Manual for the Child Behavior Checklist/4–18 and 1991 Profile.* Burlington, VT: University of Vermont, Department of Psychiatry.

Achenbach, T. M. (1991b). *Manual for the Teacher's Report Form and 1991 Profile.* Burlington, VT: University of Vermont, Department of Psychiatry.

Anderson, J. M. (1998). Mental retardation general intelligence and modularity. *Learning and Individual Differences,* 10, 159–178.

Anderson, S. W., Barrash, J., Bechara, A. & Tranel, D. (2006a). Impairments of emotion and real-world complex behavior following childhood- or adult-onset damage to ventromedial prefrontal cortex. *Journal of the International Neuropsychological Society,* 12, 224–235.

Anderson, V. A. & Catroppa, C. (2005). Recovery of executive skills following paediatric traumatic brain injury (TBI): a 2 year follow-up. *Brain Injury,* 19, 459–470.

Anderson, V. A. & Moore, C. (1995). Age at injury as a predictor of outcome following pediatric head injury: a longitudinal perspective. *Child Neuropsychology,* 1, 187–202.

Anderson, V. A., Catroppa, C., Rosenfeld, J., Haritou, F. & Morse, S. A. (2000). Recovery of memory function following traumatic brain injury in pre-school children. *Brain Injury.* 14, 679–692.

Anderson, V. A., Catroppa, C., Haritou, F., Morse, S., Rosenfeld, J. & Stargatt, R. (2001a). Predictors of acute child and family outcome following traumatic brain injury in children. *Pediatric Neurosurgery.* 34, 138–148.

Anderson, V. A., Catroppa, C., Morse, S., Haritou, F. & Rosenfeld, J. (2001b). Outcome from mild head injury in young children: a prospective study. *Journal of Clinical and Experimental Neuropsychology,* 23, 705–717.

Anderson, V. A., Morse, S. A., Catroppa, C., Haritou, F. & Rosenfeld, J. V. (2004). Thirty month outcome from early childhood head injury: a prospective analysis of neurobehavioural recovery. *Brain*, **127**, 2608–2620.

Anderson, V. A., Catroppa, C., Morse, S., Haritou, F. & Rosenfeld, J. (2005a). Functional plasticity or vulnerability after early brain injury? *Pediatrics*, **116**, 1374–1382.

Anderson, V. A., Catroppa, C., Morse, S., Haritou, F. & Rosenfeld, J. (2005b). Identifying factors contributing to child and family outcome at 30 months following traumatic brain injury in children. *Journal of Neurology, Neurosurgerys, and Psychiatry*, **76**, 401–408.

Anderson, V. A., Catroppa, C., Dudgeon, P., Morse, S. A., Haritou, F. & Rosenfeld, J. V. (2006b). Understanding predictors of functional recovery and outcome 30 months following early childhood head injury. *Neuropsychology*, **20**, 42–57.

Ashwal, S., Babikian, T., Gardner-Nichols, J., Freier, M. C., Tong, K. A. & Holshouser, B. A. (2006). Susceptibility-weighted imaging and proton magnetic resonance spectroscopy in assessment of outcome after pediatric traumatic brain injury. *Archives of Physical Medicine and Rehabilitation*, **87**, 50–58.

Barkley, R. A. (1997). Behavioral inhibition, sustained attention, and executive functions: constructing a unifying theory of ADHD. *Psychological Bulletin*, **121**, 65–94.

Barlow, K. M., Thomson, E., Johnson, D. & Minns, R. A. (2005). Late neurologic and cognitive sequelae of inflicted traumatic brain injury in infancy. *Pediatrics*, **116**, e174–e185.

Barnes, M. A. & Dennis, M. (2001). Knowledge-based inferencing after childhood head injury. *Brain and Language*, **76**, 253–265.

Barnes, M. A., Dennis, M. & Wilkinson, M. (1999). Reading after closed head injury in childhood: effects on accuracy, fluency, and comprehension. *Developmental Neuropsychology*, **15**, 1–24.

Barry, C. T., Taylor, H. G., Klein, S. & Yeates, K. O. (1996). The validity of neurobehavioral symptoms in children with traumatic brain injury. *Child Neuropsychology*, **2**, 213–226.

Beebe, D. W., Krivitzky, L., Wells, C. T., Wade, S. L., Taylor, H. G. & Yeates, K. O. (2007). Parent report of sleep behaviors following moderate or severe pediatric traumatic brain injury. *Journal of Pediatric Psychology*, **32**, 845–850.

Beery, K. E. (1989). *Revised Administration, Scoring, and Teaching Manual for the Developmental Test of Visual-Motor Integration*. Cleveland, OH: Modern Curriculum Press.

Bigler, E. D. (2008). Neuropsychology and clinical neuroscience of persistent post-concussive syndrome. *Journal of the International Neuropsychological Society*, **14**, 1–22.

Bijur, P. E. & Haslum, M. (1995). Cognitive, behavioral, and motoric sequelae of mild head injury in a national birth cohort. In S. Broman & M. E. Michel, eds. *Traumatic Head Injury in Children*. Oxford, UK: Oxford University Press, pp. 147–164.

Bittigau, P., Sifringer, M., Pohl, D. *et al.* (1999). Apoptotic neurodegeneration following trauma is markedly enhanced in the immature brain. *Annals of Neurology*, **45**, 724–735.

Bloom, D. R., Levin, H. S., Ewing-Cobbs, L. *et al.* (2001). Lifetime and novel psychiatric disorders after pediatric traumatic brain injury. *Journal of the American Academy of Child and Adolescent Psychiatry*, **40**, 572–579.

Bonnier, C., Marique, P., Van Hout, A. & Potelle, D. (2007). Neurodevelopmental outcome after severe traumatic brain injury in very young children: role for subcortical lesions. *Journal of Child Neurology*, **22**, 519–529.

Brenner, T., Freier, M. C., Holshouser, B. A., Burley, T. & Ashwal, S. (2003). Predicting neuropsychologic outcome after traumatic brain injury in children. *Pediatric Neurology*, **28**, 104–114.

Brown, G., Chadwick, O., Shaffer, P., Rutter, M. & Traub, M. (1981). A prospective study of children with head injuries: III. Psychiatric sequelae. *Psychological Medicine*, **11**, 63–78.

Byles, J., Byrne, C., Boyle, M. H. & Offord, D. R. (1988). Ontario Child Health Study: reliability and validity of the General

Functioning Scale of the McMaster Family Assessment Device. *Family Process*, **27**, 97–104.

Catroppa, C. & Anderson, V. (2005). A prospective study of the recovery of attention from acute to 2 years post pediatric traumatic brain injury. *Journal of the International Neuropsychological Society*, **11**, 84–98.

Catroppa, C. & Anderson, V. (2007). Recovery in memory function, and its relationship to academic success, at 24 months following pediatric TBI. *Child Neuropsychology*, **13**, 240–261.

Catroppa, C., Anderson, V. A., Morse, S. A., Haritou, F. & Rosenfeld, J. V. (2008). Outcome and predictors of functional recovery 5 years following pediatric traumatic brain injury. *Journal of Pediatric Psychology*, **33**, 707–718.

Cattelani, R., Lombardi, F., Brianti, R. & Mazzucchi, A. (1998). Traumatic brain injury in childhood: intellectual, behavioural and social outcomes into adulthood. *Brain Injury*, **12**, 283–296.

Dacey, R., Dikmen, S., Temkin, N., McLean, A., Armsden, G. & Winn, H. (1991). Relative effects of brain and non-brain injuries on neuropsychological and psychosocial outcome. *Journal of Trauma*, **31**, 217–222.

Delis, D., Kramer, J., Kaplan, E. & Ober, B. (1986). *The California Verbal Learning Test: Children's Version*. San Antonio, TX: Psychological Corporation.

Dennis, M. & Barnes, M. A. (2001). Comparison of literal, inferential, and intentional text comprehension in children with mild or severe closed head injury. *Journal of Head Trauma Rehabilitation*, **16**, 456–468.

Dennis, M., Guger, S., Roncadin, C., Barnes, M. & Schachar, R. (2001). Attentional-inhibitory control and social-behavioral regulation after childhood closed head injury: do biological, developmental, and recovery variables predict outcome? *Journal of the International Neuropsychological Society*, **7**, 683–692.

Dennis, M., Yeates, K. O., Taylor, H. G. & Fletcher, J. M. (2007). Brain reserve capacity, cognitive reserve capacity, and age-based functional plasticity after congenital and acquired brain injury in children. In Stern, Y., ed. *Cognitive Reserve*. New York: Taylor & Francis, pp. 53–83.

Donders, J. & Woodward, H. R. (2003). Gender as a moderator of memory after traumatic brain injury in children. *Journal of Head Trauma Rehabilitation*, **18**, 106–115.

Ewing-Cobbs, L. & Barnes, M. (2002). Linguistic outcomes following traumatic brain injury in children. *Seminars in Pediatric Neurology*, **9**, 209–217.

Ewing-Cobbs, L., Levin, H., Fletcher, J., Miner, M. & Eisenberg, H. (1990). The Children's Orientation and Amnesia Test: relationship to severity of acute head injury and to recovery of memory. *Neurosurgery*, **27**, 683–691.

Ewing-Cobbs, L., Fletcher, J. M., Levin, H. S., Iovino, I. & Miner, M. E. (1998). Academic achievement and academic placement following traumatic brain injury in children and adolescents: a two-year longitudinal study. *Journal of Clinical and Experimental Neuropsychology*, **20**, 769–781.

Ewing-Cobbs, L., Barnes, M., Fletcher, J. M., Levin, H. S., Swank, P. R. & Song, J. (2004a). Modeling of longitudinal academic achievement scores after pediatric traumatic brain injury. *Developmental Neuropsychology*, **25**, 107–133.

Ewing-Cobbs, L., Prasad, M. R., Landry, S. H., Kramer, L. & DeLeon, R. (2004b). Executive functions following traumatic brain injury in young children: a preliminary analysis. *Developmental Neuropsychology*, **26**, 487–512.

Ewing-Cobbs, L., Prasad, M. R., Kramer, L. *et al.* (2006). Late intellectual and academic outcomes following traumatic brain injury sustained during early childhood. *Journal of Neurosurgery*, **105**, 2887–2896.

Fay, G. C., Jaffe, K. M., Polissar, M. L., Liao, S., Rivara, J. B. & Martin, K. M. (1994). Outcome of pediatric traumatic brain injury at three years: a cohort study. *Archives of Physical Medicine and Rehabilitation*, **75**, 733–741.

Fletcher, J. M., Ewing-Cobbs, L., Miner, M., Levin, H. & Eisenberg, H. (1990).

Behavioral changes after closed head injury in children. *Journal of Consulting and Clinical Psychology*, **58**, 93–98.

Fletcher, J. M., Ewing-Cobbs, L., Francis, D. J. & Levin, H. S. (1995). Variability in outcomes after traumatic brain injury in children: a developmental perspective. In S. H. Broman & M. E. Michel, eds. *Traumatic Head Injury in Children*. New York: Oxford University Press, pp. 3–21.

Fletcher, J. M., Levin, H. S., Lachar, D. *et al.* (1996). Behavioral outcomes after pediatric closed head injury: relationships with age, severity, and lesion size. *Journal of Child Neurology*, **11**, 283–290.

Gerring, J. P., Brady, K. D., Chen, A. *et al.* (1998). Premorbid prevalence of ADHD and development of secondary ADHD after closed head injury. *Journal of the American Academy of Child and Adolescent Psychiatry*, **37**, 647–654.

Green, M. L., Foster, M. A., Morris, M. K., Muir, J. J. & Morris, R. D. (1998). Parent assessment of psychological and behavioral functioning following pediatric acquired brain injury. *Journal of Pediatric Psychology*, **23**, 289–299.

Hanten, G., Dennis, M., Zhang, L. *et al.* (2004). Childhood head injury and metacognitive processes in language and memory. *Developmental Neuropsychology*, **25**, 85–106.

Hedeker, D. & Gibbons, R. D. (1997). Application of random-effects pattern-misture models for missing data in longitudinal studies. *Psychological Methods*, **2**, 64–78.

Jonsson, C. A., Horneman, G. & Emanuelson, I. (2004). Neuropsychological progress during 14 years after severe traumatic brain injury in childhood and adolescence. *Brain Injury*, **18**, 921–934.

Keenan, H. T. & Bratton, S. L. (2006). Epidemiology and outcomes of pediatric traumatic brain injury. *Developmental Neuroscience*, **28**, 256–263.

Kinsella, G., Prior, M., Sawyer, M. *et al.* (1995). Neuropsychological deficit and academic performance in children and adolescents

following traumatic brain injury. *Journal of Pediatric Psychology*, **20**, 753–768.

Kinsella, G., Prior, M., Sawyer, M. *et al.* (1997). Predictors and indicators of academic outcome in children 2 years following traumatic brain injury. *Journal of the International Neuropsychological Society*, **3**, 608–616.

Kinsella, G., Ong, B., Murtagh, D., Prior, M. & Sawyer, M. (1999). The role of the family for behavioral outcome in children and adolescents following traumatic brain injury. *Journal of Consulting and Clinical Psychology*, **67**, 116–123.

Kirkwood, M., Janusz, J., Yeates, K. O. *et al.* (2000). Prevalence and correlates of depressive symptoms following traumatic brain injury in children. *Child Neuropsychology*, **6**, 195–208.

Kirkwood, M. W., Yeates, K. O., Taylor, H. G., Randolph, C., McCrea, M. & Anderson, V. A. (2008). Management of pediatric mild traumatic brain injury: a neuropsychological review from injury through recovery. *The Clinical Neuropsychologist*, **22**, 769–800.

Levi, R. B., Drotar, D., Yeates, K. O. & Taylor, H. G. (1999). Posttraumatic stress symptoms in children following orthopedic or traumatic brain injury. *Journal of Clinical Child Psychology*, **28**, 232–243.

Levin, H. S. & Hanten, G. (2005). Executive functions after traumatic brain injury in children. *Pediatric Neurology*, **33**, 79–93.

Levin, H. S., Mendelsohn, D., Lilly, M. A. *et al.* (1997). Magnetic resonance imaging in relation to functional outcome of pediatric closed head injury: a test of the Ommaya–Gennarelli Model. *Neurosurgery*, **40**, 432–441.

Levin, H. S., Song, J., Ewing-Cobbs, L. & Roberson, G. (2001). Porteus maze performance following traumatic brain injury in children. *Neuropsychology*, **15**, 557–567.

Levin, H. S., Zhang, L., Dennis, M. *et al.* (2004). Psychosocial outcome of TBI in children with unilateral frontal lesions. *Journal of the International Neuropsychological Society*, **10**, 305–316.

Levine, B., Kovacevic, N., Nica, E. I. *et al.* (2008). The Toronto Traumatic Brain Injury Study: injury severity and quantified MRI. *Neurology*, **70**, 771–778.

Luis, C. A. & Mittenberg, W. (2002). Mood and anxiety disorders following pediatric traumatic brain injury: a prospective study. *Journal of Clinical and Experimental Neuropsychology*, **24**, 270–279.

Mangeot, S., Armstrong, K., Colvin, A. N., Yeates, K. O. & Taylor, H. G. (2002). Long-term executive function deficits in children with traumatic brain injuries: assessment using the Behavior Rating Inventory of Executive Function (BRIEF). *Child Neuropsychology*, **8**, 271–284.

Massagli, T. L., Jaffe, K. M., Fay, G. C., Polissar, N. L., Liao, S. & Rivara, J. B. (1996). Neurobehavioral sequalae of severe pediatric traumatic brain injury: a cohort study. *Archives of Physical Medicine and Rehabilitation*, **77**, 223–231.

Max, J. E., Levin, H. S., Landis, J. *et al.* (2005a). Predictors of personality change due to traumatic brain injury in children and adolescents in the first six months after injury. *Journal of the American Academy of Child and Adolescent Psychiatry*, **44**, 434–442.

Max, J. E., Schachar, R. J., Levin, H. S. *et al.* (2005b). Predictors of secondary attention-deficit/hyperactivity disorder in children and adolescents 6 to 24 months after traumatic brain injury. *Journal of the American Academy of Child and Adolescent Psychiatry*, **44**, 1041–1049.

McCarthy, M. L., MacKenzie, E. J., Durbin, D. R. *et al.* (2006). Health-related quality of life during the first year after traumatic brain injury. *Archives of Pediatric and Adolescent Medicine*, **160**, 252–260.

McCauley, S. R. & Levin, H. S. (2004). Prospective memory in pediatric traumatic brain injury: a preliminary study. *Developmental Neuropsychology*, **25**, 5–20.

McDermott, P. A. (1995). Sex, race, and other demographics as explanations for children's ability and adjustment: a national appraisal. *Journal of School Psychology*, **33**, 75–91.

McKinlay, A., Dalrymple-Alford, J. C., Horwood, L. J. & Fergusson, D. M. (2002). Long term psychosocial outcomes after mild head injury in early childhood. *Journal of Neurology, Neurosurgery, and Psychiatry*, **73**, 281–288.

Pennington, B. F. (1994). The working memory function of the prefrontal cortices: implications for developmental and individual differences in cognition. In M. M. Haith, J. Benson, R. Roberts & B. F. Pennington, eds. *The Development of Future Oriented Processes*. Chicago, IL: University of Chicago Press, pp. 243–289.

Prasad, M. R., Ewing-Cobbs, L., Swank, P. R. & Kramer, L. (2002). Predictors of outcome following traumatic brain injury in young children. *Pediatric Neurosurgery*, **36**, 64–74.

Raz, S., Lauterbach, M. D., Hopkins, T. L. *et al.* (1995). A female advantage in cognitive recovery from early cerebral insult. *Developmental Psychology*, **31**, 958–966.

Ruijs, M. B. M., Keyser, A. & Gabreels, F. J. M. (1994). Clinical neurological trauma parameters as predictors for neuropsychological recovery and long-term outcome in paediatric closed head injury: a review of the literature. *Clinical Neurology and Neurosurgery*, **96**, 273–283.

Salorio, C. F., Slomine, B. S., Grados, M. A., Vasa, R. A., Christensen, J. R. & Gerring, J. P. (2005). Neuroanatomic correlates of CVLT-C performance following pediatric traumatic brain injury. *Journal of the International Neuropsychological Society*, **11**, 686–696.

Satz, P., Zaucha, K., McCleary, C., Light, R., Asarnow, R. & Becker, D. (1997). Mild head injury in children and adolescents: a review of studies (1970–1995). *Psychological Bulletin*, **122**, 107–131.

Schachar, R., Levin, H. S., Max, J., Chen, S. & Purvis, K. (2004). Attention deficit hyperactivity disorder and inhibition deficit after closed head injury in children: do preinjury behavior, injury severity, and recovery variables predict outcome? *Developmental Neuropsychology*, **25**, 179–198.

Serra-Grabulosa, J. M., Junque, C., Verger, K., Salgado-Pineda, P., Maneru, C. & Mercader, J. M. (2005). Cerebral correlates of declarative memory dysfunctions in early traumatic brain injury. *Journal of Neurology, Neurosurgery, and Psychiatry*, 76, 129–131.

Sesma, J. W., Slomine, B. S., Ding, R. & McCarthy, M. L. (2008). Executive functioning in the first year after pediatric traumatic brain injury. *Pediatrics*, 121, e1686–e1695.

Sparrow, S., Bolla, D. & Ciccetti, D. (1994). *Vineland Adaptive Behavior Scales.* Circle Pines, MN: American Guidance Service.

Stancin, T., Kaugars, A. S., Thompson, G. H. et al. (2001). Child and family functioning 6 and 12 months following a serious pediatric fracture. *The Journal of Trauma: Injury, Infection, and Critical Care*, 51, 69–76.

Stancin, T., Drotar, D., Taylor, H. G., Yeates, K. O., Wade, S. L. & Minich, N. M. (2002). Health-related quality of life of children and adolescents after traumatic brain injury. *Pediatrics*, 109, 34, http://www.pediatrics. org/cgi/content/full/109/2/e34.

Taylor, H. G. & Alden, J. (1997). Age-related differences in outcomes following childhood brain insults: an introduction and overview. *Journal of the International Neuropsychological Society*, 3, 1–13.

Taylor, H. G., Drotar, D., Wade, S., Yeates, K. O., Stancin, T. & Klein, S. (1995). Recovery from traumatic brain injury in children: the importance of the family. In S. Broman & M. E. Michel, eds. *Traumatic Head Injury in Children*. Oxford UK: Oxford University Press, pp. 188–216.

Taylor, H. G., Yeates, K. O., Wade, S. L., Drotar, D., Klein, S. K. & Stancin, T. (1999). Influences on first-year recovery from traumatic brain injury in children. *Neuropsychology*, 13, 76–89.

Taylor, H. G., Yeates, K. O., Wade, S. L., Drotar, D., Stancin, T. & Burant, C. (2001). Bidirectional child–family influences on outcomes of traumatic brain injury in children. *Journal of the International Neuropsychological Society*, 7, 755–767.

Taylor, H. G., Yeates, K. O., Wade, S. L., Drotar, D., Stancin, T. & Minich, N. (2002).

A prospective study of long- and short-term outcomes after traumatic brain injury in children: behavior and achievement. *Neuropsychology*, 16, 15–27.

Taylor, H. G., Yeates, K. O., Wade, S. L., Drotar, D., Stancin, T. & Montpetite, M. (2003). Long-term educational interventions after traumatic brain injury in children. *Rehabilitation Psychology*, 48, 227–236.

Taylor, H. G., Swartwout, M. D., Yeates, K. O., Walz, N. C., Stancin, T. & Wade, S. L. (2008). Traumatic brain injury in young children: post-acute effects on cognitive and school readiness skills. *Journal of the International Neuropsychological Society*, 14, 1–12.

Teasdale, G. & Jennett, B. (1974). Assessment of coma and impaired consciousness: a practical scale. *Lancet*, 2, 81–84. demonstrated in a controlled study. *Brain Injury*, 19, 511–518.

Verger, K., Junque, C., Jurado, M. A. et al. (2000). Age effects on long-term neuropsychological outcome in paediatric traumatic brain injury. *Brain Injury*, 14, 495–503.

Wechsler, D. (1991). *WISC-III: Wechsler Intelligence Scale for Children. 3rd Edition Manual.* San Antonio, TX: Psychological Corporation.

Wilde, E. A., Chu, Z., Bigler, E. D. et al. (2006). Diffusion tensor imaging in the corpus callosum in children after moderate to severe traumatic brain injury. *Journal of Neurotrauma*, 23, 1412–1426.

Wilde, E. A., Bigler, E. D., Hunter, J. V. et al. (2007). Hippocampus, amygdale, and basal ganglia morphometrics in children after moderate-to-severe traumatic brain injury. *Developmental Medicine and Child Neurology*, 49, 294–299.

Woodcock, R. & Mather, N. (1989). *Woodcock–Johnson Tests of Achievement-Revised – Standard and Supplemental Batteries.* Allen, TX: DLM Teaching Resources.

Woodward, H., Winterbalther, K., Donders, J. et al. (1999). Prediction of neurobehavioral outcome 1–5 years post pediatric traumatic head injury. *Journal of Head Trauma Rehabilitation*, 14, 351–359.

167

Yeates, K. O. (2000). Pediatric closed-head injury. In K. O. Yeates, M. D. Ris & H. G. Taylor, eds. *Pediatric Neuropsychology: Research, Theory, and Practice*. New York, NY: Guilford, pp. 92–116.

Yeates, K. O. & Taylor, H. G. (1997). Predicting premorbid neuropsychological functioning following pediatric traumatic brain injury. *Journal of Clinical and Experimental Neuropsychology*, **19**, 825–837.

Yeates, K. O. & Taylor, H. G. (2005). Neurobehavioral outcomes of mild head injury in children and adolescents. *Pediatric Rehabilitation*, **8**, 5–16.

Yeates, K. O. & Taylor, H. G. (2006). School-based behavior problems and their educational correlates in children with traumatic brain injury. *Exceptionality*, **14**, 141–154.

Yeates, K. O., Taylor, H. G., Drotar, D. *et al.* (1997). Pre-injury family environment as a determinant of recovery from traumatic brain injuries in school-age children. *Journal of the International Neuropsychological Society*, **3**, 617–630.

Yeates, K. O., Taylor, H. G., Barry, C. T., Drotar, D., Wade, S. L. & Stancin, T. (2001). Neurobehavioral symptoms in childhood closed-head injuries: changes in prevalence and correlates during the first year post-injury. *Journal of Pediatric Psychology*, **26**, 79–91.

Yeates, K. O., Taylor, H. G., Wade, S. L., Drotar, D., Stancin, T. & Minich, N. (2002). A prospective study of short- and long-term neuropsychological outcomes after traumatic brain injury in children. *Neuropsychology*, **16**, 514–523.

Yeates, K. O., Swift, E. E., Taylor, H. G. *et al.* (2004). Short- and long-term social outcomes following pediatric traumatic brain injury. *Journal of the International Neuropsychological Society*, **10**, 412–426.

Yeates, K. O., Armstrong, K., Janusz, J. *et al.* (2005). Long-term attention problems in children with traumatic brain injury. *Journal of the American Academy of Child and Adolescent Psychiatry*, **44**, 574–584.

Yeates, K. O., Bigler, E. D., Dennis, M. *et al.* (2007). Social outcomes in childhood brain disorder: a heuristic integration of social neuroscience and developmental psychology. *Psychological Bulletin*, **133**, 535–556.

Ylvisaker, M., Turkstra, L., Coehlo, C. *et al.* (2007). Behavioural interventions for children and adults with behaviour disorders after TBI: a systematic review of the evidence. *Brain Injury*, **21**, 769–805.

Chapter 9

Neuropsychological rehabilitation in children with traumatic brain injuries

Ingrid van't Hooft

It is of importance to underline that traumatic brain injuries (TBI) in children affects cognitive, social, behavioral, and emotional functioning. Each of these domains interacts with the other, and need to be considered simultaneously within the field of neuropsychological rehabilitation (Sohlberg & Mateer, 2001). The goals of neuropsychological rehabilitation are to promote recovery and to work with the injured child and his/her family to compensate for residual deficits, to understand and treat cognitive, social, and behavioral impairments, to recognize the role of these impairments in functional disabilities, and to monitor and support the family in managing their child's needs. Working with the emotional reactions to frustration and loss is another integral part of effective treatment (Prigatano, 1999; Wilson, 2003; Ylvisaker, 1998; Ylvisaker & Feeney, 2002). Parents play a key role in the rehabilitation process and education for parents is essential in the rehabilitation program (Braga, 2000).

Plasticity versus vulnerability in brain development

Traumatic injury to the developing brain is distinct from adult traumatic brain injury in many ways. One major difference is that the developing brain is more plastic, often considered as an advantage with regard to recovery of function. However, children who suffer TBI are well known to develop chronic cognitive and behavioral disturbances (Taylor & Alden, 1997). Plasticity may be defined as a both structural and functional process (Dennis, 2000). Structural plasticity refers to the anatomical, chemical, and electrical properties of the brain following TBI. Functional plasticity refers to the cognitive and behavioural competencies that may recover following TBI. Plasticity may be considered "good" or "bad" for recovery. On one side, studies both on animals and humans have shown that enriched environments may have a positive influence on brain development, with regards to memory and the ability to learn. This experience-dependent "good" plasticity was first noted by Hebb (1949). Kandel *et al.* (2000) and Kolb and Wishaw (2004) have further demonstrated induced beneficial plasticity in both neocortex and hippocampus by functional exercises, associated with behavioral changes.

On the other side, animal research has demonstrated that TBI-induced alterations in brain development may perturb normal developmental plasticity, including altered neurotransmission, alterations in molecular responses, cell death, changes in neuronal connectivity and function, inhibition of experience-dependent "good" plasticity, and activation of

Pediatric Traumatic Brain Injury: New Frontiers in Clinical and Translational Research, ed. V. Anderson and K. O. Yeates. Published by Cambridge University Press. © Cambridge University Press 2010.

self-propagating "bad" plasticity (Giza & Prins, 2006). "Neuroplasticity seems to be a complex series of molecular, cellular and physiological events that must be carefully orchestrated for optimal developmental outcome" (Giza & Prins, 2006a, b).

Normal developmental neuroplasticity in humans may occur through many age-specific processes, and our understanding of how the recovery after TBI can influence developmental neuroplasticity at a neuroscience level is only beginning to emerge. However, advances in cognitive neuroscience (for example, functional brain imaging) provide a platform for better understanding what happens to the brain during neuropsychological recovery and rehabilitation. More specifically, these techniques can demonstrate post-injury processes that have previously been considered speculatative at best.

While generally viewed as a process advantageous to recovery after TBI, in children the concept of neuroplasticity needs to be considered in the light of vulnerability due to the still developing immature brain. While plasticity or vulnerability perspectives appear to represent opposite extremes along a continuum, they may be better understood as more or less relevant explanations of outcome, depending on a range of factors, including injury characteristics (severity, lesion location), developmental considerations (age at injury), and environmental influences (social advantage, family function). Further, it could be that age at presentation is important in understanding these issues, for example, different structures may subserve emerging versus established skills. If an area is functionally immature at the time of injury, deficits may not be observable until the functions that depend on that particular damaged region are expected to develop (Anderson & Moore, 1995; Anderson *et al.*, 2000). In early childhood it is likely that many brain regions are not yet dedicated to certain functions (Lenneberg, 1967). Despite the potential for significant plasticity in early childhood this neural environment may lead to greater vulnerability in the context of injury. With diffuse, widespread, or bilateral injury in particular, the mechanisms for plasticity may not be available (Kolb, 1995). The significant deficits associated with early brain injury can also be understood in the context of rapid development of important skills during childhood. Ewing-Cobbs *et al.* (2004) suggest that these developing skills are more vulnerable to brain injury at different ages, because rates of skill acquisition vary with age. Early injury may disrupt acquisition of basic competencies (e.g. expressive language, visuospatial skills) that provide necessary foundations for later development (Dennis, 2000).

As the child moves through later childhood and adolescence, the nature of impairment comes to resemble the adult picture more closely, reflecting the more mature CNS, and the associated reduction in plasticity/flexibility for recovery and reorganization (Anderson, 2003).

The implications of these developmental issues for rehabilitation are significant. If neural circuits are more plastic at a young age, rehabilitation efforts for young children should be designed to facilitate these plastic changes. In principle, there are two ways in which the brain might form plastic changes supporting recovery: (1) through the reorganization of remaining undamaged circuits, indicating that the brain could "do more with less." This reorganization could be stimulated by application of different treatments that would facilitate synaptic formation; and (2) the application of different treatments that would facilitate formation of new, functionally adequate synaptic connections (Kolb & Wishaw, 2004). If plasticity is time limited, then the application of early intervention could maximize recovery. Knowledge of child development is critical in the design and implementation of cognitive rehabilitation programs for children. A challenge for future rehabilitators will be the identification of the optimal timing of cognitive training or behavioural therapy methods, which would influence development and reparative processes in the injured brain (Ponsford, 2004; Prigatano, 1999; Sohlberg & Mateer, 2001).

Cognitive rehabilitation

Cognitive remediation, rehabilitation and retraining are all terms that refer to systematic therapeutic efforts designed to improve cognitive functions (Cappa *et al.*, 2003; Carney *et al.*, 1999; Cicerone, 2000; Cope, 1995; Ponsford *et al.*, 1997; Ponsford, 2004; Sohlberg & Mateer, 2001). Cognitive rehabilitation may be considered as a specific component of neuropsychological rehabilitation and involves *internally focused* interventions: the direct process-specific training of a function, for example, attention and/or memory training where the aim of the intervention is *restorative*, seeking to reestablish impaired function or *substitute* where intact abilities are utilized to reroute skills that have been disrupted. Other aspects of internally focused interventions often included in cognitive rehabilitation programs involve learning compensatory techniques and instruction in the use of meta-cognitive strategies as well as the facilitation of insight and self-awareness with regard to cognitive abilities.

In addition to direct process-specific training, cognitive rehabilitation programs may also involve *externally focused* interventions, for example, adapting to environmental demands, environmental modifications, and the use of specialized teaching strategies.

All these aspects need to be included in a broad definition of cognitive rehabilitation. Reviews of a large number of studies on the effectiveness of cognitive rehabilitation for adults after stroke or TBI have provided support for several forms of cognitive rehabilitation. In particular, a positive effect of attention training in the post-acute phase of rehabilitation has been established along with support for compensatory memory training (Cicerone *et al.*, 2000).

Cognitive rehabilitation in children

Assessing recovery after cognitive rehabilitation in children is a particularly complex task with improvement in performance alone not sufficient to imply recovery, because developmental expectations assume ongoing increments in abilities through childhood.

The timing of the insult, the nature of the injury, the stage of skills development, and the social context of the child interact to determine outcome for the child (Ylvisaker & Feeney, 2002). This interaction between development and brain injury is sometimes referred to as "growing into deficits" (Mateer, 1999). Furthermore, the pre-injury cognitive profile of the child, and the psychosocial context and family function, are known to play an important role for recovery following TBI in children (Anderson *et al.*, 2001).

The few existing studies on cognitive rehabilitation with children are based on small samples and frequently include no control conditions (Mateer *et al.*, 1996). Moreover, currently available training methods for children are often versions of material designed for adults (Warschausky *et al.*, 1999), and thus may lack validity and interest for children. The Attention Process Training (APT) materials, based on the hierarchical model of attention from Sohlberg and Mateer (2001), is a process-specific method originally developed for adults. In a study of children with attention deficit/hyperactivity disorder (ADHD), Kerns evaluated a child-oriented version of this programme, called "Pay Attention," and demonstrated significant improvement on several psychometric measures of sustained, selective, and higher levels of attention as well as academic efficiency in seven children with ADHD as compared to seven controls matched by age, sex, and medication status (Kerns et al., 1999). Similarly, Klingberg et al. (2002) showed enhanced performance on visuospatial working memory as well as on Raven's matrices with directed, computerized process-specific training for working memory on seven children with ADHD as compared to seven controls.

Butler and Copeland (2002) reported positive effects with their broader Cognitive Remediation Program (CRP) in a pilot study on ten children post-brain tumor treatment. The program consisted of approximately 50 hours of treatment, over the course of six months, utilizing attention process training, meta-cognitive strategies, and cognitive behavioral therapy. Following treatment there was statistically significant higher performance within the CRP training group on the Digit Span Test, Sentence Memory, and Continuous Performance Test.

A review from Limond and Leeke (2006) on cognitive rehabilitation in children found no publications of randomized controlled trials in the child TBI literature, and only 11 studies with quasi-experimental designs, highlighting the difficulties in meeting current demands of evidence-based practice and arguing the importance of considering multiple research designs to measure the impact of time-consuming rehabilitation activities.

A more recent systematic evidence-based review of published studies between 1980 and 2006 (Laatsch et al., 2007) examined cognitive and behavioral rehabilitation treatment in children with acquired brain injury. These authors identified 28 studies which they divided into four treatment domains: comprehensive, attention and memory, speech and language, and behavior. These studies were then classified as Class 1 to Class IV, where Class I, II, and III are randomized controlled trials, with Class I being those with the most robust designs. Class IV studies involved no control group or utilized case studies or clinical case series. Eight published studies met the criteria for integrated comprehensive cognitive rehabilitation studies. Many of these studies involved meta-cognitive training in memory and attention, and problem solving. A further eight studies on cognitive interventions for attention and memory were reviewed and classified but none of these fulfilled the criteria for Class I. Within Class II there were two studies identified, those of Butler and Malhern (2005) described above, and a study from our team (van't Hooft, 2005). The CRP has further been evaluated in a randomized multi-center clinical trial on survivors of childhood cancer ($N = 161$) who manifested an attentional deficit. The results indicated improved attention according to parents' reports and statistically significant increases in academic achievement (Butler & Malhern, 2005).

The study by vant Hooft et al. (2005) aimed to evaluate the Amsterdam Memory and Attention Training for Children (Amat-c), which is a cognitive training program developed by Hendriks (1996) and initially used with children surviving cancer. This program consists of both internally and externally focused interventions and is based on a modified model from Sohlberg and Mateer (2001), which differentiates attention on three levels: sustained attention, selective attention, and mental tracking. Hendriks and van den Broek (1996) equally differentiated the memory processes on three levels: the sensory register, the short-term or working memory, and the long-term memory. The interaction between attention and memory is most evident at the level of mental tracking (Lezak, 2004), which is defined as the ability to coordinate and integrate sustained and selective attention, as well as to divide, alternate, and shift attention.

The Amat-c method involves a combination of daily practice and games on the one hand, and exercises in specific attention and memory techniques on the other. Additional behavior modification techniques are incorporated in the program. These techniques focus on learning strategies for use in daily life and in the accomplishment of school tasks. Skills for enhancing both visual and auditory modalities are trained. Daily exercises of 30 minutes during 17 weeks are conducted with a gradual increase in the level of difficulty according to the three phases mentioned below. Children perform the exercises with a coach (teacher or parent) at school or at home. Written instructions and a diary complement the exercises. Once a week, the child and his/her coach are seen for feedback and reinforcement sessions, which provide the opportunity for therapeutic intervention beyond that encompassed by the specific training tasks, and enable the child to share his/her cognitive, emotional, and behavioral experiences. There are two versions of the Amat-c method, one for children between 8 and 12 years of age and one for adolescents aged 13 or older.

First phase: training sustained attention

The training techniques in this phase include only one or two auditory or visual stimuli, with only one response alternative. One example of this technique is "listening to the ticking of a clock", or listening to the radio and registering sounds, it is intended to train the ability to focus attention consciously. The results are registered in the diary, which then provides the basis for discussion during the weekly therapeutic session. This first treatment phase supports the child in learning to focus attention step-by-step and in inhibiting impulses and also simultaneously acts as a time for establishing an alliance between trainer and child.

Second phase: training selective attention

During the second phase of the program the focus is on selective attention skills. Once again, responses have to be further inhibited or activated. Distracting stimuli are introduced that need to be distinguished from the relevant stimuli. The second part of the selective attention phase trains the child's ability to divide his or her attention between different stimuli and alternate activation of responses. The differences between relevant and irrelevant stimuli have a higher level of complexity in this phase. An example of an exercise in this phase is the letter maze. The child is required to track down specific words one by one: find one word, cross it through and ignore all the other words or combinations of letters. After the exercise, the child is asked to write down all the different ways in which he/she found the words, to increase the awareness of meta-cognitive strategies.

Third phase: training mental tracking

The third and final phase of training involves a combination of mental tracking and training of internal compensatory strategies for semantic and episodic memory. The overlapping functions of attention and memory are especially clear in this phase and are trained in combination. This phase includes verbal, visual, and spatial memory exercises, starting with simple encoding techniques, such as repetition, and then progressing into semantic encoding strategies and finally combining all the techniques and strategies. The children's capacity for retrieval is trained by association, recognition, free recall, cued recall, as well as recall with vanishing cues. The exercises are mixed with interactive games that include incidental learning, visual imagery, and semantic processing. Several stimuli patterns are processed sequentially. Children consciously learn to organize encoding in order to improve retrieval by using different conceptual search strategies. In addition to memory techniques, they learn step-wise strategies in how to deal with new information, and with situations demanding self-regulation, i.e. executive functions.

Studies on the cognitive intervention with SMART

The Amat-c has recently been translated into Swedish and renamed the Swedish version of Memory and Attention Re Training (the SMART method). Our group initially tested the feasibility of the new version with three children with TBI. Results indicated that the method had the potential to improve cognitive efficieny in children with TBI (van't Hooft, 2003).

The direct and long-term effect of the SMART was then evaluated in a randomized controlled trial of 38 children with acquired brain injuries (ABI) (van't Hooft, 2005).

Results revealed that children with ABI significantly improved their performance on tests of complex attention and memory functions after training as compared to the control group.

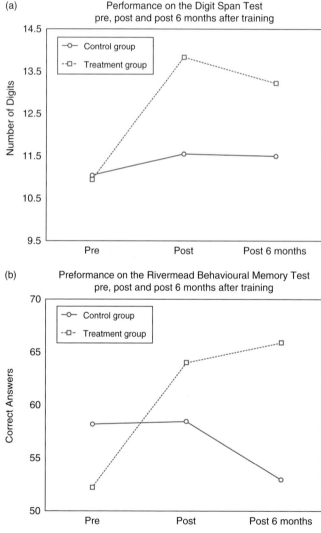

Fig. 9.1. Teachers' ratings (sum scores) of school performance before training, directly after training, and at 6-month follow-up.

Six months after completed training the effects were maintained (van't Hooft & Lindahl-Norberg, in press). Children, parents, and teachers all completed questionnaires on behavior before and directly (see Fig. 9.1) after training, as well as six months after completed training. This questionnaire for children, parents, and teachers contained questions about attention, executive functions, social behavior, and school performance. According to the teachers' ratings, a significant positive change was observed in attention and executive functions as well as in school performance after training. Parents and children described the same tendency. However, there were no significant effect on social behavior (van't Hooft, 2007).

In summary, although based on relatively small samples, the studies suggest that there is a direct potential benefit in children with ABI from cognitive training on their cognitive functions as well as a maintained effect six months after completion of the training. Of note, the benefits also appear to transfer to behavior at school, and to attention-related and executive functions (Tables 9.1, 9.2).

Table 9.1 Estimates (restricted) of relative training effect in % based on teacher's ratings

Questions	Group	After training			6-mo follow-up			p
		M	SE	n	M	SE	n	
School performance (> 42)[a]	Training	12.3	4.6	13	17.3	4.4	15	0.012
	Control	1.3	3.3	19	1.8	3.5	17	
Attention and executive functions (45–65)	Training	15.7	6.7	7	16.5	6.4[b]	8	0.001
	Control	−2.0	3.0	9	−3.5	3.0	9	
Social behavior (> 65)	Training	5.4	4.1	9	1.8	3.8	11	0.100
	Control	−1.6	1.9	17	−3.4	2.0	15	

Notes:
[a]Numbers in this column are sum score limits before training.
[b]One extreme value (outlier) was deleted because it had a large Cook's distance. This deletion does not affect the p value but yields a more reliable estimate of the training effect.

Table 9.2 Estimates (restricted) of relative training effect in % based on parents' ratings

Questions	Group	After training			6-mo follow-up			p
		mean	SE	n	mean	SE	n	
School performance (45–75)[a]	Training	6.1	5.0	12	8.1	4.8	13	0.41
	Control	1.5	4.2	19	3.4	4.3	18	
Attention and executive functions (> 45)	Training	−5.6	6.4	9	−4.5	6.1	10	>0.50
	Control	−3.6	2.9	20	−3.6	3.0	18	
Social behavior (> 60)	Training	5.6	3.2	13	7.0	3.1	14	0.11
	Control	0.1	2.5	20	0.7	2.5	18	

Notes:
[a]Numbers in this column are sum score limits before training.

The combination of hierarchical practice to retrain a dysfunction, and the adoption of learning skills and strategy acquisition, as well as the individual's weekly contact with a professional and the active involvement of the parents and teachers all appear to have contributed to the rehabilitative benefit.

Conclusion and future direction

Questions that remain concern the optimal length of training, the ideal mode of administration (individual or group), the timing (acute or post-acute phase), the possibility of avoiding the need to travel great distances between the homes of the children and their families and rehabilitation units (for example, use of the internet). Since many children with ABI show behavioral dysfunction during development and no effect from this training method was found on social measures, the SMART method could possibly be complemented by a cognitive behavioral modification approach. Our group is in the process of addressing some of these issues.

With regards to the length of training, the efficacy of an abbrevated version was tested out in a pilot study of four children treated for medulloblastomas with irradiation and chemotherapy. The cognitive training was reduced to 10 weeks without excluding exercises and combined with a parents coaching program including 5 × 1 hour sessions. Pre- and post-test measures addressed the same areas as the original study. Preliminary results indicate an improvement on outcome measures both with regard to the children's test performances and their parents' stress level. In addition the children showed improved self-image (van't Hooft, submitted).

A next step to validate the theoretical and practical consequence of these studies could be to test the SMART method in more specific diagnostic groups as well as in larger groups of children from multiple rehabilitation units.

In order to achieve evidence-based interventions in the clinic and better understand the effectiveness of intervention, future research on cognitive rehabilitation in children with TBI is dependent on the collaboration between investigators with expertise in areas such as neuropsychology, neuropathology, and neuroimaging.

References

Anderson, V. (2003). Outcome and management of traumatic brain injury in childhood: the neuropsychologist's contribution. In Wilson, B (ed). *Neuropsychological Rehabilitation*. Lisse: Swets & Zeitlinger, pp. 217–252.

Anderson, V. & Moore, C. (1995). Age at injury as a predictor following paediatric head injury: a longitudinal perspective. *Child Neuropsychology*, 1, 187–202.

Anderson, V., Catroppa, C., Morse, S., Haritou, F. & Rosenfeld, J. (2000). Recovery of intellectual ability following TBI in childhood: impact of injury severity and age at injury. *Pediatric Neurosurgery*, 32, 282–290.

Anderson, V., Northam, E., Hendy, J. & Wrennal, J. (2001). *Developmental Neuropsychology: A Clinical Approach.* Hove and New York: Taylor & Francis Psychology Press.

Braga, L. (2000). Rehabilitation and the role of the family. *Brain Injury*, 17, 1–9.

Butler, R. W. & Malhern, R. (2005). Neuro-cognitive effects of treatment for childhood cancer. *Journal of Pediatric Psychology*, 30, 65–78.

Cappa, S. F., Benke, T., Clarke, S., Rossi, B., Stemmer, B. & van Heugten, C. M. (2003). Guidelines on cognitive rehabilitation:

report of an EFNS task force. *European Journal of Neurology*, **10**, 11–23.

Carney, N., Chesnut, R. M. & Maynard, H. (1999). Effect of cognitive rehabilitation on outcomes for persons with traumatic brain injury: a systematic review. *Journal of Head Trauma Rehabilitation*, **14**, 277–307.

Cicerone, K. D., Dahlberg, C., Kalmar, K. *et al.* (2000). Evidence-based cognitive rehabilitation: recommendations for clinical practice. *Archives of Physical Medicine and Rehabilitation*, **8**, 1596–1615.

Cope, D. N. (1995). The effectiveness of traumatic brain injury rehabilitation: a review. *Brain Injury*, **9**, 649–670.

Dennis, M. (2000). Developmental plasticity in children: the role of biological risk, development, time, and reserve. *Journal of Communication Disorders*, **33**, 321–332.

Ewing-Cobbs, L., Barnes, M., Fletcher, J. M., Levin, H. S., Swank, P. R. & Song, J. (2004). Modeling of longitudinal academic achievement scores after pediatric traumatic brain injury. *Developmental Neuropsychology*, **25**, 107–133.

Giza, C. & Prins, M. I. (2006). Is being plastic phantastic? *Developmental Neuroscience*, **28**(4–5), 364–79.

Hebb, D. O. (1949). *The Organization of Behaviour. A Neuropsychological Theory.* New York: John Wiley & Sons, Ltd.

Hendriks, C. M. (1996). Attention and memory training in childhood cancer survivors. *European Cancer Society Newsletter*, **5**, 13–14.

Hendriks, C. M. & van den Broek, T. M. (1996). *Amat-c Manual and Workbook*. Lisse: Swets & Zeitlinger.

Kandel, E. R., Schwartz, J. H. & Jessell, T. M. (2000). *Principles of Neural Science*, 4th edition. New York: McGraw-Hill.

Kerns, K. A., Eso, K. & Thomson, J. (1999). Investigation of a direct intervention for improving attention in young children with ADHD. *Developmental Neuropsychology*, **16**, 273–295.

Klingberg, T., Westerberg, H. & Forssberg, H. (2002). Training of working memory in children with ADHD. *Journal of Clinical and Experimental Neuropsychology*, **24**, 781–791.

Kolb, B. (1995). *Brain Plasticity and Behaviour*. Mahwah, NJ: Erlbaum.

Kolb, B. & Wishaw, I. Q. (2004). *Fundamentals of Human Neuropsychology*, 5th edition. New York: Worth/Freeman-Koskinen.

Laatsch, L., Harrington, D., Hotz, G. *et al.* (2007). An evidence-based review of cognitive and behavioral rehabilitation treatment studies in children with acquired brain injuries. *Journal of Head Trauma Rehabilitation*, **22**, 248–256.

Lenneberg, E. H. (1967). *Biological Foundations of Language*. New York: John Wiley & Sons, Ltd.

Lezak, M. (2004). *Neuropsychological Assessments*, 4th edition. New York: Oxford University Press.

Limond, J. & Leeke, R. (2006). Practitioner review: cognitive rehabilitation for children with acquired brain injury. *Journal of Child Psychology and Psychiatry*, **46**, 339–352.

Mateer, C. A. (1999). Executive function disorders: rehabilitation challenges and strategies. *Seminars in Clinical Neuropsychiatry*, **4**, 50–59.

Mateer, C. A., Kerns, K. A. & Eso, K. L. (1996). Management of attention and memory disorders following traumatic brain injury. *Journal of Learning Disabilities*, **6**, 618–632.

Ponsford, J. (2004). *Cognitive and Behavioral Rehabilitation: From Neurobiology to Clinical Practice*. New York: The Guilford Press.

Ponsford, J., Willmott, C., Rothwell, A. *et al.* (1997). Cognitive and behavioural outcome following mild traumatic brain injury in children. *Journal of the International Neuropsychological Society*, **3**, 225.

Prigatano, G. P. (1999). *Principles of Neuropsychological Rehabilitation*. New York: Oxford University Press.

Sohlberg, M. M. & Mateer, C. A. (2001). *Cognitive Rehabilitation: An Integrative*

Neuropsychological Approach. New York: Guilford Press.

Taylor, H. G. & Alden, J. (1997). Age related differences in outcomees following childhood brain insults: an introduction and overview. *Journal of the International Neuropsychological Society*, **3**, 555–567.

van't Hooft, I., Andersson, K., Sejersen, T., Bartfai, A. & von Wendt, L. (2003). Attention and memory training in children with acquired brain injuries. *Acta Paediatrica*, **92**(8), 935–940.

van't Hooft, I., Andersson, K., Bergman, B., Sejersen, T., von Wendt, L. & Bartfai, A. (2005). Beneficial effects from a cognitive training programme on children with acquired brain injuries demonstrated in a controlled study. *Brain Injury*, **19**, 511–518.

van't Hooft, I., Andersson, K., Bergman, B., Sejersen, T., von Wendt, L. & Bartfai, A. (2007). A randomized controlled trial on children with acquired brain injuries reveals sustained favorable effects of cognitive training. *Neurorehabilitation*, **22**, 109–116.

van't Hooft, I., Brodin, U., Sejersen, T., von Wendt, L. & Bartfai, A. (in press).

Measuring effects on behaviour after cognitive training in children with acquired brain injuries.

van't Hooft, I. & Lindahl-Norberg. (in press). Cognitive training and parental coaching in 3 children with medullablastoma.

Warschausky, S., Kewman, D. & Kay, J. (1999). Empirically supported psychological and behavioural therapies in pediatric rehabilitation of TBI. *Journal of Head Trauma Rehabilitation*, **14**, 373–383.

Wilson, B. (2003). *Neuropsychological Rehabilitation, Theory and Practice*. Lisse, the Netherlands: Swetz & Zeitlinger.

Ylvisaker, M. & Feeney, T. (2002). Executive functions, self-regulation, and learned optimism in paediatric rehabilitation: a review and implications for intervention. *Pediatric Rehabilitation*, **5**, 51–70.

Ylvisaker, M., Szekeres, S. F. & Feeney, T. (1998). Cognitive rehabilitation: executive functions. In Ylvisaker, M. ed. *Traumatic Brain Injury Rehabilitation: Children and Adolescents*, revised edition. Boston: Butterworth-Heinemann, pp. 221–269.

Chapter 1

Psychosocial interventions

Shari L. Wade

Developing and testing psychosocial interventions for pediatric TBI requires answering the key questions of: who, what, when, where, and how. As in middle school journalism, the answers to these questions fundamentally shape the story, or in this case, the nature of the intervention. This chapter focuses specifically on interventions or treatments that have been developed to address the psychosocial problems following TBI in children and adolescents. Within this scope, I have considered treatments to improve child and family adaptation including executive functions and behavior. However, interventions targeting memory and cognitive problems (i.e. cognitive retraining) are considered elsewhere in this volume. In considering the answers to the five questions, we will examine all levels of evidence from Class 1: double-blinded randomized trials to Class 4: uncontrolled descriptive studies (Edlund *et al.*, 2004). The existing intervention literature is examined with an eye toward promising new approaches and avenues for further investigation.

Who?
Injury severity
Given that this is a volume on pediatric TBI, the answer to the question of "who" seems deceptively simple children with traumatic or acquired brain injury. However, upon further consideration the answers are considerably more varied and complex. First, there is the question of which children with respect to injury severity. The psychosocial sequelae of TBI vary widely depending on the severity of injury, and thus the nature and targets of intervention will vary correspondingly. Although most published interventions have focused on more severe injuries because they are associated with the most profound and persistent psychosocial consequences, others have targeted preventing secondary symptoms following mild TBI (Ponsford *et al.*, 2001) or have sought to address the broad spectrum of injuries (Wade *et al.*, 2006).

Developmental considerations
The age of the child will also shape the nature and targets of the intervention. Interventions to improve behavioral outcomes in an infant or young child will likely focus on the responsiveness and behavior management skills of the adult caregivers (Schuhmann *et al.*, 1998). Conversely, interventions for adolescents with TBI may place greater emphasis on self-awareness and self-regulation and relatively less emphasis on parenting skills (Wade

Pediatric Traumatic Brain Injury: New Frontiers in Clinical and Translational Research, ed. V. Anderson and K. O. Yeates. Published by Cambridge University Press. © Cambridge University Press 2010.

et al., 2008b). Thus, it is unlikely that any single intervention approach will be effective across the entire pediatric age range.

Key individuals or pathways for intervention

The question of who also pertains to the individuals involved in the intervention. Potential targets for intervention include the injured child, his or her parents, and siblings and extended family. Involving the family in psychosocial interventions is important from two perspectives. First, parent and family functioning are adversely affected by TBI (Rivara *et al.*, 1996; Wade *et al.*, 2002; Wade *et al.*, 2006d), thus it is important to consider interventions that facilitate family functioning. Moreover, family functioning and resources are important predictors of the child's behavioral recovery, with poor family functioning contributing to less recovery over time (Kinsella *et al.*, 1999; Max *et al.*, 1998; Taylor *et al.*, 1999; Yeates *et al.*, 1997). Thus, improving parent and family functioning should contribute to improved child outcomes. Moreover, parents can provide critical environmental supports or scaffolding for the child's behavior, particularly for children with more severe injuries. From this perspective, parents can function as the interventionist as well as the target of the intervention (Braga *et al.*, 2005). Children develop in the broader ecological contexts of the school and community (Bronfenbrenner & Morris, 2006) and thus these also constitute targets for intervention. For school-age children, teachers may serve as a particularly critical target for intervention (Ylvisaker *et al.*, 2001).

What?
Targets for intervention
Child behavior

TBI can cause or exacerbate a wide range of both internalizing and externalizing behavior problems in children (Max *et al.*, 1997; Schwartz *et al.*, 2003). Externalizing symptoms include impulsivity, executive dysfunction, emotional lability, anger/aggression, and concomitant attention and conduct difficulties. Although less common, internalizing symptoms, such as depression and anxiety, are also present following pediatric TBI and can serve as the targets for intervention (Vasa *et al.*, 2002; 2004). Social competence and self-esteem may also be adversely affected following TBI (Janusz *et al.*, 2002; Yeates *et al.*, 2004). Thus, interventions targeting behavioral concerns may incorporate a broad range of treatment approaches from anger management to social skills training.

Parent distress and family functioning

Parents or adult caregivers also experience increased burden and distress as a consequence of the injury (Wade *et al.*, 1998). Differing parental perceptions regarding the severity of the injury and how to respond to the child may contribute to communication difficulties and exacerbate marital conflicts. For example, one parent may be worried over the child's re-injury whereas the other emphasizes letting the child "get back to normal." Parents may also harbor feelings of guilt or blame toward the other spouse (Fig. 10.1). Family functioning can also deteriorate following TBI due to increased burden, role strain, and associated tensions (Wade *et al.*, 2006d). Anecdotally, siblings may experience worries about their sibling's recovery, increased responsibility for household chores, and reductions in parental attention which in turn contribute to depression and/or acting out behaviors. Thus, siblings may also benefit from supportive or cognitive behavioral interventions.

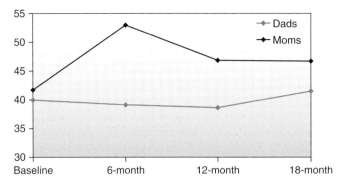

Fig. 10.1. Mother's vs. father's ratings of parenting disagreements over time following severe TBI in young children.

Although there is limited evidence that parenting skills are adversely affected by TBI (Wade *et al.*, 2008a), they may be targeted in interventions for infants or younger children.

Remediation versus compensatory approaches

Interventions also vary to the extent that they emphasize remediating or relearning the lost skill versus developing strategies for compensation. For example, with respect to EF skills such as working memory, a remediation approach may focus on sharpening memory skills; whereas a compensatory approach might encourage the use of graphic organizers or other external memory aids. By its nature, remediation directly involves the injured child. Compensatory strategies, however, may focus on modifying the home and/or school environment to enable the child to function more effectively.

Single versus multiple skills

As outlined previously, TBI can result in a range of child, caregiver, and family difficulties. As such, interventions to improve psychosocial outcomes may target single issues or problems (i.e. anger management) or multiple behaviors. Because sequelae vary widely from individual to individual, interventions emphasizing multiple problems or skills must be sufficiently flexible to accommodate differing child and family needs. Conversely, because most children with severe TBI experience difficulties in multiple domains, an intervention targeting a single skill may be inadequate for many children and families.

When?

The limited literature on treatment studies provides no information on the optimal timing of interventions. Intervening early in the recovery process may prevent the subsequent emergence of problems (Ponsford *et al.*, 2001). However, the nature and extent of behavioral and social difficulties may not be apparent early on, and, as a consequence, families may be resistant to treatment. Thus, the timing of intervention involves a tradeoff between intervening early to reduce longer term problems versus waiting until the child and family has some awareness of residual problems or concerns. Mounting versus diminishing stress and difficulties over time following severe TBI (Wade *et al.*, 2006d) suggest that both acute and long-term intervention may be appropriate for some children and families.

Where?

Traditionally, psychosocial treatments for pediatric TBI have been provided in the hospital or outpatient clinic. However, children with TBI receive treatment at centralized pediatric trauma and rehabilitation centers with service areas spanning hundreds of miles. Thus, it may be impossible or unduly time-consuming to return to the inpatient rehabilitation facility for ongoing treatment. Conversely, community providers may lack familiarity or experience with TBI, thereby resulting in potentially inappropriate diagnoses and treatments. As a consequence, families must often choose between traveling long distances to obtain services or forgoing them altogether. Tele-rehabilitation approaches such as video-conferencing or web-based treatments (Rotondi et al., 2005; Wade et al., 2006a,b) may provide an alternative to clinic-based treatments, enabling families to receive services in their homes. Schools also constitute an important, if under-utilized, treatment venue.

How?

An overview

How you intervene is determined by who you are intervening with and what you want to change. Several recent review articles provide a sense of the range of psychosocial interventions for pediatric TBI (Catroppa & Anderson, 2006; Laatsch et al., 2007; Ylvisaker et al., 2005; 2007). As noted by Laatsch and colleagues (2007), this literature yields few, if any, guidelines for practice based on Class 1 randomized clinical trials (RCT). The one exception is the recommendation that family members be considered as active treatment providers based on the RCT by Braga and colleagues (2005). However, this study examined the relative efficacy of caregivers versus professionals in delivering an intervention to improve the child's physical and cognitive functioning. Thus, it does not strictly constitute an intervention to improve psychosocial or behavioral outcomes. Ylvisaker (2006), evaluating an overlapping, but not identical, literature using different criteria, noted converging evidence for the efficacy of interventions emphasizing positive behavioral supports, which will be described in greater detail below.

There are a number of reasons for the dearth of evidence-based guidelines. First, TBI is a "low incidence" disorder making it difficult to conduct an adequately powered trial at a single site. As a result, there have been only a handful of randomized trials. Second, the varied and multi-faceted nature of TBI-related difficulties makes it difficult to identify homogeneous samples for targeted treatments. While some children present with internalizing symptoms such as anxiety and depression following TBI (Kirkwood et al., 2000; Vasa et al., 2002; 2004), others experience difficulties with EF (Levin & Hanten, 2005), personality changes (Max et al., 2000), or externalizing symptoms (Schwartz et al., 2003). Evaluation of parental needs following TBI consistently highlight the desire for additional information about the medical consequences of TBI (Aitken et al., 2004), whereas psychosocial concerns are considered less important. These informational needs often translate into a desire for greater specifics about their child's recovery trajectory and long-term prospects rather than more information about brain injury in general. Given this perspective, parents may have difficulty recognizing their needs for psychosocial treatment, thereby reducing the likelihood of participation in programs targeting child or family adjustment. Parents of both young children and adolescents may also have difficulty distinguishing the behavioral consequences of injury from typical development. While parents of pre school-age children may fail to link academic difficulties to the earlier injury; those of adolescents may misattribute emotional lability and poorly controlled anger to adolescence rather than TBI. Taken together, these factors underscore the difficulty of conducting adequately powered trials for psychosocial interventions and point to the need for multi-center collaboration.

Given the barriers to conducting an adequately powered RCT, some researchers and clinicians (Ylvisaker *et al.*, 2007) have argued that a different standard of evidence (i.e. multiple, well-designed single-case studies) may be more appropriate. Depending on the nature of the intervention, multiple baseline or reversal designs, in which an intervention is implemented then removed, may provide crucial evidence regarding the responsiveness of target behaviors to a specific intervention. However, for interventions which were designed to generalize across behaviors or settings (i.e. most cognitive behavioral approaches), traditional behavioral paradigms are inappropriate. Thus, whether investigation by RCT is necessary or appropriate depends to some extent on the nature of the intervention approach. However, as the evidence base continues to evolve, it will be important to continue to consider findings from appropriately designed single-case studies.

Specific treatment approaches

Much of the rest of this chapter focuses on *how* various clinical researchers have intervened to improve psychosocial outcomes following pediatric TBI. This review is not intended to be exhaustive, but rather to highlight approaches that show promise and may provide a foundation for subsequent research. The reader is referred to a series of recent review articles for more extensive consideration of psychosocial treatments for pediatric TBI (Catroppa & Anderson, 2006; Laatsch *et al.*, 2007; Ylvisaker *et al.*, 2007).

Preventive approaches

Ponsford *et al.* (2001) conducted an RCT examining the efficacy of information/anticipatory guidance in reducing behavior problems following mild TBI in children. This study is unique in its focus on mild TBI and its emphasis on prevention rather than amelioration. They found that parents of children with mild TBI who received an informational pamphlet in the emergency department regarding the acute effects of TBI and common post concussive symptoms reported fewer symptoms on the Child Behavior Checklist at three months post-injury than those receiving standard care. These findings suggest that even a limited, educational intervention can be effective in reducing some behavioral sequelae of mild TBI, although more intensive interventions are likely to be necessary to improve functioning following more significant injuries.

Positive behavioral supports

In response to the limitations of traditional behavioral treatment paradigms for children with frontal lobe injuries that limit their ability to benefit from consequences, Ylvisaker and colleagues (2003) developed an intervention model incorporating positive behavioral supports and antecedent behavior control to improve on-task behaviors/task completion and reduce aggressive and disruptive behaviors. Their approach engages the child's parents, teachers, or other everyday communication partners in identifying and addressing environmental antecedents to problem behaviors and providing appropriate supports and scaffolding to the child to ensure successful task completion. Principles include negotiating with the child to make tasks interesting, meaningful and doable, providing frequent support and feedback early on and then fading over time, and structuring the environment to maximize successes. Although limited to multiple, well-designed single-case studies, the growing evidence base for positive behavioral supports suggests that it can be an effective approach for addressing behavioral issues in the school and home. The reader is referred to Ylvisaker and colleagues (2003) for a more thorough description of this approach.

Cognitive behavioral approaches

Although less numerous in the literature than traditional behavioral treatment designs, investigations suggest that cognitive behavioral interventions emphasizing awareness and implementation of meta-cognitive strategies such as self-monitoring (Selznick & Savage, 2000), self-regulation, and self-reinforcement (Suzman *et al.*, 1997) may be effective in improving self-awareness and problem solving skills. Ylvisaker (2006) has also described a model of self-coaching for adolescents with TBI that expands upon positive behavioral support approaches described above by placing greater emphasis on self-awareness and having routines or scripts to implement in potentially problematic situations. This self-coaching model employs a problem solving heuristic (Goal-Obstacle-Plan-Do-Review) that encourages individuals to systematically develop and implement a plan for achieving their goals.

Family-centered approaches

My colleagues and I have conducted a series of RCTs examining the efficacy of family problem solving treatment in improving functioning in both the injured child and his or her family. Previous research demonstrated that cognitive behavioral stress management interventions were superior to supportive approaches in reducing parental distress following TBI (Singer *et al.*, 1994). Problem solving therapy equips parents, as well as the injured child, with the coping skills they need to respond to challenges arising from the TBI as well as other concerns facing the family. The problem solving program that we developed integrated education regarding the consequences of TBI with training in problem solving, communication skills, and positive behavioral supports to reduce parental burden and distress as well as child behavioral problems. We adopted a family-centered approach, including the child with TBI as well as siblings in the treatment, with the expectation that positive changes in the child's behavior could occur either as a result of improvements in parent functioning/parenting skills or through the child directly acquiring the target skills.

In an initial face-to-face study of families of children aged 5–17 who sustained a moderate to severe TBI in the past 24 months, those randomly assigned to the family problem solving treatment reported a significant reduction in internalizing symptoms on the Child Behavior Checklist relative to the usual psychosocial care comparison group (Wade *et al.*, 2006c). However, no group differences in externalizing behaviors or parent distress were found.

To address issues raised following this initial trial regarding accessibility, developmental differences among the participants, and the need for greater repetition of core content, we developed an online version of the family problem solving program (OFPS). By providing the treatment online, we obviated the need for families to return to the hospital for sessions, thereby reducing time and logistic constraints. OFPS integrated self-guided, web-based didactic sessions with synchronous videoconferences with a trained therapist to assist

Fig. 10.2. Sample webpage listing six steps for controlling anger.

families in implementing the problem solving process around family goals. The web-based sessions included didactic information, video clips modeling skills, and exercises giving the family an opportunity to apply the skills that they were learning, thereby affording repeated exposure to intervention content through different modalities (Fig. 10.2).

In the initial RCT of OFPS, families of 40 school-age children with moderate to severe TBI were randomly assigned to OFPS or an internet resource comparison group (IRC). During the 6-month treatment period, all families received computers and high-speed internet access to online resources for TBI including chat rooms; however, only the OFPS families received the specific skill-building content and synchronous videoconferences. OFPS resulted in significantly greater reductions in parental depression, anxiety, and distress than the IRC (Wade *et al.*, 2006a) (Fig. 10.3). Improvements in child behavior problems and self-management skills were also demonstrated with greater effects among older and economically disadvantaged children (Wade *et al.*, 2006b). These studies are among the few randomized clinical trials demonstrating significant improvements in both parent and child adjustment following TBI providing evidence that cognitive behavioral approaches that have demonstrated efficacy for other conditions (D'Zurilla & Nezu, 1999) may be beneficial following TBI.

Parents as advocates

Another approach to improving psychosocial outcomes following TBI is training parents to serve as more effective advocates for their children. Glang and colleagues (2007) implemented this approach in an RCT examining the efficacy of a CD-ROM-based program that

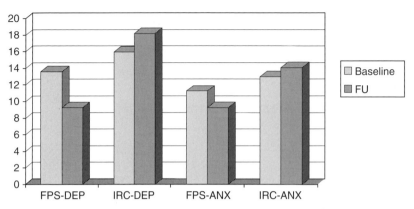

Fig. 10.3. Findings from RCT (*n* = 40): changes in depression and anxiety from pre- to post-treatment.

taught parents communication and advocacy skills for working with school personnel. Parents receiving the Brain Injury Partners CD demonstrated greater improvements than the comparison group on measures of knowledge, application, and attitudes. However, the groups did not differ in their intention to use the skills or self-efficacy. Like the education-based intervention by Ponsford and colleagues (2001) described previously, this project underscores the potential value of self-directed, information-based interventions for addressing targeted skills or outcomes.

Where are we?

Depending on the answers to the questions: who, what, when, where, there are a number of potentially promising approaches for how to intervene. The heterogeneity of the psychosocial concerns following pediatric TBI coupled with the range of pre- and post-injury family issues makes the advent of a single "one-size-fits-all" intervention unlikely. However, educational interventions, traditional behavioral interventions, positive behavioral supports, and cognitive behavioral approaches have each demonstrated efficacy with at least some of the psychosocial and behavioral consequences of TBI. Family-centered interventions that seek to facilitate parent and child coping as well as family communication and adaptation may be able to address a broader range of issues facing children and families following TBI. However, it is not clear whether such broad spectrum approaches are equally as effective as more targeted approaches at improving specific behaviors (i.e. anger management).

Where do we need to go?

As the discussion above suggests, further research is needed to determine what type of approach is most effective for a particular target problem and to identify which individuals and families are most likely to benefit from a particular intervention. For example, in my own research, we found that older children showed greater improvements as a result of OFPS. This led us to speculate that older children and adolescents may be better equipped to directly learn and apply the problem solving and communication skills; whereas a different approach targeting parent rather than child skills may be more effective with younger children. Multi-site, randomized trials comparing different treatments would afford an opportunity to begin to address these issues. Toward this end, I recently completed a two-center trial comparing OFPS to online family support and information (Rotondi *et al.*, 2005). Although we are still analyzing the data, inadequate statistical power due to smaller than planned sample size will likely limit our ability to draw conclusions about the relative merits of these treatment approaches for various individuals. This suggests that future multi-site trials will likely need to involve several sites that have previously demonstrated the ability to recruit and retain adequate numbers of participants.

Future intervention efforts should also place greater emphasis on the child's developmental level and the relationship between the child's age/development, the injury sequelae, and the nature of the intervention. Most of the interventions described previously, including my own work, involved children across the age span. However, we know that the cognitive capabilities of a 6-year-old and a 16-year-old are vastly different. Likewise, markedly different developmental and social challenges face each. Thus, it only makes sense that TBI intervention programs should be tailored to address the specific developmental abilities and concerns of the children involved. Toward this end, we have been developing and testing an intervention for adolescents that builds upon OFPS by placing more emphasis on self-monitoring and self-awareness in social situations. At the other end of the age spectrum, we have developed a parenting skills program to address behavior problems in younger children (Fig. 10.4.).

Fig. 10.4. Live coaching of parenting skills using videoconferencing and Bluetooth earpieces.

It will also be important to design studies examining the timing of intervention delivery (acute versus chronic phase of recovery) and the relative ability of treatments to prevent the emergence of secondary problems versus ameliorating existing ones. To address the issue of secondary/tertiary prevention, studies will need to include children without clearly identified sequelae; however, this approach will also necessitate larger samples since children without existing symptoms cannot, by definition, improve as a function of the treatment (ceiling effects).

The term translational enjoys wide use in academic medicine, although its meaning varies widely according to the context. With respect to psychosocial interventions for pediatric TBI, we have the potential to translate interventions that have been developed for another population or problem for use with children with TBI. TBI shares many of the behavioral characteristics of Attention Deficit/Hyperactivity Disorder including inattention, impulsivity, executive dysregulation, and an inability to anticipate consequences. As such, we might consider translating efficacious treatments for ADHD (Barkley, 2002) for use with TBI. Evidence-based treatments for depression, anxiety, and anger control may also provide intervention models for TBI.

Advances in neuroimaging may afford opportunities for interdisciplinary research, while allowing us to redefine how we measure improvement following psychosocial interventions. For example, if a problem solving intervention successfully changes how the adolescent approaches problem solving, this change should potentially be reflected in altered neural activation during problem solving paradigms. Thus, we may be able to more tangibly determine intervention effects.

Challenges moving forward

A major challenge to developing evidence-based guidelines for treating psychosocial and behavioral concerns following pediatric TBI is the lack of sensitive and ecologically valid outcome measures. The studies reviewed in this chapter used a range of treatment outcome measures including behavioral counts, standardized checklists, and specialized assessments of knowledge and skills. However, it is unclear whether any of these approaches corresponds to improved functioning in everyday settings. While identifying sensitive and meaningful outcome measures is an issue for all treatment research, it is a more significant problem in TBI research, given the wide range of behavioral and family sequelae and inconsistent symptom profiles across individuals and over time.

In a time of diminishing federal funding, finding the resources to conduct multi-site clinical trials is a daunting task. It is incumbent upon professionals in the field to raise the profile of pediatric TBI and to help funding agencies appreciate the significant mental health consequences and the tremendous societal costs when these consequences go untreated (Osberg et al., 1997). We must also work to de-stigmatize brain injury for families so that they are more willing to lobby for funding for such work rather than denying that their child suffered a brain trauma ("it was a "head" injury not a brain injury"). To move forward, we must also find ways to collaborate rather than compete.

Despite these challenges, the future holds considerable promise for identifying more homogeneous groups of patients (via imaging and brain chemistry) and building upon the existing foundation of intervention research to develop evidence-based guidelines for pediatric TBI in the coming decades.

References

Aitken, M. E., Mele, N. & Barrett, K. W. (2004). Recovery of injured children: parent perspectives on family needs. *Archives of Physical Medicine and Rehabilitation*, **85**, 567–573.

Barkley, R. A. (2002). Psychosocial treatments for attention deficit hyperactivity disorder. *Journal of Clinical Psychiatry*, **63**, S36–S43.

Braga, L. W., Da Paz, A. C. & Ylvisaker, M. (2005). Direct clinician versus indirect family-supported rehabilitation of children with traumatic brain injury: a randomized clinical trial. *Brain Injury*, **19**, 819–831.

Bronfenbrenner, U. & Morris, P. A. (2006). The bioecological model of human development. In Lerner, R. M., ed. *Theoretical Models of Human Development*. Volume **1** of *Handbook of Child Psychology*, 6th edition. Hoboken, NJ: John Wiley & Sons, Ltd.

Catroppa, C. & Anderson, V. (2006). Planning, problem-solving and organizational abilities in children following TBI: intervention techniques. *Pediatric Rehabilitation*, **9**, 89–97.

D'Zurilla, T. J. & Nezu, A. M. (1999). *Problem-solving Therapy: A Social Competence Approach to Clinical Intervention*, 2nd edition. New York: Springer Publishing Co.

Edlund, W., Gronseth, G., So, Y. & Franklin, G. (2004). *AAN Clinical Practice Guideline Process Manual*. St Paul, MN: American Academy of Neurology.

Glang, A., McLaughlin, K. & Schroeder, S. (2007). Using interactive multimedia to teach parent advocacy skills: an exploratory study. *Journal of Head Trauma Rehabilitation*, **22**, 198–205.

Janusz, J. A., Kirkwood, M. W., Yeates, K. O. & Taylor, H. G. (2002). Social problem-solving skills in children with traumatic brain injury: long-term outcomes and prediction of social competence. *Child Neuropsychology*, **8**, 179–194.

Kinsella, G. J., Ong, B., Murtagh, D., Prior, M. & Sawyer, M. (1999). The role of the family for behavioral outcome in children and adolescents following traumatic brain

injury. *Journal of Consulting and Clinical Psychology*, **67**, 166–123.

Kirkwood M., Janusz J., Yeates K. O. *et al.* (2000). Prevalence and correlates of depressive symptoms following traumatic brain injuries in children. *Child Neuropsychology*, **6**, 195–208.

Laatsch, L., Harrington, D., Hotz, G. *et al.* (2007). An evidence-based review of cognitive and behavioral rehabilitation treatment studies in children with acquired brain injury. *Journal of Head Trauma Rehabilitation*, **22**, 248–256.

Levin, H. S. & Hanten, G. (2005). Executive functions after traumatic brain injury in children. *Pediatric Neurology*, **33**, 79–93.

Max, J. E., Robin, D. A., Lindgren, S. D. *et al.* (1997). Traumatic brain injury in children and adolescents: psychiatric disorders at two years. *Journal of American Academy of Child and Adolescent Psychiatry*, **36**, 1278–1285.

Max, J. E., Koele, S. L., Smith, W. L. *et al.* (1998). Psychiatric disorders in children and adolescents after severe traumatic brain injury: a controlled study. *Journal of American Academy of Child and Adolescent Psychiatry*, **37**, 832–840.

Max, J. E., Koele, S. L., Castillo, C. C. *et al.* (2000). Personality change disorder in children and adolescents following traumatic brain injury. *Journal of the International Neuropsychological Society*, **6**, 279–289.

Osberg, J. S., Brooke, M., Baryza, M. J., Rowe, K., Lash, M. & Kahn, P. (1997). Impact of childhood brain injury on work and family finances. *Brain Injury*, **11**, 11–24.

Ponsford, J., Willmott, C., Rothwell, A. *et al.* (2001). Impact of early intervention after mild traumatic brain injury in children. *Pediatrics*, **108**, 1297–1303.

Rivara, J. B., Jaffe, K. M., Polissar, N. L., Fay, G. C., Liao, S. & Martin, K. M. (1996). Predictors of family functioning and change 3 years after traumatic brain injury in children. *Archives of Physical Medicine and Rehabilitation*, **77**, 754–764.

Rotondi, A. J., Sinkule, J. & Spring, M. (2005). An interactive web-based intervention for persons with TBI and their families: use and evaluation by female significant others.

Journal of Head Trauma Rehabilitation, 2, 173–185.

Schuhmann, E. M., Foote, R. C., Eyberg, S. M., Boggs, S. R. & Algina, J. (1998). Efficacy of parent–child interaction therapy: interim report of a randomized trial with short-term maintenance. *Journal of Clinical Child Psychology*, 27, 34–45.

Schwartz, L., Taylor, H. G., Drotar, D., Yeates, K. O., Wade, S. L. & Stancin, T. (2003). Long-term behavior problems after pediatric traumatic brain injury: prevalence, predictors, and correlates. *Journal of Pediatric Psychology*, 28, 251–264.

Selznick, L. & Savage, R. C. (2000). Using self-monitoring procedures to increase on-task behavior with three adolescent boys with brain injury. *Behavioral Interventions*, 15, 243–260.

Singer, G. H. S., Glang, A., Nixon, C. *et al.* (1994). A comparison of two psychosocial interventions for parents of children with acquired brain injury: an exploratory study. *Journal of Head Trauma Rehabilitation*, 9, 38–49.

Suzman, K. B., Morris, R. D., Morris, M. K. & Milan, M. A. (1997). Cognitive-behavioral remediation of problem-solving deficits in children with acquired brain injury. *Journal of Behavior Therapy ad Experimental Psychiatry*, 28, 203–212.

Taylor, H. G., Yeates, K. O., Wade, S. L., Drotar, D., Klein, S. K. & Stancin, T. (1999). Influences on first-year recovery from traumatic brain injury in children. *Neuropsychology*, 13, 76–89.

Vasa, R. A., Gerring, J. P., Grados, M. *et al.* (2002). Anxiety after severe pediatric closed head injury. *Journal of the American Academy of Child and Adolescent Psychiatry*, 41, 148–156.

Vasa, R. A., Grados, M., Slomine, B. *et al.* (2004). Neuroimaging correlates of anxiety after pediatric traumatic brain injury. *Biological Psychiatry*, 55, 208–216.

Wade, S. L., Taylor, H. G., Drotar, D., Stancin, T. & Yeates, K. O. (1998). Family burden and adaptation following traumatic brain injury (TBI) in children. *Pediatrics*, 102, 110–116.

Wade, S. L., Taylor, H. G., Drotar, D., Stancin, T., Yeates, K. O. & Minich, N. M. (2002). A prospective study of long-term caregiver and family adaptation following brain injury in children. *Journal of Head Trauma Rehabilitation*, 17, 96–111.

Wade, S. L., Carey, J. & Wolfe, C. R. (2006a). The efficacy of an online cognitive-behavioral, family intervention in improving child behavior and social competence following pediatric brain injury. *Rehabilitation Psychology*, 51, 179–189.

Wade, S. L., Carey, J. & Wolfe, C. R. (2006b). The efficacy of an online family intervention to reduce parental distress following pediatric brain injury *Journal of Consulting and Clinical Psychology*, 74, 445–454.

Wade, S. L., Michaud, L. & Brown, T. M. (2006c). Putting the pieces together: preliminary efficacy of a family problem-solving intervention for children with traumatic brain injury. *Journal of Head Trauma Rehabilitation*, 21, 50–60.

Wade, S. L., Taylor, H. G., Yeates, K. O. *et al.* (2006d). Long-term family adaptation following pediatric brain injury. *Journal of Pediatric Psychology*, 31, 1072–1083.

Wade, S. L., Taylor, H. G., Walz, N. C. *et al.* (2008a). Parent–child interactions during the initial weeks following brain injury in young children. *Rehabilitation Psychology*, 53, 180–190.

Wade, S. L., Walz, N. C., Carey, J. C. & Williams, K. M. (2008b). Preliminary efficacy of a web-based family problem-solving treatment program for adolescents with traumatic brain injury. *Journal of Head Trauma Rehabilitation*, 23, 369–77.

Yeates, K. O., Taylor, H. G., Drotar, D. *et al.* (1997). Pre-injury family environment as a determinant of recovery from traumatic brain injuries in school-age children. *Journal of the International Neuropsychological Society*, 3, 617–630.

Yeates, K. O., Swift, K., Taylor, H. G. *et al.* (2004). Short- and long-term social outcomes following pediatric traumatic brain injury. *Journal of the International Neuropsychological Society*, 10, 412–426.

Ylvisaker, M. (2006). Self-coaching: a context-sensitive, person-centered approach to social communication after traumatic brain injury. *Brain Impairment*, 7, 246–258.

Ylvisaker, M., Todis, B., Glang, A. *et al.* (2001). Educating students with TBI: themes and recommendations. *Journal of Head Trauma Rehabilitation*, **16**, 76–93.

Ylvisaker, M., Jacobs, H. E. & Feeney, T. (2003). Positive supports for people who experience behavioral and cognitive disability after brain injury: a review. *Journal of Head Trauma Rehabilitation*, **18**, 7–32.

Ylvisaker M, Turkstra L. & Coelho C. (2005). Behavioral and social interventions for individuals with traumatic brain injury: a summary of the research with clinical implications. *Seminars in Speech and Language*, **26**, 256–67.

Ylvisaker, M., Turkstra, L., Coehlo, C. *et al.* (2007). Behavioral interventions for children and adults with behavioral disorders after TBI: A systematic review of the evidence. *Brain Injury*, **21**, 769–805.

Pediatric TBI: challenges for treatment and rehabilitation

Cathy Catroppa and Vicki Anderson

Introduction

Permanent disability can often result from childhood traumatic brain injury (TBI) (Adelson *et al.*, 2003; Goldstein & Levin, 1987; Jennett, 1996; Kraus, 1987; 1995; Mazurek, 1994). There is increasing evidence that the young child's brain may be particularly vulnerable to early trauma due to: (i) physiological factors – the child's neck control is poor and the head is proportionally large, leading to greater diffuse injury and interruption to cerebral development (Hudspeth & Pribram, 1990); and (ii) developmental factors – children possess few well-consolidated and established skills and so future acquisition of these skills may be compromised (Dennis, 1989).

It is therefore not surprising that cognitive abilities may be compromised following brain injury at a critical developmental stage. A number of studies have identified impairments in cognitive areas that affect the individual's successful functioning in everyday life: (i) attention; (ii) memory; (iii) executive functioning and; (iv) social functioning, which impinge on educational progress, adaptive skills, and quality of life (Anderson & Catroppa, 2005; Anderson *et al.*, 2005b; Carney & Gerring, 1990; Catroppa & Anderson, 2002; 2005; Chadwick *et al.*, 1981; Chevignard *et al.*, 2000; Cooley & Morris, 1990; Dennis *et al.*, 1995; Donders, 1993; Ganesalingam *et al.*, 2007; Hawley, 2003; 2004; Hawley *et al.*, 2004; Kinsella *et al.*, 1995; 1997; Levin *et al.*, 1982; Nelson & Kelly, 2002; Savage *et al.*, 2005; Yeates *et al.*, 2004; Ylvisaker *et al.*, 2005).

Characteristics of "high-risk" post-TBI include: (i) more severe injuries at a younger age (Anderson & Moore, 1995); (ii) pre-injury history of developmental or behavioral problems (Ponsford *et al.*, 1997); and (iii) living in poorer functioning and less advantaged families (Rivara *et al.*, 1994); professionals report only small numbers of injured children having access to rehabilitation resources (Cronin, 2000; Di Scala *et al.*, 1997). At this point we are able to effectively assess and diagnose the child post-TBI, we have some confidence in long-term recovery patterns, and we have increasing knowledge pertaining to predictors of outcome, but our knowledge of rehabilitation and prevention is limited.

The aim of this chapter is to: (i) provide a summary of acute rehabilitation and models of intervention; (ii) discuss methodological issues and obstacles to collaborative work in the intervention domain; (iii) provide an overview of intervention studies being conducted in our laboratory and; (iv) discuss integrative and translational aspects of research in this area.

Recovery following traumatic brain injury in childhood

During the acute and post-acute stages post-injury, how does the child with brain injury recover, and so be able to benefit from intervention programs? Following brain insult, the

Pediatric Traumatic Brain Injury: New Frontiers in Clinical and Translational Research, ed. V. Anderson and K. O. Yeates. Published by Cambridge University Press. © Cambridge University Press 2010.

proposed mechanisms of recovery can be grouped into two general classes: restitution theories and substitution theories. Restitution of function suggests that spontaneous physiological recovery occurs after brain damage, as damaged brain tissue heals, neural pathways are re-activated and so functions are restored (Cannon & Rosenbleuth, 1949; Rothi & Horner, 1983). These processes are potentially amenable to the impact of early medical intervention such as hypothermia treatment and pharmacological approaches. In contrast, substitution theories refer to more functional restoration via system reorganization or compensation, with the assumption of transfer of functions from damaged brain tissue to healthy sites (Kolb & Wishaw, 1996; Lashley, 1929; Luria, 1963; Munk, 1881; Rothi & Horner, 1983). While the prevailing views have argued that the young child's brain is preferentially able to take advantage of these recovery processes, it is unclear whether underlying neural recovery actually translates into functionally better outcome.

Models of intervention

To date, much rehabilitation has taken a disciplinary approach, with clinicians from various disciplines (e.g. medical, pharmacological, physical, speech, psychological) implementing specific interventions and working toward their individual goals, with little reference to the "whole" child and the child and family goals. More recent models argue for an interdisciplinary approach, with the focus on the goals of the patient and the family, rather than those of therapy. This has led to an integration of approaches and a more holistic evaluation of the child's progress post-injury (Barnes, 1999; Hostler, 1999; Semlyen et al., 1998; Swaine et al., 2000). Using this model, rehabilitation may be divided into restitution ("direct") and substitution ("indirect") approaches. (See Table 11.1 for a summary of Phases/models of intervention).

Table 11.1 Phases/models of intervention

Phase	Intervention
1. During coma	Sensory stimulation
2. Short-term post-injury (e.g. 6 hours)	Hypothermia research
3. Post-coma/PTA	Intervention for difficulties in cognition and behavior
4. Outpatient therapy	Intervention to assist re-entry into home/school/community:
	Direct approach
	Behavioral compensation
	Environmental modifications and supports
	Behavioral interventions
	Psych-educational approaches
	pharmacological treatments
	Family-based interventions

Adapted from Catroppa & Anderson (in press).

Direct approach

Using this model, lost functions must be retrained and impaired functions must be maximally stimulated in order to be maintained (Rothi & Horner, 1983). As mentioned earlier, in order to treat secondary effects (e.g. raised intracranial pressure), hypothermia has been introduced (Sahuquillo & Vilalta, 2007) and is argued to reduce risk factors that cause poor outcome. Once the child is stable, there is focus on feeding, commencement of any physical therapy, and management of any behavioral challenges. This is followed by a focus on facilitation of recovery and compensation for difficulties identified in movement, language and cognition, and behavior, again highlighting the need for cross-discipline cooperation. While such therapies offered by disciplines such as occupational therapy, physiotherapy, and speech therapy are well established, to date, evaluation studies are few, and so effectiveness is unclear. In some cases, a pharmacological approach may be taken to alleviate identified difficulties, for example, Mahalick (2004) found that psycho-stimulants may be beneficial for treating attentional deficits post-TBI.

When using a direct approach, the child may be trained using specific exercises focusing on impaired cognitive abilities or processes, in an attempt to improve these skills, as well as to impact more generally on all cognitive functions. Adult results suggest that such approaches may be more effective in certain cognitive domains (e.g. attention), with small, non-significant improvements reported in other domains (Diller & Gordon, 1981; Gray et al., 1992; Mateer et al., 1996; Robertson, 1990). Such intervention techniques have been used for "memory" difficulties, implementing memory strategy training versus drill or repetitive practice on memory tasks and errorless learning (Wilson et al., 1994; Wilson & Moffat, 1992). To date, there is little evidence that this "direct" approach has a high level of effectiveness in children, or that it generalizes to other cognitive domains (Miller, 1992; Park & Ingles, 2001; Ponsford et al., 1995; Wilson, 1997; Wood, 1988) or to daily functions.

With regard to child-based research, Brett and Latch (1998) report increases in neuro-psychological scores following implementation of a cognitive intervention focused on development of meta-cognition. Thompson (1995) and Thompson and Kerns (2000), using both case study and group research and implementing the Attention Process Training (APT) paradigm, found inconsistent results, yet some subjects did show improvements. Case studies have also been reported by Glang et al. (1992). They recruited three children who had suffered severe TBI one year previously, and provided direct instruction programs (problem solving) as a form of intervention. Improvements were reported in areas such as self-monitoring and mathematics. In a study by Suzman et al. (1997), five children with TBI between the ages of 6 and 11 years who presented with problem solving difficulties were provided with meta-cognitive training, self-instructional training, self-regulation training, attribution training, and reinforcement. A computerized problem solving task (Think Quick, 1987) was used to evaluate the intervention program and substantial improvements were documented on trained tasks. Ogberg and Turktra (1998) employed an elaborative encoding paradigm with two severely injured adolescents and demonstrated improvements on the trained task post-intervention. Further, Lawson and Rice (1989) demonstrated improved list learning ability after direct training. In a recent randomized control trial conducted in Sweden, researchers (Van't Hooft et al., 2005 – described in detail in this volume) conducted a weekly training intervention to enhance children's attention skills. Findings showed improvements in neuropsychological measures of attention and memory function post-treatment for the treatment group; however, generalization of skills remains uncertain, highlighting the need for studies in this area to employ more so functional outcome measures.

Indirect approaches: behavioral compensation

This approach emphasizes cognitive strengths, and how they can be maximized in order to ensure optimal performance in everyday life. Children are taught to perform various activities using alternative strategies, compensating for cognitive deficits, in order to achieve specified behaviors. Such approaches have been used successfully for children with developmental disorders and are most effective when the impairment is mild, as a global deficit makes it hard to identify an intact modality to focus upon in the intervention (Rourke, 1989).

Environmental modifications and supports

To a great extent, the emphasis of pediatric rehabilitation is on modifying the child's environment (family and school) to ensure that the context is conducive to best level of function. These externally focused interventions use highly structured environments for learning and include the removal of potential distractions, simplification of tasks, increasing time allocation to complete a given task, the use of external aids or cues, such as lists, diaries, alarms, or paging systems, and the reduction of noise (Mateer, 1999). Such interventions rely heavily on the availability of resources, and the full support of the child's family, school, and community. While appealing, few studies have formerly evaluated this type of intervention.

A recent study by Wilson et al. (2001) targeted memory, attention, planning, and organizational problems, and included a small number of children and adolescents. The intervention comprised a radio-paging system where reminders were transmitted to each individual on their pager. Results showed that the pager system significantly reduced everyday problems in memory and planning for participants with brain injury. Another example of such an approach has been reported by Wright and Limond (2004) who describe implicit (e.g. skills and habits such as walking) and explicit (e.g. recollection of a piece of knowledge) memory, with the latter including working memory. In the case of younger children, these authors suggest the use of passive rehabilitation strategies, with emphasis on improving retrieval of learned information using much environmental support as offered by parents and teachers. Support for the efficacy of this approach has been provided in a study by Selznick and Savage (2000), in which three adolescents with a history of brain injury were trained using an auditory cueing paradigm, with the aim of improving on-task behavior and self-regulation. Outcomes from the intervention suggested skills improvement and some evidence of generalization to related situations.

Behavioral interventions

Behavioral interventions aim to overcome cognitive deficits via the use of behavioral strategies, such as the use of positive reinforcement and the implementation of token economies. In a study by Burke et al. (1988), a group of five adolescents with primarily frontal injuries, were given cognitive training to address poor attention and concentration, reduced memory and problem solving skills, and poor social judgement. Training to improve attention and concentration specifically involved self-control strategies and antecedent control and small groups were taught via self-instructional training, modeling and role-playing, reinforcement, and group feedback. Following this intervention, four out of five adolescents returned home to live with parents, and were able to successfully return to public schools. Crowley and Miles (1991) conducted an adolescent intervention case study, where a 16-year-old male was provided with a behaviorally based intervention. Forty one-hour sessions, over a period of 8 weeks, were used to improve self-monitoring via the use of saturated cues and by charting progress. Results suggested some improvement in the outcome measures of algebra and completion of homework, but perhaps expected given such an intensive treatment protocol.

Feeney and Ylvisaker (2003) investigated the effects of a cognitive behavioral intervention program on two young children who presented with frontal lobe impairment and severely challenging behavior. These children demonstrated organization and planning problems in the classroom which contributed to their behavioral problems. The authors argued that intervention should involve the child as well as the caregivers at home and at school, with the intervention focusing on: (i) daily routine; (ii) positive momentum; (iii) reduction of errors; (iv) escape communication; (v) adult communication style; (vi) graphic advance organizers and; (vii) goal-plan-do-review routine, with staff trained in a number of these areas. Post-intervention challenging behaviors had significantly decreased in intensity and were almost eliminated, with maintenance of skills in the longer term. Similarly, Mottram and Berger-Gross (2004) evaluated a behavioral intervention program for three children with brain injury aged 8–14 years. A multiple baseline design across individuals was employed, and the experimental group's disruptive behavior was seen to decrease by 69% during the intervention phase, with maintenance at follow-up. This study suggested that the use of program rules, a token economy with response cost and mystery motivators, was well received and resulted in long-term improvements. Overall, it appears that behavioural interventions have a positive impact, but are very time-consuming and intensive, and the importance of appropriate outcome measures is again highlighted.

Psycho-educational approaches

The basis of these approaches is to provide information about a specific area of relevance. With regard to TBI, psycho-educational approaches are often used with adults, with inconsistent results reported with children. Beardmore et al. (1999) demonstrated that parents did appear to show improved understanding of their child's difficulty, in comparison to little benefit shown for the child with TBI, from a single information session. Ponsford et al. (2001) assessed a group of children with mild TBI. Those in the intervention group were seen at one week post-injury and were given an information booklet regarding coping strategies post-TBI. Both intervention and non-intervention groups were seen at 3 months post-injury, and results suggest that the provision of an information booklet reduced anxiety and lowered the incidence of ongoing problems. While not evaluated empirically, clinical experience indicated that at the level of the school and community, it is important that significant others are provided with information regarding the child's likely deficits and how these may limit the child's ability to cope with routine expectations (Anderson, 2003).

Pharmacological interventions

Management approaches addressing the emotional (e.g. depression), social (e.g. social isolation), and behavioral consequences (e.g. inattention) of childhood TBI have been poorly documented and evaluated (Lewis et al., 2000; Ylvisaker et al., 2005). Potential interventions in this domain may include traditional behavioral methods and psychotherapy; however, pharmacological approaches are employed more frequently with generally positive results (Napolitano *et al.*, 2005). With regard to TBI, improved mental health has been cited to propranolol (Williams *et al.*, 1982), respiradone (Ylvisaker, 2005), and sedating seratonin re-uptake inhibitors (Silver, 1987) in children, while Mahalick (2004) found that psycho-stimulants may be effective in the treatment of attentional deficits secondary to acquired brain injury.

Family-based interventions

Recent literature stresses the important role of caregivers in the recovery process following brain injury (Bedell *et al.*, 2005; Feeney & Ylvisaker, 2003; Mottrom & Berger-Gross, 2004; Ylvisaker *et al.*, 2001). In a randomized controlled trial Braga and colleagues (2005) explored the effectiveness of a clinician-delivered versus a family-supported intervention. While both clinician and family-supported intervention groups showed improvement, only those in the family-supported intervention group demonstrated both statistically and clinically significant improvements across both physical and cognitive domains. In our laboratory, the "Signposts for Building Better Behavior" program, originally designed for use with children with learning disabilites (Gavidia-Payne & Hudson, 2002; Hudson *et al.*, 2003; Sanders, 1999), has been adapted to suit a pediatric population post-ABI. We expected that parents of children with ABI would also benefit from the program. Preliminary post-intervention results have demonstrated significant reductions in total problem behaviors for children in each severity group, and significant reductions in parental stress for each severity group (Woods *et al.*, 2009).

Wade *et al.* (2005a,b) -described in more detail in this volume, examined the feasibility and efficacy of a web-based family problem solving intervention for children with TBI. Results suggested that an internet-based intervention was promising with regard to improvement in both parent and child outcomes following TBI. In addition, Wade *et al.* (2006) investigated a problem solving family intervention, administered at a clinic or in the home, using a randomized control trial. The intervention was reported to hold promise for reducing child behavior problems. In a research study by Glang *et al.* (2007), parents of children with brain injury were trained in educational advocacy skills, using an interactive multi-media intervention. Those parents in the randomized trial scored higher in the areas of application, knowledge, and attitudes in comparison to the control group.

Summary

For many years child-based rehabilitation models have been idiosyncratic, reflecting the particular delivery context and the skills of the treating team. Only recently have attempts been made to evaluate various strategies employed by rehabilitationists in order to provide objective information about the most effective approaches, so that best outcome for the individual can be achieved. It remains challenging to categorize studies into any one approach as most intervention programs incorporate a combination of approaches. The major obstacles in this field include: (i) lack of an integrated "interdisciplinary" model; (ii) the medical model often employed does not sufficiently consider functional outcome; (iii) clinical therapies including speech and occupational therapy do not routinely evaluate outcomes; (iv) most evaluations have failed to account for spontaneous recovery, and; (v) outcome measures are often inappropriate and do not tap into improvements in functional "everyday" skills. Despite these significant hurdles, recent research evidence of the benefit of intervention suggests a positive trend, providing ideas for future research (Hall & Cope, 1995; Mills *et al.*, 1992).

Evaluating child-based interventions

Given the previous discussion, it is not surprising that evidence regarding treatment outcomes is scarce. To summarise, evaluative research is hindered by: (1) heterogeneity of the pediatric TBI population with respect to injury factors, age, and pre-injury function; (2) difficulties accounting for the effects of spontaneous recovery in measuring change; (3) ethical restrictions leading to problems in implementing best practice research design and withholding treatments during important recovery periods; (4) limitations with respect to valid and reliable outcome measures; (5) practical impediments to implementation of standardized interventions; and (6) developmental variations across childhood, which result in the need for age-specific approaches (Anderson & Catroppa, 2006).

With these obstacles and limitations in mind, some attempts have been made to evaluate research in the intervention area. Using established protocols, behavioural intervention studies have been classified according to the level of evidence provided (Edlund *et al.*, 2004) as follows: (i) Class I – requires a prospective randomised controlled trial, with masked outcome assessment, in a representative population; (ii) Class II – these studies are similar to Class I but also include a prospective, matched group cohort without a masked outcome, and studies with less adequate control procedures (e.g. no clearly defined exclusion/ inclusion criteria); Class III – studies involving well-defined natural history controls, or patients serving as their own controls; Class IV – no control group is utilized, and individual case studies or clinical case series are included.

Laatsch *et al.* (2007) conducted a review of cognitive and behavioral rehabilitation treatment studies following ABI in childhood, with the inclusion of 28 studies (1 Class I, 5 Class II, 6 Class III, 16 Class IV). The Clinical Practice Guideline Process Manual (Edlund *et al.*, 2004) was utilized to make specific treatment recommendations, which require evidence from Class I or II studies. The evidence-based recommendation that could be made was a practice guideline for considering provision of attention remediation. In addition, a practice guideline involving the family in the intervention process, was based on Classification II and III, and a practice option, made on inconclusive or conflicting evidence, noting that families of children seen in emergency would most likely benefit from a TBI information booklet.

Ylvisaker *et al.* (2007) have also systematically reviewed the evidence for the effectiveness of behavioral interventions for children and adults with behavior disorders following TBI. Evidence-based recommendations included a guideline: provision of a behavior intervention (not a specific intervention) for children and adults; and an option: traditional applied behavior analysis and positive behavior interventions and support may be considered an evidence-based treatment option. No practice standards (based on Class I or strong Class II evidence) could be made. In a review of treatment strategies to manage motor impairments post-ABI, Marshall *et al.* (2007) concluded that, although a variety of treatment strategies were in use, most were supported by limited evidence (e.g. non-RCT or a single-group intervention). These reviews highlight the lack of RCTs in the child literature (Limond & Leeke, 2005), most likely due to practical limitations of such designs in this group, and emphasize the importance of considering multiple research designs (e.g. single-case study experimental designs) for evaluating intervention programs.

Overcoming obstacles and limitations

In order to progress the field of intervention research, current scientific approaches argue that the most appropriate design for treatment evaluation is the randomised control trial, as it is better able to handle factors such as developmental trajectories, spontaneous recovery, and sample heterogeneity. Despite the advantages of the gold standard approach, feasibility of implementing such designs needs to be considered. In the area of early recovery from TBI, a number of ethical considerations arise. A major concern is the justification for delaying treatment if one is assigned to a wait list control group, particularly in the light of clinical research suggesting the early period post-TBI is critical for brain plasticity and may be a critical period for intervention. Furthermore, implementing Class I and II studies is often time-consuming and labour intensive, and so impractical for clinicians in the midst of clinical responsibilities, highlighting the need for Class III and IV research studies to provide crucial information regarding the efficacy of an intervention program. There is also a need for future intervention studies to broaden outcome measures from "more laboratory-based" clinical measures to theoretically driven ecological measures. It is important to also investigate intervention models already available for adults and other disease groups, and where relevant to adapt these existing models/programs to suit a child TBI population. A multidisciplinary approach and collaborations, both national and international, are also essential to move the intervention area forward.

Our research

As part of our emerging model of care for children with TBI, our center is implementing an evidence-based approach which emphasizes: (i) the importance of focusing on the rehabilitation goals of the child and the family; (ii) an interdisciplinary rehabilitation model where specific disciplines work collaboratively and employ multidisciplinary therapeutic techniques; (iii) identifying the key outcome as improvement of overall day-to-day function, participation, and quality of life. This approach to care facilitates the application of a research-based program for the evaluation of intervention programs. Below are examples of the implementation of this collaborative model.

Intervention programs trials
Signposts program

Research has found that child behavior problems post-injury, while related to injury factors such as injury severity and presence of persisting disability, are more directly related to parent mental health and coping strategies (e.g. Anderson *et al.*, 2005a; Yeates *et al.*, 1997). The program "Signposts for Building Better Behavior" was developed to provide parent support to families of children with intellectual and developmental disabilities (Hudson *et al.*, 2003). The aim of the Signposts program is to help parents identify the purposes of their children's difficult behavior, develop effective ways of managing that behaviour, and prevent more difficult behavior developing in the future. The five parenting skills addressed in the program include: (a) monitoring children's behavior; (b) systematic use of daily interactions; (c) replacing difficult behavior with useful behavior; (d) planning for better behavior; and (e) developing more skills in children. Three additional modules cover: (a) introductory material about the program; (b) dealing with stress in the family; and (c) the family as a team.

As mentioned earlier, in our laboratory we have devised an additional module specific to a pediatric ABI population, and have now completed a pilot study using the modified Signposts program. Pilot results (Woods *et al.*, 2007) as in the case of an 8-year-old boy with attention deficit/hyperactivity disorder (ADHD), as well as a mild TBI, suggest improvements in both children and parent functioning. At two months post-injury, this young boy presented with fatigue, heightened irritability, sensitivity to light, poor concentration, and difficulty falling asleep. Following the Signposts intervention, there were reductions in externalising behavior, total problem behavior, meta-cognitive and emotional behavioral problems. The parent reported a lowering of stress, anxiety, and depression, with an improvement in parenting skills. Preliminary results from a recently completed larger trial (Woods *et al.*, 2009) have also shown significant improvement in both child behavior and parent coping and parent stress levels. A RCT trial, using different modes of delivery of the program, is now also in progress.

Executive functioning (EF) intervention

Recently, a pilot intervention program was developed (Catroppa *et al.*, in press), which aimed to develop and implement an intervention program for adolescent/young adults in the chronic phase post-TBI, and to teach strategies to improve EF (e.g. planning, organizing, problem solving, maintaining positive self-esteem). The intervention consisted of six one-hour weekly sessions, with the content and delivery of the intervention based on both cognitive behavioral and psycho-educational/instructional approaches, with a focus on increasing understanding and developing EF skills.

Findings indicated little benefit of intervention on standardized measures of EF, with no consistent improvements from pre- to post-intervention. In contrast, some change was evident on functional measures, suggesting that the content and delivery of the intervention may be efficacious at the level of day-to-day function. The pilot study has highlighted the need to incorporate more relevant measures of functional outcome, in both pre- and post-intervention phases, so that subtle changes, that can have a large impact on everyday functioning, are measured and evaluated.

Conclusions and future directions

While research into the area of rehabilitation/intervention with children following acquired brain injury is in its infancy, with many obstacles hindering progress (Laatsch *et al.*, 2007), descriptive research has made great progress in identifying the consequences from child TBI, and in targeting children who are at high risk for long-term difficulties. Our next challenge is to grapple with establishing an evidence base for treating and managing the problems these children experience. Based on this knowledge, several specific goals need to be addressed:

(i)   To extend research into the development of programs specific for children with regards to developmental needs of the child and practical needs of the family – keeping in mind the importance of a model where the child is viewed "holistically," where treatment goals are agreed upon with the family, a multi-dimensional approach is utilized, and where functional measures that are relevant to rehabilitation goals are utilized.

(ii) To modify and adapt both adult-based interventions and those originally developed for other child groups for a pediatric group.

(iii) To promote interdisciplinary collaboration and multi-center research (both nationally and internationally) in the development of intervention programs specific to a pediatric post-TBI population.

(iv) To go beyond the current scientific focus on RCT studies, which have limited feasibility and ethical pitfalls in child TBI, and so consider other methods of evaluating interventions that may be better suited to progressing knowledge in the field.

(v) To further develop pharmacological approaches to intervention that may act in isolation or facilitate behavioral interventions (e.g. Bakker *et al.*, 2008 -conducted in our research center).

In conclusion, the ultimate challenge for research in the intervention area is to: (a) develop/ adapt intervention programs specifically for a child/adolescent population with TBI (and perhaps for subgroups within this population); (b) pilot the programs; (c) evaluate the efficacy of the intervention, with goals focusing on improvement in functional outcome; (d) make adjustments to the program based on pilot data, with the ultimate goal of implementing the programs into standard clinical care. The intervention area is challenging, and yet interventions are beneficial for all – the individual with TBI, the family, significant others, and the community at large, as cost savings and benefits will continue for years to come (Aranow, 1987; Davis *et al.*, 1997; Eames *et al.*, 1995), as these individuals will be better able to function in society. Hence the importance of expanding our knowledge and expertise in the area of pediatric intervention post-TBI.

References

Adelson, P., Bratton, S. L., Camey, N. *et al.* (2003). Guidelines for the acute medical management of severe traumatic brain injury in infants, children and adolescents. *Pediatric Critical Care Medicine*, 4, 2–75.

Anderson, V. (2003). Outcome and management of traumatic brain injury in childhood. In Wilson, B, ed. *Neuropsychological Rehabilitation: Theory and Practice*. Lisse, The Netherlands: Swets & Zeitlinger, pp. 217–252.

Anderson, V. & Catroppa, C. (2005). Recovery of executive skills following paediatric traumatic brain injury (TBI): a two year follow-up. *Brain Injury*, 19(6), 459–470.

Anderson, V. & Catroppa, C. (2006). Advances in post-acute rehabilitation after childhood acquired brain injury: a focus on cognitive, behavioural and social domains. *American Journal of Physical Medicine and Rehabilitation*, 85(9), 767–787.

Anderson, V. & Moore, C. (1995). Age at injury as a predictor following pediatric head injury: a longitudinal perspective. *Child Neuropsychology*, 1(3), 187–202.

Anderson, V., Catroppa, C., Haritou, F., Morse, S. & Rosenfeld, J. (2005a). Identifying factors contributing to child and family outcome at 30 months following traumatic brain injury in children. *Journal of Neurology, Neurosurgery, and Psychiatry*, 76, 401–408.

Anderson, V., Catroppa, C., Morse, S., Haritou, F. & Rosenfeld, J. (2005b). Attentional and processing skills following traumatic brain injury in early childhood. *Brain Injury*, 19(9), 699–710.

Aranow, H. U. (1987). Rehabilitation effectiveness with severe brain injury: translating research into policy. *Journal of Head Trauma and Rehabilitation*, 2(3), 24–36.

Bakker, K., Waugh, M. C., Epps, A. *et al.* (2008). *Efficacy of Stimulant Medication in Paediatric Acquired Brain Injury. Report to the Motor Accidents Authority.* New South Wales, Australia.

Barnes, M. P. (1999). Rehabilitation after traumatic brain injury. *British Medical Bulletin*, 55(4), 927–943.

Beardmore, S., Tate, R. & Liddle, B. (1999). Does information and feedback improve children's knowledge and awareness of deficits after traumatic brain injury? *Neuropsychological Rehabilitation,* **9,** 45–62.

Bedell, G. M., Cohn, E. S. & Dumas, H. M. (2005). Exploring parents' use of strategies to promote social participation of school-age children with acquired brain injuries. *The American Journal of Occupational Therapy,* **59**(3), 273–284.

Braga, L. W., Da Paz, A. C., Jr. & Ylvisaker, M. (2005). Direct clinician-delivered versus indirect family-supported rehabilitation of children with traumatic brain injury: a randomized controlled trial. *Brain Injury,* **19**(10), 819–831.

Brett, A. W. & Laatsch, L. (1998). Cognitive rehabilitation therapy of brain-injured students in a public high school setting. *Pediatric Rehabilitation,* **2,** 27–31.

Burke, W. H., Wesolowski, M. D. & Guth, M. L. (1988). Comprehensive head injury rehabilitation: an outcome evaluation. *Brain Injury,* **2**(4), 313–322.

Cannon, W. & Rosenbleuth, A. (1949). *The Supersensitivity of Denervated Structures.* New York: Macmillan.

Carney, J. & Gerring, J. (1990). Return to school following severe closed head injury: a critical phase in pediatric rehabilitation. *Pediatrician,* **17,** 222–229.

Catroppa, C. & Anderson, V. (2002). Recovery in memory function in the first year following TBI in children. *Brain Injury,* **16**(5), 369–384.

Catroppa, C. & Anderson, V. (2005). A prospective study of the recovery of attention from acute to 2 years post pediatric traumatic brain injury. *Journal of the International Neuropsychological Society,* **11,** 84–98.

Catroppa, C. & Anderson, V. (In press). Traumatic brain injury in childhood: rehabilitation considerations. *Developmental Neurorehabilitation.*

Catroppa, C., Anderson, V. & Muscara, F. In press. Rehabilitation of executive skills post childhood traumatic brain injury (TBI): a pilot intervention study. *Developmental Neurorehabilitation.*

Chadwick, O., Rutter, M., Brown, G., Shaffer, D. & Traub, M. (1981). A prospective study of children with head injuries: II. Cognitive sequelae. *Psychological Medicine,* **11,** 49–61.

Chevignard, M., Pillon, B., Pradat-Diehl, P. *et al.* (2000). An ecological approach to planning dysfunction: script execution. *Cortex,* **36,** 649–669.

Cooley, E. L. & Morris, R. D. (1990). Attention in children: a neuropsychologically based model for assessment. *Developmental Neuropsychology,* **6**(3), 239–274.

Cronin, A. F. (2000). Traumatic brain injury in children: issues in community function. *American Journal of Occupational Therapy,* **55,** 377–384.

Crowley, J. A. & Miles, M. A. (1991). Cognitive remediation in paediatric head-injury: a case study. *Journal of Paediatric Psychology,* **16,** 611–627.

Davis, C. H., Fardanesh, L., Rubner, D., Wanlass, R. L. & McDonald, C. M. (1997). Profiles of functional recovery in fifty traumatically brain-injured patients after acute rehabilitation. *American Journal of Physical Medicine and Rehabilitation,* **76**(3), 213–218.

Dennis, M. (1989). Language and the young damaged brain. In T. Boll & B. Bryant, eds. *Clinical Neuropsychology and Brain Function: Research, Measurement and Practice.* Washington: American Psychiatric Association.

Dennis, M., Wilkinson, M., Koski, L. & Humphreys, R. P. (1995). Attention deficits in the long term after childhood head injury. In S. H. Broman & M. E. Michel, eds. *Traumatic Head Injury in Children.* New York: Oxford University Press, 165–186.

Diller, L. & Gordon, W. (1981). Rehabilitation and clinical neuropsychology. In S. Filskov & T. Boll, eds. *Handbook of Clinical Neuropsychology.* New York: John Wiley & Sons Ltd, pp. 702–733.

Di Scala, C., Osberg, S., Savage, R. C. (1997). Children hospitalised for traumatic brain injury: transition to post-acute care. *Journal of Head Trauma Rehabilitation,* **12,** 1–10.

Donders, J. (1993). Memory functioning after traumatic brain injury in children. *Brain Injury*, 7(5), 431–437.

Eames, P., Cotterill, G., Kneale, T. A., Storrar, A. L. & Yeomans, P. (1995). Outcome of intensive rehabilitation after severe brain injury: a long-term follow-up study. *Brain Injury*, 10(9), 631–650.

Edlund, W, Gronseth, G., So, Y. & Franklin, G. (2004). *AAN Clinical Practice Guideline Process Manual*. St. Paul, Minn: American Academy of Neurology.

Feeney, T. J. & Ylvisaker, M. (2003). Context-sensitive behavioural supports for young children with TBI. Short-term effects and long-term outcome. *Journal of Head Trauma and Rehabilitation*, 18(1), 33–51.

Ganesalingam, K., Sanson, A., Anderson, V. & Yeates, K. (2007). Self-regulation as a mediator of the effects of childhood traumatic brain injury on social and behavioral functioning. *Journal of the International Neuropsychological Society*, 13, 298–311.

Gavidia-Payne, S. T. & Hudson, A. (2002). Behavioural supports for parents of children with an intellectual disability and problem behaviours: an overview of the literature. *Journal of Intellectual and Developmental Disability*, 27, 31–55.

Glang, A., Singer, G., Cooley, E. & Tish, N. (1992). Tailoring direct instruction techniques for use with elementary students with TBI. *Journal of Head Trauma Rehabilitation*, 7(4), 93–108.

Glang, A., McLaughlin, K. & Schroeder, S. (2007). Using interactive mulitmedia to teach parent advocacy skills: an exploratory study. *Journal of Head Trauma Rehabilitation*, 22(3), 198–205.

Gray, J., Robertson, I., Pentland, B. & Anderson, S. (1992). Micro-computer based attentional training after brain damage: a randomised group controlled trial. *Neuropsychological Rehabilitation*, 2, 97–115.

Hall, K. M. & Cope, D. N. (1995). The benefit of rehabilitation in traumatic brain injury: a literature review. *Journal of Head Trauma Rehabilitation*, 10(1), 1–13.

Hawley C. A. (2003). Reported problems and their resolution following mild, moderate and severe traumatic brain injury amongst children and adolescents in the UK. *Brain Injury*, 17(2), 105–129.

Hawley C. A. (2004). Behaviour and school performance after brain injury, *Brain Injury*, 18(7), 645–659.

Hawley, C. A., Ward, A. B., Magnay, A. & Long, J. (2004). Outcomes following childhood head injury: a population study. *Journal of Neurology, Neurosurgery, and Psychiatry*, 75(5), 737–742.

Hostler, S. L. (1999). Pediatric family-centered rehabilitation. *Journal of Head Trauma Rehabilitation*, 14(4), 384–393.

Hudson, A., Matthews, J., Gavidia-Payne, S., Cameron, C., Mildon, R. & Radler, G. (2003). Evaluation of an intervention system for parents of children with intellectual disability and challenging behaviour. *Journal of Intellectual Disability Research*, 47, 238–249.

Hudspeth, W. & Primram, K. (1990). Stages of brain and cognitive maturation. *Journal of Educational Psychology*, 82, 881–884.

Jennett, B. (1996). Epidemiology of head injury. *Journal of Neurology, Neurosurgery, and Psychiatry*, 60, 362–369.

Kinsella, G., Prior, M., Sawyer, M. *et al.* (1995). Neuropsychological deficit and academic performance in children and adolescents following traumatic brain injury. *Journal of Pediatric Psychology*, 20, 753–767.

Kinsella, G. J., Prior, M., Sawyer, M. *et al.* (1997). Predictors and indicators of academic outcome in children 2 years following traumatic brain injury. *Journal of the International Neuropsychological Society*, 3, 608–616.

Kolb, B. & Wishaw, Q. (1996). *Fundamentals of Human Neuropsychology*, 4th edition. New York: W.H. Freeman.

Kraus, J. F. (1987). Epidemiology of head injury. In Cooper, P. R., ed. *Head Injury*, 2nd edition. Baltimore: Williams and Wilkins, pp. 1–19.

Kraus, J. F. (1995). Epidemiological features of brain injury in children: occurrence, children at risk, causes and manner of injury, severity, and outcomes. In S. Broman & M. E. Michel, eds. *Traumatic Head Injury in Children*: New York: Oxford University Press, pp. 22–39.

Laatsch, L., Harrington, D., Hotz, G. *et al.* (2007). An evidence-based review of cognitive and behavioral rehabilitation treatment studies in children with acquired brain injury. *Journal of Head Trauma Rehabilitation*, 22(4), 248–256.

Lashley, K. (1929). *Brain Mechanisms and Intelligence*. Chicago: University of Chicago Press.

Lawson, M. J. & Rice, D. N. (1989). Effects of training in use of executive strategies on a verbal memory problem resulting from closed head injury. *Journal of Clinical and Experimental Neuropsychology*, 6, 842–854.

Levin, H. S., Eisenberg, H. M., Wigg, N. R. & Kobayashi, K. (1982). Memory and intellectual ability after head injury in children and adolescents. *Neurosurgery*, 11, 668–673.

Lewis, J., Morris, M., Morris, R., Krawiecki, N. & Foster, M. (2000). Social problem solving in children with acquired brain injuries. *Journal of Head Trauma Rehabilitation*, 15, 930–942.

Limond, J. & Leeke, R. (2005). Cognitive rehabilitation for children with acquired brain injury. *Journal of Consulting and Clinical Psychology*, 46, 339–352.

Luria, A. R. (1963). *Restoration of Function After Brain Injury*. New York: Macmillan.

Mahalick, D. (2004). Psychopharmacological treatment of acquired attentional disorders in children with brain injury. *Pediatric Neurosurgery*, 85, 1732–1755.

Marshall, S., Teasall, R., Bayona, N. *et al.* (2007). Motor impairment rehabilitation post acquired brain injury. *Brain Injury*, 21(2), 133–160.

Mateer, C. (1999). Executive function disorders: rehabilitation challenges and strategies. *Seminars in Clinical Neuropsychiatry*, 4, 50–59.

Mateer, C., Kerns, K. & Eso, K. (1996). Management of attention and memory disorders following traumatic brain injury.

Journal of Learning Disabilities, 29, 6118–6132.

Mazurek, A. J. (1994). Epidemiology of paediatric injury. *Journal of Accident and Emergency Medicine*, 11, 9–16.

Miller, E. (1992). Psychological approaches to the management of memory impairments. *British Journal of Psychiatry*, 160, 1–6.

Mills, V. M., Nesbeda, T., Katz, D. I. & Alexander, M. P. (1992). Outcomes for traumatically brain-injured patients following post-acute rehabilitation programmes. *Brain Injury*, 6(3), 219–228.

Mottram, L. & Berger-Gross, P. (2004). An intervention to reduce disruptive behaviours in children with brain injury. *Pediatric Rehabilitation*, 7(2), 133–143.

Munk, H. (1881). *Ueber die funktion der grosshirnrinde. Gesammelte aus den Jahren.* Berlin: Hirschwald, 1877–1880.

Napolitano, E., Elovic, E. P. & Qureshi, A. I. (2005). Pharmacological stimulant treatment of neurocognitive and functional deficits after traumatic and non-traumatic brain injury, *Medical Science Monitor*, 11(6), 212–220.

Nelson, J. E. & Kelly, T. P. (2002). Long-term outcome of learning and memory in children following severe closed head injury. *Pediatric Rehabilitation*, 5(1), 37–41.

Ogberg, L. & Turkstra, L. (1998). Use of elaborative encoding to facilitate verbal learning after adolescent traumatic brain injury. *Journal of Head Trauma Rehabilitation*, 13, 44–62.

Park, N. & Ingles, J. (2001). Effectiveness of attention rehabilitation after acquired brain injury: a meta-analysis. *Neuropsychology*, 15, 199–210.

Ponsford, J., Sloan, S. & Snow, P. (1995). *Traumatic Brain Injury: Rehabilitation for Everyday Adaptive Living.* Hove, UK: Lawrence Erlbaum Associates.

Ponsford, J., Willmott, C., Rothwell, A. *et al.* (1997). Cognitive and behavioural outcome following mild traumatic brain injury in children. *Journal of the International Neuropsychological Society*, 3, 225.

Ponsford, J., Willmott, C., Rothwell, A. *et al.* (2001). Impact of early intervention on outcome after mild traumatic brain injury in children. *Pediatrics*, **108**(6), 1297–1303.

Rivara, J. M. B., Jaffe, K. M., Fay, G. C. *et al.* (1994). Family functioning and children's academic performance and behaviour problems in the year following traumatic brain injury. *Archives of Physical Medicine and Rehabilitation*, 75, 369–379.

Robertson, I. (1990). Does computerised cognitive rehabilitation work? A review. *Aphasiology*, 4, 381–405.

Rothi, L. & Horner, J. (1983). Restitution and substitution: two theories of recovery with application to neurobehavioral treatment. *Journal of Clinical Neuropsychology*, 3, 73–81.

Rourke, B. P. (1989). *Nonverbal Learning Disabilities*. New York: Guilford Press.

Sahuquillo, J. & Vilalta, A. (2007). Cooling the injured brain: does moderate hypothermia influence the pathophysiology of traumatic brain injury. *Current Pharmaceutical Design*, 13, 2310–2322.

Sanders, M. (1999). Triple P positive parenting program: towards an empirically validated multilevel parenting and family support strategy for the prevention of behavior and emotional problems in children. *Clinical Child and Family Psychology Review*, 2, 71–90.

Savage R. C., DePompei R., Tyler J. & Lash M. (2005). Paediatric traumatic brain injury: a review of pertinent issues. *Pediatric Rehabilitation*, 8(2), 92–103.

Selznick, L. & Savage, R. C. (2000). Using self-monitoring procedures to increase on-task behavior with three adolescent boys with brain injury. *Behavioral Interventions*, 15, 243–260.

Semlyen, J. K., Summers, S. J. & Barnes, M. P. (1998). Traumatic brain injury: efficacy of multidisciplinary rehabilitation. *Archives of Physical Medicine and Rehabilitation*, 79, 678–683.

Silver, J. (1987). Neuropsychiatric aspects of traumatic brain injury. In Hales, R., ed. *The American Psychiatric Press Textbook of Psychiatry*. Washington DC: American Psychiatric Association, pp. 173–184.

Suzman, K. B., Morris, R. D., Morris, M. K. & Milan, M. A. (1997). Cognitive behavioural remediation of problem solving deficits in children with acquired brain injury. *Journal of Behavior Therapy and Experimental Psychiatry*, 28(3), 203–212.

Swaine, B. R., Pless, I. B., Friedman, D. S. & Montes, J. L. (2000). Effectiveness of a head injury program for children. *American Journal of Physical Medicine and Rehabilitation*, 79(5), 412–420.

Think Quick. (1987). Fremont, CA: The Learning Company.

Thompson, J. (1995). Rehabilitation of high school individuals with traumatic brain injury through utilization of an attention training program. *Journal of the International Neuropsychological Society*, 1, 149.

Thompson, J. & Kerns, K. (2000). Mild traumatic brain injury in children. In S. A. Raskin & C. A. Mateer, eds. *Neuropsychological Management of Mild Traumatic Brain Injury*. New York: Oxford University Press, pp. 233–251.

Van't Hooft, L., Andersson, K., Bergman, B., Sejerson, J., von Wendt, L. & Bartfai, A. (2005). Beneficial effect from a cognitive training programme on children with acquired brain injuries demonstrated in a controlled study. *Brain Injury*, 19, 511–518.

Wade, S., Michaud, L. & Maines-Brown, T. (2006). Putting the pieces together. Preliminary efficacy of a family problem-solving intervention for children with traumatic brain injury. *Journal of Head Trauma Rehabilitation*, 1, 57–67.

Wade, S., Wolfe, C. R., Maines-Brown, T. & Pestian, J. P. (2005a). Can a web-based family problem-solving intervention work for children with traumatic brain injury? *Rehabilitation Psychology*, 50(4), 337–345.

Wade, S., Wolfe, C. R., Maines-Brown, T. & Pestian, J. P. (2005b). Putting the pieces together: preliminary efficacy of a family problem-solving intervention for children with traumatic brain injury. *Journal of Pediatric Psychology*, 30(5), 437–442.

Williams, D., Mehl, R. & Yudofsky, S. (1982). The effect of propranolol on uncontrolled rage outbursts in children and adolescents with organic brain dysfunction. *Journal of the Academy of Child Psychology*, **21**, 129–135.

Wilson, B. A. (1997). Cognitive rehabilitation: how it is and how it might be. *Journal of the International Neuropsychological Society*, **3**, 487–496.

Wilson, B. A. & Moffat, M. (1992). *Clinical Management of Memory Problems*. London: Chapman & Hall.

Wilson, B. A., Baddeley, A. & Evans, J. (1994). Errorless learning in the rehabilitation of memory impaired people. *Neuropsychological Rehabilitation*, **4**(3), 307–326.

Wilson, B. A., Emslie, H., Quirk, K. & Evans, J. (2001). Reducing everyday memory and planning problems by means of a pager system: a randomised control crossover study. *Journal of Neurology, Neurosurgery, and Psychiatry*, **70**, 477–482.

Wood, R. (1988). Attention disorders in brain rehabilitation. *Journal of Learning Disabilities*, **21**, 327–332.

Woods, D., Catroppa, C., Anderson, V. *et al.* (2007). Treatment acceptability of a family-centered intervention for parents of children with an acquired brain injury (ABI) – Pilot study. *New Fontiers in Pediatric Traumatic Brain Injury*, San Diego, California, 8–10 November: poster.

Woods, D., Catroppa, C., Anderson, V., Matthews, J., Giallo, R. & Barnett, P. (2009).

Efficacy for a family-centered behavioural intervention for parents of children with acquired brain injury (ABI). *Meeting of the International Neuropsychological Society (INS)*, Boston, February: poster.

Wright, I. & Limond, J. (2004). A developmental framework for memory rehabilitation in children. *Pediatric Rehabilitation*, **7**(2), 85–96.

Yeates, K. O., Taylor, H. G., Drotar, D. *et al.* (1997). Pre-injury family environment as a determinant of recovery from traumatic brain injuries in school-age children. *Journal of the International Neuropsychological Society*, **3**, 617–630.

Yeates, K. O., Swift, E., Taylor, H. G. *et al.* (2004). Short- and long-term social outcomes following pediatric traumatic brain injury. *Journal of the International Neuropsychological Society*, **10**, 412–426.

Ylvisaker, M., Todis, B., Glang, A. *et al.* (2001). Educating students with TBI: themes and recommendations. *Journal of Head Trauma and Rehabilitation*, **16**(1), 76–93.

Ylvisaker, M., Adelson, P. D., Willandino-Braga, L. W. *et al.* (2005). Rehabilitation and ongoing support after pediatric TBI twenty years of progress. *The Journal of Head Trauma Rehabilitation*, **20**, 95.

Ylvisaker, M., Turkstra, L., Coehlo, C. *et al.* (2007). Behavioral interventions for children and adults with behavior disorders after TBI: a systematic review of the evidence. *Brain Injury*, **21**(8), 769–805.

Chapter 12

Integrating multidisciplinary research for translation from the laboratory to the clinic

Bryan Kolb, and Robbin Gibb

An important development in behavioral neuroscience in the last 20 years has been the demonstration that it is possible to stimulate functional recovery after brain injury in laboratory animals. A significant challenge for the next 20 years is the translation of this work to improve the outcome from brain injury and disease in humans. Rodent models of early brain injury provide a tool for developing such rehabilitation programs. The models include analyses at different levels including detailed behavioral paradigms, electrophysiology, neuronal morphology, protein chemistry, and epigenetics. Our goal here is to synthesize this multidisciplinary work to provide a platform for moving to the clinic.

The road to translation begins with a search for an understanding of brain development and the factors that modify "normal" development. This allows us to outline a series of principles of cerebral plasticity that provide a framework from which to launch a search for rehabilitation treatments for animals with injuries of varying etiologies. By necessity this requires an investigation of behavior, neuronal morphology, neurophysiology, protein chemistry, and genetics/epigenetics. By using this strategy, we have been able to identify a variety of factors that influence functional recovery and brain plasticity, including the demonstration that both pre-natal factors and peripheral stimulation can profoundly influence functional outcome after perinatal brain injury.

Background
Assumptions and hypotheses

The underlying assumption of our experiments is that there are critical periods during development in which the brain is more able to reorganize, and others where it is less able to reorganize, to allow restoration of function after cerebral injury. The general idea is that the critical periods are constrained by the ongoing developmental processes that are occurring at the time of injury. For example, when there is proliferation of neurons (such as on embryonic day 18 (E18) in rats) or astrocytes (such as on postnatal day 8 (P8)), the brain can recruit these proliferative processes to facilitate processes leading to functional recovery. In contrast, if the brain is shedding synapses or neurons, injury may lead to an enhancement of this process, which may exacerbate the effects of injury. Two hypotheses flow from this general theoretical framework.

The first hypothesis is that the reason for critical period(s) for functional restoration is related to the fact that when the developing brain is injured, two different processes are initiated:

Pediatric Traumatic Brain Injury: New Frontiers in Clinical and Translational Research, ed. V. Anderson and K. O. Yeates. Published by Cambridge University Press. © Cambridge University Press 2010.

processes related to *degeneration* and those related to *regeneration*. It is the balance between these two sets of processes that defines critical periods for recovery (or not) after early brain injury.

The second hypothesis is that it is possible to shift the critical periods by pre- and/or postnatal treatments. If so, then it should be possible to partially stimulate functional restoration at times that it would not normally occur. It is proposed that the effectiveness of treatments for early brain injury will vary depending upon how they might influence the degenerative and regenerative processes respectively.

A final hypothesis is that the timing and duration of different interventions will vary depending upon the precise time of injury. Treatments that are highly effective after injury at one point in a critical period may be less effective at a different time point.

The challenge of neurodevelopmental disorders

Neurodevelopmental disorders are estimated to account for about 25% of all health conditions causing disability in developed countries. These conditions include cerebral palsy, mental retardation, epilepsy, learning disabilities, ADHD, autism spectrum disorders, and drug-related disorders such as fetal alcohol spectrum disorders. The cause of these disorders remains uncertain but hypoxic episodes are common at birth and a recent study reported a 26% incidence of intracranial hemorrhage in a random sample of infants from vaginal births (Looney *et al.*, 2007). What is remarkable about this latter study is that the affected infants were asymptomatic at the time of the MRI.

The interaction between hypoxia, cerebral bleeds, and other perinatal risk factors in the developmental trajectories of children is not known, however. The combination of pre-natal events (e.g. infection, intrauterine insufficiency, drug exposure, stress) and hemorrhage is likely to predispose infants to more severe neurobehavioral disabilities than any single event. It is likely that a large number of children with developmental disabilities experience a complex "double-hit" that leads to neurological compromise and later behavioral problems. In view of the importance of interactions both in understanding the outcomes of early mild brain injury and the development of rehabilitation programs, we have attempted to include such interactions in our animal studies.

In order to identify principles that will inform the development of rehabilitation programs we designed a four-part strategy:

1. We systematically varied lesion size, location, and age-at-injury.
2. We used a wide range of behavioral measures that included sensory, motor, cognitive, emotional, and social measures.
3. We looked for anatomical correlates of recovery and non-recovery.
4. Because correlation is an inherent route to causation, when we have found correlations we have tried to manipulate both brain and behavioral outcomes to determine if the correlations are maintained. For example, we have attempted to block recovery after injury with the goal of seeing if the anatomical changes correlated with recovery change in the absence of recovery.

Principles of recovery from early cortical injury
Precise age-at-injury is critical

It was generally assumed up until the 1970s that the earlier brain injury occurred during development, the better the outcome would be. This idea dates back to the late nineteenth century when Broca and others noticed that children rarely had persistent aphasia after damage to the cortical language zones. Beginning in the 1930s studies by Margaret Kennard confirmed this general notion of "earlier is better." She made unilateral motor cortex lesions in infant and adult monkeys. The behavioral impairments in the infant monkeys were milder than those in the adults, which led Kennard to hypothesize that there had been a change in cortical organization in the infants and these changes supported the behavioral recovery. In particular, she hypothesized that, if some synapses were removed as a consequence of brain injury, "others would be formed in less usual combinations" and that "it is possible that factors which facilitate cortical organization in the normal young are the same by which reorganization is accomplished in the imperfect cortex after injury" (Kennard, 1942: 239). Although intuitively appealing, Donald Hebb's studies of children with early brain injury in the 1940s led to a different conclusion (Hebb, 1947; 1949). Hebb noticed that children with frontal lobe injuries often had worse outcomes than adults with similar injuries and proposed that the early injuries prevented a normal initial organization of the brain, thus making it difficult for the child to develop many behaviors, especially socio-affective behaviors. Thus, whereas Kennard hypothesized that recovery from early brain damage was associated with reorganization into novel neural networks that supported functional recovery, Hebb postulated that the failure to recover was correlated with a failure of initial organization that prevented the normal development of many behaviors. Extensive studies of both cats and rats with cortical injuries have shown that both views are partially correct (e.g. Kolb, 1995; Schmanke & Villablanca, 2001; Villablanca et al., 1993). It is the precise developmental age at injury that predicts the Kennard or Hebb outcome.

The critical relationship between age-at-injury and functional outcome can be illustrated in our studies looking at the effect of cortical injury at ages ranging from birth to adulthood. The behavioral and anatomical effects of focal cortical injury in the rat are tightly tied to the precise time of injury, a time that we can loosely refer to as a "critical period" for early injury. In rats, this critical period is described by a U-shaped function in which injury to presumptive cortical areas on embryonic day 18 or between postnatal days 7–12 leads to excellent functional outcome relative to adult lesions whereas similar lesions between birth and day 5 is associated with a dismal functional outcome. This U-shaped function of recovery applies to all neocortical regions (e.g. Kolb, 1995).

A similar pattern of results can be seen in parallel studies of the effects of cortical lesions in kittens by Villablanca and his colleagues (e.g. Villablanca et al., 1993), although, because the rat and cat develop at different rates, the precise ages are different in the two species. Specifically, damage in the first few weeks after birth in the cat is equivalent to damage in the second week in the rat, and thus is associated with a relatively good outcome, whereas damage in the last few pre-natal weeks in the cat is equivalent to damage in the first week in the rat and is associated with a very poor functional outcome. The key point here is that birth date is irrelevant – it is the stage of neural development that is important.

Given that pre-natal factors can influence later brain development in the rat we have wondered how pre-natal cortical injury would influence brain and behavioral development. We made pre-natal lesions in putative frontal cortex and concluded that damage during the period of neurogenesis, which in the rat cortex is from about E12 to E20, appears to be associated with a good functional outcome (see also Hicks & D'Amato, 1961) provided there is no hydrocephalus (Kolb et al., 1998). We hasten to point out, however, that our injuries were relatively focal and it is possible that more diffuse injuries that might be seen in head trauma, ischemia, or response to teratogens could have a different outcome.

Behaviors are not all the same

Early in the development of our models we discovered that behaviors differentially recover from early injury. Whereas cognitive behaviors, such as those measured by neuropsychological tests in rats, show dramatic critical periods for recovery, the pattern of recovery for other behaviors is more capricious. Motor and sensory behaviors show only partial recovery at best and social behaviors show no recovery at all. For example, rats with frontal cortex injuries at any age show marked deficits in a range of social behaviors including play and agonistic behavior (e.g. Pellis *et al.*, 2006).

These results are reminiscent of the effects of early injuries in children: it is rare indeed to see aphasia after early injury but social behaviors are especially sensitive to early injury. The differential recovery of different classes of behavior is important for assessment of rehabilitative success. It would be quite misleading to measure a single outcome and generalize about the effectiveness of interventions. Curiously, whereas clinical researchers would rarely generalize from a single measure, it is common in studies of laboratory animals for researchers to focus on a narrow range of behavioral measures, and especially cognitive measures.

Cortical regions show differential recovery

It follows from principle 2 that, if different behaviors are differentially sensitive to early injury, then this sensitivity is likely related to the precise region of injury. As a general statement we can say that there is better recovery after P10 injury from prefrontal and cingulate cortex lesions than motor and sensory cortex lesions and the poorest recovery is seen after posterior parietal cortex injuries. The extent of recovery is correlated with differential anatomical reorganization as well (see below).

In contrast to the effects of focal lesions, hemidecortication shows a different critical period for functional recovery. The best time for optimal functional recovery after hemidecortication is on the day of birth, with the extent of recovery decreasing with lesions thereafter (e.g. Kolb & Tomie, 1988). The reason for this radically different pattern of recovery from hemidecortications is unknown, but we believe it to be related to different degenerative and regenerative processes in the extensive decortications.

There are neuronal changes that correlate with recovery

Regardless of the time of injury (pre-natal or in the first 3 postnatal weeks) there is always a reduction in overall brain size relative to similar injuries later in life. Thus, given that we have seen that age-at-injury leads to very different outcomes, it must be some difference in the synaptic organization of the brain that is key – rather than simply brain size. Indeed it is.

The critical period for recovery is characterized by a fundamentally different set of molecular changes that is seen after earlier or later injury. These former changes include neurogenesis, gliogenesis, changes in protein and gene expression, and synaptic proliferation, with the details varying with the location of injury. Many of these changes are simply an exaggeration, or re-initiation, of normal developmental processes. In contrast, the molecular changes associated with day 1–5 lesions include increased apoptosis, abnormal cell migration, and a failure of normal synaptogenesis. These changes reflect an interruption of normal developmental processes or an acceleration of degenerative processes that would usually occur later.

Golgi analyses of cortical neurons from rats with perinatal lesions consistently show a general atrophy of dendritic arborization and a drop in spine density across the cortical mantle (e.g. Kolb *et al.*, 1994). In contrast, rats with cortical lesions around 10 days of age show an increase in dendritic arbor and an increase in spine density relative to normal control littermates. Thus, animals with the best functional outcome show the greatest synaptic increase whereas animals with the worst functional outcome have a decrease in synaptic space relative to control animals.

We might expect that the changes in dendritic organization are related to obvious changes in cortical connectivity. Indeed, the elegant work on the effects of perinatal cortical lesions in the visual system of kittens by Payne and his colleagues (e.g. Payne & Cornwell, 1994; Payne & Lomber, 2001) have shown a major rewiring of thalamo-cortical and cortico-cortical connections of the visual system. Although there are certainly behavioral deficits in these animals, there is an impressive visual functional sparing.

Unilateral injuries show a different pattern of morphological changes

Given that rats with focal bilateral injuries show extensive dendritic remodeling, it is reasonable to expect similar changes in the injured hemisphere of animals with unilateral lesions. Indeed, in our initial study of dendritic remodeling we studied animals with small frontal lesions on P1 in one hemisphere and on P10 in the other hemisphere and found, relative to normal controls, dendritic atrophy in the P1-operated hemisphere and hypertrophy in the P10-operated hemisphere (Fig. 12.1). Animals with just a unilateral injury at P1 or P10 showed a different pattern of results, however. For example, the P10 operates did not show hypertrophy in the injured hemisphere, but rather showed an increase in cortical thickness in the normal hemisphere. This thickness is not due to increased dendritic fields, however, because the neurons actually had a reduced dendritic field relative to controls. It appears that there are more neurons in the intact hemisphere, although we are not yet sure whether this reflects reduced apoptosis or neurogenesis. Rats with neonatal hemidecortications are different yet. They show a 15% increase in cortical thickness and an increased dendritic arborization across the intact hemisphere (Kolb *et al.*, 1992). The increase in cortical thickness is particularly impressive given that there are no callosal connections. It is our hypothesis that the reason for the different patterns of reactive neuronal organization is related differences in degenerative and regenerative processes. Bilateral lesions result in degenerative and regenerative processes in both hemispheres; unilateral focal injuries lead to degenerative and regenerative processes in the injured hemisphere but only regenerative processes in the intact hemisphere; hemidecorticates have only regenerative processes in the intact hemisphere.

Parallel studies in rats and cats with unilateral motor cortex injuries have shown there is a major expansion of the ipsilateral cortico-spinal pathway from the undamaged hemisphere, which is correlated with partial recovery of skilled forelimb use (e.g. Castro, 1990; Whishaw & Kolb, 1988; Villablanca & Gomez-Pinella, 1987). It appears, however, that the anomalous cortico-spinal projections sometimes may be formed at a significant cost. Careful behavioral studies have shown that, although rats with expanded ipsilateral pathways may show partial recovery measured by success in obtaining food items on skilled reaching tasks, there are marked abnormalities in the details of the movements. Furthermore, rats with hemidecortications show large ipsilateral pathways that support some recovery of the limbs contralateral to the surgery but the "normal" ipsilateral limbs show impairments.

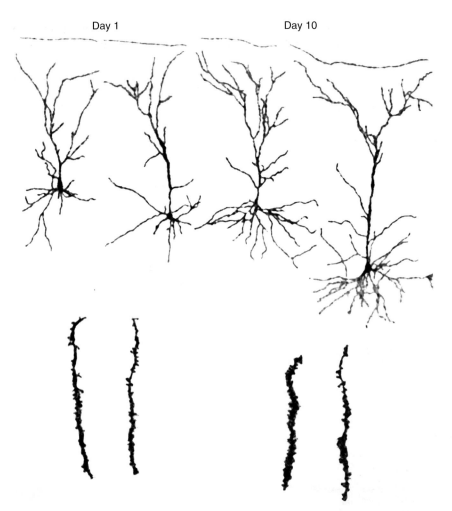

Fig. 12.1. Dendritic changes after perinatal frontal lesions. A medial prefrontal lesion on postnatal day 1 led to generalized dendritic atrophy and reduced spine density of cortical pyramidal neurons whereas lesions on day 10 led to hypertrophy.

The possibility that the development of anomalous ipsilateral pathways may be problematic has led Eyre *et al.* (2007) to propose that rather than representing "reparative plasticity," increased ipsilateral projections from the non-infarcted cortex compound disability by competitively displacing surviving contralateral cortico-spinal projections from the infarcted cortex. This may provide a pathophysiological explanation for why signs of hemiplegic cerebral palsy appear late and progress over the first two years of life.

Early lesions alter cortical maps

Both sensory and motor maps have proven to be remarkably plastic in response to a wide range of experiences. The idea that cortical maps may shift in response to cortical injury comes from studies by Rasmussen and Milner (1977) showing that early injuries that invade either the anterior or posterior speech zone in human infants cause the language maps to move either to the opposite hemisphere or to other regions of the left hemisphere. By using intracortical microstimulation of the motor cortex in our rats with cortical lesions we have been able to show that perinatal cortical lesions cause maps to shift or change size, even if the injuries do not actually invade the maps. Figure 12.2 shows a typical map from a control animal. There are two representations of the forelimbs, one referred to as the caudal forelimb area and the other as the rostral forelimb area. Although the precise function of the two regions is still under debate, these regions change in response to motor experience (Kleim *et al.*, 1998).

There are several different effects on the motor maps. First, if the motor cortex is removed in the first 10 days of life, the maps shifts more posteriorly into the posterior parietal cortex where the representation is abnormal, as shown in Fig. 12.2. Second, if the medial prefrontal cortex is injured unilaterally the map does not shift but is very small as shown in Fig. 12.2 (Williams *et al.*, 2006). In contrast, the map on the intact hemisphere is normal in size but it is distorted and missing the rostral forelimb area (P. Williams, N. Sherren, & B. Kolb unpublished observations). Third, if the medial prefrontal cortex is damaged bilaterally, the maps do not shrink as they do after unilateral lesions. They are

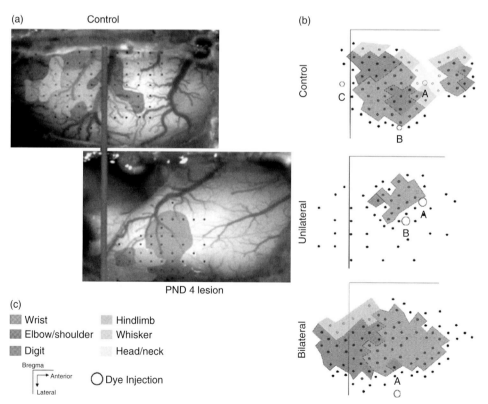

Fig. 12.2. Motor maps after perinatal cortical lesions. (a) Removal of motor cortex on postnatal day 2 caused the map to shift posterior into the posterior parietal region (J. Kleim & B. Kolb, unpublished photograph). (b) Unilateral medial prefrontal lesions that do not invade the motor cortex still alter the motor maps. Unilateral lesions lead to very small maps on the ipsilateral side whereas bilateral lesions produce large maps that have no rostral forelimb area. (After Williams *et al.*, 2006.) See color plate section.

somewhat distorted, however, and again are missing the rostral forelimb area. The distortions in the maps are especially interesting because we have found that, whenever the map is abnormal (including all of the distortions noted above), the performance on skilled reaching tasks is abnormal.

We have not mapped sensory regions, but it seems likely that maps of visual, somatosensory, or auditory space will be distorted too. This is especially true in cases where the motor maps have shifted more posterior into sensory regions of the posterior parietal cortex. The shifts in map organization are important not only in understanding symptoms of early injury, but also in evaluating the rehabilitative programs both in laboratory animals and children.

Early lesions can lead to cell genesis

In the course of studies of the effect of restricted lesions of the medial frontal cortex or olfactory bulb we discovered that midline telencephalic lesions on postnatal day 7–12 led to spontaneous regeneration of the lost regions, or at least partial regeneration of the lost regions. Lesions elsewhere in the cerebrum did not produce such effects. Similar injuries either before or after this temporal window did not produce such a result. Analysis of the medial frontal region showed that the area contained newly generated neurons that formed at least some of the normal connections of this region (Kolb et al., 1998). Furthermore, animals with this regrown cortex appeared virtually normal on many, although not all, behavioral measures (Kolb et al., 1998). Curiously, lesions lateral or posterior to the medial frontal cortex did not show neurogenesis, the sole exception being posterior cingulate lesions that showed some neurogenesis, provided the medial frontal cortex was removed as well (Gonzalez et al., 2002).

Additional studies showed that if we blocked regeneration of the tissue with pre-natal injections of the mitotic marker bromodeoxyuridine (BrdU), the lost frontal tissue failed to regrow and there was no recovery of function (Kolb et al., 1998), a result that implies that the regrown tissue was supporting recovery. Parallel studies in which we removed the regrown tissue found complementary results: removal of the tissue eliminated the functional recovery (Dallison & Kolb, 2003). Thus, in the absence of the regrown tissue, either because we blocked the growth or because we removed the tissue, function was lost. Furthermore, we were able to show in vitro that mice that had day 8 medial frontal lesions and later had the subventricular zone removed had an impaired capacity for the generation of stem cells, as did cells taken from animals with pre-natal (E12) treatment with bromodeoxyuridine (BrdU) (Kolb et al., 1999). More recently, we have shown in mice that x-radiation intended to kill stem cells after day 7 lesions blocks both regeneration and functional recovery (G. Silasi & B. Kolb, unpublished observations). In sum, it appears that neurogenesis can be re-initiated after frontal or olfactory bulb lesions on postnatal days 7–12. Why this time and place is special is unclear, but these results do suggest that regeneration of lost tissue is possible. One hypothesis is that the mitosis is stimulated by endogenous upregulation of growth factors such as Fibroblast Growth Factor -2 (FGF-2), which shows a rapid increase in cortical expression about 7 days of age (Monfils et al., 2006a) (see below).

There are changes in protein and gene expression

The production of new cells, new pathways, and new synapses requires the production of proteins. We have used Western blots to look for changes in protein expression and global gene methylation. The working hypothesis is that there should be differential changes after injuries at different times in the critical periods for recovery. There are. We have shown, for example, that there is an enhanced expression of FGF-2, glial fibrillary acidic protein (GFAP, a marker for astrocytes), and glucocorticoid receptor after prefrontal injuries at P10 but not at P3 (Gibb, 2004). There are also differential changes in the patterns of gene methylation after the injuries at the two age points (Gibb *et al.*, 2006).

Although our studies of changes in protein and gene expression are still nascent, the results are intriguing because they not only give us additional markers of the effects of treatments, they also have the potential to provide specific targets for rehabilitation. It is our working hypothesis that the mechanism(s) underlying the effectiveness of certain rehabilitation treatments will be found in differential expression of proteins and genes.

Modulating recovery

The pattern of critical periods for recovery after early cortical injury provides us with a nice model to investigate the effects of a wide range of factors on brain development and reorganization after injury. We have taken advantage of the poor outcome after injury in the first week of postnatal life in the rat to look for factors that would *facilitate* recovery and have contrasted this to the effect of factors that *interfere* with recovery after injury in the second week. We hasten to point out that we are not simply talking about *post-injury* factors but also *pre-natal* factors that can modulate the outcome of a brain injury that occurs much later in development. Because most of our studies on modulating factors have been using rats with medial frontal lesions, our discussion will focus on this preparation with appropriate reference to other lesions where appropriate.

Behavioral therapies

Although it is generally assumed that behavioral therapies will improve recovery from cerebral injury in humans, there have been few direct studies of how this might work, when the optimal time for therapy might be, or even whether it is actually effective (e.g. Kwakkel *et al.*, 1997). There have been many studies of the effects of various types of experience on functional outcome after cerebral injury in adult laboratory animals, with the most studied and effective treatment being complex housing (e.g. Will & Kelche, 1992). There are surprisingly few studies using animals with perinatal cortical injuries, however, and the few that are available have not reported any anatomical or physiological correlates. We therefore began our studies by looking at the effects of the pre-natal and postnatal experiential treatments that we had found to influence cortical development in intact animals and in each case we collected anatomical measures to see if they might provide insight into why the treatments did or did not work. There were two general results. First, nearly all treatments enhanced functional outcome after P4 cortical injuries (Table 12.1). Second, there were morphological correlates of the enhanced recovery.

Our behavioral studies have taken two basic forms. In the first, animals were placed in complex environments either pre-natally (i.e. the pregnant mom was in the environment), immediately after weaning, or in adulthood. In the second, animals received tactile stimulation three times daily with a soft brush either directly after their cortical injury or pre-natally via stimulation of the pregnant mom. The general finding was that both pre- and postnatal treatments were effective in stimulating functional recovery and enhanced synaptogenesis (e.g. Gibb & Kolb, 2009b; Kolb & Elliott, 1987; Kolb & Gibb, 2009). The

Table 12.1 Modification of the effects of early frontal cortical injury by experiential treatments

Treatment	Result	Basic Reference
Complex housing at weaning	Enhanced recovery after P1–7 injury	Kolb & Elliott (1987)
Complex housing in adulthood	No functional recovery after P1–5 injury	Comeau *et al.* (2008)
Complex housing prenatally	Enhanced recovery after P4 injury	Gibb & Kolb (2009a)
Post-injury tactile stimulation	Enhanced recovery after P4 injury	Kolb & Gibb (2009a)
Pre-natal tactile stimulation	Enhanced recovery after P4 injury	Gibb & Kolb (2009b)
Postnatal handling	No effect on behavior	Gibb & Kolb (2005)

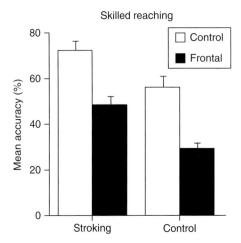

Fig. 12.3. Tactile stimulation in infancy (stroking) facilitates performance on a skilled reaching test in both control and medial prefrontal injured rats.

strong impact of complex housing was not too surprising given the well-documented effects of this housing on cerebral organization (e.g. Kolb & Whishaw, 1998), but the effect of tactile stimulation was far greater than we had anticipated (see Fig. 12.3). Animals with either pre-natal tactile stimulation, and thus the treatment was before the injury, or postnatal tactile stimulation after the injury, showed remarkable functional recovery on both cognitive and motor tasks. This was correlated with a variety of morphological changes such as increased brain weight, and increased dendritic length and/or spine density in cortical pyramidal neurons.

One unexpected finding was that the morphological changes in the intact and injured brain were often different. For example, whereas tactile stimulation *reduced* spine density in intact animals, there was an *increase* in spine density in brain-injured animals. It appears that the intact and injured brain respond differently to the same experiences. In addition, the morphological correlates of tactile stimulation-induced functional improvement varied with lesion locus. Rats with medial prefrontal lesions showed an increase in spine density in cortical pyramidal neurons, whereas rats with posterior parietal lesions showed an increase in dendritic length, but no increase in spine density. Both morphological changes would produce increased synaptic space but in different ways.

The timing of the behavioral therapies after perinatal cerebral injury has not been studied systematically but we have reason to believe that earlier is better than later. When we compared the effects of putting rats with P2 frontal lesions in complex environments at weaning versus in adulthood, there was a large effect of the early housing on cognitive recovery but no advantage for the adult treatment (Comeau *et al.*, 2008). This result is not definitive, however, as a parallel study found motor benefits from the adult housing (Williams *et al.*, 2006). There clearly need to be more studies of the timing of treatments because many infants are likely to miss the early treatments and we need some idea of how to treat adults with early injuries.

Diet

It is generally presumed that the body heals better when it is given good nutrition so it is reasonable to predict that recovery from cortical injury might be facilitated by vitamin and/ or mineral supplements. Although there is little study of this possibility after early brain injury, dietary choline supplementation during the perinatal period produces a variety of changes both to behavior and brain of laboratory rats (Meck & Williams, 2003). For example, perinatal choline supplementation leads to enhanced spatial memory in various spatial navigation tests (e.g. Meck *et al.*, 1988; Tees & Mohammadi, 1999) and increases the levels of nerve growth factor (NGF) in hippocampus and neocortex (e.g. Sandstrom *et al.*, 2002). Halliwell *et al.* (2009) added choline to the drinking water of pregnant rats and continued the treatment until weaning. Rats with P4 prefrontal lesions and the choline treatment did as well on various cognitive tasks as rats with day 10 lesions, effectively shifting the critical period earlier. The functional recovery was correlated with dendritic growth in cortical pyramidal cells. In a follow-up study, dams and later their pups were given a diet enriched with vitamins and minerals using a formula that had been found to be beneficial in treating human bipolar patients (Kaplan *et al.*, 2001; 2004). Like the choline treatment, there was a facilitation of recovery correlated with dendritic growth in cortical pyramidal cells (C. Halliwell & B. Kolb, unpublished observations). In addition, the lesions in the diet-enhanced animals were significantly smaller, suggesting that either the diet was neuroprotective or the critical period for the initiation of compensatory neurogenesis had been shifted earlier.

The possibility that diet might be important for stimulating recovery after early cortical injury is further supported by a study by Dabyhdeen *et al.* (2008). Human neonates with perinatal brain damage were randomly allocated to receive either a high (120% recommended average intake) or average (100% recommended average intake) energy and protein diet. The effect on recovery was so dramatic that the study was terminated before completion so that all infants could be placed on the higher energy diet. Although direct anatomical measurements of synaptic growth could not be done in such a study, non-invasive imaging showed that axonal diameters in the cortico-spinal tract, length, and weight were also significantly increased.

FGF-2

Fibroblast growth factors are a class of growth factors that are involved in embryonic development, angiogenesis, and wound healing. FGF-2 is particularly interesting because in vitro it can stimulate stem cell division from cells taken from the subventricular zone in the brain. FGF-2 is virtually absent in the rat cortex at birth but shows a rapid increase in expression at about seven days of age – the time that the critical period for recovery from cortical injury begins (Monfils *et al.*, 2006). Furthermore, FGF-2 expression is increased by many factors that enhance cortical plasticity, including complex housing and psychomotor stimulants.

In the course of trying to determine how stimulating the skin might facilitate brain repair, we discovered that FGF-2 levels were increased in skin and brain after tactile stimulation in infant rats and that there was also an increase in FGF-2 receptor in the brain (Gibb & Kolb, 2009b). The increased expression of FGF-2 in skin and brain in response to tactile stimulation led us to conclude that the mechanism underlying the benefits of tactile stimulation was via the production of FGF-2 in the skin, which in turn travelled in the blood stream to the brain to stimulate cerebral plastic processes that facilitated recovery.

The FGF-2 expression studies led us to administer FGF-2 directly as a therapy. In our first series of studies we gave animals with day 4 medial frontal or posterior parietal lesions FGF-2 either pre-natally, post-injury, or both (e.g. Comeau *et al.*, 2007; Comeau *et al.*, 2008). All three treatment regimens proved to be beneficial, with the combined pre-natal and postnatal treatments being the most advantageous.

In a second series of studies Monfils and colleagues (2005; 2006a; 2008) gave FGF-2 to rats with P10 motor cortex lesions. This treatment not only stimulated functional recovery but it also led to regrowth of the lost tissue, much as we had seen spontaneously after medial prefrontal lesions (Fig. 12.4). The regenerated tissue was abnormal in its gross appearance, but it grew functional cortico-spinal projections

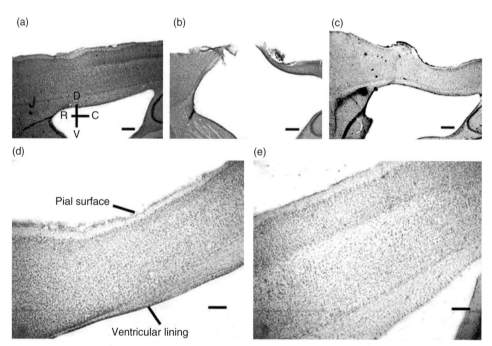

Fig. 12.4. Sagittal brain sections illustrating the extent of the lesion, as well as the distribution of cells within the filled region, in rats that received motor cortex aspiration lesions at postnatal day 10 and FGF-2 treatment. Lesion rats that did not receive FGF-2 show a prominent lesion cavity (b) relative to no lesion controls (a), whereas those that received a lesion + FGF-2 show a filling of the previously lesioned area with cells (c). Compared to that of a no lesion rat (e), the filled region in the lesion-FGF-2-treated rats did not show clear laminar distribution (d). (After Monfils *et al.*, 2006).

and if the new tissue was removed in adulthood there was an immediate loss of the recovered functions.

The administration of growth factors such as FGF-2 to infants with brain injuries could certainly carry some risks – such as the development of brain tumors given the neurogenic properties of FGF-2. Nonetheless, treatments that act to increase endogenous FGF-2 production, such as tactile stimulation, would seem to be quite safe and have an experimental basis.

Psychoactive drugs

There is a long history of using stimulants to stimulate recovery after adult cortical lesions but until recently there was no obvious mechanism for any beneficial actions of the drugs. It has become clear, however, that repeated exposure to virtually all psychoactive drugs, including psychomotor stimulants (amphetamine, cocaine, nicotine) and prescription drugs (SSRIs, anxiolytics, antipsychotics) induce major remodeling of both cortical and subcortical circuits in both adulthood and childhood development (e.g. Robinson & Kolb, 2004). We therefore wondered if we could shift the critical period for recovery by pre- or postnatal drug treatments.

We had shown that very low doses of nicotine could stimulate recovery from adult prefrontal or motor cortex lesions and that this was correlated with dendritic growth in both cortex and striatum (e.g. Gonzalez et al., 2006) so we gave pregnant rats a very low dose of nicotine (roughly equivalent to the nicotine content of one cigarette per day in humans) throughout pregnancy and then administered a similar dose to infant rats with P4 prefrontal lesions. Animals given the nicotine either pre-natally or post-injury fared better behaviorally than saline-treated rats. We have not completed the anatomical studies but our expectation is that nicotine-treated brains will show effects similar to those seen in adults with cortical strokes. Curiously, however, animals given the nicotine but not given the later lesions fared worse than saline controls (McKenna et al., 2000). Once again, it appears that events can have different effects on the intact and injured brains.

In a second series of studies we gave pregnant rats the SSRI, fluoxetine (Prozac), or the anxiolytic, diazepam (Valium). Because fluoxetine has neurogenic effects in the hippocampus and also enhances the expression of brain-derived neurotrophic factor (BDNF) we expected the treatment to enhance recovery from P4 cortical lesions. Not only did it not prove beneficial, it actually blocked recovery from P10 prefrontal lesions. The brains of these animals, and controls, were smaller than normal (Kolb et al., 2008). Dendritic analysis showed a reduction in dendritic length in cortical pyramidal cells (Fig. 12.5). Diazepam has been shown to shift the critical period for visual development earlier in mice (Morishita & Hensch, 2008) so it seemed possible that a similar phenomenon might occur for the critical period of recovery from early prefrontal lesion. In fact, in contrast to the effect of fluoxetine, diazepam facilitated recovery from P4 lesions and this was correlated with increased dendritic length in cortical pyramidal cells (see Fig. 12.5).

The use of psychoactive drugs for infants with brain injury would be premature at this point but it is clear that such drugs can have a powerful influence on recovery from cortical lesions. Of special importance is our finding that fluoxetine had deleterious effects not only in brain-injured rats but also in their intact siblings. We have shown too that exposure to both typical and atypical antipsychotics at developmental times equivalent to the third trimester in humans produces a widespread atrophy of cortical pyramidal cells in mice

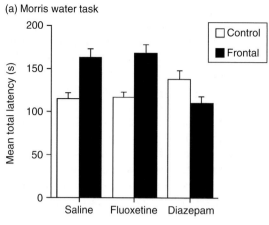

(a) Morris water task

Fig. 12.5. The effect of prescription drugs on recovery from perinatal injury. (a) Performance on the Morris Water Task. Diazepam reversed the lesion deficit whereas fluoxetine did not. (b) Diazepam reversed the lesion-induced loss in dendritic length (in microns). Fluoxetine led to a loss in dendritic length.

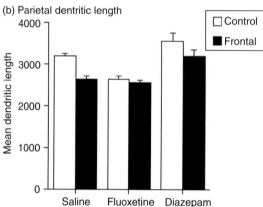

(b) Parietal dentritic length

(Frost *et al.*, 2009). Such changes would likely have significant impact upon the developmental trajectories of infants with perinatal cerebral injury.

Postscript: translating from the laboratory to children

Animal models of early brain injury have allowed us to identify some basic principles underlying recovery from early injury. In particular, studies using rats and cats have shown that there are critical periods for recovery and that the idea that "earlier is better" cannot be supported. It is difficult to translate developmental ages directly to children but it does appear that like the laboratory animals, children show differential recovery from injury depending upon age-at-injury. Anderson *et al.* (2009) showed, for example, that children with head trauma prior to the age of 2 showed significant cognitive deficits whereas children with head trauma between the ages of 3 and 6 years had a more favorable outcome. Children with similar injuries later than 6 years did more poorly suggesting a critical period for the best recovery at 3–6 years in children.

The application of rehabilitation strategies based upon the laboratory animal studies has yet to be realized, but the laboratory animal studies should give rehabilitation specialists and families cause for optimism because there appears to be far more capacity for functional recovery than had previously been recognized. Non-invasive treatments such as tactile stimulation would be easy to implement and without any obvious risks. In fact, there is a general consensus that tactile stimulation is important in normal human development and especially in cases in which the infants are compromised such as from premature birth. The application of complex housing in rats can be translated into the use of a wide range of games and activities to stimulate the infant's brain, and especially the use of reading to infants and young children [54, 63]. Older children may benefit from web-based treatment programs [61]. The advantage of reading is that it can provide tactile, cognitive, and social stimulation simultaneously. There are pilot programs now under way in which children with perinatal brain injuries go to summer camps for several weeks in order to participate in intense multi-modal rehabilitation programs (C. Mateer, personal communication). We noted too that enriched diets have been found to be extremely beneficial in infants with brain injuries and, based upon our animal studies, we would expect the diets to work even with older children.

In sum, perhaps the major contribution of the animal studies to date is to demonstrate that a wide range of rehabilitation programs can work after early brain injury and that there are identifiable mechanisms that account for the beneficial effects of many rehabilitation regimes. The importance of understanding the mechanisms underlying recovery cannot be understated. Understanding how the brain can compensate for early injury will allow a more rationale choice of novel rehabilitation strategies that are targeted to stimulating recovery. It is our hunch that, as we continue to study the molecular underpinnings of rehabilitation treatments, we will have a better handle on how to shift critical periods after brain injury. This would allow us to selectively target processes that will stimulate regenerative processes and reduce the parallel degenerative processes. This may prove especially important for those infants who may be presumed to be at risk either because of poor pre-natal care, maternal distress or other maternal health issues, disadvantaged socio-economic status, and so on.

References

Adkins, D. L., Boychuk, J., Remple, M. S. & Kleim, J. A. (2006). Motor training induces experience-specific patterns of plasticity across motor cortex and spinal cord. *Journal of Applied Physiology*, **101**, 1776–1782.

Anderson, V., Spencer-Smith, M., Leventer, R. *et al.* (2009). Childhood brain insult: can age at insult help us predict outcome? *Brain*, **132**, 45–56.

Bao, S., Chang, E. F., Woods, J. & Merzenich, M. M. (2004). Temporal plasticity in the primary auditory cortex induced by operant perceptual learning. *Nature Neuroscience*, 7, 974–981.

Castro, A. (1990). Plasticity in the motor system. In B. Kolb & R. Tees, eds. *Cerebral Cortex of the Rat*. Cambridge, MA: MIT Press, pp. 563–588.

Comeau, W., Hastings, E. & Kolb, B. (2007). Differential effect of pre and postnatal FGF-2 following medial prefrontal cortical injury. *Behavioral Brain Research*, **180**, 18–27.

Comeau, W., Gibb, R., Hastings, E., Cioe, J. & Kolb, B. (2008). Therapeutic effects of complex rearing or bFGF after perinatal frontal lesions. *Developmental Psychobiology*, **50**, 134–146.

Dabydeen L., Thomas, J. E., Aston, T. J., Hartley, H., Sinha, S. K. & Eyre, J. A. (2008). High-energy and -protein diet increases brain and corticospinal tract growth in term and preterm infants after perinatal brain injury. *Pediatrics*, **12**, 181–182.

Dallison, A. & Kolb, B. (2003). Recovery from infant frontal cortical lesions in rats can be reversed by cortical lesions in adulthood.

Behavioral Brain Research, **146**, 57–63.

Day, M., Gibb, R. & Kolb, B. (2003). Prenatal fluoxetine impairs functional recovery and neuroplasticity after perinatal frontal cortex lesions in rats. *Society for Neuroscience Abstracts*, **29**, 459.**10**.

Driscoll, I., Monfils, M.-H., Flynn, C., Teskey, G. C. & Kolb, B. (2007). Neurophysiological properties of cells filling the neonatal medial prefrontal cortex lesion cavity. *Brain Research*, **1178**, 1209–1218.

Eyre, J. A., Smith, M., Dabydeen, L. *et al.* (2007). Is hemiplegic cerebral palsy equivalent to amblyopia of the corticospinal system? *Annals of Neurology*, **62**, 493–503.

Frost, D. O., Page, S., Carroll, C. & Kolb, B. (2009). Early exposure to haloperidol or olanzapine induces long-term alterations of dendritic form. *Synapse, in press.*

Gibb, R. (2004). Perinatal experience alters brain development and functional recovery after cerebral injury in rats. Unpublished Ph.D. thesis, University of Lethbridge.

Gibb, R. & Kolb, B. (2005). Neonatal handling alters brain organization but does not influence recovery from perinatal cortical injury. *Behavioral Neuroscience*, **119**, 1375–1383.

Gibb, R. & Kolb, B. (2009a). Prenatal tactile stimulation alters brain and behavioral development and facilitates recovery from perinatal brain injury, Manuscript in submission.

Gibb, R. & Kolb, B. (2009b). Tactile-stimulation that facilitates functional recovery after perinatal cortical injury is mediated by FGF-2, Manuscript in revision.

Gibb, R. L., Kovalchuk, O., Halliwell, C. & Kolb, B. (2006). Prenatal stress affects recovery and DNA methylation patterns after postnatal day 10 frontal cortex lesions in rats. *Society for Neuroscience Abstracts*, 832.25.

Gibb, R., Gonzalez, C. L. R. & Kolb, B. (2009). *Complex environmental experience during pregnancy facilitates recovery from perinatal cortical injury in the offspring*, Manuscript in submission.

Gonzalez, C. L. R., Gibb, R. & Kolb, B. (2002). Functional recovery and dendritic

hypertrophy after posterior and complete cingulate lesions on postnatal day 10. *Developmental Psychobiology*, **40**, 138–46.

Gonzalez, C. L. R., Gharbawie, O. A. & Kolb, B. (2006). Chronic low-dose administration of nicotine facilitates recovery and synaptic change after focal ischemia in rats. *Neuropharmacology*, **50**, 777–787.

Halliwell, C., Tees, R. & Kolb, B. (2009). *Prenatal choline treatment enhances recovery from perinatal frontal injury in rats*, Manuscript in submission.

Hebb, D. O. (1947). The effects of early experience on problem solving at maturity. *American Psychologist*, **2**, 737–745.

Hebb, D. O. (1949). *The Organization of Behavior*. New York: McGraw-Hill.

Hicks, S. & D'Amato, C. J. (1961). How to design and build abnormal brains using radiation during development. In W. S. Fields & M. M. Desmond, eds. *Disorders of the Developing Nervous System*. Springfield, Ill: Thomas, pp. 60–79.

Kaplan, B. J., Simpson, J. S., Ferre, R. C., Gorman, C. P., McMullen, D. M. & Crawford, S. G. (2001). Effective mood stabilization with a chelated mineral supplement: an open-label trial in bipolar disorder. *Journal of Clinical Psychiatry*, **62**, 936–944.

Kaplan, B. J., Fisher, J. E., Crawford, S. G., Field, C. J. & Kolb, B. (2004). Improved mood and behavior during treatment with a mineral-vitamin supplement: an open-label case series of children. *Journal of Child Adolescence and Psychopharmacology*, **4**, 115–122.

Kennard, M. (1942). Cortical reorganization of motor function. *Archives of Neurology*, **48**, 227–240.

Kleim, J. A., Barbay, S. & Nudo, R. J. (1998). Functional organization of the rat motor cortex following motor skill learning. *Journal of Neurophysiology*, **80**, 3321–3325.

Kolb, B. (1995). *Brain Plasticity and Behavior*. Mahwah, NJ: Erlbaum.

Kolb, B. & Elliott, W. (1987). Recovery from early cortical damage in rats: II. Effects of experience on anatomy and behavior following frontal lesions at 1 or 5 days of age. *Behavioral Brain Research*, **26**, 47–56.

Kolb, B. & Gibb, R. (2009). *Tactile stimulation after posterior parietal cortical injury in infant rats stimulates functional recovery and altered cortical morphology*, Manuscript in submission.

Kolb, B. & Tomie, J. (1988). Recovery from early cortical damage in rats: IV. Effects of hemidecortication at 1, 5, or 10 days of age. *Behavioral Brain Research*, **28**, 259–274.

Kolb, B. & Whishaw, I. Q. (1998). Brain plasticity and behavior. *Annual Review of Psychology*, **49**, 43–64.

Kolb, B., Gibb, R. & van der Kooy, D. (1992). Neonatal hemidecortication alters cortical and striatal structure and connectivity. *Journal of Comparative Neurology*, **322**, 311–324.

Kolb, B., Gibb, R. & van der Kooy, D. (1994). Neonatal frontal cortical lesions in rats alter cortical structure and connectivity. *Brain Research*, **645**, 85–97.

Kolb, B., Petrie, B. & Cioe, J. (1996). Recovery from early cortical damage in rats: VII. Comparison of the behavioral and anatomical effects of medial prefrontal lesions at different ages of neural maturation. *Behavioral Brain Research*, **79**, 1–13.

Kolb, B., Cioe, J. & Muirhead, D. (1998a). Cerebral morphology and functional sparing after prenatal frontal cortex lesions in rats. *Behavioral Brain Research*, **91**, 143–155.

Kolb, B., Gibb, R., Gorny, G. & Whishaw, I. Q. (1998b). Possible brain regrowth after cortical lesions in rats. *Behavioral Brain Research*, **91**, 127–141.

Kolb, B., Martens, D. J., Gibb, R., Coles, B. & van der Kooy, D. (1999). Proliferation of neural stem cells in vitro and in vivo is reduced by infant frontal cortex lesions or prenatal BrdU. *Society for Neuroscience Abstracts*, **25**, 296.1.

Kolb, B., Gibb, R., Pearce, S. & Tanguay, R. (2008). Prenatal exposure to prescription medication alters recovery from early brain damage in rats. *Society for Neuroscience Abstracts*, 349.5.

Kwakkel, G., Wagenaar, R. C., Koelman, T. W., Lankhorst, G. J. & Doetsier, J. C. (1997). Effects of intensity of rehabilitation after stroke: a research synthesis. *Stroke*, **28**, 1550–1556.

Looney, C. B., Smith, J. K., Merck, L. H. *et al.* (2007). Intracranial hemorrhage in asymptomatic neonates: prevalence on MR images and relationship to obstetric and neonatal risk factors. *Radiology*, **242**, 535–541.

McKenna, J. E., Brown, R. W., Kolb, B. & Gibb, R. (2000). The effects of prenatal nicotine exposure on recovery from perinatal frontal cortex lesions. *Society for Neuroscience Abstracts*, **26**, 653.17.

Meck, W. H., Smith, R. A. & Williams, C. L. (1988). Pre- and postnatal choline supplementation produces long-term facilitation of spatial memory. *Developmental Psychobiology*, **21**, 339–353.

Monfils, M.-H., Driscoll, I., Vandenberg, P. M. *et al.* (2005). Basic fibroblast growth factor stimulates functional recovery after neonatal lesions of motor cortex in rats. *Neuroscience*, **134**, 1–8.

Monfils, M.-H., Driscoll, I., Kamitakahara, H. *et al.* (2006a). FGF-2-induced cell proliferation stimulates anatomical, neurophysiological, and functional recovery from neonatal motor cortex injury. *European Journal of Neuroscience*, **24** 739–749.

Monfils, M.-H., Driscoll, I., Melvin, N. & Kolb, B. (2006b). Differential expression of basic fibroblast growth factor in developing rat brain. *Neuroscience*, **141**, 213–221.

Monfils, M.-H., Driscoll, I., Vavrek, R., Kolb, B. & Fouad, K. (2008). FGF-2 induced functional improvement from neonatal motor cortex injury via corticospinal projections. *Experimental Brain Research*, **185**, 453–460.

Morishita, H. & Hensch, T. K. (2008). Critical period revisited: impact on vision. *Current Opinion in Neurobiology*, **18**, 101–107.

Payne, B. R. & Cornwell, P. (1994). System-wide repercussions of damage of immature visual cortex. *Trends in Neuroscience*, **17**, 126–130.

Payne, B. R. & Lomber, S. (2001). Reconstructing functional systems after lesions of the cerebral cortex. *Nature Reviews, Neuroscience*, **2**, 911–919.

Pellis, S. M., Hastings, E., Takeshi, T. *et al.* (2006). The effects of orbital frontal cortex damage on the modulation of defensive responses by rats in playful and non-playful social contexts. *Behavioral Neuroscience*, **120**, 72–84.

Rasmussen, T. & Milner, B. (1977). The role of early left-brain injury in determining lateralization of cerebral speech functions. *Annals of the New York Academy of Sciences*, **299**, 355–367.

Robinson, T. E. & Kolb, B. (2004). Structural plasticity associated with drugs of abuse. *Neuropharmacology*, **47** Suppl 1, 33–46.

Sandstrom, N. J., Loy, R. & Williams, C. L. (2002). Prenatal choline supplementation increase NGF levels in the hippocampus and frontal cortex of young and adult rats. *Brain Research*, **947**, 9–16.

Schmanke, T. D. & Villablanca, J. R. (2001). A critical maturational period of reduced brain vulnerability to injury. A study of cerebral glucose metabolism in cats. *Developmental Brain Research*, **26**, 127–141.

Tees, R. C. & Mohammadi, E. (1999). The effects of neonatal choline dietary supplementation on adult spatial and configural learning and memory in rats. *Developmental Psychobiology*, **35**, 226–240.

Tropea, D., van Wart, A. & Sur, M. (2009). Molecular mechanisms of experience-dependent plasticity in visual cortex. *Philosophical Transactions of the Royal Society, London. Biological Sciences*, **364**, 341–345.

Villablanca, J. R. & Gomez-Pinilla, F. (1987). Novel crossed corticothalamic projections after neonatal cerebral hemispherectomy. A quantitative autoradiography study in cats. *Brain Research*, **410**, 2119–2231.

Villablanca, J. R., Hovda, D. A., Jackson, G. F. & Infante, C. (1993). Neurological and behavioral effects of a unilateral frontal cortical lesion in fetal kittens: II. Visual system tests, and proposing a 'critical period' for lesion effects. *Behavioral Brain Research*, **57**, 79–92.

Whishaw, I. Q. & Kolb, B. (1988). Sparing of skilled forelimb reaching and corticospinal projections after neonatal motor cortex removal or hemidecortication in the rat: support for the Kennard Doctrine. *Brain Research*, **451**, 97–114.

Will, B. & Kelche, C. (1992). Environmental approaches to recovery of function from brain damage: a review of animal studies (1981 to 1991). In F. D. Rose & D. A. Johnson, eds. *Recovery from Brain Damage: Reflections and Directions*. New York: Plenum, pp. 79–104.

Williams, P. T., Gharbawie, O. A., Kolb, B. & Kleim, J. A. (2006). Experience-dependent amelioration of motor impairments in adulthood following neonatal medial frontal lesions in rats is accompanied by motor map expansion. *Neuroscience*, **141**, 1315–1326.

Index

Locators for headings which also have subheadings refer to general aspects of the topic.

Locators in **bold** refer to major entries.

Locators in *italic* refer to figures/tables.

235